A HISTORY
OF THE
GERMAN LANGUAGE

A HISTORY

OF THE

GERMAN LANGUAGE

*With Special Reference to the Cultural and Social
Forces that Shaped the Standard Literary Language*

REVISED EDITION

By JOHN T. WATERMAN

UNIVERSITY OF WASHINGTON PRESS

Seattle and London

Copyright © 1966 by the University of Washington Press
Library of Congress Catalog Number 66-13542
ISBN 0-295-73807-3
Printed in the United States of America
Revised edition, 1976
Second printing, 1986

To My Brothers

DR. CHARLES ROBERT WATERMAN
DR. SIDNEY PAUL WATERMAN

Preface

Two histories of the German language written in English are currently in print and available: Robert Priebsch and William E. Collinson, *The German Language*; and Arthur Kirk, *An Introduction to the Historical Study of New High German*. Neither of these is printed in the United States, and only the former makes an occasional reference to monographs and articles by American scholars. The latter is quite brief (eighty-five pages) and is meant to serve only as an introductory survey—a goal it fulfills admirably.

Also available of course are the German texts. Some of them can be highly recommended, such as Adolf Bach's standard treatise (*Geschichte der deutschen Sprache*), thorough and well-documented, but written in a style that is almost inaccessible to any but the advanced student of the language. Then there is Hugo Moser's readable and neatly organized *Deutsche Sprachgeschichte*. And ranking high on the list of acceptable texts is the necessarily condensed but otherwise excellent Göschen volume by Hans Sperber and Wolfgang Fleischhauer, *Geschichte der deutschen Sprache*.

My reasons for adding another title to those just listed are several. Kirk's book is too brief. The Priebsch and Collinson text is in general very good—but highly technical, a bit cluttered, and, by its topical presentation, obscures, to my way of thinking, the chronological sequence of events which does so much to articulate and make meaningful any historical study.

The German texts labor under two disadvantages from an American point of view. First of all, they are written in a language which is not easily read by many who for one reason or another may want to know something about the history of the German language. Secondly, and probably of greater significance, they are almost all intended for the

German university student. But most students reared and educated in the United States simply do not have the historical, cultural, and linguistic background quite naturally taken for granted by the German authors. Our students need a generous amount of peripheral and introductory information before they can deal intelligently with the central themes of a history of the language.

Of all the texts so far mentioned—both English and German—none gives the reader an adequate foundation in the methods, goals, and results of historico-comparative linguistics (or philology, if you prefer) as they apply to the German language and its historical antecedents. In most universities and colleges in this country, an undergraduate student majoring in German will usually be required to take only one philology course: a history of the language. This may be (and frequently is) his sole opportunity to learn something of the nomenclature, methods, and accomplishments of this particular discipline. If a student goes on to graduate school, he often finds himself enrolled in the first semester in a course in Middle or Old High German, Old Norse, Old English, or perhaps Gothic. And unless he has had some prior orientation in the philological background common to all these subjects, he will muddle through with only a foggy idea of what he is supposed to understand and to learn.

My goal, therefore, has been to prepare a text broad enough in scope to provide the advanced undergraduate or beginning graduate student with both an introduction to the more specialized philology courses and a reasonably comprehensive account of the historical development of the modern standard language. I have tried above all to keep the American-reared and American-schooled student in mind, including for this reason much more information of a general encyclopedic nature than is found in the standard German handbooks. The bibliography, with its emphasis upon the journals printed in the United States—and therefore available in any college library—I consider an important pedagogical adjunct to the body of the text.

My indebtedness to the standard German texts is everywhere evident and usually noted. To Professors Harold von Hofe and Richard H. Lawson, who carefully read and commented upon most of the manuscript, I owe a special debt of gratitude. My thanks also to Dr. Günther Gottschalk for preparing the maps used in Appendix II. And for her constant and willing help in so many ways, I express my deep appreciation to my wife.

J. T. W.

Los Angeles, 1965

Preface to the Revised Edition

THE principal changes in the revised edition are in Chapter Seven: "The New High German Period from 1800," and in the bibliography. Map 5, which has been added to Appendix II, is reprinted from Harry Steinhauer, *Kulturlesebuch für Anfänger* (2nd ed.; New York: Macmillan, 1967), with the kind permission of author and publisher.

I am especially indebted to the following graduate students for helping me prepare the material for this edition: Linda Frisch, Frank Hudson, Monika Johansson, Judy McCaslin, Rolf Scheel, Jacoba Van Staveren, Kim Vivian, and Jill Warnecke. My thanks also to my colleague, Professor Rolf Linn, for giving me of his knowledge and counsel, and to Mr. Peter Johansson for his help in revising the Bibliography. To colleagues everywhere, who have alerted me to errors or weaknesses in the first edition, I extend my grateful appreciation.

J.T.W.

Santa Barbara, 1975

ABBREVIATIONS

Alem.	Alemannic	MG	Middle German
Arab.	Arabic	MHG	Middle High German
Bav.	Bavarian	NHG	New (Modern) High German
Du.	Dutch	NGmc.	North Germanic
Eng.	English	OE	Old English
ENHG	Early New High German	OFr.	Old French
Finn.	Finnish	OHG	Old High German
Fr.	French	ON	Old Norse
Franc.	Franconian	OS	Old Saxon
Ger.	German	Pers.	Persian
Gk.	Greek	PGmc.	Proto-Germanic
Gmc.	Germanic	PIE	Proto-Indo-European
Go.	Gothic	Russ.	Russian
HG	High German	Skt.	Sanskrit
IE	Indo-European	Slav.	Slavic
Iran.	Iranian	Span.	Spanish
Ital.	Italian	UG	Upper German
Lat.	Latin	WGmc.	West Germanic
Lith.	Lithuanian		

Contents

	Page
Abbreviations	x

CHAPTER ONE
Indo-European   3

The Indo-European Languages	4
Proto-Indo-European	13
The Technique of Linguistic Reconstruction	15
The Indo-European Homeland	16
Linguistic Evidence for Location of the Indo-European Homeland .	17
The Centum-Satem Division of the Indo-European Dialect Area .	18

CHAPTER TWO
Germanic   20

The Germanic Homeland	20
Proto-Germanic	20
Germanic Loanwords in Latin	21
Testimony of Early Inscriptions	21
Germanic Loanwords in Finnish	22
Stress Accent in Germanic	23
Alliteration	23
The Germanic Sound Shift	24
Verner's Law	26
The Chronology of the Germanic Sound Shift	27
Causes of the Germanic Sound Shift	28
Structural Changes in Proto-Germanic	29
" Weak " and " Strong " Adjectival Declensions	31
The Germanic Preterite	33
The Vocabulary of Proto-Germanic	35
Classification of the Germanic Languages	37
The Homeland of the Germanic Peoples—Evidence from Archeology	39
The Arrival of the Indo-Europeans	39
Lexico-Statistical Dating	42
Migrations from the Early Germanic Homeland	42
The Validity of the " West Germanic " Concept	45
West Germanic Similarities	46
Gothic (East Gmc.)—Old Norse (North Gmc.)	46
West Germanic and North Germanic (Old Norse)	47
Old High German—Gothic (East Gmc.)	48
Anglo-Frisian	49
Recent Attempts at Classification	49

Page

CHAPTER THREE

The Old High German Period from the Beginnings to 1050   52

Chronology 52
Upper German—Middle German 53
Low German 53
Old Saxon 54
Linguistic Boundaries 55
The High German Consonant Shift 56
Chronology and Points of Origin of the High German Consonant Shift   59
Causes of the High German Consonant Shift 62
Influence of the Franks on the Development of High German . . 64
Similarities Between Old French and Old High German . . . 67
High German Made Up of Many Elements 68
The Gothic Mission 68
The Anglo-Saxon Mission 70
The Influence of the Monasteries 70
The Emergence of German as a Written Language . . . 73
Was There a Standardized OHG Written Language ? . . . 75
The Word " Deutsch " 77
The Old High German Vernacular 78
Notker Labeo of St. Gall 79
The Decline of German as a Written Language 80
Specimen Texts 81

CHAPTER FOUR

The Middle High German Period, 1050–1350   83

Early Middle High German : 1050–1170 83
High Medieval or " Classic " Middle High German : 1170–1250 . 84
     Principal Differences Between OHG and MHG, 85 ; The Language of Knighthood (*Die Rittersprache*), 88 ; French Influence, 89 ; Linguistic Influences from the Netherlands, 92 ; Language and the Ideals of Chivalry, 92 ; The Language of the Court Poets (*Die Höfische Dichtersprache*), 93
Late Middle High German : 1250–1350 97
     Early Prose Works, 97 ; The Preachers, 98 ; The Medieval Mystics, 100

CHAPTER FIVE

The Early New High German Period, 1350–1600   102

Principal Differences Between Middle High German and New High German 102
     Phonology, 102 ; Morphology, 103
Orthography 106

                                                                        Page
Major Dialects of Early New High German 107
Die Kanzleisprachen 110
    Das Gemeine Deutsch—Ostmitteldeutsch, 117 ; *Mittelniederdeutsch,*
    118 ; *Mittelniederländisch,* 119 ; Yiddish, 119 ; Pennsylvania
    " Dutch," 119
Foreign Influences 120
    Latin, 120 ; Eastern Europe, 122 ; The Near East, 122 ;
    Northern Europe, 123
Specialized Dialects (*Sondersprachen*) 123
    Trade and Commerce, 123 ; The Language of the Seaman, 125 ;
    The Language of the Soldier, 125 ; The Language of the Miner,
    126
The Invention of Printing 127
Martin Luther 128
    The Spread of Luther's German, 133
The Nature and Character of Early New High German .   .   . 135

CHAPTER SIX

The New High German Period from **1600** *to* **1800**   137

Renewed French Influence 137
Die Sprachgesellschaften 139
The Grammarians 140
Spread and Acceptance of a Standard Literary Language .   . 145
Literary Influences 147
    Baroque, 148 ; Pietism, 150 ; The Enlightenment, 152 ; Bodmer
    and Breitinger, 153 ; Rococo and *Empfindsamkeit,* 154 ; Klop-
    stock, 156 ; Wieland and Lessing, 158 ; Storm and Stress, 161 ;
    Summary, 162

CHAPTER SEVEN

The New High German Period from **1800**   163

Literary Influences 163
    Classicism (*Goethe and Schiller*), 163 ; Romanticism, 166 ;
    Romanticism and the Beginnings of German Philology, 167 ;
    Beyond Romanticism, 169
Toward a Standard Orthography 171
Toward a Standard Pronunciation 173
Foreign Influences 175
    French, 175 ; English, 177 ; American, 178 ; Russian, 181 ;
    Political, Industrial, and Military Influences, 183
Die Umgangssprache 185
Principal High German Dialects 187
    Low German, 188 ; Middle German, 188 ; Upper German, 190 ;
    The German Speech Atlas, 192
New Directions in German Grammar 193

PAGE

CHAPTER EIGHT

A Brief Description of the Sounds of German 201

Consonants 203
Vowels 207
Semivowels 207
Diphthongs 207
Some Features of Coarticulation 208

Appendix I : Plates 211

Appendix II : Maps 225

Selected Bibliography 233

Index 275

A HISTORY
OF THE
GERMAN LANGUAGE

CHAPTER ONE

Indo-European

EVEN the casual student soon becomes aware of many similarities
between German and English. Vocabulary correspondences are perhaps
the most obvious, but after a while he notices that the two also have much
in common structurally—the manner in which the comparative and
superlative degrees of the adjective are expressed, the agreement between
the forms of many of the pronouns, and the striking parallels in the verbal
systems, to mention just a few of the congruent features. Nor are these
similarities fortuitous, since English and German are closely related, both
belonging to the so-called "Germanic" family of languages, a relationship
shared also by Danish, Icelandic, Norwegian, Swedish, Frisian, Flemish,
and Dutch.

On an even broader scale, those students who have studied Latin are
struck by the fact that the grammar of German seems often more akin to
Latin than to English. And such comparisons could be expanded to point
up similarities to such languages as Greek, Sanskrit, and Russian. In
other words, it would soon become clear that German is related not only to
that group of languages we have called "Germanic," but also—even if
usually less obviously—to other and more distant tongues. In fact, the
Germanic languages are related to the following linguistic groups: Albanian,
Armenian, Baltic, Celtic, Greek, Hittite, Indic, Iranian, Italic, Slavic, and
Tocharian (in addition to certain other less available languages of
antiquity). These languages—or language groups—are subsumed under
the term "Indo-European." The German language, therefore, in point of

its broadest generic classification, is an Indo-European language belonging to the Germanic group.

THE INDO-EUROPEAN LANGUAGES

Geographically the speakers of the Indo-European languages are located for the most part in lands that extend from India to Europe, although certain languages—such as English—have been carried far beyond these borders by later migrations.

The term "Indo-European" implies linguistic relationship only and should not be used in an ethnographic sense—the principal reason why the older expression "Aryan" has been abandoned. In Germany and in the Scandinavian countries, most writers still employ the synonym "Indo-Germanic," though the geographical restriction implied by the second half of the compound makes it less suitable than "Indo-European," the preferred term in English.

If we limit ourselves to the major languages, we may divide the Indo-European family of languages into twelve groups:

Albanian

Clearly an IE language, although not much is known about its more immediate affinities. It is today the national language of Albania, a tiny country on the Adriatic bordered by Greece and Yugoslavia. Although its earliest records date only from the fourteenth century of our era, some scholars consider Albanian to be related either to ancient Illyrian or Thracian.

Armenian

Except for a few lines of poetry, the oldest documents in Armenian date from a fifth-century A.D. Bible translation. Tradition has it that the Armenians descended from the ancient Phrygians of Asia Minor, but there is little historical confirmation of this. Because its vocabulary is so heavily tinctured with Persian borrowings, scholars long felt that Armenian was but a dialect of the large Indo-Iranian linguistic group. We now recognize it as an independent branch of Indo-European, although the tragic political history of the Armenians has brought their language at various times under the influence not only of Persian but also of Syrian, Turkish, and Greek. At one time Armenian underwent a series of sound changes similar to the ones we refer to collectively as the Germanic sound shift, a complex of phonetic mutations primarily responsible for the emergence of the linguistic subdivision of Indo-European known as "Germanic."

Baltic

Under this geographical term (referring to the Baltic Sea), we group Lithuanian, Latvian (or Lettish as it is sometimes called), and an extinct language, Prussian, which died out in the seventeenth century (note that Prussian is not a Germanic but a Baltic language). Lithuanian and Latvian are of special interest to linguists because they have preserved certain archaic features, such as the dual number and, in a general way, the system of pitch accent represented in written Greek by the acute, grave, and circumflex accent marks. Furthermore, the suffixes used to distinguish their seven grammatical cases are still similar in appearance to those assumed for the parent language. The records of both Lithuanian and Latvian are not old, dating as they do from the sixteenth century of the Christian era.

Celtic

This group breaks down into two main divisions: Goidelic (also known as q-Celts) and Brythonic (or p-Celts). To the former are reckoned Irish, Scots Gaelic, and Manx; to the latter, Welsh, Cornish, Gaulish, and Breton. Both Gaulish and Cornish are extinct (the latter, however, only since about 1800), and Manx—perhaps still spoken by just a few people on the Isle of Man—seems doomed to imminent oblivion. Gaulish, sometimes called Continental Celtic, has the most ancient recorded history, its oldest inscriptions dating from the third century B.C. Once spoken throughout much of Europe and, indeed, as far east as the Black Sea, Gaulish did not survive the influences of later conquests by foreign peoples, especially the Romans and the Germanic tribes. Nonetheless, St. Jerome (331–420 A.D.) tells us that the Galatians (compare the Latin *Galli*) of Asia Minor and the Gauls of Trier (Trèves) spoke almost identical languages, even though the fourth century must have marked a late date in the waning existence of Continental Celtic. The Breton language, incidentally, is not a continuation of Gaulish, but was brought to the old Gaulish province of Armorica (Brittany) by the emigrants from southern Britain, especially Cornwall, in the fifth and sixth centuries.

The most important of the Celtic languages to the linguist is Irish, primarily because of its relatively copious records, but also because the language shows a minimum of Latin influence (Ireland never became a Roman province).

The Celtic languages long resisted satisfactory investigations. Trying to establish the correspondences in the phonology to the other IE languages, for instance, proved to be a most difficult task. And likewise the morphology, especially of the verb, was analyzed only after painstaking researches extending over many years. This group of languages, though unmistakably of Indo-European extraction, sometimes diverges from what we might consider the standard IE prototype, perhaps because Celtic had been separated from the parent language for a much longer time than some of the more "typical" Indo-European languages. It may also have been influenced by the unknown idioms of the aboriginal inhabitants of what later became Celtic territory. We do know that the Celts were already a great and powerful people at a time when the Germanic tribes first became known, and long before the Slavs emerge upon the historical scene.

Germanic

Since the next chapter is devoted to a discussion of the Germanic languages and their speakers, we shall limit ourselves at this time to a simple enumeration of the principal languages belonging to this group, subdividing them according to geographical location into North, East, and West Germanic.

To North Germanic are reckoned the Scandinavian languages, which in turn may be further divided into a western and eastern group. The former includes Icelandic, Norwegian, and Faroese; the latter, Gothlandic, Swedish, and Danish. Although their manuscript tradition begins late (twelfth century), there is a rich treasury of inscriptions, the earliest of which may be assigned to the fourth century A.D. These inscriptions—carved in runes—constitute our earliest firsthand records of Germanic.

East Germanic is represented chiefly by Gothic, an extinct language preserved for the most part in the fourth-century Bible translation of Ulfilas, bishop to the Western Goths (Visigoths). His episcopal see was in Dacia, roughly present-day Rumania. Since Gothic is the Germanic language for which we possess the oldest sizable body of text, it is of obvious importance to the historical linguist.

West Germanic (the student is again reminded that this is primarily a convenient geographical grouping) may be divided into High German, Low German, Low Franconian (Dutch), Frisian, and English. The written records of English and German go back to approximately the late seventh century. The relationship of these "West Germanic" languages to one another is a subject of some controversy among scholars, and will be discussed in the following chapter.

Greek

Although today confined to the political boundaries of Greece, the

Greek language in ancient times was spoken over a much broader area that extended to the west and south along the Mediterranean coasts of Europe and Africa, as far north as the Black Sea, and eastward to much of the Levant, including such countries as Syria, Palestine, and the Isle of Cyprus. After the conquests of Alexander the Great (356–323 B.C.), Greek became for a time the reigning world language.

Until recently the most ancient records of Greek were thought to be inscriptions from approximately the eighth century B.C. In 1952, however, Michael Ventris published the results of his efforts to decipher the so-called Linear B script of some ancient tablets which had been discovered on the Isle of Crete and also on the mainland of Greece. Archeologists have assigned the years 1450–1200 B.C. to these tablets. Ventris demonstrated that the language of the tablets is Greek, now usually referred to as Mycenaean Greek.

Ancient Greek is known to us in a variety of dialects for which there is no satisfactory classification, although in a general way we can group them geographically into North Greek (Boeotian, Thessalian, and Lesbian—known collectively as Aeolic), South Greek (Arcadian, Cyprian, and—perhaps—Mycenaean), West Greek (Doric and Achaean), and East Greek (Ionian and Attic). Only the most important dialects are listed in parentheses; almost all of what is usually called Classical Greek literature was written in Ionic-Attic.

By the time of Christ the ancient dialects had given way to a common Greek speech—the *Koiné*—based predominantly upon the Attic dialect. From this common Greek (with the single exception of the Doric Tsaconian) the modern language is derived. After the conquest of Greece by the Turks in the fifteenth century, this more or less homogeneous language began breaking down again into dialects that can today be classified roughly into a northern and southern group.

In the comparative study of the IE languages, Greek—especially since the decipherment of the Linear B script—must be accorded a place of primary importance, for it not only preserves more faithfully than all the others the vocalism of the parent language, but at least rivals the rest in the fidelity with which it reflects both the verbal structure and the accentual system of Proto-Indo-European.

Hittite

This ancient language was lost to the modern world until approximately the turn of the last century, when excavations at Boghaz-köi near Ankara in present-day Turkey unearthed thousands of clay tablets containing cuneiform inscriptions in a strange idiom that was later shown to have many features in common with the Indo-European languages. Archeologists had here discovered the ruins of a city known to the Assyrians as *Hatti*, the capital of a people who ruled over Asia Minor and Syria throughout much of the second millennium B.C. Of uncertain racial origins, they were known to the Hebrews as *Hittites*. Many languages were spoken within their borders, but inasmuch as the unnamed language of the inscriptions had enjoyed an official status, scholars called it "Hittite," even though the word actually refers to a city and not to a people.

The status of Hittite as an Indo-European language is still disputed. Although all are agreed that it shows unmistakable affinities to the IE languages, there are both chronological and linguistic reasons why some scholars prefer to consider it not as a *descendant* of Proto-Indo-European but as a *contemporary*, and to assume that both Hittite and PIE are derived from still an earlier proto-language[1] which may be called "Proto-Indo-Hittite." This view, once quite popular, has lost favor in recent years. Most linguists today include Hittite within the Indo-European family of languages, even though certain features of its phonology and morphology sometimes make such a classification seem a bit forced.

The discovery and subsequent analysis of Hittite has been of critical importance to historico-comparative linguists. Of special significance was the identification in Hittite of a symbol that apparently stood for a phonetic reflex (that is, a "descendant") of a vowel-like guttural sound known to linguists as a "laryngeal *sonant*" (= voiced sound) not previously assumed for Proto-Indo-European. The orthographies of the other languages had no comparable symbol. However, upon inspection of the forms that corresponded to the appropriate Hittite words, the following situation was found to prevail: whenever Hittite showed a *short* vowel in the immediate vicinity of the "laryngeal," the other languages evinced only a *long* vowel with *no* symbol that could be matched to the Hittite laryngeal. This raised the interesting possibility that at least some (if not all) of the etymologically long vowels of the historical languages were derived from *short vowels plus laryngeals*, and that Hittite alone had preserved direct evidence of the situation as it had prevailed in Proto-Indo-European.

This—most briefly—is the essence of the so-called "laryngeal theory." Its implications are far-reaching. A re-evaluation of the phonology and

---

[1] In comparative linguistics, the prefix *proto-*—when applied to a language—designates the latest common ancestor of two or more related languages. Some linguists employ *proto-* to refer only to reconstructed languages. This is an arbitrary and unwarranted restriction, since the prefix serves equally well to designate either recorded or assumed ancestral languages.

morphology of the parent language in the light of this new evidence has forced many scholars to adopt a revised version of what they assume to have been the structure of Proto-Indo-European.

Indic

When Sanskrit first became generally known to the philologists of the western world in the early decades of the nineteenth century, they thought they had discovered the parent language from which Latin, Greek, Gothic, and all the other then-known IE languages had developed. They were led to this conclusion primarily by the great antiquity of its literature and by the richness of its morphology, although a certain romantic enthusiasm about this new "light from the Orient" no doubt contributed to their thinking.

Today we know that Sanskrit is neither the Indo-European parent language nor, for that matter, even the oldest representation of the Indic group. That distinction belongs rather to the language of the *Rig-Veda*, a collection of more than a thousand hymns, dating in composition from approximately 1500 to 500 B.C. Since these hymns are not specifically dated and are known to us only through later manuscripts, the time of composition must be determined by indirect evidence.

This Vedic language has come down to us largely in poetic form, prose making its first extensive appearance around 500 B.C. in commentaries to the religious hymns of the various *Vedas*. These commentaries, known as *Brâhmaṇas*, are for the most part written in a simplified and somewhat divergent type of Old Indic called *Sanskrit*. This language, probably not directly descended from the Vedic, was apparently spoken in north-western India by the upper classes in roughly the fourth century B.C. It grew in prominence, eventually becoming not only the liturgical language of the Brahmin religion, but also the standard vehicle for literature and scholarship throughout all of Brahmin India. Indeed, it is still spoken and written by the learned in India today, occupying a position somewhat analogous to Latin in the Roman Catholic church.

Curiously enough, the oldest dated records of Indic speech are the relatively late, third-century B.C. inscriptions of King Aśoka, written in several of the vernacular languages—called *Prâkrits*—that are reckoned to the so-called Middle Indic era. Two of these Prâkrits, Pali and Jaina Magadhi, became the religious languages of Buddhism and Jainism, respectively.

In India today about 322 million people speak the many modern Indic languages, of which the following are numerically most prominent: Bengali, Bihari, Hindi (Western and Eastern), Gujarati, Marathi, Oriya, Panjabi, and Rajasthani. All these languages derive in an indirect way from one or another of the Middle Indic Prâkrits.

Old Indic, as represented by Vedic and—to a lesser extent—by Sanskrit, is of singular importance to the linguist. Among all the Indo-European languages, it most faithfully preserves the accentual system that prevailed in late Proto-Indo-European. Not only does the orthography of the Vedic hymns include accent marks, but the native grammarians tell us that until about 400 B.C. the accent was one of pitch rather than stress, a situation corroborated by evidence from the Greek and the Balto-Slavic languages. Furthermore, both the nominal and verbal systems of Proto-Indo-European are remarkably well preserved in Old Indic. And the earlier stages of word composition so important to an understanding of the morphology of the IE languages are known to us in large degree from a study of the Vedic and Sanskrit.

Iranian

This group of the Indo-European languages is represented in its most ancient form by Old Persian and Avestan. Our records of the former are chiefly the rock inscriptions of their kings. Carved in a wedge-shaped script known as "cuneiform," these inscriptions may be dated roughly from 500–300 B.C. The second of the two Iranian languages is preserved for us in the *Avesta*, the sacred text of the Zoroastrian religion. Some scholars believe Avestan to have been the language of the ancient Medes; at any rate, it was probably extinct by 400 B.C. Although portions of the *Avesta* may have been composed as early as 600 B.C., the manuscripts are comparatively late and are written in a script which has undergone such drastic changes that scholars cannot be sure to what extent it reflects the Avestan language itself.

Old Persian was continued as Middle Persian, called either *Pehlevi* or *Pahlavi*. Discoveries from around 1900 in Chinese Turkestan brought to light a religious literature composed during the eighth and ninth centuries of our era in three other Middle Iranian languages, namely, Parthian, Sogdian, and Sakian.

From one of the Middle Persian dialects, *Parsik*, has descended Modern Persian, which itself may be subdivided into several dialects. Related to Modern Persian are other Modern Iranian dialects, such as Kurdish, Afghan, and Osseti (spoken in the Caucasus).

The oldest stages of Indic and Iranian are so similar that scholars assume them to be immediate descendants of a common *Indo-Iranian* language. For this reason, it is customary to group them together under this rubric whenever we list the various linguistic groups that make up the Indo-European family of languages.

Italic

This is the name used to designate a group of closely related languages, all belonging to the Indo-European family and all once spoken in various parts of Italy. The principal representatives of this group are Latin and Oscan-Umbrian.

Our oldest Latin inscription is carved on an ornamental gold clasp fashioned some time around 600 B.C. The wording on this clasp (called the "Prenestine fibula," after the locality in which it was found) is: *Manios med fhefhaked Numasioi* "Manius made me for Numasios." In Classical Latin this would read: *Manius mê fêcit Numerio.* There are other fragmentary remains of Latin from the sixth and fourth centuries, too, but not until the third century B.C. do the inscriptions become numerous. In fact, the most important of the Early Latin inscriptions—the *Senâtus consultum dê Bacchânâlibus*—is dated as late as 186 B.C.

We know Oscan and Umbrian only from inscriptions, there being almost nothing of a literary nature that has come down to us. Both these languages have so much in common with Latin that we must assume a period of common Italic development for all three. Although their phonology and morphology are in general more archaic than those of Latin—and hence especially valuable to the linguist—the Oscan and Umbrian inscriptions are relatively late, going back no further than about 200 B.C. Of special interest are seven bronze tablets that were found in present-day Gubbio (ancient Iguvium), upon which are inscribed about four thousand words of Umbrian.

The most important member of the Italic group, Latin, was originally but one of the dialects spoken in Latium, a small area along the mouth of the Tiber on the west coast of central Italy. This Italic dialect was fated to become the language of Rome and, ultimately, of the Roman Empire.

Latin is customarily divided into several major periods, terminating in what is often called the Vulgar Latin era, extending from the death of Marcus Aurelius in 180 A.D. to the time when Latin disappeared as a vernacular. To the degree that Vulgar Latin reflected the *spoken* language of the day, we can correctly refer to it as "vulgar" or—to use a currently more acceptable synonym—"colloquial." In most of the literature from these centuries, however, the influence of Classical Latin is still strong, so that we must not suppose that the literary style of, say, Saint Augustine (354–430) reliably represents the kind of native and colloquial Latin spoken in his North African homeland. The vernacular shines through, as it were, but the written Latin of this era was to an extent an artificial language. Exactly when Latin ceased to exist as a "living" tongue, and when its descendants, the Romance languages, came into being cannot be stated with precision. Our earliest document in a Romance language is the Old French version of the Straßburg Oaths, recited on February 14, 842, by Louis the German in the presence of the French-speaking troops of his brother, Charles the Bald, when the two had decided to make common cause against a third brother who was trying to wrest their inherited lands from them. By this time the Franks west of the Rhine spoke a language that was no longer Latin, but rather an early form of what we now call French. Certainly we may assume that this Old French had existed as a linguistic entity long before 842.

In addition to French, Italian, Portuguese, and Spanish, we also include the following languages in the Romance group: Catalan, spoken in eastern Spain; Provençal in southern France; Sardinian, spoken on the Isle of Sardinia in the Mediterranean Sea; Rhaeto-Romanic or Ladin, limited to parts of Switzerland and Italy; Rumanian, far to the east in the Balkans; and an extinct language, Dalmatian, spoken in Italy until 1898.

Slavic

Documentary evidence of the Slavic languages is comparatively late, there being nothing of consequence prior to the ninth-century translation of the Scriptures into Old Bulgarian or Old Church Slavic. Modern Bulgarian, along with Serbo-Croatian and Slovenian, constitute the South Slavic group. Great Russian, Little Russian (Ukrainian), and White Russian are customarily grouped together, either as North Slavic or East Slavic. A third group, West Slavic, is made up of Polish, Sorbian (Wendic), Czech, and Slovak.

Old Church Slavic has an unbroken history as the liturgical language of the Eastern Orthodox church in Russia, Bulgaria, and Serbia. Even in this limited and in a sense artificial form, however, it has undergone many changes from that time in the ninth century when it lived as the vernacular of the Macedonian Slavs.

To the comparative Indo-European linguist, the Slavic languages offer a most profitable area of study. In the inflection of the noun and adjective, for instance, are preserved most of the features of these categories in the parent language. The verbal system, too, reflects certain Proto-Indo-

European distinctions of tense and aspect. Along with Indic, Greek, and the Baltic languages, the Slavic group—especially Russian and Serbian—illuminates the accentual conditions characterizing various periods of the proto-language. Because of many similarities in their linguistic systems, the Slavic and Baltic languages are assumed by most scholars to have undergone a period of mutual development. Some texts group them together under the name "Balto-Slavic."

Tocharian

This language shares with Hittite the distinction of having been "discovered" only in recent times. Excavations at the turn of the last century in Chinese Turkestan brought to light a wealth of material written in the Brahmi script of India, though the language thus recorded was not Indic. Two distinct and quite different dialects were established, since named East Tocharian or Tocharian A, and West Tocharian or Tocharian B. The former was centered near present-day Karashahr, the latter near Kucha; both towns are in Sinkiang Province. The documents are not especially old, extending in time from the sixth to the eighth centuries.

Scholars have established that Tocharian is an Indo-European language, and that it shows special resemblances to Italic and Celtic, the two most westerly of the Indo-European languages. Oddly enough, it shows no special similarities to its nearest neighbors, Indic and Iranian. The discovery of an Indo-European language in far-off China—agreeing as it does with the western representatives of the family—admittedly poses many problems. The location of Tocharian so far to the east is most likely due to early migration, probably from an area approximately between the Caspian Sea and the Black Sea, just north of the Caucasus.

PROTO-INDO-EUROPEAN

We have no documents written in the parent language from which the various Indo-European idioms are presumed to have descended. Although historical linguists refer freely to this Indo-European parent language, it is in fact a "reconstructed" language, existing only as the product of the comparative method; its forms are labeled with an asterisk in order to inform the reader that they are reconstructed and not recorded—that is, that they do not actually occur. We refer to this "language" as Proto-Indo-European, abbreviated to *PIE* or—if the reference is quite clear—simply to *IE*.

This reconstructed Proto-Indo-European is of value to the extent that it is based upon documented forms of real languages and reflects the correspondences that obtain between these documented forms. The individual reconstruction—the "starred form"—has the status of a formula constructed for the purpose of summarizing sound changes in a group of related languages; it is not necessarily identical with a word that may once have existed.

When we say that two or more languages are "related," we mean that they have descended from a common and single ancestor. Their degree of relationship depends upon the number and type of features they share, as demonstrated by the comparative method, a procedure based upon the postulate that similarities between languages result from a common ancestor or origin, whereas the differences are assumed to have arisen during periods of independent growth. Since the method seeks to go back in time, it depends for its data upon the older recorded versions (if available) of a given language or language group. The most decisive evidence of linguistic relationship is a systematic correspondence between the sounds (as recorded in the writings) of the languages being compared. Similarities in the vocabulary and—of far greater reliability—in the morphology are also significant, but *phonetic correspondences* present the most convincing evidence that the languages being compared do indeed stem from a common prototype.

As an example of what is meant by the term "systematic phonetic correspondences," let us consider the third person singular, present indicative of the verb "to be" as it occurs in various Indo-European languages:

Sanskrit	Greek	Latin	Lithuanian	Old Church Slavic	Gothic
ásti	estí	est	ēsti	jestъ	ist

That these words are "cognates" (words resembling one another in form and meaning) is obvious. What is not so apparent, but of much greater significance, is that a certain kind of *e*-vowel in Greek, Latin, Lithuanian, or Old Church Slavic corresponds to *a* in Sanskrit and *i* in Gothic. This is substantiated by such additional sets of cognates as the following:

Sanskrit	Greek	Latin	Lith.	Old Slavic	Gothic	
saptá	heptá	septem	septynì	sedmъ	sibun	"seven"
mádhyas	mésos	medius			midjis	"middle"
váhâmi		vehô	vežù	vezq	*wiga	"I travel"
sánas	hénos	senex	sēnas		sineigs	"old"

In this same manner we can establish the correspondences that obtain between the consonants, as for instance the following systematic correspondences between *bh, f,* and *b* in Sanskrit, Latin, and Gothic, respectively:

Sanskrit	Latin	Gothic		
bhárāmi	*ferô*	*baíra*	"I carry"	
bhinádmi	*findo*	*beita*	"I split" "I bite"[2]	
bhrắtar	*fráter*	*brôþar*	"brother"	

THE TECHNIQUE OF LINGUISTIC RECONSTRUCTION

Once we are able to establish such sets of systematic phonetic correspondences between two or more languages, we conclude that they are related to one another; that is, we assume that they have descended from a common linguistic ancestor. And by comparing the correspondences according to certain definite principles, we can also tentatively establish the form which the word had in the proto-language. To illustrate: the four words—Old Latin *loucos* "grove" (> Classical Latin *lûcus*),[3] Sanskrit *lôkas* "open space," Lithuanian *laũkas* "field," and Old High German *lôh* "clearing in the forest"—constitute a set of cognates adequate for reconstructing the Proto-Indo-European word from which they all presumably descend.[4]

The consonants *l* and *k* occur in all four instances, thus assuring their presence in the parent language (the change in Old High German from *k* to the corresponding spirant—written here as *h*—is quite regular). We may also confidently reconstruct *s* in final position, preserved as it is in Sanskrit, Lithuanian, and Latin. Its absence in the German form is in order: IE word-final -*s* eventually disappeared in Germanic, as can be seen by comparing such cognates as Latin *piscis*—Old High German *fisk* "fish"; Latin *hostis*—Old High German *gast* "guest." The German example *lôh* has also lost the unstressed vowel of the final syllable, so that we must turn to the other languages in our illustration to determine its Indo-European quality. Sanskrit and Lithuanian show an orthographic *a*. Unfortunately, the class of sound represented by this symbol may be of various origins in both languages: Sanskrit *a* may derive from IE *a*, *e*, or *o*; a Lithuanian *a* may stem from IE *a* or *o*. However, from this evidence we may at least conclude that the original vowel was not *e*. And since Old Latin has an *o* of unquestioned historicity, we determine that the *a* of Sanskrit and Lithuanian is in both cases a secondary development, thus permitting us to reconstruct an *o* as the original vowel of the second syllable.

---

[2] The Sanskrit and Latin words—each containing a nasal infix in the root—are to be glossed in English as "I split"; the Gothic form means "I bite."

[3] The symbol < means "derives from"; > means "becomes."

[4] This illustration is taken from Hans Krahe, *Indogermanische Sprachwissenschaft* (Sammlung Göschen, No. 59 [Berlin: Walter de Gruyter & Co., 1962]), I, 34–36 *passim*.

With respect to the vowel of the root syllable, Sanskrit *ô* may be a reflex of an older *au, eu,* or *ou;* in a similar fashion may Lithuanian *au* serve as a continuation of any one of these same three Indo-European diphthongs. Latin *ou,* however, can derive only from *eu* or *ou,* allowing us to strike *au* from the list of possible antecedents. Old High German *ô* reflects either an earlier *au* or *ou,* but just as *au* has already been eliminated, so must *eu* now likewise be rejected, leaving *ou* as our only acceptable choice. That is to say: *ou* is the only alternative whose selection does not conflict with the evidence presented by the verifiable forms that occur in the various Indo-European languages. We therefore reconstruct **loukos* as the common ancestor of the four words we have been comparing;[5] we assume that its original meaning was something like "a clearing in the forest." Our reconstruction is *phonemic,* that is, each letter stands for a given *class* of sounds made up of the phonetic variants or *allophones* as reflected in the historical languages. This means, among other things, that we cannot determine the exact pronunciation of the reconstructed form.

In an analogous fashion, historico-comparative linguists also attempt to reconstruct the morphology and even the syntax of the parent language. Much of the scholarship in this field is currently concerned with refining the research methods, an effort that has been abetted in recent years by contributions from structural linguistics.

The comparativist encounters many obstacles. He must always decide whether a given form is indigenous or whether it was at one time borrowed. If borrowed, at what time relative to certain sound changes was it adopted? One of the most difficult tasks is determining whether the evidence is sufficient to attribute a linguistic feature to Proto-Indo-European in its broadest sense, or whether its occurrence might have been restricted to something less than the total area.

THE INDO-EUROPEAN HOMELAND

We are unable to determine the exact or even the approximate geographical location of the Indo-European homeland. From the standpoint of ancient history and tradition, the Indo-European languages seemingly had their origins in a language spoken by people inhabiting eastern Asia Minor perhaps two or three thousand years before Christ. The chronology is fluid and uncertain, hinging in part upon dates assigned in ancient times to the reigns of the Egyptian pharaohs, in part upon the dates ascribed to certain artifacts (utensils, weapons, and so forth) recovered by

---

[5] In the technical vocabulary of historico-comparative linguistics, words related to one another in this way are often referred to as *congeners.* The word from which a set of congeners presumably derives is called an *etymon* (pl. *etyma*).

archeologists. The cultural time level of the Indo-European civilization is usually considered to be Late Stone Age—or about 2500 to 2000 B.C.—for the area and people under consideration.

We are even less certain about the pedigree of the speakers of this language: did they constitute a race, a nation, or simply a loosely knit tribal organization? There are references in Egyptian and Hebrew records to contemporary non-Semitic peoples, such as the Hittites, and we know that at least one of the languages spoken within the Hittite empire belonged to the Indo-European stock. But whether the Hittites were *the* Indo-Europeans, or whether, more improbable yet, the so-called Hittite language is the original Indo-European language—these are questions for which we have no sure answers.

Linguistic Evidence for Location of the Indo-European Homeland

Basing their conclusions chiefly upon linguistic evidence rather than upon ancient history and tradition, scholars are more inclined to locate the Indo-European homeland farther to the west, some favoring an area north and west of the Black Sea, others preferring those lands bordering on the Baltic. This method of drawing historico-cultural inferences from linguistic material consists in the main of studying the vocabulary of related languages, assuming that cognate lexical items guarantee the presence in their respective cultures of the corresponding objects. If the fundamental postulate of the comparative method is correct—that a feature common to all or most of the daughter languages must have been inherited from the parent language—then we may also draw certain inferences about the environment of the speakers of this parent language: what metals they knew, the kind of crops they grew, the animals they raised, the climate in which they lived, and so forth. Of course, this method must be used with extreme caution, since it would be quite unsafe to assume that the *absence* of a given word may be taken as proof that the object itself did not exist in that particular culture: the "argument from silence" carries little weight.

As an example of this sort of linguistic detective work, we might cite the well-known attempt to deduce the geographical location of the parent language from the occurrence in the various Indo-European languages of a word with the original meaning "beech tree." Cognates of this word are found in five of the IE language groups:

Gmc.	Italic	Greek	Iran.	Slav.
ON *bôk*	Lat. *fāgus*	*phêgós*	*bûz*	Russ. *buziná*
OE *bôc*				*boz*

These words are all customarily derived from a PIE root with two possible forms, *bha(u)g* and *bhûg*. Although we cannot here go into a full discussion, it seems most likely that the meaning of the IE etymon (see note 5) was "beech tree." But of the five linguistic groups quoted, only two—Germanic and Italic—preserve the original meaning; the other three use their cognate to refer to other kinds of trees. Now, the beech tree is not indigenous to the territories anciently occupied by the Greeks, Persians, and Slavs. We assume, therefore, that when these "Indo-Europeans" arrived in the lands that were to become their permanent home, they transferred the superfluous "tree word" to a local species for which their language had no native term. If this is so, then we may conclude that the Indo-European homeland lay west of a line that would run between Kaliningrad (formerly Königsberg) and the Crimea, for the beech is not native to the soil east of this longitude.

The Centum-Satem Division of the Indo-European Dialect Area

Another example of using linguistic evidence in an attempt to locate the IE homeland has to do with the development in the daughter languages of three sets of velar stops assigned to Proto-Indo-European: the palatal series $\hat{k}$, $\hat{k}h$, $\hat{g}$, $\hat{g}h$; the velar series k, kh, g, gh; and the labiovelars q^w, q^wh, g^w, g^wh.

We direct our attention first to the palatals, which merged with the velars in certain of the daughter languages, but developed into sibilants in others. This is the familiar "centum-satem" division of the Indo-European languages, based upon the congeners of the reconstructed PIE form for the word "hundred," namely *$\hat{k}m̥tóm$*. To the *centum* languages (in addition to Latin *centum*) we assign Greek *he-katón*, Old Irish *cêt*, Gothic *hund* (IE k > Gmc. h), and West Tocharian *känte*. Forms for "hundred" in the *satem* languages are: Sanskrit *śatám*, Avestan *satəm*, Lithuanian *šim̃tas*, and Old Church Slavic *sъto* (Russian *sto*).

In what must be regarded as a parallel development, the *centum* group preserved the lip-rounding characteristic of the labiovelar series, whereas in the *satem* languages the labiovelars became pure velars: IE *q^wi-*q^wo- (stems of the interrogative pronouns meaning "who," "what") > Latin *quis, quid*; Welsh *pwy*; Gothic *hwas*; Greek *póte* ("when"); West Tocharian *kuse*; Hittite *kuis*. The *satem* cognates are: Sanskrit *kás*; Albanian *kɛ*; Lithuanian *kas*; Old Church Slavic *kъto*.

This twofold development of the palatals and the labiovelars would seem to provide evidence of two old but distinct dialect areas, one to the east and the other to the west. The discovery in recent times of Hittite and

Tocharian—*centum* languages deep in *satem* territory—has tended to discredit this interpretation, although there is apparently no reason why one may not assume a series of early migrations eastward. This east–west cleavage may still be accepted as reflecting in a general way the *relative* geographical positioning of these dialects probably not long after the period of Indo-European linguistic unity. And pertinent to this observation is another: the *centum* languages would seem to show a more conservative treatment of this and other instances of phonetic change than does the *satem* group, that is, the innovations are more numerous in the eastern dialects, the western ones reflecting more faithfully the phonology of Proto-Indo-European. This may mean, therefore, that linguistically we would again be obliged to consider an area west of, say, the Caucasus as the original home of the Indo-Europeans.

It might also be noted that the parent language had words for "snow" and "winter," thus presumably ruling out a homeland in a tropical or subtropical climate. Proto-Indo-European also had a word, the meaning of which has been preserved in Germanic, Italic, Celtic, and Balto-Slavic as "sea"—Gothic *marei*, Latin *mare*, Old Irish *muir*, Lithuanian *mãres*, Old Church Slavic *morje*. But comparative and historical studies of these cognates reveal that the Indo-European etymon **mori* meant an inland sea. This is one of the major arguments for selecting an area around the Black Sea or the Baltic Sea as the Indo-European homeland.

Examples such as these could be multiplied many times, but the end result would be the same—we cannot do more than guess intelligently about who the Indo-Europeans were, where they lived, or how old their language is.

One last point: there have always been those scholars who have sought to go further back into prehistory and link Indo-European to other large linguistic groups, especially to the Semitic. Indeed, some linguists even in modern times have attempted to trace all languages back to one single source (monogenesis). Now, it may well be that the world's languages did develop in this way; linguistic science, however, can neither verify nor disprove the hypothesis. It would seem that the Indo-European languages may be related to the Semitic and perhaps even to the Finno-Ugrian families,[6] but even this theory—though not completely lacking in evidence—must be considered conjectural in the light of our present knowledge.

[6] The Finno-Ugrian (also known as *Uralic*) linguistic family includes Finnish, Lappish, Estonian, and Hungarian, in addition to several other less well-known languages.

CHAPTER TWO

Germanic

THE GERMANIC HOMELAND

THE prehistoric homeland of the Germanic people comprised an area including the southern part of the Scandinavian peninsula, Denmark, Schleswig-Holstein, and northern Germany from the Weser to the Oder rivers. By 500 B.C. the east–west boundaries had been extended to the Vistula and the Rhine, respectively, whereas the southward expansion had reached the mountain ranges of central Germany. The following centuries witnessed further encroachments to the south upon territory occupied by the Celts and Illyrians. In the last pre-Christian century Germanic tribes and Roman legions met in the first of the many battles that were to determine the Celtic, Germanic, and Roman boundaries for some time to come. The battle of Mulhouse in 56 B.C. established the Rhine as the boundary separating Celtic and Germanic tribes in the west. The south-western border was assured by the *limes*—a fortified wall that extended from the Rhine just above Koblenz southeastward to Regensburg near the Danube. These boundaries were generally successful in containing the Teutonic tribes until the third century of the Christian era and the onset of the vast and overwhelming migrations (*Völkerwanderungen*) brought on by overpopulation, inundations, and by the invasions of the Slavs in the east.

PROTO-GERMANIC

The language spoken by the Germanic tribes dwelling within the prehistoric homeland as outlined above is known as *Proto-Germanic* (abbreviated to *PGmc.*). Although we possess no documents, save perhaps a few of the runic inscriptions, written in this earliest form of a Germanic language, we nevertheless have both direct and indirect evidence of its phonology, morphology, and vocabulary. Moreover, we have the testimony of the comparative method, established—as we saw in the last chapter— by the systematic comparison of those languages which descended from Proto-Germanic and which are preserved for us in writing.

GERMANIC LOANWORDS IN LATIN

Certain Roman authors from the centuries just before and after the birth of Christ constitute a source of information about this language. Julius Caesar, for example, quotes the Germanic words for "bison" and "elk": *ûrus* and *alcês*. The historian Pliny records the words *ganta* "goose" and *sâpo* "cosmetics" (related to our word "soap"). And in the *Germania* of Tacitus we learn that the Germanic word for "amber" was *glêsum* (compare English "glass"), and that when going into battle the Teutonic warriors joined in a fear-inspiring chant or song called *barditus*. Both Tacitus and Caesar, especially, have given us additional linguistic informa- tion by recording the approximate Germanic names of places, rivers, tribes, and the like.

TESTIMONY OF EARLY INSCRIPTIONS

In addition to the testimony of the Roman writers, there is the scant but valuable evidence afforded by a few inscriptions, chief among which is found on one of twenty-six bronze helmets unearthed in 1812 at Negau near the Austro-Yugoslavian border. This helmet—referred to as Helmet B—has inscribed on its brim in rune-like letters the words *harigasti teiwai*. Though the precise meaning of these two words is in doubt, they are Germanic: *hari* (compare German *Heer*) is derived from an Indo- European noun **koris* "war" (compare Old Lithuanian *karis* "war"); *gasti* is the dative case of a Proto-Germanic **gastiz*, related to such words as Old Church Slavic *gosti* and Latin *hostis*. This word, by way of long semantic meanderings, developed meanings ranging from "stranger" to "friend" to "enemy." *Teiwai*, also in the dative case, means "god"; compare Old Norse *tîvi* "god." Many scholars believe that the compound word *harigasti* is used here as a proper name, and they suggest as a translation of the entire inscription, "to the god Harigast." The dates assigned to this archeological find range from the third century B.C. to the beginning of the Christian era.

Another discovery of great linguistic importance was a golden drinking horn found in 1734 near the Danish village of Gallehus in Jutland (see Plate 1). Inscribed in runic characters beneath the lip of the horn were the words *ek hlewagastiR holtigaR horna tawido* (R in the northern runic alphabets denotes a special kind of *r*-sound), which may be roughly translated: "I, Hlewagast of the Holting clan, made the horn." The language is a primitive form of Old Norse (*Urnordisch*), in general more archaic in phonology and morphology than the oldest historical stages of the Germanic languages that have come down to us. This same phrase in fourth-century Gothic, for instance, would read: *ik hliugasts hultings horn tawida*. The final syllables, especially, show a weakening or sloughing off when compared with the language of the inscription. Scholars assign the Golden Horn of Gallehus to about the end of the fifth century A.D. Unfortunately, it was stolen from the Danish Royal Museum in 1802, but not before several careful drawings had been made.

Germanic Loanwords in Finnish

Additional evidence of the structure of Proto-Germanic is found in a sizable number of loanwords which were taken over at an early date into such languages as Continental Celtic, Latin, Lithuanian, and—of unique importance—into Finnish. This latter language has undergone remarkably little change over the past two thousand years, so that we may assume that the Germanic words frozen into the Finnish vocabulary are preserved in almost the same form in which they were first borrowed during the Proto-Germanic period, an era that extends far back into prehistory. Compare the following Germanic loanwords as they are found today in Finnish with the corresponding reconstructed forms of the words *ring, king, soap,* and *gladly*:

Finn. *rengas*–Gmc. **hrenga–* (OHG, OS *hring*, ON *hringr*, OE *hring*)
Finn. *kuningas*–Gmc. **kuningaz* (OHG, OS *kuning*, ON *konungr*, OE *cyning*)
Finn. *saippjo*–Gmc. **saipôn–* (OHG *seiffa*, OE *sâpe*)
Finn. *kernas*–Gmc. **gernaz* (OHG, OS *gerno*, OE *georne*)

Significantly, the Finnish examples show in each instance a more archaic form than do any of the Germanic cognates: the Finnish words maintain from the ultimate syllable either the vowel or the consonant or both, whereas the Germanic instances exhibit additional degrees of attrition. This results from the fixing of the stress accent on the root syllable sometime during the Proto-Germanic period.

Stress Accent in Germanic

Of the many happenings which set apart PGmc. from the parent IE language, few had a greater and more profound effect than the stabilizing of the accent upon the root syllable of a word. This accent was movable in Proto-Indo-European (as it continued to be, for example, in Greek, Sanskrit, Lithuanian, and Russian) and in the early stages of PGmc., but it eventually settled on the root syllable. This caused a progressive sloughing off of the phonetic elements in final position. Compare, for instance, the Latin word *hostis* "stranger"—which preserves the full force of the terminal syllable—with the following Gmc. cognates: Gothic *gasts*, the Old Norse *gastiR*. and Old High German *gast*. The Old Norse still preserves the vowel and shows a final consonant that is regularly derived from a voiced sibilant. The Gothic form has lost the vocalic element, but still reflects the IE case ending (but compare the compound *gasti-gôps* "hospitable," which has preserved the *i*). In Old High German the attrition is complete. After contrasting the Indo-European congeners with the full set of Germanic cognates, we can reconstruct a PGmc. **gastiz*.

Returning now to the loanwords in Finnish, our examples must have been borrowed at a time prior to the perceptible weakening of final syllables—in other words, at a time prior to the onset of those changes in stress which later brought about such wholesale modifications of the phonology and morphology of the Germanic languages.

Alliteration

Another consequence of fixing the dynamic accent on the root syllable was the development in Germanic of what is known as "alliteration" (*Stabreim*), that is, the recurrence of the same consonant sound or vowel sound initially in accented syllables. This became a formal principle of Germanic verse, which employed alliteration as a poetic device: "in a *somer seson* whan *soft* was the *sonne*" (*Piers Plowman*); "ich *will* durch dinen *willen wagen* ere unde lip" (*Nibelungenlied*).

This principle played a role in the giving of Germanic family names: Chlodwig, Chlothar, Chlodomer; Heribrant, Hiltibrant, Hadubrant; Gunther, Gernôt, Gîselher. The force and compelling charm of alliteration has left its mark on all Germanic languages in the many noun doublets preserved, especially in the idiom of the vernacular: black and blue, hearth and home, bag and baggage; or such German expressions as *Wind und Wetter*, *Nacht und Nebel*, *Haus und Hof*, and so forth. Alliteration, of course, is not limited to those languages in which the stress accent became fixed on the root syllable, but only under those accentual conditions could it develop into such a dominant feature.

THE GERMANIC SOUND SHIFT

This Proto-Germanic language, as revealed to us by linguistic science, history, and archeology, is distinguished above all else by a phonological structure that sets it off sharply from Proto-Indo-European. Those sound changes which brought about the emergence of this new and distinct language, we group together under the heading "the Germanic sound shift." Although the vocalic structure was also modified, the most dramatic changes involved the consonants; and specifically those consonants we classify as "stops" (also known as "occlusives"), articulations characterized by the occluding or stopping of the breath-flow. Because of the fundamental importance of the Germanic sound shift, we must examine it in some detail.[1]

Ignoring certain aspects of Indo-European phonology not pertinent to Germanic, we may schematize the principal features of the sound shift as follows:

Indo-European	Germanic
Voiceless stops *p, t, k*	Voiceless spirants *f. þ. χ*
Voiced aspirated stops *bh, dh, gh*	Voiced spirants *ƀ, đ, ǥ* (emerging as the voiced unaspirated stops *b, d, g* in certain phonetic environments in the historical languages)
Voiced unaspirated stops *b, d, g*	Voiceless unaspirated stops *p, t, k*

In order to appreciate the significance of these observations, we must emphasize one point: the changes under discussion are *phonemic* changes, that is, they affect a particular *class* of sounds (voiceless stops, for example) at all points of articulation (here limited to labial, dental, and velar). With this point in mind, we may now inspect illustrations of each of these changes from Indo-European to Germanic. The Germanic examples are quoted in Gothic, it being the language which most closely conforms to PGmc.; the IE examples, unless otherwise noted, are from Latin.

The PIE voiceless stops *p, t, k* became in PGmc. the corresponding voiceless spirants *f, þ, χ*:

---

[1] The student would do well at this time to turn to Chapter Eight and review the material on phonetics given there.

> *pecu–faíhu* "cattle"
> *trés–þreis* "three"
> *cornû–haúrn* "horn" (Gothic *h* equals χ)

These consonants were not subject to spirantization if they were preceded by a voiceless sibilant:

> Lat. *con-spicere* "gaze at"–OHG *spehôn* "to spy"
> Gk. *skiá* "shadow"–Go. *skeinan* "shine"
> Lat. *(ve)-stîgium* "footstep"–Go. *steigan* "mount"

The PIE voiced aspirated stops *bh, dh, gh*, via an intermediate spirantal stage in Proto-Germanic (*b̄, d̄, ḡ*), later emerge as either the voiced spirants or the voiced stops *b, d, g*, depending upon their distribution. Whether Proto-Indo-European actually possessed this series is open to question. At any rate, of all the Indo-European languages, only Sanskrit has preserved such a series, and there is some reason to assume that it borrowed these sounds from non-Indo-European sources. However, since most of the handbooks assume voiced aspirated stops in the parent language, this text somewhat reluctantly follows the traditional presentation.

English does not include this class of sounds in its phonemic inventory, although we approximate the strongly aspirated pronunciation in such compounds as *abhor, adhere,* and *foghorn.* Two of the IE examples are taken from the Sanskrit; a third—because of a subsequent change that must be assumed for Indic—is quoted in its reconstructed IE form:

> *bhárâmi–baíran* "carry"
> *mádhyas–midjis* "middle"
> **ghóstis–gasts* "guest"

The PIE voiced unaspirated stops *b, d, g* became voiceless—*p, t, k*—in PGmc. There are no completely satisfactory examples illustrating the labial series (*b > p*), since convincing evidence for this change is restricted to comparisons between the Germanic and the Balto-Slavic languages. However, the clear testimony of the dental and velar series would seem to warrant the conclusion that PIE also possessed the unaspirated voiced bilabial stop:

> Lat. *lûbricâre* "make slippery"–Go. *(s)liupan* "slip"
> Lat. *decem*–Go. *taíhun* "ten"
> Lat. *genu*–Go. *kniu* "knee"

The Germanic sound shift was first described by the Danish philologist Rasmus Rask in an essay published in 1818. A few years later, in 1822, the German scholar Jacob Grimm set forth in his comparative Germanic grammar what is usually considered to be the definitive statement of this sound shift, coining the term *Lautverschiebung* (literally "sound shift") to describe the systematic and regular transition from one sound to another. A later generation assigned the expression "Grimm's Law" to the sum of the phonetic changes here discussed.

Verner's Law

Even as Rask, Grimm, and other early nineteenth-century scholars set about trying to systemize the phonetic changes that distinguished the Germanic languages from an earlier Indo-European stage, they became aware of certain "exceptions" to the patterns they had established. One such exception seemed to involve the PIE voiceless stops *p, t, k*. Instead of appearing in Gmc. as the corresponding voiceless spirants *f, þ, χ*, they occasionally emerged as the voiced spirants *ƀ, đ, ǥ* (usually not distinguished in conventional scripts from *b, d, g*). For instance, as opposed to a regular development as illustrated by the cognates Skt. *bhrā́tar*–Go. *brôþar*, there were such apparently irregular correspondences as Skt. *pitā́*–Go. *fadar* (*d* equals *đ*). Examples of this sort are fairly numerous.

The conditions governing this curious interchange were first established by the Dane, Karl Verner, who determined that the regulatory factor had been the variable position of the stress accent in late PIE and in early PGmc. If the affected consonants stood in speech-initial position, or if the stressed syllable immediately preceded the consonants in question, then the ensuing shift was to the corresponding *voiceless* spirant. If, on the other hand, the accent fell on any other syllable, then the change was to the *voiced* spirant. As can be determined by inspecting the examples given above, the stress marks of the Sanskrit words correspond to the shifting phonetic pattern of the Germanic cognates.

This interplay is especially striking when we examine the Germanic verbal system, comparing it to, say, Sanskrit, which reflects the accentual conditions of Proto-Indo-European. Consider, for instance, these forms of the Sanskrit verb "to turn" and their Germanic cognates:

Sanskrit	Old English	
vártāmi	*weorþe*	"I become"
vavárta	*wearþ*	"I became"
vavṛtimá	**wurdum*	"we became"
vavṛtāná	*worden*	"become" (past participle)

(The form with the asterisk does not actually occur. The third person plural of the preterite—*wurdon*—had replaced a regular **wurdum* before the historical period of Old English.)

What Verner first called an "exception" to the Germanic sound shift was, therefore, not that at all, but simply the effects of stress accent upon the shift. His explanation was accepted as valid, and was soon honored with the title "Verner's Law"—the term we still use today.

THE CHRONOLOGY OF THE GERMANIC SOUND SHIFT

Efforts to determine the chronology of the Gmc. sound shift have not been successful, though this is not to say that scholars have been reluctant to try. Archeologists, for example, cite evidence of an early Bronze Age civilization in Scandinavia dating from the latter half of the second pre-Christian millennium (see pages 39–42 for details). Since this civilization was presumably Germanic, we could say that the sound shift must have had its beginnings sometime around 2000 B.C. However, such a statement is inferential and without foundation in fact. We assume that some of those dialectal differences which eventually took on significant proportions probably characterized the language even of that early day. The assumption is reasonable, but unproved.

Historical evidence bearing upon the chronology of the sound shift is extremely sparse. One of the few bits of information has to do with the word for "hemp" borrowed by the Greeks as *kánnabis* from a neighboring language in about the fifth century before Christ. We have the authority of a contemporary Greek historian, Herodotus, that the word and the product were unknown to the Greeks prior to that time. Now, the word appears in the Germanic language in such forms as Old Saxon *hanap* and Old Norse *hampr*. A comparison with the Greek *kánnabis* will show that the IE consonants k and b have been shifted to χ (written h) and p. We must therefore conclude that the word for hemp was in the Germanic vocabulary *prior* to the onset of the sound shift, or at least prior to the time when the forces causing the shift had become inactive. If we accept the authority of Herodotus, then this word could not have been in the vocabulary before his time, and since it underwent the same phonetic change as all other Germanic words containing these sounds, we must assume that it was in the language prior to the transition of k to χ and b to p. In short, as of the fifth century B.C., the Germanic sound shift had either not yet occurred, or at any rate was not yet completed. We must also assume, of course, that hemp was introduced to the western Indo-European peoples via the Greeks, and then, through them, either directly or indirectly had become known to the Germanic tribes.

The inscription of the Negau helmet also enters into attempts to date the sound shift. As shown earlier, the words of the inscription are Germanic, which means that the shift was essentially completed at the time the inscription was made. Scholars are not in agreement as to the time, some of them selecting the third century B.C., others preferring a date as late as 6–9 A.D. The most convincing arguments, however, would seem to favor a time late in the second pre-Christian century.

In addition to efforts aimed at fixing the absolute or "metric" chronology, there is also the problem of the "inner chronology," that is, the problem of determining the sequence in which the various changes occurred. We must assume three major phases, extending possibly over several centuries. The precise order in which these phases took place cannot be determined, except to note that the IE voiceless stops *p, t, k* must already have become spirants—either voiceless or voiced—by the time that the IE voiced stops *b, d, g* had begun their transition to the *Germanic* voiceless stops *p, t, k*. Otherwise, of course, hopeless semantic confusion would have resulted.

As is obvious from the statements in the preceding paragraphs, we do not know when the Germanic sound shift occurred. However, on the basis of the inadequate information at our disposal, the general consensus of scholars is that it began probably not much before the fifth century B.C., and that it was essentially completed by the last pre-Christian century. This much at least is certain: not a single Latin loanword in any Germanic language shows indisputably the effect of the sound shift. Of course, we cannot know just when and where a specific Germanic tribe borrowed a word from the Romans, but contact between the two linguistic groups was well established by the time of Julius Caesar (102/100–44 B.C.).

Causes of the Germanic Sound Shift

The many explanations of the cause of the sound shift have one feature in common—inadequacy. In this area our ignorance is almost complete. There are, to be sure, a number of reasonable assumptions we may make, as well as a few observations of probable significance. For instance, it is reasonable to assume that a non-Germanic substratum had some influence upon the language of those Indo-Europeans who migrated to the area in northern Europe which later became the Germanic homeland. But what language or languages were spoken in that region prior to the arrival of the Indo-Europeans is not specifically known, so of course it is impossible to measure the degree of any supposed influence. One may, as far as that is concerned, look for an even earlier substratal influence prior to the time when the tribes in question reached northern Europe. In this connection it is interesting to note that another IE language, Armenian, otherwise quite foreign to the Germanic type, underwent in its transition from

Proto-Indo-European a series of consonantal changes much like those which characterized Proto-Germanic. This could mean, if we were to assume the same sort of influence, that the substratum should be sought far to the southeast in ancient Germanic territory, or perhaps even in Asia Minor itself.

Another explanation—and one that has been growing steadily in favor —is that similar phonetic changes may occur spontaneously at different times and in different languages. Let us take Armenian and Germanic as an example. In both languages the IE voiced unaspirated stops *b, d, g* appear as the corresponding voiceless stops *p, t, k*. A phonetic tendency toward devoicing might have occurred independently and spontaneously in both languages, resulting in an identical phonological pattern. It is not necessary, according to this view, to assume any causal relationship between Armenian and Germanic or between either or both of these languages and a substrate.

Other scholars, although recognizing the possibility of similar or identical changes in geographically separated and genetically unrelated languages, insist that there is a dynamic interconnectedness governing all such transformations, contending that there are indeed universally valid "laws" or principles according to which all languages change. They would posit the existence of certain forces operating to offset the equilibrium in any group of languages, in a single language, or even in a dialect. This view, advanced by Marxist linguists, is, as the reader may determine, the doctrine of dialectical materialism applied to linguistics. This doctrinaire approach to the problem of sound change, though producing an elaborate theoretical superstructure, has yielded distressingly little of a factual nature.

STRUCTURAL CHANGES IN PROTO-GERMANIC

Whatever the causes or reasons may have been, the result of such phonetic changes as the sound shift, Verner's Law, and the like, was that Proto-Germanic underwent many structural modifications. In other words, the sound changes brought about form changes. The effect on the inflectional pattern of moving (and subsequently fixing) the stress accent to the root syllable, for instance, can be seen by comparing certain singular case-forms of one class of nouns in Sanskrit and Gothic:

	Sanskrit	Gothic
Nominative	*devá-s* "god"	*dag-s* "day"
Genitive	*devá-sya*	*dagi-s*
Accusative	*devá-m*	*dag*

Or compare the conjugation of the verb in the present indicative active of the same two languages (in the first person singular, Gothic follows a pattern reflected by Greek rather than by Sanskrit):

Sanskrit	Gothic
(*bhárā-mi*) Greek *phér-ô*	*baír-a* "I carry"
bhára-si	*baíri-s*
bhára-ti	*baíri-þ*
bhárā-mas	*baíra-m*
bhára-tha	*baíri-þ*
bhára-nti	*baíra-nd*

Even without a detailed explanation—and leaving aside certain problems —it is obvious that the Gothic inflectional endings have suffered various degrees of attrition. With respect to the noun, this loss of formal markers (case endings) indicating syntactic relationships wrought decisive changes in the declensional pattern. Where PIE had distinguished between the forms of the ablative, dative, instrumental, and locative cases, the processes of phonetic attrition due to lack of stress caused these inflectional distinctions to be largely obliterated in the emerging Germanic languages. For instance, again taking the Sanskrit word *devás* "god," its case forms in the sequence just given are *devất*, *deváya*, *devéna*, and *devé*. Gothic, on the other hand, shows only the dative, which—for this declension—is characterized by an *a*-ending, *daga*. What we call the "dative" case in Germanic is merely a cover-name for the vestigial remains of four Indo-European cases; in fact, certain Germanic dative forms most likely reflect even a fifth case, the Indo-European genitive.

This weakening or loss of inflectional endings, resulting from phonetic tendencies, worked many fundamental changes in the structure of the Germanic languages. Indeed, so drastic were these changes that the affected languages must in large part be reclassified from "synthetic" to "analytic." In Latin, as an example of a synthetic language, the single formant *portấbantur* is translated into English as "they were (being) carried." Latin "synthesizes" the root *portâ-* and the bound elements *-ba-* "imperfect tense," *-nt-* "third person plural," and *-ur* "passive voice" into one complex grammatical form. Modern English or German, however, no longer possessing such wealth of bound suffixal elements, uses three or four free forms (words) to express the same thoughts. The sequence has been "analyzed," as it were, into its discrete and independent elements.

Referring back briefly to the loss of declensional suffixes which had been used to indicate case relationships, we saw that this in turn caused dramatic structural changes, and what had once been expressed by a case ending now required another signaling device altogether, namely, a preposition.

The synthetic Latin, for example, can express in one word—*sagittâ* "by (means of) an arrow"—what the analytic English or German must translate with a prepositional phrase. The older Germanic languages were more synthetic in structure than their later versions, though even in their earliest historical stages they fell short of the highly synthetic nature of such languages as Sanskrit, Greek, and Latin.

"Weak" and "Strong" Adjectival Declensions

In addition to the many internal changes that marked the transition from Proto-Indo-European, the Germanic dialects also developed or acquired a number of features either not found in the proto-language, or— if present—not yet so specialized as to function. For instance, there had been no structural difference between nouns and descriptive adjectives in the parent language. Such adjectives were declined according to the same pattern as nouns, the adjective agreeing in gender with the noun it modified. The inflectional paradigm of a Latin phrase such as "good friend" will illustrate this:

	Singular		Plural	
Nominative	bonus	amîcus	bonî	amîcî
Genitive	bonî	amîcî	bonôrum	amîcôrum
Dative	bonô	amîcô	bonîs	amîcîs
Accusative	bonum	amîcum	bonôs	amîcôs
Vocative	bone	amîce	bonî	amîcî
Ablative	bonô	amîcô	bonîs	amîcîs

The Germanic languages departed from this traditional structural pattern, introducing a distinction not observed in the parent language, namely, that between the "strong" and the "weak" adjectival declensions. The strong declension is a mixture of nominal and *pronominal* elements, whereas the weak declension is—as in the parent Indo-European—purely nominal. The inflectional suffixes of the pronominal adjective (the demonstrative pronoun) had, even in PIE, been partly nominal and partly pronominal, but in Germanic this pattern was extended to the descriptive adjective, thus establishing a new morphological category. In the paradigm below, the Gothic word for "holy" is declined as a strong adjective modifying the masculine noun "day"; the pronominal endings are in roman type and are followed in parentheses by the corresponding case of the personal pronoun of the third person masculine:

	Singular	Plural
Nominative	weihs dags	weihái (eis) dagôs
Genitive	weihis dagis	weiháizê (izê) dagê
Dative	weihamma (imma) daga	weiháim (im) dagam
Accusative	weihana (ina) dag	weihans dagans

The Germanic weak adjectival declension, on the other hand, is the direct continuation of an Indo-European nominal type, characterized by the addition to the root of an *n*-suffix (IE *-ên/ôn*, used to form nouns of agent and attributive nouns). An instance of this declensional type is the Latin *homô* "man," which is inflected as follows (note the presence of the *n*-suffix preserved in all cases save the nominative singular):

	Singular	Plural
Nominative	*homô*	*hominês*
Genitive	*hominis*	*hominum*
Dative	*haminî*	*hominibus*
Accusative	*hominem*	*hominês*
Ablative	*homine*	*hominibus*

The IE declensional pattern from which the Latin example derives was also continued in the Germanic languages; it is the familiar "weak" noun declension. Whereas the plural forms of the Latin and Gothic show internal developments that would require considerable explanation, the singular forms are obviously similar, as in the case of Gothic *guma* "man":

	Singular	Plural
Nominative	*guma*	*gumans*
Genitive	*gumins*	*gumanê*
Dative	*gumin*	*gumam*
Accusative	*guman*	*gumans*

In several of the Indo-European languages—Latin and Germanic among others—the addition of this *n*-suffix to the root of a nominal imparted to the basic meaning of the word the added notion of "permanent quality." Thus, Latin *catus* "sly" could be changed to *catô* (genitive *catônis*) "the sly one," and *rufus* "red" occurs in the *n*-declension as *rufô–ônis* "the red (headed) one"; Gothic examples are: *dwals* "foolish"– *dwala* "fool"; *liuts* "hypocritical"–*liuta* "hypocrite"; *weihs* "holy"–*weiha* "priest." The noun-forms are declined like *guma*.

The most frequent syntactic function of such nominals (there being no morphological distinction between adjectives and nouns), that of attributive modifier of another nominal, came to be identified structurally by the *n*-stem inflectional pattern. In Germanic this pattern resulted in the emergence of a special category, the "weak" adjectival declension, so that a noun phrase that at one time must have consisted simply of two nouns in apposition ("The holy one–The day") was now felt to consist of a noun and its modifiers: "The holy day." In the following paradigm, notice that the adjective is declined exactly the same as the noun *guma*:

	Singular	Plural
Nominative	*sa weiha dags* "the holy day"	*þái weihans dagôs*
Genitive	*þis weihins dagis*	*þizê weihanê dagê*
Dative	*þamma weihin daga*	*þáim weiham dagam*
Accusative	*þana weihan dag*	*þans weihans dagans*

Jacob Grimm introduced the terms "strong" and "weak" into Germanic grammar. Romantic and impressionistic, these words reflect the age in which he lived. His reasons for using the term "weak" for what is more properly called the "*n*-stem" declension, include the observations that the weak declension cannot express as many case distinctions as the strong, and that the former "decays" more rapidly than the latter (that is, the various vocalic elements following the suffixal *n*—compare the inflection of Latin *homô*—were largely lost in Germanic). In spite of all objections, however, Grimm's terminology continues to be employed by the writers of most German grammars.

THE GERMANIC PRETERITE

Likewise, in the structure of the verbal system, Proto-Germanic developed much that was different from the pattern in Proto-Indo-European. The Germanic general past tense, for instance, is such an innovation. This tense—called the "preterite"—is, in the case of the strong (or "primary") verb, a fusion and simplification of what in the parent language had been a complex pattern that involved both temporal and aspectual considerations. Tense distinctions in the Germanic strong verb are signaled by a regular and systematic alternation of the root vowel, as in *sing–sang, give–gave*. This vocalic alternation—usually referred to as *Ablaut* or "apophony"—was also a feature of the Indo-European verb, reflected for example in such Latin forms as *factus* "made"—*fêcî* "I made"; *stâre* "to stand"—*stetî* "I stood." In Greek these interchanges are likewise easy to demonstrate:

	peíthein "to persuade"	*dérkomai* "I look, see"
Present	*peíthô*	*dérkomai*
Perfect	*pépoitha*	*dédorka*
Aorist	*épithon*	*édrakon*

In the Germanic languages, however, this vocalic alternation developed into a full-fledged and regular grammatical system for signaling the distinction between the present and the past tense.

Historical grammars of the Germanic languages classify the strong verbs according to their ablaut patterns, assigning them to one of six or seven "classes." Here are examples of verbs of the first five *Ablautreihen* in Gothic and Old High German:

		Present	Preterite Singular	Preterite Plural	Past Participle
1.	Go.	*reitan*	*rait*	*ritum*	*ritans* "reiten"
	OHG.	*rîtan*	*reit*	*ritum*	*giritan*
2.	Go.	*biugan*	*baug*	*bugum*	*bugans* "biegen"
	OHG.	*biogan*	*boug*	*bugum*	*gibogan*
3.	Go.	*bindan*	*band*	*bundum*	*bundans* "binden"
	OHG.	*bintan*	*bant*	*buntum*	*gibuntan*
4.	Go.	*niman*	*nam*	*nêmum*	*numans* "nehmen"
	OHG.	*nëman*	*nam*	*nâmum*	*ginoman*
5.	Go.	*giban*	*gaf*	*gêbum*	*gibans* "geben"
	OHG.	*gëban*	*gaf*	*gâbum*	*gigëban*

The formation of the weak preterite by means of a dental suffix added to the verb stem (Gothic *nasj-an* "to save"—*nasi-da* "he saved") is probably a Germanic innovation, though other Indo-European languages show broadly parallel constructions, such as the suffixal *-t* of the Latin perfect participle, e.g., *amâ-t(-us)*.

Many scholars, however, hold that the preterite of the weak verb consists of the verbal stem plus what at one time must have been a past tense of the verb "to do," so that in Proto-Germanic there would have developed verbal compounds roughly analogous to something like "work-he did." Gothic provides us with the strongest support for this precarious theory. The conjugation of the preterite of a regular weak verb of the first class in Gothic is:

	Singular	Plural
1st Person	*nasida*	*nasidêdum*
2nd Person	*nasidês*	*nasidêduþ*
3rd Person	*nasida*	*nasidêdun*

Our attention is drawn to the plural (and to the second singular), which does indeed seem to be compounded of the stem-form of *nasjan* "to save" and another verbal element that can be matched etymologically with Greek *ti-thê-mi* "I place" and Latin *fêcî* (perfect of *facio* "I make"), both of which may be regularly derived from an IE root **dhê-*. Furthermore, the plural past tense of the verb "to do" in Old Saxon and Old High German is *dâdun*, *tâtun* (third plural), respectively. Since Gmc. *ê* became *ê* in Gothic and *â* in both Old Saxon and Old High German, it would appear as if the Gothic weak preterite might contain the reflex of an Indo-European root meaning "do." Unfortunately, though, as is so often the

case in historical linguistics, there are several factors which complicate
this seemingly neat solution to the problem. For one thing, this hypothesis
does not explain the first and third singular forms of the Gothic, which
show no long vowel; nor does it in the least clarify the composition of the
weak preterite in the other Germanic languages, no one of which has a long
vowel in the verbal suffix: OE *nerede,* OS *nerida,* OHG *nerita* (Old Norse
does not record this particular verb, but it can be reconstructed as **nerada*).

The difficulties—and there are still others—are insurmountable, so that
the problem of the origin of the Gmc. weak preterite remains one of the
thorniest of all.

THE VOCABULARY OF PROTO-GERMANIC

We shall conclude this brief description of some of the most outstanding
features of the Proto-Germanic language with a few remarks about its
vocabulary. Here, as in the case of its phonology and morphology,
Germanic is an interesting blend of the old and new. Certain common and
widely used Indo-European words (such as "to drink" and "to give") were
lost, for reasons which today escape us. On the other hand, contact with
the Roman civilization resulted in the borrowing of countless terms. A
brief list of such borrowings reveals those aspects of Roman culture which
were of most interest to the Germans. We may assume that many of these
words were borrowed during the period of Germanic linguistic unity:

German	Latin[2]
Fenster	*fenestra*
Kampf	*campus*
Kauf(en)	*caup(ô)*
Kelch	*calix*
Keller	*cellârium*
Kelter	*calcatûra*
Kessel	*catînus*
Kirsche	*ceresia*
Küche	*coquîna*
Kümmel	*cumînum*
Mauer	*mûrus*
Maul(tier)	*mûlus*
Meile	*mîlia (passum)*
Pfeffer	*piper*
Pfeil	*pîlum*
Pfirsich	*persica*

[2] No attempt is made to account for the phonetic changes from the Latin to the
German. For details, the student should consult a recent edition of Friedrich Kluge's
Etymologisches Wörterbuch der deutschen Sprache.

German	Latin
Pforte	*porta*
Pfund	*pondô*
Rettich	*râdix*
Senf	*sinâpis*
Sims	*sîmâtus*
Straße	*(via)strâta*
Tisch	*discus*
Wein	*vînum*
Ziegel	*têgula*

In addition to incorporating many extraneous elements, however, the Proto-Germanic language, no doubt from its very beginnings, had drawn and continued to draw heavily upon its own resources, substantially enriching its native vocabulary, especially in the areas of agriculture, animal husbandry, hunting, and warfare. Authorities have estimated that from approximately a fourth to a third of the Modern German vocabulary is uniquely Germanic in origin, no Indo-European cognates of these words having been found. Here is a sampling of such terms from the various fields just mentioned:[3]

Agriculture

Beere	*Hechel*
Bohne	*Hede*
Brot	*Pflug*
Distel	*Speiche*
Dung	*Wachs*
Harke	*Weizen*

Animal husbandry

Ente	*Krippe*
Fleisch	*Lamm*
Gans	*Leder*
Hahn	*Mähre*
Hengst	*Ross*
Henne	*Schaf*
Herd	*Schinken*
Huhn	*Speck*
Kalb	*Talg*

Hunting

Habicht	*Reh*
Iltis	*Reiher*
Marder	*Storch*
Rabe	*Wiesel*

[3] The examples to follow are excerpted from Alfred Schirmer, *Deutsche Wortkunde*, ed. Walther Mitzka (Sammlung Göschen, No. 929 [4th ed.; Berlin: Walter de Gruyter & Co., 1960]), pp. 42–45.

Warfare

Bogen	*Schleuder*
Fehde	*Spieß*
Friede	*Schwert*
Helm	*Waffe*
Schild	

Legal institutions and practices of the early Germanic tribes as well as the political and social stratifications of their society came through in these purely Germanic words:

Adel	*Herzog*
Bann	*König*
Dieb	*schwören*
Ding (a case tried before a court of law)	*sühnen*
Graf	*Volk*
Herr	*Wirt*

As would be expected from people living near large bodies of open water, they contributed many items dealing with seafaring and with fishing:

Aal	*Netze*
Dorsch	*Reede*
Ebbe	*Rogen*
Hafen	*Schiff*
Haff	*schwimmen*
hissen	*See*
Jolle	*Segel*
Kahn	*Steuer*
Kiel	*Stint*
Lee	*Sturm*
Luke	*Takel*
Möwe	*Tran*
Nachen	*Wrack*

(as well as the cardinal points of the compass)

CLASSIFICATION OF THE GERMANIC LANGUAGES

As stated earlier, this Proto-Germanic language is largely reconstructed, even though we have been able to retrieve bits and pieces of it in the ways previously mentioned. Those Germanic dialects for which we possess adequate historical records emerge considerably later as the languages of various tribes or tribal groupings (*Stammessprachen*), classified under three headings: North Germanic (Old Norse), East Germanic (Gothic, Burgundian, Vandalic), and West Germanic (Anglo-Frisian, Old Saxon, Old High German, Old Low Franconian, Langobardic).[4]

---

[4] Some texts group North and East Germanic together, using some term such as "Gotho-Nordic."

This particular grouping resulted from the efforts of nineteenth-century scholars who, in the manner of the natural scientists (botanists especially), had attempted to trace the pedigree of the Germanic languages by drawing up a "family tree," which supposedly reflected the actual derivations and developments of the various members. We may schematize these proposed filiations in this way:

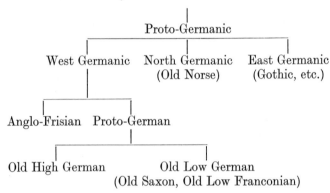

The principle underlying this attempt to establish a linguistic pedigree is that upon which the comparative method itself is based: similarities between languages are assumed to bear witness to a common ancestor, and those languages sharing the greatest number of features are assumed to be the most closely related.

This tripartite division of the Germanic languages (or bipartite, in case North and East Germanic are grouped together) is no longer accepted by many scholars. The difficulty centers on the term "West Germanic,"[5] for the older viewpoint would have us believe that Anglo-Frisian and Proto-German (from which descended Old Low German and Old High German) both derive from the same immediate proto-language. Especially objectionable is the traditional statement that High German and Low German are but later stages of an earlier, undifferentiated *Urdeutsch*. This is not to deny that the West Germanic languages have much in common with one another, but they also, individually, have much in common with the other Germanic languages. Furthermore, the traditional linguistic groupings—and this criticism extends to the entire Germanic complex— are often at variance with what we know about the historical location and migrations of the tribes who spoke these languages. Indeed, contemporary

---

[5] The student must not suppose that the words "north," "east," and "west" imply merely geographical relationship, in which sense they are generally acceptable; but according to the family tree concept they are used in conjunction with the word "Germanic" to designate *proto-languages*.

scholars are turning more and more to the testimony of archeology and history, realizing that the neat family-tree diagram is nothing more than a convenient schematization of possible but not necessarily historical linguistic relationships. The results of this reoriented approach, though they leave many problems unsolved, are at least more in consonance with what we know about the speakers of these languages, and the picture we get is to that extent several shades closer to reality.

Let us, therefore, review briefly the archeological and historical findings about the origins and later geographical disposition of the early Germanic tribes. Then we can examine the more prominent linguistic features shared by the various Germanic dialects, attempting finally to correlate our two sets of findings. By this method we can ascertain the most probable development of the *German* language.

The Homeland of the Germanic Peoples— Evidence from Archeology

As stated earlier, the prehistoric homeland of the Germanic people comprised an area including the southern part of the Scandinavian peninsula, Denmark, Schleswig-Holstein, and northern Germany from the Weser to the Oder rivers. In a narrower sense, though, it would be accurate to pinpoint the Germanic "heart land" in present-day Denmark and southern Sweden.

We do not know how long this area has been inhabited by man. The earliest generally acceptable evidence of human habitation stems from the early postglacial age, roughly 10,000 B.C. In the clay strata that mark this period, weapons made from reindeer horn and arrowheads crudely fashioned from flint have been recovered. From the following millennia, constituting what archeologists call the Paleolithic and Mesolithic Ages (*ca.* 10,000–3000 B.C.), the race or races of men who inhabited the Germanic heartland have left, imbedded in the soil and peat bogs, additional traces of their obscure existence: usually bone or stone artifacts, but now and then such things as a wooden arrow shaft, a canoe paddle, or some rudely fashioned pottery. From the refuse dumps surrounding their simple huts have been recovered the skeletons of marine life and land animals, dried fruits and berries, seeds of several varieties, and other remains of what at one time was food for these primitive peoples.

The Arrival of the Indo-Europeans

There is nothing from either the Paleolithic or Mesolithic eras that sheds any light whatsoever on the question of what language or languages were spoken in the Germanic homeland. On the other hand, the findings from the next archeological period, called Neolithic (late Stone Age)— roughly 2500–1500 B.C.—are quite pertinent, for during this era at least three culturally distinct elements arrived in Scandinavia from various parts of central and eastern Europe. Named after that feature of their culture by which archeologists most readily identify them, these three peoples are known as: (1) the food gatherers, (2) the megalithic builders, and (3) the battle-axe people (known also as the people of the separate graves).

Prior to the arrival of the food gatherers, a population of fishers and hunters inhabited the southern Scandinavian area. The newcomers, how- ever, raised domestic animals and planted grain. To clear sections of the forest, they slashed the bark of the trees, allowed it to dry out enough to burn easily, and then set fire to it. Some of the cleared land was used for grazing, some was planted in grain that was later harvested and stored in large earthenware vessels.

The megalithic builders arrived somewhat later. They are named after their practice of building communal graves from huge flat boulders (Greek *mégas* "great"—*líthos* "stone") arranged usually in the shape of a rectangle and roofed over with a massive block of stone. These people also developed their own style of pottery, both in shape and ornamentation (*Bandkeramiker*). They were farmers, kept dairy animals, and knew how to weave sheep's wool into cloth.

At a time when the communal graves were still being used, a new culture made its appearance in Scandinavia. Its bearers were not farmers but rather stock breeders. In addition to the practice of burying their dead in single graves, they brought with them a new kind of pottery ornamentation (*Schnurkeramiker*) and also a new kind of weapon, the battle-axe—for which reason theirs is also referred to as the "battle-axe culture." Archeological remains of this culture cover a wide territory extending across central and eastern Europe. Whatever their ultimate origins, they had little in common with the other two groups, and succeeded eventually in dominating and absorbing them, so that by the beginning of the Bronze Age (*ca.* 1500 B.C.) their culture predominated throughout the Germanic area.

Probably most archeologists and anthropological linguists accept the view that the battle-axe people were the first of the Scandinavian elements to possess a distinctly Indo-European culture. Scholars of this persuasion, therefore, date the beginnings of "Germanic" from the time that the battle-axe people reached what was to become their historical homeland;

in other words, approximately 2000 B.C. To quote from the authoritative work by Haakon Shetelig and Hjalmar Falk, *Scandinavian Archeology*:

> We have no direct evidence as to which race these battle-axe people belonged to, since no sufficient number of skeletons has been preserved in their graves in the north. But by indirect inferences an hypothesis has been reached which has at least strong probability on its side. It has been observed that the battle-axe culture in its expansion over large areas of Europe carried with it those forms which philological researchers declare to be characteristic of the earliest Indo-European culture, and it may be deduced from this that the spread of the battle-axe marks the expansion of the oldest Indo-European people. The immigration of the battle-axe people into the north must then be the starting point of the Germanic-speaking people known in later times in Scandinavia.[6]

Although this is the view most generally adopted by German and Scandinavian scholars, it must be admitted that there is no direct evidence compelling us to accept this interpretation. Indeed, the testimony of archeology could suggest another date for the introduction of an Indo-European language into the Germanic area: sometime around 1200 to 1100 B.C., when the so-called "urnfield" culture—and possibly also the *people* whose culture it was—penetrated the north country.

The practice of decorating the graves of an urnfield (that is, cemetery) with headstones and bronze decorations apparently had its origins in eastern Europe. At any rate, the custom can be traced from the Caucasus, across central Europe, up into Scandinavia, and as far west as the British Isles. Now, perhaps only the *custom* spread—one of the results of the Bronze Age with its emphasis on metal ornamentation—but there is always the possibility that the representatives of this culture had migrated down through the passes of the Caucasus, crossed the Danubian plains, and eventually reached even the outer fastnesses of western and northern Europe. What language (or languages) they spoke we know not, but it was probably different from that of the peoples they found in Scandinavia. It *could*, of course, have been a related language, even though separated in time by a good five hundred years. We must bear in mind that the two cultures were distinct—at least when judged by those features according to which the archeologists reconstruct prehistorical cultures. However, we should not make the mistake of equating race and language, nor—for that matter—social customs and linguistic types. The only conclusion we may safely draw is that an Indo-European language *could* have been introduced into the area as late as the arrival of the urnfield culture. As mentioned

[6] Trans. E. V. Gordon (Oxford: Oxford University Press, 1937), pp. 71–72.

earlier, this interpretation of the linguistic significance of this migration has few adherents.

LEXICO-STATISTICAL DATING

Pertinènt to our discussion are the results of a new technique of anthropological linguistics that seeks not only to establish the degree to which cognate languages are related, but also attempts to determine the age of a given language. This technique is known as lexico-statistical dating.[7] Those who accept the validity of this procedure (and there are many who do not) tell us that sometime between 2000 and 1800 B.C. the language we call Proto-Germanic emerged as an independent offshoot of Indo-European. They would also establish that the dialectal subgroup to which Germanic belongs is the same as the one from which the Slavic languages are derived. The method in fact posits a period of Germanic-Slavic unity that ended about 2000 B.C.

In terms of people and places, this information would mean that in the early centuries of the second millennium, speakers of an Indo-European dialect had reached northern Germany and Scandinavia, having migrated there from an area subsequently inhabited by Slavic-speaking people. In this particular instance the findings of a lexico-statistical analysis are in accord with the conclusions reached by the school of linguistic and cultural historians that favors the theory that the battle-axe people were indeed the first Indo-Europeans to arrive in the Germanic homeland. We shall adopt this interpretation in this book.

MIGRATIONS FROM THE EARLY GERMANIC HOMELAND

During the next two millennia, prehistory gradually merges into history. Archeologists distinguish the late Bronze Age (*ca.* 1000–500 B.C.), the Iron Age (*ca.* 500 B.C.–500 A.D.), and the Viking Period (*ca.* 500–1000 A.D.). Roughly two centuries before the beginning of the Christian era there occur the first faint *historical* allusions to the Germanic tribes. Although we must wait another six centuries for documents written in any of their languages, we begin to find references to the people in the writings of Roman and Greek historians, and—from the early Christian centuries— we have the valuable testimony of the runes: letters carved on bone, stone, and metal by the Germanic people themselves. On the basis of all available information, we can reconstruct the following account of the

[7] See my *Perspectives in Linguistics* (2d ed.; Chicago, Ill.: University of Chicago Press, 1970), pp. 57ff.; also Winfred P. Lehmann, *Historical Linguistics* (New York: Holt, Rinehart and Winston, 1963), chap. 7.

earliest migrations of those Germanic tribes that left the Scandinavian homeland.

Sometime within the early Bronze Age the lands touching upon the Baltic Sea were settled—perhaps as far to the east as the Oder River. By 800 B.C. northern Germany from the Ems to the general vicinity of the Vistula was inhabited by Germanic tribes, an area corresponding to the historical linguistic boundaries of Low German. Some two centuries later, tribes from around the mouth of the Elbe moved southward, following the course of the river into Upper Saxon territory. Then, in the last pre-Christian century, the Vandals, Burgundians, and Goths left Scandinavia, beginning their long trek eastward.

By the first Christian century this Germanic dispersion had resulted in five archeologically identifiable tribal groupings (see Map 1). One was of course made up of those elements that had stayed on in the Scandinavian epicenter (*Nordgermanen*). Another constituted the units that had migrated to the territory between the Oder and Vistula rivers (*Ostgermanen* or *Oder-Weichsel-Germanen*). The other three—traditionally lumped together as *Westgermanen*—were settled in northern Europe in an area of varying depth extending from the Netherlands to the Elbe. Taking their terminology from the topography, German scholars refer to these tribal groups as the *Nordsee-Germanen*, *Weser-Rhein-Germanen*, and *Elb-Germanen*. In his *Germania* (98 A.D.) Tacitus tells us that the ancient Germans themselves called the people nearest the North Sea *Ingaevones*, those of the "center" *Herminones*, and the remainder *Istaevones*. In conventional German spelling these words appear as *Ingwäonen*, *Irminonen*, and *Istwäonen*, and are now used as near-synonyms for the North Sea Germans, the Elbe Germans, and the Weser-Rhine Germans, respectively. The Herminones or *Elb-Germanen* correspond in general to the Suebi of Tacitus, described by him as a generic term for a number of distinct tribes, the most important of which were the Alemanni, the Langobardi, the Hermunduri, the Marcomanni, and the Quadi.

Starting with this last-mentioned subgrouping of the *Elb-Germanen*, we may trace the subsequent migrations of its five major tribal groups approximately as follows.[8] Beginning in the third century A.D. the Alemanni spread out into southwestern Germany, where they remained until Chlodwig, king of the Franks, drove them even farther south (some of them migrating as far south and east as the Iberian peninsula). The Hermunduri settled in present-day Thuringia. The Langobardi, after

[8] The following summary is in the main a free translation of pp. 88–89 of Hugo Moser's *Deutsche Sprachgeschichte* (4th ed.; Stuttgart: Curt E. Schwab, 1961).

crossing the Hungarian plains, found their way into Italy, where, in the second half of the sixth century, they established the kingdom of Lombardy; by the tenth century they were completely Romanized.

The Main River served as the southwestern boundary of the territory ruled by the Marcomanni and Quadi. In 8 B.C. the latter tribe began a migration that took it into Upper Hungary, where the Quadi subsequently disappeared as a distinct people. The Marcomanni, defeated in battle by the Romans in 9 B.C., withdrew into the Bohemian forests, where they dwelt until their final migration into southern Bavaria in the sixth century A.D. As a result of these converging southward movements, the Alemannic Suebi, the Bavarians (that is, the Marcomanni), and the Langobardi are often referred to collectively as *Alpengermanen*.

The Weser-Rhine Germans emerged later as the Franks and Hessians, occupying present-day Franconian territory in Germany, as well as the Netherlands, parts of Belgium, and northern France. Elements of them also merged with the North Sea Germans, who appear first as Frisians, Angles, and Saxons; later as Anglo-Saxons (occupying England in the fourth and fifth centuries), Saxons (*Niedersachsen*), and Frisians.

The *Nordgermanen* remained in Scandinavia, whereas the *Ostgermanen* —the Goths, Vandals, and Burgundians—undertook the most extensive migrations of any of the Germanic tribes, caught up as they were in the swirling cross-currents of population movements that swept across Europe throughout the early Christian centuries.

By the middle of the third century, the Goths had reached the Black Sea. From there, in 348, a band of them—known to us as the Visigoths (West Goths)—crossed the Danube into Lower Moesia (present-day Bulgaria). In the fifth century, pressures from the east again forced them to migrate, this time as far west as France and Spain, where Visigothic kings ruled until 711, succumbing ultimately to the armed might of the Saracens. Other Goths—the Ostrogoths (East Goths)—established a short-lived empire in Italy (493–554) under Theodorich, the greatest of their chiefs. Remnants of the Goths apparently lived on in the Balkans and in the Crimea, for a ninth-century historian mentions their presence in an area near the Black Sea, and a Flemish nobleman, while living in Constantinople from 1550 to 1565, recorded some words and phrases in a latter-day Gothic dialect now usually called "Crimean Gothic" (*Krimgotisch*), extinct since the middle of the seventeenth century.

About A.D. 400 another East Germanic tribe, the Vandals, left their homeland in northern Hungary and started on their long series of conquests that took them to Gaul, Spain, and finally to Africa, where, in 429 under their chieftain Geiserich, they established an empire that was to endure until it was crushed in 533 by the Byzantine general, Belisarius.

The Burgundians had a fate less spectacular than that of the Goths and the Vandals. They had settled in the third century along the upper reaches of the Main, pushing on a century later even farther up-river to Worms (*Nibelungenlied!*). However, after being beaten by the Huns in 437, they moved on into southeastern Gaul, soon became thoroughly Romanized, and in 534 were conquered by the Franks.

THE VALIDITY OF THE "WEST GERMANIC" CONCEPT

This brief discussion recaps the general archeological and historical theories about the origins, interrelationships, and migrations of the Germanic tribes. Unfortunately, when we try to derive from this information some scheme of *linguistic* development, we are at once faced with difficulties. For instance, we must assume—for quite valid reasons—that by the beginning of the Christian era the Proto-Germanic language community had broken up into several clearly defined dialect areas. Written evidence supporting this assumption, however, is long in coming: Gothic is known to us from the fourth-century Bible translation of Bishop Ulfilas; from the same century we have a few runic inscriptions in a primitive form of Old Norse. But for the rest, for the "West Germanic" languages, aside from words preserved in Latin works, written records do not begin until the eighth century.

If we try to relate the findings of archeology to our traditional concept of the West Germanic "pedigree" (page 38), we find it most difficult to reconcile this scheme with the complicated migration patterns of those tribal groups who later emerge as speakers of Old English, Old Frisian, Old High German, and Old Saxon. The reason for our difficulty, of course, is that the conventional charting of the West Germanic family tree depends for its validity upon findings which presumably prove that Old High German and Old English, for example, have many more features in common than, say, Old High German and Gothic. But this is by no means so certain; in fact, a careful tally reveals that the "West Germanic" languages—though admittedly having much in common—may also in several important features be paired separately with either the North or the East Germanic languages, or both, thus suggesting that there never was a single West Germanic proto-stage from which they all descended. An inspection of the following sets of comparisons will reveal why such a hypothesis must be considered suspect. We may begin by mentioning certain features shared by Old English, Old Frisian, Old Low

Franconian, and Old German (that is, Old Saxon and Old High German) to the exclusion of the Gothic and Old Norse.

WEST GERMANIC SIMILARITIES

1. Every consonant except *r* was lengthened when immediately followed by *j* (and sometimes by *m, n, r, l, w*). This phenomenon is known as "gemination" (*Konsonantenverdoppelung*), perhaps the most striking of the features shared by the West Germanic languages. In the following examples, the Gothic forms reflect the PGmc. situation, whereas the Old Saxon equivalents illustrate the changes wrought in the West Germanic consonantism by the following *i*-vowel:

Gothic	Old Saxon	
wilja	*willio*	"will"
sibja	*sibbia*	"relationship"
satjan	*settian*	"to set"

2. The second person singular of the WGmc. preterite shows an *i*-ending attached to a reflex of an IE optative form (in contrast to a reflex of a regular IE perfect tense form in Gothic and Old Norse; compare the corresponding Gothic forms given in parentheses). The examples are taken from Old Saxon:

	geban	*drîban*	*helpan*
First and third	*gab*	*drêf*	*halp*
Second	*gâbi* (*gaft*)	*dribi* (*draift*)	*hulpi* (*halft*)

3. Final Gmc. -*s* is usually dropped in WGmc. This phenomenon is especially obvious when one compares the declension patterns of Gothic nouns with those of the WGmc. dialects:

	Gothic	Old Saxon	
	dags	*dag*	"day"
Nominative singular	*fisks*	*fisk*	"fish"
	gasts	*gast*	"guest"

4. The noun-forming suffixes -*heit*, -*schaft*, and -*tum* are common to all the WGmc. dialects but are lacking in North and East Germanic.

5. Many vocabulary items are peculiar to the WGmc. languages:

Baum	*Knecht*
Faust	*Messer*
Geist	*Schaf*

GOTHIC (EAST GMC.)—OLD NORSE (NORTH GMC.)

It is generally assumed that Gothic and Old Norse are more closely related to one another than is either of them to any of the West Germanic languages. This assumption is based to a considerable extent upon the following observations:

1. Proto-Germanic frequently lengthened the articulation of the semi-vowels *j* and *w* after short vowels; this is indicated in print by doubling the symbols: *jj, ww*. In the WGmc. dialects, the preceding vowel and the lengthened semivowel unite to form a diphthong plus a semivowel: *ejj* > *eij; eww* > *euw*. In Gothic and Old Norse, however, the lengthened semi-vowels appear as stops plus semivowel: PGmc. *jj* > Go. *ddj*, ON *ggi* (the divergent spellings attempt to reflect what at one time was probably pronounced as some variety of a voiced palatal stop followed by a vocalic off-glide); PGmc. *ww* appears as *ggw* in both Gothic and Old Norse.[9]

Skt.	*dvayôs* "of two"		
Go.	*twaddjê*	*triggwa*	"alliance"
ON	*tueggia*	*tryggue*	"trust"
OHG	*zweiio*	*triuua*	"faith"
IE	**drewâ*		

2. The second person singular of the preterite in both Gothic and Old Norse has -*t* as a personal ending (Go., ON *gaft* "you gave"), which is affixed to a verb-stem that may be regularly derived from an Indo-European perfect tense.

3. A further similarity between Gothic and Old Norse is that only in these languages did those weak verbs formed by means of an *n*-suffix (Go. *gawak-nan*, ON *vak-na*) persist as an independent type, the so-called "class 4." The West Germanic languages preserve only traces of these verbs.

West Germanic and North Germanic (Old Norse)

The Gothic–Old Norse unity discussed above loses some of its signi-ficance when we discover that the WGmc. dialects *also* have certain features in common with Old Norse to the *exclusion* of the other Gmc. languages, thus—according to the family-tree concept—pointing to a period of mutual development:

1. The partial assimilation of *a* to a following *i*-vowel (*i*-umlaut) is an important feature shared only by these two groups. Actually, this is but one of several types of umlaut or mutation which occur in, and are limited to, West and North Germanic. In the examples, the Gothic words show the nonmutated vowel; the plural form shows a suffixal *i* or *j*. The Old Saxon and Old Norse equivalents exhibit umlaut:

---

[9] This statement of the development of PGmc. *jj, ww*, in the various Germanic languages is still sometimes referred to as "Holtzmann's Law." A generally acceptable explanation of the conditions governing these changes has yet to be found.

Gothic	Old Saxon	Old Norse
manna–mans[10] "man"	*man–men*	*mann–menn*
handus–handjus "hand"	*hand–hendi*	*hand–hendr*

2. Gmc. *ê* appearing as *â* is another feature characterizing these two dialect groups (Gothic again represents PGmc.):

Gothic	Old Saxon	Old Norse
(*manna-*)*sêþs* "mankind"	*sâd* "seed"	*sâd* "seed"
gêbum "we gave"	*gâbum*	*gâfum*

3. The voiced sibilant *z* appears as *r* (rhotacism; see note 11):

Gothic	Old Saxon	Old Norse
máiza "more"	*mêro*	*meiro*
áusô "ear"	*ôra*	*eyra*

4. Gmc. *þl-* corresponds to WGmc. and NGmc. *fl-*:

Gothic	Old Saxon	Old Norse
þliuhan "flee"	*fliôhan*	*flyja*

5. A significant number of words are restricted in their occurrence to these two linguistic groups: *Kohle, sagen, Segel, sterben,* and so forth.

Old High German—Gothic (East Gmc.)

The basis for a special West Germanic classification is further weakened when we find that the *individual* dialects constituting this proposed subgroup sometimes show marked affinities to one or another of the *non*-WGmc. languages. For instance, considerable significance is attached to the fact that Old High German has several features which it alone shares with the principal witness for the East Germanic group, namely, Gothic:

1. The personal pronouns in these languages show certain similarities not shared by Old English, Old Saxon, and Old Frisian:

Gothic	Old High German	Old Saxon	Old English
is	*er*[11]	*he*	*he*
weis	*wir*[11]	*wi*	*we*
mis	*mir*	*mi*	*me*

2. Both Gothic and Old High German preserve the dental nasal before *f, þ* (OHG *d*), and *s*, whereas it is lost in Old English and Old Saxon:

---

[10] The plural derives from a PGmc. **manniz*

[11] The *r* of the OHG forms is a regular phonetic development from a PGmc. voiced sibilant. When this sound—conventionally written as *z*—occurred in final position in Gothic, it tended to become voiceless (*s*). The technical term for the change to *r* is *rhotacism*, after the Greek letter *rho* (*r*).

Gothic	Old High German	Old Saxon	Old English	
fimf	*fimf*	*fîf*	*fîf*	"five"
anþar	*ander*	*âđar*	*ôder*	"other"
uns	*uns*	*ûs*	*ûs*	"us"

3. These two languages have preserved all three persons in the preterite plural, whereas Old English, Old Frisian, and Old Saxon have but one ending for all three persons: the common plural.

ANGLO-FRISIAN

Another telling argument against the supposed West Germanic unity is that Old English and Old Frisian (Anglo-Frisian) agree in certain features not shared by the *German* dialects. In the examples that follow, Old Saxon represents the German group, Old English the Anglo-Frisian:

1. WGmc. *a* usually appears in Anglo-Frisian as *e* (recorded as *æ* in Old English):

Old Saxon	Old English	
dag	*dæg*	"day"
fadar	*fæder*	"father"
akar	*æcer*	"acre"

2. When followed by a nasal, WGmc. *a* often appears as *o* in Anglo-Frisian:[12]

Old Saxon	Old English	
gangen	*gongan (gangan)*	"go"
lang	*long (lang)*	"long"
namo	*noma (nama)*	"name"

As is obvious from the preceding material, special resemblances can be found to obtain between any two of the Germanic languages, so that all attempts to plot their precise linguistic relationship based solely or even mainly upon phonetic, morphological, or lexical likenesses must be regarded as inconclusive. This applies especially to the traditional grouping of German and Anglo-Frisian as "West Germanic."

RECENT ATTEMPTS AT CLASSIFICATION

In recent decades scholars have been turning more and more to the evidence of archeology, history, and dialect geography in order to account

---

[12] "In the oldest English manuscripts it was written *a*, in the ninth century it was mostly written *o*, and in late OE mostly *a* again, but in some parts of Mercia it seems to have become *o* which has been preserved in many of the Midland dialects down to the present day." Joseph Wright and Elizabeth Mary Wright, *Old English Grammar* (3rd ed.; London: Oxford University Press, 1925), p. 42. See also Alistair Campbell, *Old English Grammar* (Oxford, 1959), pp. 51–52.

for the degrees of similarity obtaining among the languages of the various Germanic tribal groups. Among the best-known of these efforts—and also one of the earliest—is that of the eminent dialectologist, Ferdinand Wrede, who, in 1924, propounded his *Ingwäonentheorie*, which assumes that the so-called "West Germanic" linguistic community consisted in fact only of Anglo-Frisian (a grouping he preferred to call "Ingvaeonic") and that the *German* language arose later as a result of strong Gothic influences exerted upon an Ingvaeonic speech area which at that time extended as far south as the Alps.

Wrede was especially struck by the fact that High German—assumed to have developed from a West Germanic *Urdeutsch*—shared certain striking features with Gothic, and to that extent deviated from the pattern established by the dialects of the Ingvaeonic group. By way of explanation, he pointed out that the Swabian-Alemannic dialects of German ("High German") evince certain linguistic features which are also characteristic of the Low Saxon dialects ("Low German"), thus prompting his suggestion that the territory extending from the North Sea to the Alps had—after the withdrawal of the Roman legions from southern Germany —for a time constituted a fairly homogeneous dialect area (Ingvaeonic). This linguistic unity, according to Wrede, was disrupted when Gothic tribes from the east pushed into southwestern Germany, and the speech of the southern tribes gradually came under the strong influence of the East Germanic invaders. What we call "High German" is really, as Wrede put it, nothing but "ein gotisiertes Westgermanisch (Ingwäonisch)," whereas "Low German" is essentially a localized development of the uncontaminated Anglo-Frisian.

Unfortunately, Wrede's theory cannot be accepted. Although there is clear evidence of Gothic influence in Bavaria at that time, there is no verifiable record of a Gothic push to the western borders of central and southern Germany. Furthermore—and most damaging—those features in the phonology and morphology of the southern dialects which supposedly betray northern origins prove to be relatively late developments, post-dating the Ingvaeonic phenomena by several centuries.

Wrede's is only one of several recent attempts to broaden the scope of inquiry to include any and all factors which might have resulted in linguistic modification. Friedrich Maurer, for instance, recalling the early departure of the Goths from their northern Germanic homeland, believes that the Old High German and Old Norse likenesses stem from a period immediately thereafter, at which time the North Sea Germans and the Elbe Germans stood in close relationship to the North Germanic people.

What is called "West Germanic" would then, according to Maurer, be a later continental development, due probably to the growing political power of the Franks. The real weakness of this theory is that it fails to account satisfactorily for the language bonds uniting the continental WGmc. languages to the insular Anglo-Saxon.

Other scholars prefer to group the Germanic tribes into two large linguistic units: North Germanic (including what we have called East Germanic) and South Germanic, dividing the latter into two subgroups: (1) Weser-Rhine and Elbe—from which German ultimately derives—and (2) North Sea German, which eventually developed into Anglo-Saxon, Dutch, and Frisian. However, this division ignores the historical fact that many of the North Sea tribal groups did emerge as German-speaking.

Dialectologists point out, by the way, that this suggested juxtaposition of linguistic influences would account for many of the similarities obtaining between the Low German and the Middle Franconian dialects, as well as those features shared by Low German and the Scandinavian languages. The special High German-Gothic traits, on the other hand, could well derive from the one-time geographical proximity of the Elbe Germans (who subsequently migrated into Upper German territory) to the East Germanic tribal groups who had settled along the Baltic Sea in the early Christian centuries.

As a result of such evidence, assumptions, and arguments as these, the expression "West Germanic" as a term implying linguistic unity should probably be dropped, although it may continue to be used in a geographical sense. Certainly the notion that Old High German and Old Saxon (Low German) derive from a common and immediate prehistorical "Proto-German" must be abandoned. It now seems certain that the German language gradually took shape, from the fifth century on, as the result of the mergings and blendings of the dialects spoken by three tribal groups: the North Sea Germans (Saxons), the Weser-Rhine Germans (Franks), and the Elbe Germans (Alemannians, Bavarians, and Langobardians).

CHAPTER THREE

The Old High German Period

From the Beginnings to 1050

Chronology

IN TRACING the development of the High German language from its beginnings to approximately the fifteenth century, Germanists divide this span into an Old High German and Middle High German era, letting the former extend from the beginnings to about 1050, and assigning to the latter period the years from 1050 to, say, 1400. When greater precision is needed, they resort to such terms as "Late Old High German," "Early Middle High German," and so forth. This is, of course, an arbitrary segmentation—as is any such scheme—for language is a continuum, living on from generation to generation, undergoing gradual transitions of one sort or another, its speakers oblivious to structural changes of any kind. However, for purposes of study, some method of subdividing is necessary. One of the most satisfactory, both as to terminology and chronology, is that proposed by Hugo Moser in his *Deutsche Sprachgeschichte* ([4th ed.; Stuttgart, 1961], p. 101).

> Pre-German (second half of fifth century until 750)
> Early German (Early Medieval German; 750–1170)
> High Medieval German (1170–1250)
> Late Medieval German (1250–1500)
> New (High) German (from 1500)

The traditional division into Old High German and Middle High German (the terms were coined by Jacob Grimm) derives essentially from a study of the literature, where there are sharp distinctions between the two periods. This terminology was carried over into the linguistic field, and is used in most of the grammars and histories of the language. For this reason we retain the conventional nomenclature in this book, though calling attention to a set of terms which, if more widely adopted, would be preferable.

Since this text is in the main devoted to a history of the standard language, Old Saxon (Old Low German), Middle Low German, and Modern Low German are discussed only briefly in conjunction with their respective High German counterparts. The student is asked to consult the index and bibliography for additional references.

UPPER GERMAN—MIDDLE GERMAN

For purposes of broad classification, it is customary to designate as High German all those dialects which participate to some degree in the phonetic changes to be described on pages 56 ff. Nevertheless, the farther north one goes, the less evidence there is of this change. It is convenient, therefore, to subdivide the total High German speech area into *Upper German* (Bavarian, Alemannic) and *Middle German* (the various Franconian dialects,[1] to which were later added the different regional forms of East Middle German).

One must not imagine that there is any precise boundary line separating Upper German from Middle German (or, for that matter, separating any two dialects); there is rather a transition-zone characterized by differences in particular linguistic features. The geographic boundaries of a linguistic feature shared by some but not all of the speakers of a dialect, language, or group of related languages is indicated in dialect atlases by means of a line called an *isogloss*. Although dialectologists usually refer to a "bundle" of isoglosses which establish the boundary line between dialects, such a grouping is in reality only a summing up on a chart or map of the total differences. The effect on the traveler within a given zone is one of a gradual transition or blending of one dialect into another.

LOW GERMAN

North of the Middle German area lie those dialects which exhibit no trace of the High German consonant shift (see pp. 56–59). Historically

---

[1] Because it agrees with Alemannic and Bavarian in shifting PGmc. *p* to *pf*, and because PGmc. *þ* occasionally appears as *t*, East Franconian is usually listed as an Upper German dialect. Whereas I accept this classification for MHG and NHG, I prefer to include East Franconian with the Middle German dialects for the OHG era.

they may be subdivided into three major groupings: Low Franconian (Dutch, Flemish), Frisian, and Low German (*Niedersächsisch* or *Plattdeutsch*). Each of these is in turn made up of smaller linguistic units. Authorities differ as to the precise number of dialects in each of the major groups (it depends upon the definition of the term), but for Low German—in which we are more immediately interested—there are approximately fifteen regional groupings distinct enough in sound, structure, and vocabulary to warrant the name "dialect."

Plotted as a line on a map, the boundary separating High German from Low German begins in the west at Aachen, arches up above Cologne to the town of Benrath, then—after dipping briefly to the south—runs east by northeast just below Düsseldorf, Kassel, Magdeburg, and Frankfurt an der Oder until it reaches Slavic linguistic territory. The dialects of German to the north of this line (sometimes referred to as the "Benrath line") constitute the Low German speech area. For the Old High German period we have considerable evidence that the boundary line separating High German from Low German lay somewhat farther south. As for modern times, the student must bear in mind that the old dialect boundaries, though still extant, are everywhere much less discernible than before, due largely to a more widespread use of Standard German (*die Hochsprache*), but also—in a degree not yet fully determined—to the dialect mixtures resulting from the relocation in the west during and after World War II of millions of refugees and displaced persons from the eastern areas of prewar Germany (see p. 187 ff. for a discussion of Modern German dialects).

OLD SAXON

Our knowledge of the oldest historical form of Low German, Old Saxon, is based upon documents dated from the ninth to the twelfth centuries. By far the longest and most important work is a poetic version of the life of Christ, today preserved in two fairly complete manuscripts, one of them from the ninth century, the other from the tenth. This Gospel narrative—named *Der Heliand* (*Heiland* "Savior") by its first editor, Johann Andreas Schmeller—consists of approximately six thousand lines of alliterative verse (see p. 82 for a specimen text). Tradition holds that the poem was written by a Saxon monk at the command of the emperor, Ludwig the Pious, though there is no conclusive proof to support this otherwise probable assumption. The time of composition can be fixed at somewhere between 822 and 843.

Because it contains a curious admixture of Frisian, Old English, and Old High German elements, the language of the *Heliand* has long perplexed scholars. Mention has already been made of certain striking parallelisms between Old English and Old Saxon, accepted by Ferdinand Wrede as further evidence to support his view that Old Saxon was once an Ingvaeonic dialect (as was Anglo-Frisian); and only gradually did Old Saxon acquire certain High German characteristics resulting from southern influences which had penetrated the North Sea regions. Oddly enough, not all of the Ingvaeonic features can be traced to Middle Low German (1100–1500), which leads us to suspect that the Old Saxon of the *Heliand* contains some nonnative and probably literary accretions never present in the colloquial language. This suspicion is further heightened when we observe that the vocabulary of the *Heliand* includes many words and expressions not otherwise found in the Low German of a later era, though they *do* have their counterparts in various dialects and chronological stages of High German.

From a linguistic standpoint, the most significant observation about the *Heliand* is that it may not too accurately mirror the language spoken by the people of that time and place. For this reason Wrede prefers to call it "Bible Saxon." However, the language of the *Heliand* is clearly and unmistakably German, standing much closer in its basic structure and vocabulary to the High German dialects than to an Anglo-Frisian proto-language.

Linguistic Boundaries

As a result of the many migrations dating from the immediately preceding centuries, the German linguistic boundaries of the sixth century had undergone considerable modifications. Slavic tribes now occupied the territory east of the Elbe, while farther south other non-Germanic peoples had pushed their way across the Danubian plains to the frontiers of Bavaria.

In their own search for new territory the Germanic tribes had migrated west and south: to the west as far as the Loire River, and to the south as far as Italy (the province of Lombardy in northern Italy owes its name to the Langobards, a Germanic tribe that arrived in the sixth century). In both instances the invaders were destined to adopt the Roman culture of their new homeland, but not for several centuries and not until their own speech had left its imprint on the local Latin. French in particular shows the influence of German upon that territorial form of Latin spoken in the fifth and sixth centuries by the Romans who had settled in Gaul. This influence is especially evident in words relating to war: Fr. *guerre* "war" < Gmc. **werra*; Old French *brand* "sword" < Gmc. **brand-*; Old French *gonfalon* "battle flag" < Gmc. **gun-fanan*; Old French *heaume* "helmet" < Gmc. **helm*.

The High German Consonant Shift

The German language itself underwent a profound change during these last prehistorical centuries. Starting most probably in the southernmost reaches of the German-speaking lands sometime in the fifth century, a series of sound changes gradually resulted in the restructuring of the phonetic systems of all the southern and many of the midland dialects. Those dialects whose phonology was affected by these changes we now classify as High German; the unaffected dialects in northern Germany, on the other hand, belong to the so-called Low German group. This series of changes—known collectively as the High German consonant shift— involved the voiceless stops *p, t, k* (< IE *b, d, g*) and the voiced spirants *ƀ, đ, ǥ* (< *bh, dh, gh*) of Proto-Germanic.[2] The fate of these sounds in Old High German may be summarized as follows:

1. When occurring (a) in word-initial position, (b) medially following a consonant, (c) or in gemination (that is, when doubled), Gmc. *p, t, k* developed into their corresponding affricates: *pf, ts* (spelled *z*), and *kχ* (spelled *kh* in our examples):[3]

>   (a) Go. *páida*–OHG *pfeit* "dress"
>   Go. *twái*–OHG *zwei* "two"
>   Go. *kaúrn*–OHG *khorn*[4] "corn"
>
>   (b) ME *stampen*–OHG *stampfôn* "stamp"
>   Go. *haírto*–OHG *herza* "heart"
>   Go. *drigkan*[5]–OHG *trinkhan*[4] "drink"
>
>   (c) NE *dapper*–OHG *tapfer* "brave"
>   OE *settan*–OHG *setzan* "set"
>   OS *wekkian*–OHG *wecchan*[4] "wake"

2. In all other positions—that is, (a) medially between vowels, and

---

[2] Some scholars assume that in certain phonetic environments these spirants had shifted to the voiced stops *b, d, g* already in Proto-Germanic. I posit spirantal pronunciation in *all* positions for PGmc.

[3] In the examples that follow, the non-High German cognates—regardless of relative chronology—all reflect the consonantism that presumably prevailed in Proto-Germanic.

[4] The shift to the velar affricate was limited to the Upper German dialects.

[5] Gothic *-gk-* symbolizes phonetic [-ŋk-].

(b) in final position when immediately preceded by a vowel—the Germanic voiceless stops became the voiceless spirants *f, s, χ*:[6]

        (a) Go. *slêpan*–OHG *slâf(f)an* "sleep"
            Go. *êtum*–OHG *âzum* "(we) ate"
            Go. *mikils*–OHG *mihhil* "much"

        (b) Go. *skip*–OHG *skif* "ship"
            OE *fôt*–OHG *fuoz* "foot"
            Go. *ik*–OHG *ih* "I"

3. The Germanic voiced spirants *ƀ, đ, ǥ*, appear for the most part as orthographic *b, d, g* in the manuscripts of the various Germanic languages. Depending essentially upon phonetic environment, these symbols were pronounced now as voiced stops: [b], [d], [g]; now as voiced spirants: [ƀ], [đ], [ǥ], with a tendency toward the occluded pronunciation in all positions. In the High German dialects, this phonetic "drift" was frequently carried a step further, the voiced stops tending to become the voiceless lenis stops [b̥], [d̥], [g̥], usually written as *p, t, k*. This rather involved development is taken up in Chapter VII (see also under "Tenseness"), though the student should realize that documents written in the Upper German (especially Bavarian) dialects frequently have *p, t, k* where Middle German spellings usually show *b, d, g*:

        MG *bringan, habên*–UG *princan, hapên*
        MG *dag, fadar*–UG *tac, fater*
        MG *guod, vogel*–UG *côt, focal*

As is apparent from the examples, only the most southerly of the German dialects illustrate the full scope of the High German consonant shift. Those dialects to the north of the Bavarian and Alemannic areas exhibit progressively fewer features of the shift.[7] Indeed, the traditional and still customary division of the High German speech area into its principal dialect groupings rests upon the extent to which a given area was affected by the consonant changes just described. For the Old High

---

[6] In German manuscripts these sounds were conventionally written *ff, zz, hh* (*ch* after about 850). The letter *z* stood for both the affricate (*ts* as in *herza*) and a spirant, the precise nature of which is in doubt. Until late MHG times, at any rate, this sound was carefully distinguished from the old Germanic sibilant *s*.

[7] At this point we might mention the shift of Germanic *þ* to *d*. Since this is a change common to both the Low German and High German dialects, it cannot properly be considered part of the High German consonant shift. The transition from *þ* (usually spelled *th*) to *d* was gradual, beginning as early as the ninth century in Bavaria, not reaching Low German territory until the tenth century. In the Upper German dialects, the *d* which was derived from Gmc. *þ* was later frequently shifted to *t*. See p. 79 for a discussion of Notker's *Anlautgesetz*.

German period we recognize the following five major dialects (see also Figure 1):[8]

Bavarian

(Munich, Regensburg). In the Bavarian and Alemannic dialects we find the High German consonant shift essentially in its "classic" form as described above.

Alemannic

(High Alemannic or Swiss: Bern, Basel; Low Alemannic or Swabian: Freiburg im Breisgau, Augsburg). The High Alemannic and Upper Bavarian dialects both possessed the true velar affricate *kχ*.

East Franconian

(Nürnberg, Bamberg, Würzburg). Gmc. *k* remains unshifted under those conditions where the High German consonant shift would yield an affricate (*khalt, kalt*).

Rhenish Franconian

(Frankfurt, Mainz). Gmc. *k-*[9] remains unshifted; Gmc. *p-* frequently resists the change to the corresponding affricate *pf*.

Middle Franconian

(Koblenz, Trier).[10] The Gmc. voiceless stops *p-* and *k-* remain in general unaltered, and—in certain words of high frequency of occurrence—even Gmc. *-t-* is kept: *dat, wat* instead of *das, was*.

---

[8] This tally omits the Langobardic in upper Italy and the West Franconian in southeastern France. Both dialects participated in the High German consonant shift, but disappeared fairly early as linguistic entities—at least so far as written records go. Furthermore, this particular listing does not take into account the East Middle German dialects: Thuringian, Upper Saxon (or simply "Saxon"), and Silesian. The latter two developed later, largely as the result of colonial expansions beginning in the twelfth century.

Although the Thuringians had emerged after the migrations as one of the major tribal groups, their dialect did not become literarily significant until the Middle High German era.

[9] The use of a dash *after* a letter (*k-*) indicates the so-called "initial" position of the consonant; dashes on *both* sides of the letter (*-k-*) signify "medial" position. The term "initial" includes all positions given under 1. a, b, and c on p. 56; "medial," those given under 2. a and b on p. 57.

[10] Middle Franconian may be further divided into *Mosel Franconian* (Trier) and *Ripuarian* (Cologne). The latter dialect participated in the High German consonant shift only in a limited way, especially during the early centuries.

Figure 1. The Spread of the High German Consonant
Shift in the Old High German Dialects

PGmc.	Bav.	Alem .	East Franc.	Rhenish Franc.	Middle Franc.
p-	pf	pf	pf	—	—
t-	z	z	z	z	z
k-	kh	kh	—	—	—
-p-	ff	ff	ff	ff	ff
-t-	zz	zz	zz	zz	zz
-k-	hh	hh	hh	hh	hh

In tracing the development of the PGmc. sounds into the Old High German dialects, the conventional orthographic symbols of the German manuscripts are used: $z = ts$; $kh = k\chi$; $ss = s$; $hh = \chi$.

The blank spaces signify that the PGmc. sound comes through unshifted in that particular dialect.

CHRONOLOGY AND POINTS OF ORIGIN OF THE HIGH GERMAN CONSONANT SHIFT

In attempting to determine the chronology of the High German consonant shift, we must—as in the case of the Germanic sound shift—be content with approximations; furthermore, much of the evidence is of an indirect sort. The name *Attila* ("little father"), king of the Huns, for instance, is recorded in Middle High German documents from around 1200 as *Etzel*. The two principal changes in the MHG form are the affrication of the *t* and the partial assimilation of the back vowel *a* to the front vowel *i*, a process referred to technically as *Umlaut*. Now, in order to have undergone any sort of change, the word must first of all have been in the German language at the time when the pertinent sounds were affected. Since Attila died in 453, his name obviously could not have been known to the Germans much before then. And since there is no occurrence of the word in the manuscripts until MHG times, we cannot know just when the change in consonantism occurred, nor can we know into which of the German dialects the name of Attila was first borrowed. Our only conclusion can be that the affrication of the dental stop had not yet begun by the year 450 in at least one of the High German dialects (see p. 69 for additional testimony offered by Gothic).

Another bit of early evidence that sheds some light on our problem is found in the Latin writings of the Frankish historian, Gregory of Tours (538?–593/94). In recording certain events of the year 575, he refers to a Langobardic duke whose name he writes as *Zaban* (a thirteenth-century manuscript has the spelling *Zafan*). Etymologists tell us that this word is related to Old Norse *tafn* "sacrifice, catch." Although the purported Langobardic form would seem to show clear evidence of the High German shift ($t > z$), we cannot with certainty set the date at 575, inasmuch as Gregory's remarks are contained in a manuscript that was copied a full century later and may therefore reflect scribal changes. Taken at face value, however, such a spelling would mean that by the year 575 the Langobardic dialect had undergone at least one phase of the High German consonant shift.

Be that as it may, the Langobardic must still be considered one of our earliest sure witnesses to the consonant shift, since the *Edictus Rothari* of 643 (a codex of Lombardic law), though composed in Latin, cites many words and expressions in an unequivocally High German form. Here again, however, the earliest extant manuscript of the edicts of King Rothari dates from about 700, a good fifty years after the initial drafting of the laws, so that we cannot with complete confidence claim that Langobardic already possessed a distinctly High German consonantism as early as the middle seventh century.

Our oldest firsthand record of a High German speech form is preserved in an inscription on a spearhead found in Wurmlingen, a village near Tuttlingen in southern Württemberg (Alemannic dialect area). The inscription includes the proper name *Idorih*, a compound whose second part —related to the Gothic word *reiks* "ruler"—clearly shows the shift from stop to spirant ($h = \chi$). The date of the inscription may be placed at approximately 600.

Further evidence of High German consonantism in Alemannic territory is offered by place names quoted in Latin documents from the seventh century: *Ziaberna* "Zabern" (from a one-time Latin *ad tavernas*), *Ascapha* "Aschaffenburg," *Ziurichi* "Zürich." When added to the weight of the other testimony, instances such as these would seem to warrant a conclusion that the High German consonant shift—at least in Alemannic territory—was essentially completed by about the year 600.

Although the shift obviously had its beginnings somewhere in the southern regions of the German speech area, a more precise location of the point of origin is difficult to ascertain. The evidence just presented favors either southeastern Germany or that part of northern Italy situated between the Po River and the Brenner Pass.

In recent years the theory that the High German consonant shift received its initial impetus from the language of the Italian Goths has been growing in favor. There is, to be sure, a fair amount of evidence that the Germanic voiceless stops had undergone affrication in certain dialects of Gothic. The evidence, however, is chiefly of an indirect nature, for neither the Gothic Bible nor the other remnants of literary Gothic reflect any obvious instances of such changes. Nevertheless, Roman and Greek authors from approximately the third century on quote Gothic words—principally proper nouns—in a spelling that apparently seeks to reflect affricated sounds. The very name of the Goths themselves, for example, appears in Greek as *Gotthoi* (*Gót-thoi*) and in Latin as *Gothi* (compare earlier Greek *Goútones* and Latin *Gutones*).[11] A Latin letter written around 500 refers to *Zeia*, a Gothic king whose name in literary Gothic would be spelled *Teia* or *Teja*. Greek writers, sounding out Gothic names ending in the familiar *-reiks* "ruler," consistently adopted the spelling *reixos*, using chi rather than kappa, apparently in order to indicate an affricated velar sound. And a Latin poem from the sixth century begins with a hexameter containing several Gothic words, one of which, *matzia*, exhibits a shift from stop to spirant (compare biblical Gothic *matjan* "to eat").

On the strength of such examples as these, one might therefore assume that the language of the Italian Goths of the sixth century shows clear evidence of a sound shift affecting at least two of the Germanic voiceless stops (*t* and *k*).[12] And a final point: if the High German consonant shift was

---

[11] The *th*-spelling (in Greek the *theta*) was used to distinguish a strongly aspirated or perhaps even affricated dental stop. The symbol *t* stood for the unaspirated variety characteristic of Modern French and Spanish. Contrast the pronunciation given to the two *t*'s in English *top* and *stop*; the *t* of the latter word is pronounced without aspiration, as is the *t* of French *tasse* "cup" and Spanish *tener* "have."

[12] The OHG (Bavarian-Austrian) word *mauta*, Modern German *Maut* "tax, revenue," offers evidence of a possible exception to this statement. A loanword from Gothic (compare biblical Gothic *mota* "tax"), *mauta* would seem to point to an unshifted dental stop rather than to the affricate which we have suggested. Now, it is usually assumed that the Ostrogoths in Italy—keeping much of the Roman system of government after their own rise to power—had borrowed the term *mota* (and the practice for which it stood) from the Late Latin *mûta* "tax." But the word need not necessarily be a borrowing from the Latin, for there is reason to believe that its occurrence in Gothic was not limited to Italy. Etymologists point out that the Old Slavic word *myto* "customs, duty" (the word is still used in Modern Russian) was most likely borrowed from a Germanic language, probably from one of the eastern dialects bordering on Slavic territory. The fact that OHG *mauta* first occurs in the Bavarian-Austrian dialect may point toward contact with, not the Italian Goths, but another of the Gothic tribes, situated nearer the Balkan homeland, whose language showed no trace of the consonantal changes that had affected the Italian branch.

indeed precipitated by the Italian Gothic, then its way into Germany must have been via the kingdom of the Lombards. Significantly perhaps, the Langobardic dialect shows no trace of affrication prior to the arrival of its speakers in northern Italy (568).

The spread of the High German shift northward, whatever its ultimate provenience, took place slowly. Although we have demonstrated the occurrence of shifted forms in Alemannic territory for as early as 600, we must not suppose that this change was thoroughgoing and complete at this time. The Alemannic dialect spoken in the vicinity of Bregenz, located on the shores of Lake Constance along the Austrian-Swiss border, had unshifted *p* as late as 610. And Gregory of Tours, writing his *History of the Franks* a full decade before the year 600, spells Straßburg with an unshifted *t: Strateburgium.*[13] Moving out of Alemannic territory, Bavarian documents preserve some non-High German forms well into the eighth century and even later: the Monsee Codex of 807, for instance, records the place name *Laufen* as *Lauppa.* Still farther north, the earliest historical instances of High German influence on the Middle German dialects are preserved in late seventh-century manuscripts from the monastery at Weißenburg in Rhenish Franconia; not until a century later, however, did the transition become general in this area. And not until the ninth century did the High German consonant shift reach the Middle Franconian dialect.[14]

CAUSES OF THE HIGH GERMAN CONSONANT SHIFT

As to what caused the High German consonant shift, we can only repeat what we have already said about the causes of the Germanic sound shift: "The many explanations have one feature in common—inadequacy." Since the shift had its beginnings in an area where German tribes came in close and abiding contact with Celts and Romans (among others), it is possible that the foreign linguistic influences were strong enough to affect the phonetic structure of their language. Reasonable as this theory is, though, there is little direct evidence to support it.

The similarities between the Germanic sound shift and the High German consonant shift—in both instances the voiceless stops undergoing various

[13] Although the oldest extant manuscript of Gregory's *History* was copied a century later, it would be unreasonable to assume that a scribe at that late date—long after the consonant shift was completed in this region—would deliberately attempt to restore a pre-High German pronunciation, even if he were aware of the previous situation.

[14] For a more detailed discussion complete with bibliographical references, the student should consult Wilhelm Braune, *Althochdeutsche Grammatik*, ed. Walther Mitzka (9th ed.; Tübingen, 1959), par. 83ff.

degrees of spirantization—have, since the days of Jacob Grimm, encouraged some scholars to hold that the High German shift is simply a later phase in a cycle of phonetic modifications that began with the "first" shift. As Grimm studied the two shifts, he became aware of what seemed to him to be a fundamental principle at work, joining together the two processes in a remarkable but reasonable manner. In its simplest form, this principle may be represented by the diagram in Figure 2.

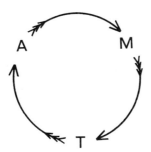

Figure 2. Jacob Grimm's Kreislauf

Grimm used the term *Kreislauf* ("revolution," "circulation") to describe the progression of the tenues (T), aspirates (A), and mediae (M)[15] in their transition from Indo-European to Germanic to Old High German. (The misleading term "aspirate" must of course be interpreted to mean "spirant.") If we refer to the material on pp. 24–25, we will see that in the change from Indo-European to Germanic each of the three series of consonants progressed through one stage or phase of the cycle.

The High German shift, according to Grimm, finished the cycle; each consonantal series in Germanic moved through another phase of the circle, thus completing the triad. In illustrating this final stage, Grimm unfortunately permitted the term "aspirate" to serve as a catch-all expression for both spirant and affricate.

Rearranging the two sound shifts in terms of their progression through the cycle, we get the following scheme:[16]

Indo-European	T	M	A
Germanic	A	T	M
Old High German	M	A	T
Examples:			
Greek	*phrátôr*	*déka*	*thygátêr*
Gothic	*brôþar*	*taíhun*	*daúhtar*
Old High German	*bruoder*	*zehan*	*tohter*

---

[15] Using the terminology of our text, we should say *voiceless stops*, *voiceless spirants*, and *voiced stops*, respectively.

[16] Quoted from my *Perspectives in Linguistics*, pp. 28–29 *passim*.

Couching his remarks in the terminology of articulatory phonetics, the late Eduard Prokosch comments as follows:

> All Indo-European stops and spirants pass through a consistent system of changes during the early history of the Germanic languages. In concrete terms, defining merely the actual result, its general course may be described as follows: in the case of *stops*, the breath is *released*. In the case of *spirants*, the breath is *checked*.[17]

While this theory makes for a neat structural explanation—and is in the main consistent with what we know about the mechanics of speech production—it is nevertheless somewhat difficult to see a generic correlation between the Germanic sound shift of *ca.* 500–100 B.C. and another set of changes (even though they exhibit what resembles a kind of cyclical progression) that took place half a millennium later, and which was apparently restricted to only one group of the Germanic dialects. Of course, if—as our previous discussions suggest—the High German consonant shift was common to certain of the *East* Germanic languages as well, then perhaps the theory that there are causal connections joining the "first" shift to the "second" may not be so improbable after all.

A third possible explanation of the High German consonant shift is that the changes took place independently and to an extent concurrently in the several dialects. Although occasional linguistic similarities can no doubt be explained in this way, the scope and complexity of the High German shift demands a more elaborate answer.

Influence of the Franks on the Development of High German

Interesting as all this theorizing may be, we must eventually admit that we do not know what caused the German dialects in the Alpine regions of Italy, Switzerland, and Germany to undergo the series of changes we refer to as the High German consonant shift. Nor can we give an entirely satisfactory explanation as to why these changes, once effected, moved northward. We know that dialects are spread by *migration* and by *diffusion*, the latter being defined as a process of language radiation from a central point. Dialectologists tell us that diffusion is intimately bound up with social—usually political—factors, the socially superior dialect in general influencing the socially inferior. This would perhaps explain the spread of the consonant shift from, say, Langobardic to Alemannic and Bavarian; it would also be a reasonable answer as to how the Italian

---

[17] *A Comparative Germanic Grammar* (Philadelphia: Linguistic Society of America, 1939), p. 50.

Gothic might have influenced Langobardic. But it would not at all clarify how the High German consonantism found its way into the Franconian dialects, for the defeat of the Alemanni at Straßburg in 496 by the Franks marked not only the approximate end of German tribal migrations, but also the beginning of Frankish political supremacy, so that subsequent linguistic diffusion from the German-speaking south could hardly have been of much consequence after that time.

Although the consonant shift is easily the most outstanding phonetic characteristic distinguishing those dialects which we now call High German, the student should bear in mind that it is only one of the changes that eventually yielded this new linguistic *Gestalt*. We are not yet dealing with a national or a literary language, but rather with a series of *Stammessprachen*, each one exerting an influence more or less proportional to its maximum political importance. In the seventh and eighth centuries these lines of influence radiated from the south and the southeast: Lombardy, Alemannia, and Bavaria. We have discussed their principal contributions in some detail. Let us now turn our attention to the Middle Rhine and consider the central and critical role played by the Franks in the development of the High German language. The subject deserves more than passing mention.

According to our classification of the tribes in primitive Germanic times, the Franks are descended from the Istvaeones or Weser-Rhine Germans. Exactly when they first crossed over into northern Gaul from their ancient home is not known, but they had begun a general southward sweep through western Europe as early as the fifth century, some of them moving along the Rhine and the Mosel in Germany, others pushing down through present-day France and eventually penetrating as far south as Aquitania. Those Franks who settled along the Rhine in an area extending roughly from Wesel (about thirty-five miles above Düsseldorf) to Koblenz are called *Ripuarian*; those who crossed over into Gaul and occupied much of modern Belgium and the northeastern tip of France are known as the *Salian* or *Salic* Franks. The latter group is historically more important, for from it developed the great Merovingian and Carolingian dynasties.

When the Weser-Rhine Germans moved northward, they must have come into close contact with the Anglo-Frisians and Low Saxons, or, to use the cover-name suggested earlier, the Ingvaeones (North Sea Germans). Now, the emerging High German language of the seventh and eighth centuries exhibits certain phonetic changes for which northern influence is assumed. These North German features were no doubt carried south by the migrating Weser-Rhine tribes.

Probably the most prominent of these features is the *i*-umlaut: the partial assimilation of a back vowel in anticipation of a following *i* or *j* (HG *trägt* < **tragit*; HG *küssen* < **kussjan*). As shown on pp. 47–48, this phenomenon is common to all the West Germanic dialects as well as to Old Norse (North Germanic), although it occurs in High German relatively late, first appearing in Rhenish Franconian around 750, but not consistently employed in the documents. The Upper German dialects tended to resist this fronting of the back vowels, especially when they were immediately followed by certain consonant combinations, so that even today Bavarian preserves un-umlauted forms like *drucken, rucken, nutzen*.

The Frankish dialects also retained in a conditional way the Low Saxon monophthongization of two Germanic diphthongs: *ai* > *ê* and *au* > *ô*, as in OS *bên* and *bôm* (HG *Bein* "leg," *Baum* "tree"). Of unlimited scope in Old Saxon, the change of *ai* to *ê* in the dialects of the Middle Rhine in general takes place only when the diphthong is followed by *h, r, w* (OHG *meist–mêr* "most–more"), and the change of *au* to *ô* only when the diphthong precedes a dental sound or the breath-spirant *h* (Go. *ráups*–OHG *rôt* "red"). The change of *ai* to *ê* is earlier, occurring in Franconian around 650, almost a century prior to its documented usage in Upper German. Both Franconian and Alemannic record the change from *au* to *ô* as of the middle of the eighth century, though we may assume that it spread from the Middle Rhine area.

It would appear, therefore, that the language of the Frankish tribes, through contact with the North Sea Germans, underwent certain changes, and that these changes—once the Franks had reached the Middle Rhine— later spread to the neighboring High German dialects to the south. The Franks, according to this interpretation, served as a linguistic link between the two great dialect areas to the north and to the south.

In certain important aspects, however, the language of the Franks— specifically the Rhenish Franconian—seems to have been the innovator rather than simply the purveyor of other linguistic features that came to be characteristic of the later stages of Old High German. For example, we have already described the conditions under which Franconian presumably reflected the change of Germanic *ai* to Low Saxon *ê*. In other surroundings, however, Rhenish Franconian (and to a lesser degree the Alemannic) as early as 750 records instances of *ei* where Germanic had *ai* and the Old Saxon shows *ê*. And fifty years later, Gmc. *au* (Old Saxon *ô*) appears in Rhenish Franconian manuscripts as *ou*:

Go.	*stáins* "stone"	*áugo* "eye"
OS	*stên*	*ôga*
OHG	*stein*	*ouga*

This particular change—in both cases it amounts to a raising of the vocalic off-glide of the original diphthong—most likely represents a Rhenish Franconian development, even though the influence of Old Saxon *ê* and *ô* would seem obvious.

Another characteristic of Franconian (again of the Rhenish dialect) is the diphthongization of Gmc. *ê* and *ô* to *ea* (later becoming *ia*, then *ie*) and *uo*, respectively; OS *hêr*–OHG *hier* (with diphthongal pronunciation) "here"; OS *brôdar*–OHG *bruoder* "brother." Both changes are reflected in documents of the eighth century.

A somewhat later and highly significant change in the phonetic structure of High German was the reduction of the vowels of the final syllables. In the tenth and eleventh centuries—again originating in Franconian territory—scribes start using forms such as *geste, leben, name, tage* (OHG *gesti* "guests," *lebên* "live," *namo* "name," *tagâ* "days"). This weakening of final unstressed vowels, incidentally, is the most obvious and characteristic change marking the transition from Old High to Middle High German. We shall refer to it again in Chapter Four.

SIMILARITIES BETWEEN OLD FRENCH AND OLD HIGH GERMAN

Because of their geographical location, the Franks came under strong Gallo-Romance influences, though to what extent their native language was modified by the Romance idiom cannot accurately be determined. Sometime prior to the eighth century, however, both French and German suffered certain innovations which would seem to point to a common model. For example, both languages began employing an old demonstrative pronoun (English *this, that*) as the definite article, and the numeral "one" as the indefinite—grammatical features lacking in both Latin and Proto-Germanic. In a similar vein, the word for "man" (OHG *man*; Lat. *homo* > Fr. *on*) came to be used as an indefinite pronoun. Even more striking is the development in the two languages of compound past tenses. Where literary Latin would express "I have done" by means of the perfect tense form *fêcî*, and where the Germanic languages would all have used an older form of what we today call the preterite or the simple past tense (*ich tat*), there developed in both German and French compound constructions (sometimes referred to as "periphrases") of the type *ich habe getan* and *j'ai fait*. The use of the verb *to be* as an auxiliary for constructing the perfect tenses of certain intransitive verbs was also a common, though somewhat later, innovation in the two languages (*ich bin gekommen, je suis venu*).

In order to explain developments such as these, we must assume that there was in all probability a period of close contact between certain dialects of Old French and of Old German. Interestingly enough, there is also some evidence from dialect geography which corroborates this assumption. For example, the French word for "beech tree"—*hêtre*—was borrowed from the Germanic, probably from the Low German; compare German *Heister*, Frisian *hêster*, Dutch *heester*. Dialectologists have established that its occurrence in French was at first limited to northern France, the Germanic cognates being originally restricted to the Netherlands, northwestern Germany, and southern Scandinavia. And Theodor Frings points to the Franconian diphthongization of Gmc. *ê* and *ô* as another instance of what he believes was a common phonetic development shared with the local French dialects. Such Old French forms as *cuër* < Vulgar Latin **côr* "heart," and *miël* < Vulgar Latin **mêl* "honey," arose—according to Frings—at approximately the same time and in about the same area as words such as OHG *guot* < Gmc. **gôd* "good" and *brief* < Vulgar Latin **brêvem* "letter."[18]

The unavoidable conclusion seems to be that beginning perhaps as early as the fifth century and extending well into the historical period, there were many points of contact and influence between Gallo-Romance and the German speech communities. It is therefore quite probable that the Franks were responsible for introducing certain French elements into the High German language. Their southward expansion into Gaul had kept them in abiding contact with Romance-speaking peoples, so that we must assume an impressive incidence of bilingualism among them. As their political might increased, so in like manner did their linguistic prestige, resulting eventually in what has been called a "Verfrankung des Deutschen."

HIGH GERMAN MADE UP OF MANY ELEMENTS

Summarizing the contents of the past few pages, we can say that what we today call the High German language is genetically a curious and complicated blend of the dialects spoken by the several major tribal groups. And the languages of these various *Stämme* not only influenced one another, but were in turn influenced by the non-German idioms with which they themselves had come in contact in the course of their various migrations: Gothic in the south (where it was no doubt influenced by Latin) and east, and Gallo-Romance in the west, to mention only the most obvious instances.

THE GOTHIC MISSION

In addition to these sundry influences, however, was the influence of the Christian religion. Precisely when the first missionaries tried to bring the

[18] "Germanisches *ô* und *ê*," *Beiträge*, 63 (1939), 1–116.

gospel of Jesus Christ to the Germans we do not know, but from the fifth century on there is an unbroken history of Christian evangelism in Germany. The first of these missions was probably the Gothic. One reason for making such an assumption is the presence in Old High German of a number of ancient Christian loanwords which derive ultimately from Greek rather than Latin. Since the Goths were Arians,[19] we assume that they brought the Greek vocabulary of the Eastern church to the Germans. Though this explanation may well be valid, it is also possible that these terms reached the Germans by way of Greek Christians living in the early Roman settlements along the Rhine and Mosel (there was a sizable Greek colony in Trier). But perhaps the strongest argument favoring the presence among the Germans of Gothic missionaries is that there are other Christian loanwords not inherited from the Greek, being related to native Gothic words which themselves are loan-translations from the Greek.[20]

Examples of Greek loanwords in German are: Vulgar Greek *kyrikón* "church" > Ger. *Kirche*; Gk. *papãs* "priest" > Ger. *Pfaffe* (the OHG *pfaffo* had no pejorative connotation, meaning simply "priest"); Gk. *ángelos* "messenger (of the Lord)" > Ger. *Engel*; Gk. *diábolos* "blasphemer" > Ger. *Teufel*; Gk. *pentêkostê* (*hêméra*) "the fiftieth (day [after Easter])" > Ger. *Pfingsten*.

Examples of Gothic loan-translations involving specifically Christian concepts are:

> Go. *dáupjan* "baptize" (translates Gk. *baptízein*) > Ger. *taufen*
> Go. *fastan* "fast" (translates Gk. *nêsteúein*) > Ger. *fasten*.

That all these words show the effects of the High German consonant shift (wherever the pertinent consonants occur, of course) is proof of their antiquity, for they must therefore necessarily have been borrowed prior to its inception. Since the Goths could hardly have sustained a mission program before the fifth century—they were themselves persecuted by unconverted elements within their own stem during the lifetime of Bishop

---

[19] The term takes its name from Arius, a native of Alexandria, who taught that Christ was not of the same essence as God the Father, but was *homoioúsios* (Gk.) "of like being." This heresy involved Christians of the Eastern rite in bitter controversy for nearly a century. The great opponent of Arius was Athanasius; he taught that God the Father and God the Son are of the same being, *homooúsios*, or, in the words of the Nicene Creed, that Christ is "true God of true God." The first Ecumenical Council of Nicea in 325 condemned Arianism, though it persisted among factions of the Eastern church for years. Both the Goths and the Lombards were Arians.

[20] A loan-translation is a word or phrase that has been translated literally from another language, and which keeps its original connotation. For example, Ger. *Ausdruck* (*aus* "out," *drücken* "to press") is a loan-translation of Latin *expressio* (*ex* "out," *pressâre* "to press").

Ulfilas (311–82)—this would be additional if indirect evidence that the shift could not have begun much before the middle of the fifth century.

THE ANGLO-SAXON MISSION

With the possible exception of a Gothic mission, all subsequent efforts to Christianize the German tribes came from the west: from the Irish,[21] the Anglo-Saxons, and—among the Germans themselves—from the Salian Franks, whose monarch Clovis (German *Chlodwig*) had embraced the Christian faith on Christmas Day of 496, after his victory over the Alemanni, when he was baptized according to the rites of the Roman church. This act not only marked the end of Arian influence in Germany, but—as the boundaries of the Frankish kingdom fanned out to the east— assured at least the nominal conversion of all vanquished German tribes.

The missionaries who followed in the wake of the victorious Frankish armies were for the most part Anglo-Saxons. Some of them became men of great religious influence: Willibrord, "Apostle to the Frisians," Liutbert, spiritual leader of the mission to Hesse, and—probably the most famous —Winfrid of Wessex (*ca.* 672–754), better known as St. Boniface, "Apostle to the Germans," who continued the work of Willibrord in Friesland, though he was especially active (at the direct invitation of Charles Martel) in central Germany. In 732 he became the first Archbishop of Mainz. He was eventually martyred by the Frisians for cutting down an *Irminsûl* or "Great Column"—a tree sacred to those among them who still practiced the ancient heathen rites.

The native language of the Anglo-Saxon missionaries, too, left its mark on German. Perhaps the most often quoted example concerns the third person of the Trinity, referred to in early south German manuscripts as *der wîho âtum* "the holy breath," a loan-translation from the Gothic. Later the term *der heilago geist* "the Holy Ghost"—modeled after the Old English *sê hâlga gâst*—gained universal currency. The Old English *godspell* "gospel" also vied with the Latin loanword *evangelio* and its Upper German translation *cuatchundida* (that is, "good news").

THE INFLUENCE OF THE MONASTERIES

The most pervasive and abiding influences exerted by the Christian mission to Germany, however, came from what is known as the *Klosterkultur*, for the role played by the medieval monasteries in shaping German

[21] As an example of the influence of the Old Irish vocabulary on German—which was indeed minimal—the word *cloc* is usually cited. This appears as OHG *glocka* (NHG *Glocke*) "bell."

culture—and, of course, the German language—was of paramount importance. The study of Old High German, certainly, is little more than a study of the manuscripts written or copied in the *scriptoria* (as the libraries were called) of such monasteries as those at St. Gall, Reichenau, Murbach, Lorsch, and Regensburg (St. Emmeram). One of these, the Benedictine monastery at Fulda, founded in 744 by St. Boniface, came to be of special importance in the history of German letters. The scribes in these islands of literacy first put to parchment the sounds of the German vernacular. They also borrowed freely from the vocabulary of the more civilized Latin, so that during this era the native language was generously enriched by the addition of Latin words from almost every sphere of activity: religion, government, agriculture, cooking, architecture, the crafts, and so on. We list a few representative terms:

German	Latin[22]
Altar	*altâria*
Kloster	*claustrum*
Mönch	**monicus (monachus)*
Nonne	*nonna*
Messe	*missa*[23]
Schule	**scôla (schola)*
Tinte	*tîncta*
predigen	*praedicâre*
firmen	*firmâre*
Kreuz	*crux*
schreiben	*scrîbere*
Tafel	*tabula*
Brief	**brêvem* (supply *libellum*)
Butter	*bûtŷrum* (< Gk. *boutŷrón*)
Brezel	**brachiatellum*[24] (*brachium*)
Zwiebel	*cêpulla*
Petersilie	*petrosilium*

[22] No attempt is made to account for the phonetic changes from the Latin to the German. In some instances we must assume that the German word was borrowed from a later, and often unrecorded, form of the Latin. Notice, however, that these words do not show the effects of the High German consonant shift, thereby affirming that they were borrowed after it was no longer operative. Conversely, the Latin loanwords listed on pp. 35–36—borrowed in Proto-Germanic times—all underwent the phonological changes which characterize High German: clear proof of their early presence in the Germanic vocabulary. For details, the student should consult a recent edition of Friedrich Kluge's *Etymologisches Wörterbuch der deutschen Sprache.*

[23] From the Latin formula *Ite, missa est* [*côntio*], "Depart [the congregation] is dismissed," addressed by the officiating priest to the congregation at the close of the Ordinary of the Mass.

[24] The term meant approximately "a little piece of dough baked in the shape of intertwined arms."

German	Latin
Lattich	*lactûca*
Eibisch	*ibiscum*
Spiegel	**spêglum (speculum)*
Regel	*rêgula*
Schuster	*sûtor*
Feier(tag)	*fêria*
Pinsel	*pênicillus*
Pelz	*pellîcia (pellis)*
Seide	*sêta*

There were also many loan-translations that came into German at this time:

German	Latin
Gewissen[25]	*conscientia*
Gemeinde[25]	*commûnio*
Gotteshaus	*domus Deî*
Mittler	*mediâtor*
barmherzig (OHG *armaherz*)	*misericors*
Wohltat	*beneficium*
Jünger	*iûnior*
Sänger	*cantor*

Another sort of influence exerted by the monastic culture was that certain native German words now took on a new and specifically Christian sense. *Tugend*, for instance, once meant approximately "fitness, usefulness" (compare Modern German *Tüchtigkeit, Tauglichkeit*), but under the influence of the Christian way of life it acquired the meaning of "virtue" (Church Latin *virtus*). The term *Laster* earlier meant simply "fault" (compare OHG *lahan* "to blame"), but it eventually came to signify a *moral* fault, that is, "vice," the equivalent of *vitium* in its theological sense. Or again: *Demut* "humility" is a compound, the first part of which means "servant" (Go. *pius* "servant"). Obviously, the term once referred to a "servile" attitude or spirit (*Mut*). Under the influence of the Church, however, the meaning shifted from *servîlitâs* to *humilitâs*, from "servility" to "humility." As a final example, OHG *sunta* at one time meant "guilt" of any kind, and only because it was employed as a translation of *peccâtum* did its meaning eventually become restricted to "sin."

Since the scribes who first wrote German were of course schooled in Latin, it was inevitable that the syntax of German as well as its vocabulary should come under the influence of the Latin model. This is all the more

[25] When used to form substantives, the prefix *ge-* gave a collective connotation to the noun: contrast *Berg–Gebirge*. In loanwords it frequently translates Latin *con- (cum)* "with."

understandable when we bear in mind that our records of Old High German consist largely of translations from the Latin. Examples of Latin syntax in early German include attempts to translate literally the familiar ablative absolute construction (using the dative case, of course): *ianuîs clausîs* "the gates having been closed," OHG *bislozzanên turin*; or *responsô acceptô* "the answer having been received," OHG *inphanganemo antwurte*. Another borrowed pattern was that of the so-called accusative with the infinitive: *dicitis ejicere me demonia* "ye say that I cast out demons," OHG *ir quedet mih werphan diuvala*. These two foreign syntactic patterns were eventually dropped, but another succeeded in insinuating itself permanently into the language, namely, the use of *zu* and the dative case of the infinitive construed with the verb *wesan* "to be" as an equivalent of the Latin gerundive: Late Latin *non credendi sunt* "they are not to be believed," OHG *ni sindun zi chilaubanne*; compare the Modern German *die sind nicht zu glauben*.

We might mention one other effect that Latin exerted upon the German language of this era. Earlier, we said that alliteration (*Stabreim*) was the formal principle of versification in the early period of all the Germanic languages. Now, influenced by the Late Latin hymns of the Roman church, this ancient poetic device deferred to the use of end-rhyme. Certain phonetic changes within the German language may already have lessened the effectiveness and tended to restrict the range of alliteration, thus making easier the transition to the new poetic form. At any rate, as of about the middle of the ninth century, alliteration as a formal poetic technique gave way almost completely to the rhyme schemes of Latin prosody.

The Emergence of German as a Written Language

With few exceptions the literary records of Old High German originated in the *scriptoria* of the monasteries. The theme of most of this material is understandably religious, extending in scope from simple prayers and catechetical aids to poetic versions of the gospel narrative.[26] Many such

---

[26] There is nothing in Old High German to compare with the Old Norse sagas or the Old English epic literature, such as *Beowulf*. For excellent introductions to the literature of this period, consult either J. Knight Bostock, *A Handbook on Old High German Literature* (Oxford, 1955), or Helmut de Boor, *Die deutsche Literatur von Karl dem Großen bis zum Beginn der höfischen Dichtung* (Munich, 1957).

For purposes of orientation and easy reference, we include a brief list of the principal OHG literary monuments arranged according to the dialect they represent (or at least most resemble), assigning to each work its date of original composition rather than the date of the manuscript(s) which has been preserved; the years given

documents owe their existence to the *Admonitio generalis* of 789 which Charles the Great (742–814) addressed to his clergy, urging them to make greater use of the vernacular in caring for the spiritual needs of the people, requesting that German translations of the Lord's Prayer, the Apostle's Creed, and other basic instruments of Christian doctrine be prepared. There also exists a fair number of devotional and theological treatises, again mostly translations of well-known Latin works, which were in turn often translations from the Greek.

Since much of their activity centered on recasting Latin into German, the scribes were constantly searching for suitable German words or expressions with which to translate the more normalized and semantically fixed Latin. In fact, the oldest German "book" in existence is a translation

---

are in most instances merely approximations. Our listing is a slightly modified version of the one to be found in *An Introduction to the Historical Study of New High German* by Arthur Kirk (Manchester: The Manchester University Press, 1923), pp. 14–15:

1. Upper German
   (a) Bavarian-Austrian
       The Wessobrunner Gebet, 770–90
       The Glossary of Hrabanus Maurus (Samanunga), 800
       The Monsee-Vienna Fragments, 800
       The Muspilli, 800
       The Exhortatio ad plebem christianam, 815
   (b) Alemannic (literary center, St. Gall)
       The Abrogans, 765–75
       The Reichenau Glosses, 775–800
       The Benediktinerregel, 800
       The Murbach Hymns, 800
       The Works of Notker Labeo of St. Gall, 1000

2. Middle German
   (a) East Franconian (literary center, Fulda)
       Tatian (Evangelienharmonie), 830
   (b) Rhenish Franconian
       Isidor (De fide catholica), 790–800
       Otfrid's *Evangelienbuch*, 863–71
       The Ludwigslied, 881
   (c) Middle Franconian
       The Trier Capitulary, 1000
       De Heinrico, 1050

3. Low German (Old Saxon)
       The Heliand, 830
       The Old Saxon Genesis, 830

A special word about two OHG documents of unique importance: the so-called *Merseburger Charms (Zaubersprüche)* and the *Hildebrandslied*. The two charms, preserved in a ninth-century manuscript otherwise devoted to religious material, are held by most scholars to be of pagan origin—the only such relics in OHG of what must surely at one time have been a considerable body of poetry. Written in a Middle

of a Latin collection of synonyms. Known as *Der Abrogans*,[27] this work was written in the latter part of the eighth century, probably in the monastery school at Fulda. Although a number of such word-lists have come down to us, the more common scribal practice was simply to jot down the German equivalent someplace on the page containing the Latin text, usually over the word or in the margin to one side. Such entries are called "glosses." Much of our knowledge of Old High German derives from a study of such material, now gathered in five large volumes totaling over four thousand pages—one of the many contributions to Germanic philology made by the German scholar, Elias Steinmeyer.[28]

Was There a Standardized OHG Written Language?

When we recall that the work of the monasteries within the Frankish empire flourished under the generous patronage and with the close cooperation of the reigning dynasty, we may ask whether the dialect of the Carolingian court might not have exerted a normalizing influence upon the German language of that time, especially upon its written form. Here again our principal reference is to the most famous of the Carolingians, Charles the Great. That he took a keen interest in things Germanic is borne out by his biographer, Einhard,[29] who tells us that the Emperor had had collected the ancient heroic songs (*barbara et antiquissima carmina*) of

German dialect of East Franconian coloration, the few lines were recorded sometime in the tenth century on a flyleaf of an older manuscript.

The *Hildebrandslied* (see Plate 3)—a fragment (sixty-eight lines) of what was probably an epic poem dealing with motifs from the Langobardic saga-cycle—is the only document of any importance in OHG literature with a theme from the Germanic past. The language of the manuscript has long been a topic of much controversy; a peculiar mixture of Low German and High German, it would seem to be the result of a rather clumsy attempt to transpose an originally High German version into what the scribes (there were two of them) thought was Old Saxon. At any rate, many problems concerning both the language and origins of the manuscript remain unresolved. The song as we have it was written on the first and last leaves of a parchment manuscript sometime in the early ninth century. The monastery at Fulda is considered by many to have been the place of copying. The two manuscript leaves containing the *Hildebrandslied* were casualties of World War II, lost or stolen from their Kassel archive in 1945. One of the leaves found its way into the hands of a New York book dealer and was returned to Germany. The other leaf, too, was finally discovered and returned in 1973.

For the sake of completeness, we have appended to our listing the principal witnesses of Old Low German (Old Saxon).

[27] The words are arranged alphabetically; *abrogans*—meaning "gentle, humble"— is the first Latin entry.

[28] Elias Steinmeyer and Eduard Sievers, *Die althochdeutschen Glossen* (Berlin, 1879–1922), 5 vols.

[29] In his *Vita Caroli Magni*, written sometime between 817 and 836.

the Germans, and that he had commissioned the writing of a German grammar. Unfortunately, nothing of these efforts has come down to us. Today we have direct knowledge of only one such project: in a passage from the twenty-ninth chapter of his biography, Einhard was inspired to write down the German names which his king had decided should be used for the months of the year and the winds of the heavens.[30]

Although the principal literary vehicle of the court was Latin, there was —as evidenced by the *Admonitio generalis*—also occasion to write in German. This, in its West Franconian dialect, was the native language of Charles the Great, though the later Carolingian monarchs spoke Rhenish Franconian. The German version of the Straßburg Oaths of 842, recited by Charles the Bald in the presence of the German-speaking troops of his brother Ludwig the German, are written in Rhenish Franconian. Even if this single fact does not prove that the Carolingian chanceries customarily employed this particular dialect, the cumulative evidence would seem to favor or at least permit such an interpretation. In any event, just as the importance of such localities as Worms and Mainz in the affairs of state and church confirms the pre-eminence of the Middle Rhine territory during the Carolingian era, so in like manner would it seem that the influence upon Alemannic and Bavarian of the dialect spoken along the Middle Rhine, Rhenish Franconian, was due in large part to its prestige as the language of the imperial court.

However, in spite of what may be called "definite tendencies" toward standardization in favor of Rhenish Franconian, the language of the Old High German manuscripts is irregular and dialectal. The situation is further complicated when we discover that the literary dialect employed by a given *scriptorium* frequently deviated from the spoken dialect characteristic of the region in which the monastery was situated. As a case in point, Fulda is in Rhenish Franconian territory, yet the *Tatian*—the monastery's most famous OHG manuscript—is composed in the East Franconian dialect. This can only mean that many of the Fulda scribes had come originally from farther east. Sometimes (as in the case of the Freisinger Manuscript of Otfrid's *Evangelienbuch*) we find the language to be a mixture of dialects; in this instance a blend of Rhenish Franconian, the home of the manuscript, and Bavarian, where it had been sent for copying.

For reasons such as these, the OHG written language tends to be a

---

[30] Some of the old Germanic terms proposed by Charles still live on in German, such as *Hornung* for February and *Brachmonat* for June.

hodgepodge of varied and frequently incongruous elements. As the philologist Karl Müllenhoff puts it: "Hardly a single document coincides completely with any other, and almost every one exhibits the language in a different form."[31] So, whatever the influences of the Carolingian court, it would be inaccurate to suppose that there resulted at this time anything substantially resembling a standard written form of Old High German.

The Word "Deutsch"

Although it may be too soon to speak of a standard language, the era of the Carolingians at least marks the emergence of a sense of linguistic as well as of political oneness. This is reflected in the history of the word *deutsch*[32] (OHG *diutisk*, Latin *theodiscus*; related to OHG *diot*, Gothic *þiuda* "folk"), which occurs for the first time in a Latin letter written in the year 786 by Wigbod, chaplain to Charles the Great, reporting to the Roman pontiff on a synodical conference held in the English province of Mercia. In this missive the pope is told that the resolutions were read *latinê quam theodicê* ("in Latin and likewise in 'Germanic'"), "so that everyone might understand." The term *theodicê* here means "Germanic" rather than specifically "German," since the reference is to the language spoken in England. But two years later, in a document summarizing the findings of a court-of-inquiry held on Bavarian soil, the expression *theodiscâ linguâ* occurs where the reference is unmistakably to the "German language."[33] And a Rhenish Franconian Gospel narrative, composed by Otfrid of Weißenburg and completed in 868 or 869, has as the heading of the first chapter the Latin sentence *Cûr scriptor hunc librum theotisce dictâverit*—"Why the author wrote this book in German." In the

---

[31] *Denkmäler deutscher Poesie und Prosa aus dem VIII–XI Jahrhundert*, ed. Karl Müllenhoff and Wilhelm Scherer (3rd ed.; Berlin, 1892), p. ix.

[32] As far as we know, the word *German* first occurs in the writings of Julius Caesar, who used the term *Germâni* to designate a group of tribes inhabiting the forests of northeastern Gaul. The word *Teutoni*, also employed by the Roman historians as a Germanic tribal name, had an adjectival form *teutonicus* which referred generally to the language spoken by the Teutons. This latter term occurs with great frequency in Latin writings from about 875 on, its meaning limited specifically to "German."

[33] A *Reichstag* convening at Ingelheim had found Duke Tassilo of Bavaria guilty of deserting his troops, *quod theodiscâ linguâ herisliz dicitur*—"which in the German language is called *herisliz* [*Heeresflucht* 'desertion']." In 801 Charles the Great, while addressing an assembly held in Italy, refers to this decree, again using the term *theudiscâ linguâ*, apparently making deliberate use of *theudiscâ* rather than the ambiguous *franciscê*, inasmuch as the latter term even then could have meant simply the language spoken by the Western Franks, that is, either Old French or Old High German.

text that follows, Otfrid also uses the word *frenkisgon* (line 34), that is, *fränkisch*—Latin *franciscê*. For a while these words were used interchangeably, but when the French and German nations appeared as distinct entities after the Treaty of Verdun in 843, the terms *fränkisch* and *deutsch* began to lose their equivalency. Both expressions had long had a limited connotation, referring only to language; not until the end of the ninth century do we find the word *diutisch* being used in a broader geographical and ethnic sense.

The Old High German Vernacular

Since so much of the Old High German which has come down to us is a translation-literature dealing with religious themes, it does not reveal to us enough of the living language of the time. No literature can incorporate more than a fraction of a living language, of course, though in the case of Old High German this fraction is distressingly small. We resort, therefore, wherever possible to indirect evidence in order to better our imperfect knowledge of this stage of the language.

Middle High German, for example, reveals a stock of native words far in excess of that contained in the OHG manuscripts. Hans Sperber calls attention to a group of weak verbs with clear Germanic cognates, many of which occur for the first time in Middle High German: verbs like *schlitzen* "slit" and *schnitzen* "carve."[34] Morphologically, these verbs are derived from the Proto-Germanic form of the strong verbs *schleißen* "split" and *schneiden* "cut," representing a class of verbs referred to in comparative Germanic grammars as "intensives." *Schneiden*, for example, is traced back to Gmc. *sneit-* "cut"; the intensive *schnitzen*, however, derives from a Germanic stem with a doubled final consonant: *snitt-* (< IE *snit-no) with the "intensified" meaning "cut up, slice." The number of such verbs in Middle High German is fairly large, yet they are but sparsely represented in Old High German, probably because their meanings were considered to be too rough or inelegant for use in religious discourse.

Aside from the scattered bits of information, almost our only direct access to the language of everyday use is provided by two fragmentary collections of words and phrases, one Latin-German, the other German-Latin. The former, usually referred to as *Die Kasseler Glossen*, is in a Bavarian dialect and was written about 800. It contains vocabulary lists and a few short sentences. The latter collection—*Die althochdeutschen Gespräche*—is the more interesting, consisting mostly of phrases, apparently compiled by a Frenchman while traveling in Germany, since

[34] *Geschichte der deutschen Sprache*, ed. Wolfgang Fleischhauer (Sammlung Göschen, No. 915 [3rd ed.; Berlin: Walter de Gruyter & Co., 1958]), p. 53.

the spelling approaches a phonetic transcription of German as it would sound to the ear of a Romance speaker. The language, which is practical and colloquial, becomes coarse and vulgar at times, reflecting the vicissitudes of travel in a strange and foreign land. A few examples: *Gimer min schelt* for *gib mir min schild* "give me my shield"; *Guaz queten ger erra?* for *waz quedet ir herre?* "what say you, master?"; *An, Ansco, Obte,* for *Hant, Hantscuoh, Houbit* "hand, glove, head."

Notker Labeo of St. Gall

Toward the end of the Old High German period we encounter several attempts to develop an orthography which would reflect the sounds of the spoken language. To be sure, various scribal conventions had grown up in the monasteries, but these represented compromises with conflicting writing traditions, and must not, therefore, be considered as serious attempts to spell in accordance with the sound-structure of the language. The most well-known of the early efforts to devise an orthography consistent with the phonetics of German was that made by Notker Labeo of St. Gall (*ca.* 950–1022).[35]

To his contemporaries he was also known as Notker Teutonicus—"The German"—because he spoke and taught in German in an age when Latin held undisputed sway in the schools. He wrote textbooks, commentaries, and translations in *Mischprosa,* a curious blend of German and Latin, intending thereby to make the material more accessible to his students. Motivated no doubt by this same desire to make learning easier, Notker set about standardizing and improving the German orthography of his day. His native dialect and that of his monastery was High Alemannic, so of course his orthography was designed specifically for the Upper German sound system.

Probably the best-known feature of his writing system bears his name: *Notker's Anlautsgesetz* (Law of Initial Consonants). Briefly put, the voiceless unaspirated Upper German equivalents of Middle German *b, d, g* are written *p, t, k* when they occur (1) at the beginning of a sentence or clause, and (2) when the preceding word ends in a voiceless sound (which included all consonants except *l, m, n, r*). Following vowels and *l, m, n, r,* however, the spellings *b, d, g* prevail.[36] For instance: *ter brûoder–únde des prûoder; tes kóldes–únde demo gólde.*

---

[35] The term *Labeo,* Latin "lip," obviously refers to a physical characteristic.

[36] The interchange of *t–d* was limited to the Old High German *d* that had developed from Germanic *þ*; Germanic *d,* on the other hand, appears in Middle German as *d,* in Upper German usually as *t*: MG *der*–UG *ter.* This Upper German *t* does not alternate with *d* under the conditions given above, thus *tes táges, temo táge* (not *dáge*). For a statement on Germanic *þ,* see p. 57.

As can be seen by the examples just quoted, Notker also made use of certain diacritics, letting the acute accent serve to identify all stressed short vowels, the circumflex all long vowels whether stressed or not.

While these are the most obvious of his innovations, his system included many other features. Taken in its entirety, it was a remarkably adequate system for writing the Alemannic dialect of Upper German. Notker himself, however, did not employ it with rigorous consistency. But most unfortunate of all, it and other pioneer efforts to devise a suitable system of orthography for the German language were soon allowed to die of neglect, leaving only traces of their former influence in the writings of later generations.

The Decline of German as a Written Language

When Charles the Great died in 814, the scepter of empire passed to the hands of his oldest surviving son, Ludwig, called "the Pious" (*Ludwig der Fromme*), a deeply religious man who did not share his late father's enthusiasm for the pagan past of his German ancestors. Nor did he approve of what he felt was a too worldly concern with classical literature in the monastery and cathedral schools. Reflecting this attitude, the Synod of Inden (near Aachen) in 817 formally limited the further use of written German to the simplest kind of practical, utilitarian prose (*Gebrauchs-prosa*). This new directive, though its effect was neither immediate nor absolute, nevertheless served to de-emphasize what had been a vigorous and increasingly successful trend toward a German national literature written in the humanistic spirit of classical antiquity. By the year 900, the literary records of Old High German dwindle away to almost nothing. There is still a literature that treats of German life and times, but its language is Latin.

From shortly after 900 until about 1050 there is—with the single and important exception of the pedagogical writings of Notker Labeo—nothing of any consequence written in German. And when, in the mid-eleventh century, compositions in the vernacular again begin to appear, the language has undergone many changes. We are, in fact, on the verge of a new linguistic era, that known as Middle High German.

Before we enter upon a discussion of certain specific and major differences between Old High German and Middle High German, the student should examine the samplings of ninth-century texts that follow, bearing in mind the information already given on pages 56–59. In order to facilitate comparison, we cite various versions of the Lord's Prayer, including the Gothic (fourth-century) and the Old Saxon (ninth-century) wordings for broader reference.

Gothic

Atta unsar þu in himinam, weihnái namô þein. Qimái þiudinassus þeins. Waírþái wilja þeins, swê in himina jah ana aírþái. Hláif unsarana þana sinteinan gif uns himma daga. Jah aflêt uns þatei skulans sijáima, swaswê jah weis aflêtam þáim skulam unsaráim. Jah ni briggáis uns in fráistubnjái, ak lausei uns af þamma ubilin; untê þeina ist þiudangardi jah mahts jah wulþus in aiwins. Amên.

Atta "father"; *weihnái* "hallowed be" (subjunctive); *Qimái* "come" (subjunctive); *þiudinassus* "kingdom"; *waírþái* "become" (subjunctive); *swê* "so"; *hláif* "bread"; *sinteinan* "daily"; *himma* "this"; *aflêt* "forgive" (imperative); *skulans* "debtors"; *sijáima* "we are" (subjunctive); *briggáis* "bring" (pronounced *bringais*); *fráistubnjái* "temptation"; *láusei* "delivery" (imperative); *ubilin* "evil"; *þiudangardi* "kingdom"; *wulþus* "glory"; *áiwins* "eternity."

As a preface to the Old High German prayers, we quote the Lord's Prayer (*Das Vaterunser* or *Paternoster*) in its traditional *New High German* wording:

Vater unser, der du bist im Himmel. Geheiligt werde dein Name. Dein Reich komme. Dein Wille geschehe, wie im Himmel, also auch auf Erden. Unser täglich Brot gib uns heute. Und vergib uns unsere Schuld, als wir vergeben unsern Schuldigern. Und führe uns nicht in Versuchung. Sondern erlöse uns von dem Übel. (Denn dein ist das Reich und die Kraft und die Herrlichkeit in Ewigkeit)[37] Amen.

Alemannic[38]

Fater unseer, thû pist in himile, wîhi [hallow, holy] namun dînan, qhueme rîhhi dîn, werde willo diin, sô in himile sôsa in erdu. Prooth unseer emezzihic [continually] kip uns hiutu, oblâz [compare *erlassen*] uns sculdi unseero, sô wir oblâzêm uns sculdîkêm, enti ni unsih firleiti in khorunka [temptation], ûzzer lôsi unsih fona ubile.

Bavarian

Fater unsêr, dû pist in himilum, kawîhit sî namo dîn, piqhueme rîchi dîn, wesa dîn willo, sama sô in himile est, sama in erdu. Pilipi unsraz emizzigaz kip uns eogawanna [always] enti flâz [farlâzzan; compare *erlassen*] uns unsro sculdi sama sô wir flâzzamês unsrêm scolôm enti ni princ unsih in chorunka, ûzzan kaneri [*ga-nerran* "save"] unsih fona allêm suntôn.

[37] This concluding sentence is contained in the version of the Lord's Prayer recited by Eastern rite Catholics and by Protestants; the Church in the Latin rite has never adopted it. For this reason it is included in the Gothic version, but missing in most pre-Reformation German paternosters.
[38] These texts are quoted from the collection found on pp. 106–8 of Hans Naumann and Werner Betz, *Althochdeutsches Elementarbuch* (Sammlung Göschen, No. 1111/1111a [3rd ed.; Berlin: Walter de Gruyter & Co., 1954]).

Rhenish Franconian

Fater unsêr, thû in himilom bist, giwîhit sî namo thîn. Quaeme rîchi
thîn. Werdhe willeo thîn, sama sô in himile endi in erthu. Broot unseraz
emezzîgaz gib uns hiutu. Endi farlâz uns sculdhi unsero sama sô wir
farlâzzêm scolôm unserêm. Endi ni gileidi unsih in costunga. Auh arlôsi
unsih fona ubile.

East Franconian

Fater unser, thû thâr bist in himile, sî giheilagôt thîn namo, queme thîn
rîhhi, sî thîn willo, sô her in himile ist, sô sî her in erdu, unsar brôt tagalîh-
haz gib uns hiutu, inti furlâz uns unsara sculdi, sô wir furlâzemês unsarên
sculdîgôn, inti ni gileitêst unsih in costunga, ûzouh arlôsi unsih fon ubile.

Old Saxon

Fadar ûsa firiho barno, thu bist an them hôhon himila rîkea, gewîhid sî
thîn namo wordo gehwilico. Cuma thîn craftag rîki. Werda thîn willeo
obar thesa werold alla, sô sama an erdo, sô thar uppa ist an them hôhon
himilo rîkea. Gef ûs dago gehwilikes râd, drohtin the gôdo, thîna hêlega
helpa, endi alât ûs, hebenes ward, managoro mênsculdio, al sô we ôdrum
mannum dôan. Ne lât ûs farlêdean lêda wihti sô ford an iro willeon, sô wi
wirdige sind, ac help ûs widar allun ubilon dâdiun.[39]

In Wilhelm Stapel's prose-translation into *Modern German* the Old
Saxon prayer reads as follows:

Vater unser, der Menschenkinder, der in dem hohen Himmelreich ist,
geweiht sei Dein Name durch jegliches Wort! Es komme Dein kraftvolles
Reich! Es geschehe Dein Wille in der ganzen Welt und auf Erden so, wie
er da oben in dem hohen Himmel ist! Gib uns jeglichen Tages Vorrat, guter
Herr, Deine heilige Hilfe, und erlaß uns, Himmelswart, die vielen Mein-
schulden, ganz wie wir es andern Menschen tun sollten. Laß uns nicht
leidige Wichte, wie sie möchten, verleiten, wie wir es wert sind, sondern
hilf uns wider alle übelen Taten.[40]

---

[39] Written in alliterative verse, this poetic version of the Lord's Prayer is taken
from *Der Heliand*. The language of course shows no traces of the High German
consonant shift.

[40] *Der Heliand*, ed. Wilhelm Stapel (Munich: Carl Hanser Verlag, 1953), p. 49.

CHAPTER FOUR

The Middle High German Period

1050–1350

Early Middle High German: 1050–1170

During the first century of what we have chosen to call the Middle High German period, the language of the manuscripts had not yet reached that stage which Hugo Moser so aptly names "High Medieval." But even to the unpracticed eye the differences between this transitional "Early Middle High German" and the language of the paternosters immediately preceding are considerable, as can be easily ascertained by a careful inspection of the two specimens that follow.

Though included in a twelfth-century manuscript collection, *Ezzos Gesang* or *Das Ezzolied* (*Ezzos Cantilêna dê mirâculîs Christî*) is older by at least a century, as proved by the existence of an eleventh-century Alemannic version. The later copy, from which we quote, shows obvious Bavarian characteristics, but internal evidence points to a possible East Franconian original. In the history of German literature this work has the distinction of being the first poem to break the "century of silence," during which nothing of a literary nature was written in the vernacular.

> Der guote biscoph vone babenberch
> der hiez machen ein vil guot werch:
> Er hiez di sîne phaphen [*Pfaffen* "priests"]
> ein guot liet machen.
> Eines liedes si begunden,
> want [since] si di buoch chunden [here: "could read"].
> Ezzo [man's name] begunde scrîben,

wille [man's name] vant die wîse [*Weise* "melody"].
Duo [when] er die wîse duo [there] gewan,
duo îlten si sich [here: "busied themselves with it"]
   alle munechen [monks].
Von êwen [eternity] zuo den êwen
Got gnâde [*sei gnädig* "be merciful"] ir aller sêle.

Reflecting the ascetic, otherworldly, and often morbid spirit of eleventh-century religious writings, a result of the strict monastic reforms of the time, the *Mementô morî* ("Remember Death") is another example of the High German of this transitional era. The dialect is Alemannic. Of special interest from a linguistic point of view is that the language—though contemporary with that of the *Ezzolied*—is more conservative in structure, especially in its treatment of the vowels of the final syllables. Such differences should serve to remind us that there was yet no such thing as a standard language, but rather simply a number of regional varieties of German (*Landschaftssprachen*).

Nû denchent, wîb unde man, war ir sulint werdan.
Ir minnont tisa brôdemi, unde wânint iermer hie sîn.
Si ne dunchet iu nie sô minnesam, eina churza wîla sund ir si hân:
Ir ne lebint nie sô gerno manegiu zît, ir muozent verwandelon disen lîb.

In Karl Wolfskehl's translation this reads as follows:[1]

Nun denket alle, Weib und Mann, was aus euch soll werden dann.
Ihr minnet der Welt Gebrechlichkeit und wähnet stets hienieden
   zu sein.
Dünkt sie euch noch so minnenswert, nur kurze Frist wird euch
   gewährt;
lebtet ihr noch so gerne manche Zeit, ihr müßt verwandeln diesen
   Leib.

HIGH MEDIEVAL OR "CLASSIC" MIDDLE HIGH GERMAN: 1170–1250

The eighty-year span from approximately 1170 to 1250 was a period of intense literary activity in Germany. In histories of literature it is often referred to as *die erste Blütezeit* (the second, of course, being the Age of Goethe). It was the Golden Age of chivalric poetry, highlighted by courtly romances and tales of knightly derring-do. Myths and legends from the Germanic past were woven anew into stately poems. Delicate lyrics of touching beauty proclaimed the pure love of a knight for his high-born lady. It was the age of Walter von der Vogelweide, greatest of the *Minnesänger*; of Wolfram von Eschenbach, Hartmann von Aue, and Gottfried

[1] *Altdeutsches Lesebuch,* ed. Kurt Bona (Frankfurt am Main: Verlag Moritz Diesterweg, 1954), p. 74.

von Straßburg; of the unknown artist who merged the stories of Siegfried, Kriemhilde, and Burgundian treachery into the grim and fateful epic of the *Nibelungen*.[2]

PRINCIPAL DIFFERENCES BETWEEN OHG AND MHG

Looking back to the last chapter, we may say that chief among the differences which distinguish Old High German from this High Medieval or "Classic" Middle High German are: (1) The spread of mutation (umlaut), and (2) the weakening of the vowels of unstressed syllables, especially when in word-final position.

As mentioned previously, indication of umlaut in High German first appears in the Rhenish Franconian dialect of around 750. Throughout the Old High German era the only vowel to suffer this partial assimilation— at least in writing—was *a*, and even this change was inhibited by certain consonant combinations.[3] But by the eleventh century, umlaut had in general spread to include also the following vowels and diphthongs: *â, o, ô, u, û, ou, uo*:

	OHG	MHG	
â > æ	*swârî*	*swære*	"*Schmerz*"
o > ö	*mohti*	*möhte*	"*möchte*"
ô > œ	*scôni*	*schœne*	"*schön*"
u > ü[4]	*suni*	*süne*	"*Söhne*"
û > û̂	*hûsir*	*hiuser (iu = û̂)*	"*Häuser*"
ou > öu	*loubir*	*löuber*	"*Läuber*"
uo > üe	*fuoren*	*füeren*	"*führen*"

The spread of umlaut did not take place at the same pace nor at the same time throughout the High German speech area. Our efforts to chart its progress are hampered by the irregular spelling practices of the medieval

[2] Of the several texts devoted to this era of German literature, one of the best introductory studies is that by Helmut de Boor: *Die höfische Literatur* (3rd ed.; Munich, 1957). The best work currently available in English is M. O'C. Walshe, *Medieval German Literature* (Cambridge, Mass., 1962).

[3] Notably *hs* and *ht*: OHG *maht*–plural *mahti*. From the twelfth century on, however, *a* begins to show mutation even in such surroundings: OHG *mahti*–MHG *mächte*. German historical grammars refer to this later mutation of an *a*-vowel in a previously restrictive environment as "secondary umlaut" (*Sekundärumlaut*), and distinguish it in print by using the symbol *ä*, reserving *e* for the "primary" umlaut (*Primärumlaut*) that had its beginnings in Old High German (*gast–gesti*). The *e*-vowel that derives from Proto-Germanic *e* is then set off in print by means of a suprascribed diacritic: *ë* (OHG *nëman*).

[4] This vowel remained (and frequently remains) unfronted in Upper German before such consonant combinations as *gg, ck, pf, tz,* and a few others. See p. 66 for examples.

scribes, who were not at all consistent either in recording the presence of an umlauted vowel or in their choice of orthographic symbols for indicating its occurrence.[5] At first limited to the *a*-vowel, the spread from Rhenish Franconian to the other dialects of German of this environmentally conditioned fronting of the back vowels covers several centuries. Exactly how long it took in at least certain instances can be illustrated by the term *Grenze*, which is a loanword from Polish (*granica*), borrowed in the mid-thirteenth century and recorded first as *granizze*, soon thereafter as *grenize*. That the *a*-vowel of the German form underwent umlaut is proof that the word was in the language (in this case in the East Middle German dialect) *prior* to the change of *a* to *e*. In tracing the spread of umlaut we must also bear in mind that certain consonant combinations either prevented or inhibited the partial assimilation of the back vowel. Except with the restriction already mentioned in the Upper German dialects (p. 66), however, the change was eventually accomplished.

The other principal phonetic change which distinguishes Middle High from Old High German—the weakening of unstressed vowels—can perhaps best be appreciated by comparing a few MHG inflectional paradigms with their OHG equivalents. In the following declensional pattern, note especially (in addition to the umlauted vowel of the root) the phonetic changes which took place in the final syllable of the Middle High German forms:

	OHG	MHG
Singular		
Nominative and Accusative	*sunt(i)a*	*sünde*
Genitive	*sunt(i)a*	*sünde*
Dative	*sunt(i)u*	*sünde*
Plural		
Nominative and Accusative	*sunt(i)â*	*sünde*
Genitive	*sunt(e)ôno*	*sünden*
Dative	*sunt(e)ôm*	*sünden*

The inflection of the verb also underwent marked phonetic modifications, as can be seen by comparing the following examples of the present indicative and past (preterite) subjunctive of the strong verb in both Old High and Middle High German:

---

[5] MHG texts as printed in most of the editions have been "normalized," that is, the editors use a conventional orthography reflecting what philologists have adopted as an acceptable form of literary MHG. The orthography of the manuscripts, however, is anything but regular or consistent. We often find *o*, *ô*, *ö*, *œ*, all rendered simply by *o*. Or *u* and *v* are used indiscriminately for *u*, *û*, *ü*, *iu*, *uo*, and *üe*.

Present Indicative

	OHG	MHG
Singular		
1st Person	*gibu*	*gibe*
2nd Person	*gibis(t)*	*gibest*
3rd Person	*gibit*	*gibet*
Plural		
1st Person	*gëbamês*	*geben*
2nd Person	*gëbet*	*gebet*
3rd Person	*gëbant*	*gebent*

Past Subjunctive

	OHG	MHG
Singular		
1st Person	*gâbi*	*gæbe*
2nd Person	*gâbîs*	*gæbest*
3rd Person	*gâbi*	*gæbe*
Plural		
1st Person	*gâbîm*	*gæben*
2nd Person	*gâbît*	*gæbet*
3rd Person	*gâbîn*	*gæben*

The consonantism of Middle High German, while not differing essentially from that of the earlier period, nevertheless was subjected to certain changes. The differences in pronunciation of the two sibilants of Old High German—*s* < PGmc. *s*; *z* < PGmc. *t* (PGmc. **etan* > OHG *ëzzan*)—was not observed by all authors in the later MHG period. And the two phonetic components of OHG *sk* merge into the single sound of the palatal spirant, usually spelled *sch*: OHG *skif*–MHG *schif*. This change had its beginnings in the Upper German dialects, spreading slowly and sporadically northward. Likewise of southern origin is the shift from alveolar to palatal pronunciation of the voiceless sibilant (*s* > *š*) when followed by *l, m, n, p, t, w*; *slange* > *schlange*, *snê* > *schnee*, *swarz* > *schwarz*, and so forth. This gradual change was not at all universal in its spread. Even today not consistently reflected in the standard orthography (as in *Spiel* and *Stein*), the palatal pronunciation has not penetrated to all the northern dialects; alveolar pronunciation is in fact one of the most distinguishing features of German as native to the region in and around the city of Hanover in Lower Saxony.

To the extent that it was put to parchment, Old High German was used chiefly for religious purposes, its form determined in the main by scribes schooled in Latin. Toward the end of the Early Middle High German era

(1130–70), the literary purview was broadened to include secular themes, though such works were still composed for the most part by clerics. Not until High Medieval times does the German language achieve full independence and unequivocal status in both speech and writing: in speech as the *Standessprache* of the most prestigious and glamorous figure of the era, the knight; in writing as the artistic medium of the court poet and minstrel.

THE LANGUAGE OF KNIGHTHOOD (DIE RITTERSPRACHE)

It would be inaccurate to assume that German as spoken by the knights[6] of this era approached in any full sense what we today think of as a standard language. Nevertheless, there were attempts to overcome the crasser features characterizing the many dialects. These features were known at least in a general way, for the knights were among the most mobile members of medieval society. Through marriage and inheritances they acquired property far from home, thus necessitating long journeys to areas in which the local dialects differed sharply from their own. Eike von Repgowe, the author of an important codification into Low German of Saxon common law (*Der Sachsenspiegel, ca.* 1222), writes that the ancestral estates of several of the landed Saxon nobles were in Franconia and Swabia. Then, too, the nature of their society brought members of the nobility into contact with their peers from all the German-speaking lands, and indeed from beyond these borders. When, over Pentecost of the year 1184, the emperor Friedrich Barbarossa (1152–90) held a festival in Mainz to celebrate the knighting of his two sons, Heinrich and Friedrich, he issued an invitation to all the knights of the realm. Upwards of seventy thousand gentlefolk were in attendance, quartered in tents and temporary wooden structures that covered the countryside along the Rhine. For three days the assembled knights and ladies were the personal guests of the emperor.

In addition to the pomp and ceremony of the tournaments, there was ample provision for entertainment of a social and literary nature. Poets

---

[6] Knighthood (*das Rittertum*), as a mark of special social and cultural status within the structure of medieval society, was conferred upon those whose nobility had been inherited, as well as upon those whose privileged position had been acquired by service. One thus distinguishes between the "higher nobility" (*der hohe Adel, der Geburtsadel, la haute noblesse*) and the "lesser nobility" (*der niedere Adel, la petite noblesse*). The "lesser" or "petty" nobility had its origins in the *Ministerialenstand* or "serving class," which, from Carolingian times, was mainly responsible for staffing the castle court and the military retinue of the older blooded families. The men-at-arms and the vassals of an earlier age emerged in later medieval society as the *Schwertadel* and the *Dienstadel*.

declaimed their verses in three languages: French, German, and Latin. And we may be sure that the Germans sought to make their speech as broadly acceptable as possible, which meant, of course, that they avoided the obvious use of dialect. But acceptability of speech involved much more than this: the language of the knight had above all else to be *socially* acceptable, or, to use the German word, it had to be *höfisch*, that is, suited to the polite parlance of the court. And this language of chivalry—indeed, the very institution of knighthood itself—was in the image of its French model.

FRENCH INFLUENCE

The prestige of French learning and culture had, even before this, been firmly established in. Germany. In the prologue to his Latin-German commentary on the Song of Solomon (*ca.* 1065), Williram, abbot of a monastery at Ebersberg in Upper Bavaria, mentions with envy the high esteem in which German men of learning held the great French scholars, notably the famous Lanfranc (*ca.* 1005–89), whose international reputation had attracted many German theologians to France to study under him. And a century later there appeared the first German poems with themes taken from Old French sources: Pfaffe Konrad's *Rolandslied*, based upon the *Chanson de Roland*, and Pfaffe Lamprecht's *Alexanderlied*, patterned after a French version of the life of Alexander the Great as written by Albéric de Pisançon. These two works, both dating from approximately 1130, mark the beginning of a period of abiding French influence upon the court epic of medieval German literature.

Not until the time of the Second Crusade (1147–49), conducted under the joint leadership of the reigning French and German monarchs— Louis VII and Konrad III, respectively—did the German knights come into extended personal contact with their French counterparts. After that time it was not at all uncommon for the German knights to visit in France, or even to seek service at one of the French courts. Nor was it unusual to find Frenchmen engaged as tutors to the children of German nobles. Thus, in a relatively brief space of time, the German language of the late twelfth and early thirteenth centuries took on many French words, expressions, and turns of speech. Several words, especially nouns, were borrowed directly:

OFr.	MHG
aventure	*âventiure*
baniere	*banier*
joste	*tjoste* (cf. Eng. *joust*)
palais	*palas*
rime	*rîm*

There was also some borrowing of French suffixal elements, most striking in those cases where the foreign suffix remained productive in the host-language. For instance, the *ie* noun-forming suffix of Old French (pronounced *î* in German) was at first limited in its occurrence to full-fledged loanwords such as *cortoisîe, partîe,* and *vilanîe.* Later, however, the use of this once-foreign suffix was extended to form nouns derived from native German words: *dörperîe, jegerîe, vischerîe, zouberîe.* When this suffix later became diphthongized to *-ei* (in Early New High German), it was no longer felt to be foreign and was used with native German nouns: *Bäckerei, Fleischerei, Heuchelei, Liebelei,* and so forth. Another suffix, *-lei* (< OFr. *lei* [Modern French *loi*] "law, kind"), was used to form indefinite numerical adjectives of the type *allerlei, mancherlei,* and *vielerlei.*

One of the most interesting borrowings is contained in the verbal suffix *-ieren,* a Germanized form of the infinitive ending of the first conjugation in Old French (Modern French *-er*). This was first used only with verbs borrowed from the French, such as *parlieren* < OFr. *parlier, loschieren* < OFr. *logier, regnieren* < OFr. *reignier.* Later its function was extended to form verbs from words of native German stock: *buchstabieren, hausieren, sinnieren, stolzieren,* and the like. That the words containing this verbal suffix—as well as those mentioned above which display nominal suffixes—are still accented on the final syllable in accordance with the native stress patterns of French rather than German, is further evidence of their foreign origins.

In addition to the many words borrowed directly from French, the language of German chivalry also contained a number of loan-translations:

Ger.	Fr.	OFr.
hövesch (höfisch)	*courtois* "of the court, courtly"	
hövescheit	*courtoisie*	
knappe	*garçon*	
ritter	*chevalier*	
dörperîe "boorish, peasant-like conduct"		*vilanîe*

It was also under the direct influence of genteel French practice that the German knights of this era began addressing one another with *ir* (NHG *Ihr*) rather than *du,* patterned after the Old French use of *vos* (Modern French *vous*).[7] This heritage from the days of knighthood still lives on in some of the more rustic dialects of German today, in which *Ihr* rather than *Sie* is the conventional form of address in polite conversation.

---

[7] Isolated instances of *ir* as the pronoun of direct address go back to OHG times, but this usage did not become widespread until the late twelfth century.

Of the many French loanwords current in the vocabulary of High Medieval German, only a fraction survived long enough to find a permanent place in the language. Most of them were obsolete by the fifteenth century. Among those that entered the standard colloquial language, however, are some words which occur with fairly high frequency:

falsch	*klar*
fehlen	*prüfen*
fein	*tanzen*[8]

As might be expected, borrowings were especially extensive in those areas predominantly concerned with knightly activities. For this reason we find the language of the hunt and of the tournament heavily tinctured with French loanwords. A sizable portion of this specialized vocabulary—some of it little more than jargon—died out along with the colorful institution of knighthood itself. Of hunting terms borrowed from the French we mention three words that are still in the language: (*Hunde-*) *Koppel* "a string (or 'leash') of dogs" < OFr. *co(u)ple*; *Pansen* "first stomach of ruminants, paunch" < OFr. *pance*; *pirschen* "to stalk game (usually deer)" < MHG *birschen* "to hunt with bow and arrow" < OFr. *berser*.

The tournament yielded a rich and varied vocabulary. Many of the words were dropped from the language long ago—words such as *garzûn* "page" < OFr. *garçon*,[9] *trunzûn* "a broken spear-shaft" < OFr. *tronce*, and *leisieren* "to ride with slackened reins" < OFr. *laissier*. Other such loanwords survived for one reason or another, living on at least in the literary language. To mention but a few: *Harnisch*,[10] *Lanze*, *Panier*, *Turnier*, *Wimpel*. Still alive, too, are a number of expressions or phrases involving this language of the tournament, though today of course they are used only in a figurative sense:

für jemand eine Lanze einlegen
jemand in Harnisch bringen
mit offenem Visier kämpfen
sich die Sporen verdienen
etwas im Schilde führen
jemand ausstechen
jemand den Fehdehandschuh hinwerfen

---

[8] < OFr. *dancer*, itself possibly a loanword from the Gmc., though this etymology is open to dispute.

[9] A word of Gmc. origin, derived from PGmc. **wrakkjo* (> HG *Recke* "warrior, hero").

[10] < OFr. *harneis*, of ultimate Germanic provenience: < Proto-Old Norse **hernest* "military equipment."

LINGUISTIC INFLUENCES FROM THE NETHERLANDS

Of the German cities bordering on Romance territory, the Alsatian Straßburg and the ancient city of Trier, situated in Lorraine next to the duchy of Luxemburg, were the two most direct points-of-entry for French culture. Another major avenue by which Gallic influences reached Germany, however, was via the Netherlands—especially by way of the old duchy of Brabant in present-day Belgium.

The Flemish-speaking knights of Brabant were most highly regarded in Germany. Indeed, their name became synonymous with courtly elegance, and for a time it was considered a mark of some distinction among the German chevaliers to lard their speech with Flemish expressions, or, as the saying went, "zuo vlæmen mit der rede."

No doubt a considerable number of French words reached Germany by way of the Netherlands, sometimes as loanwords, sometimes as loan-translations. An example of the latter process is the very term for knight, *Ritter*, which is simply a High German borrowing of Netherlandish[11] *ridder*, a loan-translation of Fr. *chevalier*. Indicative of the high esteem in which they were held, the knights of the Netherlands were also able to contribute to German a small but significant number of words native to their own speech: *wâpen* (taken into HG as *Wappen*, where it exists alongside the shifted HG variant, *Waffen*), *ors* (*Roß*), *dörper* ("*Dörfler*," "country bumpkin"), *blîde* (*happy*; compare Eng. *blithe*), were all borrowed directly into Middle High German.

LANGUAGE AND THE IDEALS OF CHIVALRY

Along with new standards of social conduct, the rise of chivalry as an institution brought about a reshaping of the old cultural and ethical patterns. In addition to smooth and courtly manners (*hövescheit*) and the striving after excellence (*tugend*), the knight sought to cultivate two other virtues: moderation in all things (*mâze*), and a disciplined and responsible conduct in his relations with others (*zuht*).

---

[11] It is difficult to hit upon an acceptable term for the Franconian dialects spoken in the Low Countries in medieval times. The inhabitants of Flanders, Brabant, and Limburg (roughly present-day Belgium) referred to their language as *Dietsc*, whereas the people of Holland called their speech *Duutsc*. Historically, both of these dialects —including Low Saxon—belong to the Low German linguistic group: that is, to those German dialects which did not participate in the High German consonant shift. The English term *Dutch*, originally applicable to both High and Low German, is now restricted to the official language of Holland. *Flemish* (*Vlaams*) is the name of the Germanic language officially used in Belgium. We may use the rather clumsy *Netherlandish* as a quasi-generic term that includes both Dutch and Flemish.

As applied to things linguistic, this meant that the knight would emulate the special parlance of courtly society, that he would avoid all boisterous, loud, and undignified speech, and that he would eschew any vulgar, odd, or unpleasant expression that might offend his listener. He would not, for instance, use words which carried connotations of brutality, violence, or moral laxity. Nor would he tolerate expressions that smacked of uncouth peasant life. Although we cannot know the precise objection which courtly society had to each of the proscribed words, we do know that many of them were associated with the old heroic sagas of the Germans, occurring in folk-epics like the *Nibelungenlied*, though studiously avoided by the court poets. These expressions were considered to be *altfränkisch* and not at all alamode; for example:

degen ⎫	*balt* "daring"
recke ⎬ "warrior"	*vrevel* "courageous"
wîgant ⎭	*mære* "famous"
wine "friend, lover"	*vruot* "clever"

The social structure of knighthood succeeded in altering the language in yet another way, namely, by modifying the meaning of certain words. A classic example is the MHG *edele* (OHG *edili*) "noble," which in the older language applied almost exclusively to nobility of birth, but whose meaning in High Medieval times was extended to include excellence of spiritual qualities. The court poet Gottfried von Straßburg uses the term in this sense: "daz edele herze" (*Tristan und Isolde*, line 4682). An example of another word, whose meaning underwent marked modification is *wîp* (= *Weib*), used in early medieval times more in the general sense of "woman, female person," the term *vrouwe* (= *Frau*) being reserved to designate a woman of gentle birth—"gentlewoman, lady." During the High Medieval period, however, *wîp* took on a common, almost vulgar tone that restricted its usage in certain circles.

THE LANGUAGE OF THE COURT POETS (DIE HÖFISCHE DICHTERSPRACHE)

If much of what we have had to say about the presumed "leveling" of the *spoken* idiom necessarily rests to a considerable extent upon deduction and inference, our remarks pertaining to the standardization of the *written* language are on the other hand based upon more positive and demonstrable evidence. Here again, though, we must not think of a standard language in terms of today, but only of a marked tendency to use speech forms (for the literature was intended to be recited) of maximum acceptability. What constituted "acceptability" was subject to change. The immediate precursors of the High Medieval court epic, for instance,

are some German adaptations from Old French sources, such as the
Alexanderlied and the *Rolandslied* already mentioned. These early works
were first written in the language of the Rhineland, especially in Middle
Franconian, a dialect bordered on the east by French and Low Franconian,
merging in its northern reaches into Low German. The nearness of the
Rhineland to France and the Low Countries no doubt did much to enhance
the status of its language as a poetic medium, for in the period immediately
prior to the High Medieval era—from roughly 1170 to 1190—there
appeared several literary works of some distinction written in Middle
Franconian. But after approximately 1190, when the court epic reached
full flower, the prevailing literary language took on features distinctive of
Lower Alemannic and East Middle German, thereby reflecting among
other things the patronage of rich and powerful princes, such as the
Hohenstaufen emperor Heinrich VI (1190–97) and Landgrave Hermann of
Thuringia (1190–1217).

Whatever its provenience and models, there did emerge for a period of
perhaps fifty years a more or less "normalized" Middle High German
literary language that enjoyed high prestige and wide currency among the
poets. Its normalizing tendencies are most obvious in its rhymes, for the
court poets of the Golden Age did not tolerate the easygoing assonance of
an earlier time, insisting rather on pure rhymes. And to a remarkable
degree they were able to use words, the final syllables of which would
correspond when transposed into any of the major High German dialects.

An example of this is provided by the works of a poet who stands at the
very beginning of the *Blütezeit*, Heinrich von Veldeke, a native of the
province of Limburg in the Netherlands, whose *Eneit* (= *Aeneid*, begun
around 1170 but not completed until approximately 1190) determined the
style, both in form and content, that was to characterize the great court
epics for the next fifty years.[12] Though he probably wrote in his native
dialect of Limburg[13] (we have no manuscript in his own hand), slightly

[12] Gottfried von Straßburg, in his *Tristan und Isolde* (lines 4738–39), praises
Heinrich in the following famous passage: "Er impete das êrste rîs in tiutescher
Zungen" (*Er impfte das erste Reis in deutscher Zunge*).

[13] Heinrich von Veldeke was native to the southern part of the old duchy of
Limburg, an area corresponding to the political boundaries of the present-day Belgian
province of Liège (Lüttich), with its capital of the same name. Linguistically, Limburg
constituted in medieval times a transitional zone between Middle Franconian to the
south and Low Franconian to the north and northwest. For purposes of identification,
dialectologists have applied the term "Ripuarian" to the language of this region.

Until about 1100, Ripuarian seems to have been a Low Franconian dialect, untouched by the effects of the High German consonant shift. After this time, however,
it is better classified as a High German dialect, but barely! Most handbooks reckon it

modified in favor of the neighboring Middle German dialects to the south and east, his choice of rhymes is such that, when converted into High German, the correspondences still hold. For example, he rhymes *tît* (*Zeit*) with *wît* (*weit*), but not with its homophone *wît*, which in High German yields *weiß*, incapable of rhyming with either *Zeit* or *weit*. In like manner he rhymes *lîden* (*leiden*) and *snîden* (*schneiden*), but not *lîden* and *rîden*, for again—though they are a pure rhyme in Low German—the High German forms *leiden* and *reiten* would not so qualify.

For the High Medieval era proper, one of the greatest of the court poets, Hartmann von Aue, of Swabian origin, attempts to rid his language of certain marked Alemannic features. In his native dialect the past tense of the verb *kommen* was *kam* in the singular, *kâmen* in the plural. In the neighboring Bavarian speech, however, the equivalent forms were *kom–kômen*. In his earlier works, Hartmann employs rhymes such as *kam–nam*. Later, he avoided rhyme-pairs involving the past tense of *kommen*, since by that time he was writing for audiences beyond the boundaries of his homeland. In declaiming his compositions before a Bavarian audience, his Swabian *kam–nam* would have to be pronounced *kom–nam*, resulting in an impure rhyme unacceptable to his listeners.

Finally, as an example of the high esteem in which this rather haphazardly normalized High German *Dichtersprache* was held, we point to its use as the literary vehicle of several prominent poets whose native dialect was *Low* German. Albrecht von Halberstadt composed his version of Ovid's *Metamorphoses* in High German (*ca.* 1210), though not without mentioning in the preface how difficult it was to convert from his native Low Saxon. And one of the greatest of the *Minnesänger*, Heinrich von Morungen, wrote his poems in High German, although Low German was the language of his North Thuringian homeland.

to the Middle Franconian, which is then subdivided, when necessary, into Ripuarian and Moselle Franconian (to the south).

As Adolf Bach suggests (*Geschichte der deutschen Sprache*, 6th ed., p. 149, note), in trying to classify the language of Heinrich von Veldeke, a more appropriate frame of reference would be the political boundaries of the Holy Roman Empire of the twelfth century. Both the province and city of Limburg were situated in Lower Lorraine, a territory that also included such cities as Aachen, Cologne, and Koblenz. The language in the northern part of Lower Lorraine had escaped the influences of the High German consonant shift, whereas the speech to the south had been affected by it in varying degrees. The dialect of Limburg, therefore, was simply a variety of German, though to call the twelfth-century idiom of Heinrich von Veldeke either "Dutch" or "German" is to risk misunderstanding and censure, burdened as the two terms are with political and nationalistic connotations. Probably the least provocative term by which to refer to his speech is simply "the dialect of Limburg," though this solution obviously begs the entire question.

As an example of the High Medieval *Dichtersprache*, we include two verses of a well-known poem by the most famous of the lyricists, Walter von der Vogelweide:

> Under der linden
> an der heide,
> dâ unser zweier bette was,
> dâ muget [*mochtet*] ir vinden
> schône [*schön*; here = *ganz*] beide
> gebrochen bluomen unde [*beide . . . unde = sowohl . . . als auch*] gras.
> vor dem walde in einem tal—
> tandaradei!
> schône sanc diu nahtegal.
>
> Ich kam gegangen
> zuo der ouwe [*Aue*],
> dô was mîn friedel [= *Schatz*] komen ê [= *schon*].
> dâ wart ich enpfangen,
> hêre frouwe! [*hohe Frau*; here = *Heilige Jungfrau*]
> das ich bin sælic iemer mê [*mehr*].
> kuste er mich? wol tûsentstunt!
> tandaradei!
> seht, wie rôt mir ist der munt.

And from the stately measures of the *Nibelungenlied*, the opening stanza of the first *Âventiure*:[14]

Uns ist in alten mæren	wunders vil geseit [gesegit]
von heleden lobebæren,	von grôzer arebeit,
von fröuden, hôchgezîten,	von weinen und von klagen,
von küener recken strîten	muget ir nu wunder hœren sagen.

During the High Medieval period the German language was fashioned into a sensitive and flexible instrument for literary expression, its form no longer patterned after Latin models. Even though they made liberal use of French loanwords, the court poets shaped a native literary idiom worthy to take its place alongside the major cultural languages of Europe. But their triumph was short-lived: the Golden Age of courtly literature faded with the waning fortunes of the Hohenstaufen dynasty, the death of Friedrich II (1250) marking the practical end of its glory. For the next three hundred years, the literary forces that contributed to the rise of a German standard language (*die Hochsprache*) emanated primarily from the imperial chanceries, from the courts of the great territorial princes, and from the city chanceries of a newly emerged and influential social class,

[14] That critics do not generally accept this stanza as belonging to the *Urtext* is in this instance of no immediate importance.

the burgher. These writings, at first less neutral than the High German *Dichtersprache*, assumed the coloring of their geographical environment, and some of them did not again achieve supraterritorial status until the Early New High German period.

LATE MIDDLE HIGH GERMAN: 1250–1350

EARLY PROSE WORKS

Because of its importance both in quality and quantity, we have so far limited our discussion to the language of poetry. Though there are a few instances of prose as early as the closing decades of the twelfth century, it does not become commonplace until Late Middle High German times. One of the earliest prose works—modeled after a Latin original—is the German *Lucidarius* (*ca.* 1190), a comprehensive account of human history written in the popular "question and answer" style of the medieval textbook.[15] In a rhymed preface, the authors declare their decided preference for verse, but state that their patron, Duke Heinrich von Braunschweig, ordered them to use prose, "for they were to write nothing but the truth." Devoted in general to a similar theme, though not in catechetical form, is the Low German *Sächsische Weltchronik* (*ca.* 1230) of Eike von Repgowe.

Another source of late medieval German prose is the city chronicle (*Stadtchronik*). Most European cities of any consequence had their chroniclers or historians, whose task it was to record events of civic interest. Once entrusted only to Latin-writing scribes, these chronicles were later written in the vernacular, at first only in rhyme, but then, beginning in the fourteenth century, also in prose. Such German prose-chronicles were especially numerous in Switzerland, starting in 1335 with Christian Kuchimeister's history of St. Gall from 1228 to 1329. Probably the most interesting and culturally significant of these early prose-chronicles is the *Limburger Chronik*, a record of the years 1336 to 1398 as written by the city clerk, Tilemann Ehlen von Wolfhagen. A valuable feature of this chronicle, reflecting the personal interest of its compiler, is the inclusion in the text of many folk songs of his day. Several of these city chronicles are written in Low German. One of the better known of these, the *Magdeburger Schöppenchronik* (begun in 1380), attempts to chronicle the events not only of the city of Magdeburg but of all Upper Saxony,

---

[15] A style technically known as "catechetical," derived from the make-up of the elementary handbooks of Christian doctrine—catechisms—used for the oral instruction of those (especially the young) who were seeking admission to communicant membership in the Church.

tracing the history of the Saxons from their reputed origins (they were thought to be descendants of the ancient Macedonians!) to the fourteenth century.

We find the use of German (in prose, of course) also gaining ground in the field of jurisprudence. The professional language of the law was Latin, but whenever it seemed appropriate to communicate directly with the laity, German came to be more and more frequently used. Probably the earliest such work—written in the first years of the thirteenth century—is the *Mülhauser Reichsrechtsbuch*, though the major break-through occurred in 1235, when Friedrich II had the imperial decree, known as the *Mainzer Reichslandfriede*, drawn up in both Latin and German.[16] This was followed in 1256 by the *Bairischer Landfriede*.

The first codifications of German common law also were compiled during later Middle High German times. We have already mentioned the best known of these: *Der Sachsenspiegel* (*ca.* 1222), written in Low German by Eike von Repgowe. Its author tells us that he first wrote the work in Latin, but then—at the request of Count Hoyer von Falkenstein—recast it in German, though he doubted at the time whether he could do it. The success of his venture is proclaimed by the nearly two hundred manuscripts of the *Sachsenspiegel* that have survived.

There appeared several other compilations of German common law, including the so-called *Schwabenspiegel* (more appropriately *Das Lehenrechtsbuch* or *Das Kaiserrecht*), which was written sometime around 1275. Contrary to its popular title, the *Schwabenspiegel* is not limited to Swabian law, but attempts to codify the law common to all the old German tribes.

THE PREACHERS

The German homilies and sermons[17] are of special interest to students of the language because they were in general meant to be read aloud before a congregation, hence their style and vocabulary tend to approximate the vernacular of the time. The most extensive collection of such material, *Das Leipziger Predigtwerk*, contains 259 sermons. The manuscript

[16] A *Landfriede* was a legal order either prohibiting the nobles from engaging in a feud, or placing certain restrictions on the conflict. Feuding was permanently outlawed by the *Ewiger Landfriede* proclaimed by an Imperial Diet in 1495.

[17] In the parlance of traditional homiletics (the study that treats of the art of preaching), the *homily* is defined as an explication of a specific text, usually a passage from Scripture. A *sermon*, on the other hand, is a religious discourse on a given theme. Unless a distinction is called for, however, we may use the word "sermon" in either sense.

is from the late fourteenth century, but the time of composition of the individual sermons ranges from the twelfth to the thirteenth centuries. Another important collection is that compiled by a monk known simply as *Der St. Georgener Prediger.* Consisting of about eighty-five sermons (the number differs in the several manuscripts) from various sources, this work was intended to be used in convents for the instruction and edification of the nuns. The language is figurative, sensuous, and laced with mystical expressions. These sermons did, in fact, have a direct and traceable influence upon the language of the German mystics of the fourteenth and fifteenth centuries.

Intimately bound up with the history of the German sermon are the missionary activities of two great religious orders: the Dominicans, a preaching order (*ôrdo frâtrûm praedicâtôrum*) founded by St. Dominic in 1216, and the Franciscans or Minor Friars (*ôrdo frâtrûm minôrum*), a mendicant order founded by St. Francis of Assisi and given papal recognition in 1223. Monks of these two orders went out among the people, preaching on street corners and in the market places, using the homely and sometimes crude idiom of the folk. The two most famous of these German-preaching evangelists are David von Augsburg (1210?–71) and Berthold von Regensburg (1210?–72), both Bavarians and both Franciscans. To our knowledge, Brother David wrote no sermons in German, though he did use the vernacular to write on a variety of religious themes. Recent studies by Kurt Ruh and Sister Francis Mary, O.C.D., have developed some effective and convincing techniques for determining the authenticity of both German and Latin works attributed to David, either by his contemporaries or by later sources.

Berthold von Regensburg was one of the great Christian evangelists of the Middle Ages. The English philosopher Roger Bacon (1214?–94) called him the greatest preacher of the century, and another contemporary reports that his audiences numbered as high as forty thousand people. We have seventy-one German sermons preached by Brother Berthold, though he himself did not write them down. His style of preaching differs radically from that of the sophisticated pulpit orator skilled in the niceties of Latin rhetoric. Speaking simply and colloquially, he used the language of the common man. One of his favorite devices—and one which makes his sermons so valuable for linguistic study—was to adopt the pose of direct address, prefacing his remarks with the personal pronoun: *dû gîtiger (Geiziger), dû ketzer, dû diep.* Or he quoted questions supposedly asked him by someone: *Bruoder Berthold, wie sülle wir uns vor in [den Ketzern] behüeten, sô lange daz sie guoten liuten sô gar glîche sint?* Not since the two fragmentary conversation manuals from Old High German times (p. 79) do we find such obvious examples of *spoken* German.

THE MEDIEVAL MYSTICS

Early German mysticism centers on the names of three women: Hildegard von Bingen (1098–1179), Elisabeth von Schönau (1129–64), and Mechtild von Magdeburg (1212?–after 1280). Of these, only the last-named wrote in German—more specifically, in Low German, though the original text has not been preserved. A High German translation of her spiritual revelations was prepared in 1344 by Heinrich von Nördlingen under the title *Das fließende Licht der Gottheit.* Cast in prose, though containing some poetry, this curiously beautiful work is one of the first and most successful attempts to put into words the ecstasies of the soul as it seeks to effect oneness with God (*ûnio mystica*). In the selection that follows, notice the frequent use of abstract nouns (formed by such suffixes as *-heit, -nisse,* and *-unge*) and the idiomatic use of the verbal prefixes. All such devices highlight the struggle for freshness of expression, for subtleties of meaning not common to a term, because, as the mystics themselves said, they were trying to "express the inexpressible."

> Die sele lobet got an fúnf dingen.
> O keyser aller eren! O crone aller fúrsten! O wisheit aller meistern! O geber aller gabe! O loeser aller gevangnisse.
>> Wie got kumet in die sele.
>> Ich kum zuo miner lieben als ein touwe vf den bluomen.
>> Wie die sele got enpfahet vnd lobet.
>> Eya vroelichú anschownge! Eya leipliche gruos! Eya minnenklichú vmbehalsunge! Herre, din wunder hat mich verwundet, din gnade hat mich verdruket. O du hoher stein, du bist so wol durgraben, in dir mag nieman nisten denne tuben vnd nahtegal.
>
>> Got gelichet die selen fúnf dingen.
>> O du schoene rose in dem dorne! O du vliegendes bini in dem honge! O du reinú tube an dinem wesende! O du schoenú sunne an dinem schine! O du voller mane an dinem stande! Ich mag mich nit von dir gekeren.

In the fourteenth and fifteenth centuries German mysticism as a movement or "school" reached its definitive proportions. Three names stand out: Meister Eckhart (1260?–1327), Johannes Tauler (1300?–71), and Heinrich Seuse or Suso (1295?–1366). Characterized by boldness of metaphor, the literary style of the mystics strove to break through to higher levels of perception and description, not hesitating at the irrational or even the bizarre. Because of their constant efforts to lend physical dimensions to the spiritual and the abstract, they frequently gave new meanings to old words. Terms such as *begreifen, bilden, einleuchten,* took on extended connotations, sometimes even losing their older physically-oriented meaning, so that *begreifen* no longer meant literally "to seize," but rather "to seize with the mind," that is, "to comprehend." Other examples of terms that took on a figurative, metaphorical meaning include the many compounds with *Ein-* as the first component: such as *Eindruck, Einfall, Einfluß,* and *Einkehr* (all loan-translations from the Latin). Of the many new abstract nouns that entered the language at this time, we mention only *Empfänglichkeit, Erleuchtung, Geistigkeit, Vereinigung,* and *Verwandlung.*

In the history of the German language, medieval mysticism played a major role, even greater in some ways than that played by the court poets, for the mystics exploited and developed to a far greater degree the native word-forming potential of the language, using its rich stock of affixes to build new words and to lend new dimensions to old ones. They enhanced the capacity of German to "express the inexpressible"—to deal in abstractions—a quality which even today marks the genius of the language.

In the following passage from Heinrich Seuse's *Büchlein der ewigen Weisheit*—considered by many to be the most elegant expression of German mysticism—note especially the figures of speech and the coining of new and unusual compounds:

Nu hoer me: Ich bin von hoher gebürt, von edlem geslechte, ich bin das minneklich wort des veterlichen herzen, in dem, nach minnerichem abgrunde miner natuerlichen sunlicheit in siner bloßen veterlicheit, heind [= *haben*] ein wunneklichs wolgevallen sine minneklichen ougen in der süeßen vfvlammenden minne des heilgen geistes. Ich bin der wunne tron; ich bin der saelden [= *Glückseligkeit*] kron. Min ougen sind so klar, min mund so zart, mine wengel so liehtvar vnd so rosenrot, vnd alle min gestalt so schoene vnd so wunneklich vnd als [= *so*] durch wol gestalt. Vnd sölt ein mensch vnz [= *bis*] an den jungsten tag in einem glüejenden oven sin, das im [= *ihm*] nuon ein anblik würde, der waer dennocht vnverdienet. Sich [= *Siehe*], ich bin als wunneklich gezieret mit liechter wat [= *Kleid*], ich bin als vinlich [= *toll*] vmbgeben mit geblüemter missevarw [= *Vielfarbigkeit*] der lebenden bluomen, von roten rosen, wißen liljen, schoenen violn vnd allerlei bluomen, das aller meijen schoeni bluost [= *Blüte*], aller liehten ouwen grüeni ris, aller schoenen heiden zarte blüemli gegen miner gezierde sind als ein ruher tistel.

CHAPTER FIVE

The Early New High German Period

1350–1600

THE CHOICE of the year 1350 from which to mark the beginning of the New High German period is, from a linguistic point of view, largely arbitrary; 1400 or even 1450 would do almost as well. However, since we are primarily interested in tracing the history of the standard language (*die Hochsprache* or *die Schriftsprache*), the mid-fourteenth century is a convenient date, for by this time those structural and phonetic features most characteristic of what was to become the standard written language had spread throughout much of the High German area, and the use of the East Middle German literary dialects began gaining in prestige at the expense of the Upper German ones. Nevertheless, in describing those features which serve to distinguish Early New High German from Middle High German, the student must not assume that such changes occurred in all the High German dialects, or that they took place at approximately the same time. Most of the phenomena to which we shall refer had their beginnings already in one or another of the dialects of Middle High (or Low) German, and their spread to other areas was gradual and selective.

PRINCIPAL DIFFERENCES BETWEEN
MIDDLE HIGH GERMAN AND NEW HIGH GERMAN

PHONOLOGY

The principal phonetic differences between MHG and ENHG are four:

1. Etymologically short vowels in open syllables were usually lengthened:

   MHG *lĕ-ben, lĕ-gen, stŭ-be, sĭ-ben* > NHG *lê-ben, lê-gen, Stû-be, sie-ben (ie = î).*

2. Etymologically long vowels in closed syllables tended to become short:[1]

   MHG *hâst, hât* > NHG *hăst, hăt.*

3. The MHG long vowels *î, û, iu* (spelled *iu*) were diphthongized to *ei, au, äu* (usually spelled *eu*):

   MHG *mîn, hûs, liute* > NHG *mein, Haus, Leute.*

4. The MHG diphthongs *ie, uo, üe* were monophthongized to the long vowels *î* (but still spelled *ie*), *û, û:*

   MHG *liep, fuoz, füeze* > NHG *lieb, Fuß, Füße.*

In addition to distinguishing Middle High German from Early New High German, these changes also serve as a basis for a more detailed classification of the Upper and Middle German dialects, for—as did all phonetic changes—they took place at a given time and in a given place. The diphthongization of *î, û, iu* had its beginning in the Austrian province of Carinthia (*Kärnten*) as early as the beginnings of the twelfth century. By 1400 this change had spread to include not only Austria and Bavaria, but also much of the *Kolonialgebiet* (see Appendix 2, Map 3). On the other hand, the monophthongization of *ie, uo,* and *üe* had apparently started in the West Middle German dialects as early as the eleventh century, spreading eastward to include Rhenish Franconian, East Franconian, Thuringian, and Upper Saxon by ENHG times. The lengthening of short vowels in open syllables originated in the Low Franconian dialects of the twelfth century, spreading to all the German dialects except High Bavarian and High Alemannic. The shortening of etymologically long vowels in closed syllables was less consistently carried through; in the ENHG era this reduction is more characteristic of the Middle German dialects.

MORPHOLOGY

The differences in the morphology between Old High German and Middle High German in large part resulted from *phonetic* changes, whereas the formal distinctions which set off New High German from Middle High German reflect the effects of analogy[2]—specifically, the regularizing or

---

[1] Especially when followed by consonant clusters, such as *ht*: MHG *brâhte, dâhte, dîhte* > NHG *brăchte, dăchte, dĭchte.*

[2] Analogy is a type of linguistic association whereby things that are alike are made more alike.

"leveling" of morphological patterns in one direction or another. The inflection of the old *i*-declension nouns is a case in point:

Singular	OHG	MHG	NHG
Nominative and Accusative	*kraft*	*kraft*	
Genitive	*krefti*	*krefte (kraft)* ⎫	
Dative	*krefti*	*krefte (kraft)* ⎭	*Kraft*
Plural			
Nominative and Accusative	*krefti*	*krefte* ⎫	*Kräfte*
Genitive	*kreft(i)o*	*krefte* ⎭	
Dative	*kreftim*	*kreften*	*Kräften*

Even though the umlauted forms in the genitive and dative singular are historically regular, they were later replaced by unmutated forms, so that today the singular in all cases has only *Kraft*. This change is documented even for MHG, though the umlauted variants still occurred with greater frequency, at least in writing.

Another example of analogical leveling is to be found in the so-called "weak" declension of feminine nouns; in the singular, the form of the nominative has spread to all the "oblique" cases:[3]

Singular	OHG	MHG	NHG
Nominative	*zunga*	*zunge* ⎫	
Genitive	*zungûn*	*zungen* ⎪	*Zunge*
Dative	*zungûn*	*zungen* ⎪	
Accusative	*zungûn*	*zungen* ⎭	
Plural			
Nominative	*zungûn* ⎫		
Genitive	*zungôno* ⎪	*zungen*	*Zungen*
Dative	*zungôm* ⎪		
Accusative	*zungûn* ⎭		

A declension that in OHG and MHG had been limited to a small group of neuter nouns was expanded in NHG. These nouns formed their plural by umlauting the root vowel and adding *-ir* (MHG *-er*) to the stem:[4] OHG *lamb–lembir*, MHG *lamp–lember*. In Early New High German we find many neuter nouns—and some masculines—forming their plurals in this manner, though historically they do not belong to this particular declension: *Haus–Häuser*, *Kind–Kinder*, *Kleid–Kleider*; and such masculine nouns as *Geist–Geister*, *Mann–Männer*, *Wald–Wälder*, *Wurm–Würmer*. The function of umlaut as a plural-marker, incidentally, spread in the

---

[3] That is, all cases except the nominative and, where it has survived, the vocative.

[4] The umlauting of the root vowel was a conditioned *phonetic* change wrought by the high front vowel of the OHG plural-marker, and—*at the time it happened*—did not constitute a formal device for indicating plurality, a function carried out solely by the *ir*-suffix.

New High German period to include many nouns that had never had an *i* in the final syllable (which would have caused mutation of the root vowel), for example, *Gärten, Gräben, Höfe, Läden, Schäden.*

The morphology of the verb also underwent considerable modification in Early New High German, again chiefly as a result of analogical forces. In the older stages of the language, for example, the strong preterite distinguished between the vowel of the singular and the vowel of the plural, as can be seen by inspecting the ablaut series of the first three classes of the strong verb in Middle High German:

	Present	Preterite Singular	Preterite Plural	Past Participle
Class I	*rîten*	*reit*	*riten*	*geriten*
II	*biegen*	*bouc*	*bugen*	*gibogen*
IIIa	*singen*	*sang*	*sungen*	*gisungen*
IIIb	*helfen*	*half*	*hulfen*	*giholfen*

New High German has leveled the vowel of the preterite in favor of either the singular or the plural, though relics of the once prevailing distinction still linger, as in the proverb, "Wie die Alten sungen, so zwitschern die Jungen." The occurrence of *ward* (Class IIIb) rather than *wurde* is not unusual, especially in elevated style. And archaic past subjunctive forms such as *stürbe* and *hülfe* (also Class IIIb verbs) still alternate with the now regularly derived *stärbe* and *hälfe*, no doubt because the latter do not differ in standard pronunciation from the present subjunctive forms, *sterbe* and *helfe.*

This leveling of the vowels of the preterite spread slowly across the High German speech area, apparently starting in the Low Alemannic and Swabian dialects around mid-fifteenth century. The Middle German dialects in general tended to resist the change. In his earlier writings, for instance, Martin Luther used singulars like *greif* and *reit* rather than *griff* and *ritt.*

Certain changes in the *formation* of the present tense were also effected during the transition to New High German. One of the more interesting cases can be demonstrated by the verb *biegen* (Class II):

Singular	OHG	MHG	ENHG
1st Person	*biugu*	*biuge*	*beuge*
2nd Person	*biugis(t)*	*biugest*	*beuchst*
3rd Person	*biugit*	*biuget*	*beucht*
Plural			
1st Person	*biogamês*	*biegen*	*biegen*
2nd Person	*bioget*	*bieget*	*bieg(e)t*
3rd Person	*biogant*	*biegent*	*biegen(t)*

The difference between the vocalic structure of the root of the singular and plural derives from changes in the Germanic diphthong *eu* (PGmc. **ƀeuǥan*), caused by certain vowels in the following syllable. When followed by an *i*-vowel, PGmc. *eu* > *iu* (*i*-umlaut). Furthermore, it is usually assumed that in Old High German and Old Saxon a following *u*-vowel could also effect the change of *eu* to *iu* (PGmc. **ƀeuǥu* > OHG *biuǥu*), so that OHG and MHG strong verbs of Class II show *iu* throughout the singular of the present tense. In the case of the plural, we must reckon with another conditional sound change: when followed by *a, e, o*, PGmc. *eu* > OHG *eo* (later *io*) > MHG *ie* > NHG *î* (spelled *ie*). This is referred to as "*a*-umlaut."

The modern language has dropped this distinction between the singular and plural of the present tense of these verbs, though some authors— especially those writing in an East Middle German dialect—continued to observe a difference until well into the sixteenth century. They did not, however, retain *iu*, since this diphthong had become *eu* in ENHG (*liute-Leute; tiutsch–deutsch*), so that MHG *biuget, kriugt, vliugt* (to quote the third person singular) appear in ENHG as *beucht, kreucht*, and *fleucht*.[5]

As might be expected, a considerable number of historically strong (that is, irregular) verbs came to be conjugated as weak (regular) verbs. Examples include:

Class I	Class II	Class III
gleisen	*bläuen*	*bellen*
keifen	*kauen*	*gellen*
kreißen	*niesen*	*hinken*
neiden	*reuen*	*schmerzen*
reihen	*schmiegen*	*schwelgen*
seihen	*sieden*	

Transfers from the other four classes could easily be added. Interestingly enough, a few historically weak verbs came to be inflected as strong verbs: *gleichen, preisen, weisen*, among others.

ORTHOGRAPHY

The spelling of German during the ENHG era was flagrantly haphazard. Even within a given chancery there was often little consistency, a vowel such as *î* being written as *ii, ij*, or *y*. The doubling or even trebling of letters (*Konsonantenhäufung*) was thought to lend elegance to the page,

---

[5] Writers sometimes use this spelling to simulate an archaic or elevated style (it occurs commonly in the Bible). Friedrich Schiller, for instance, opens Act 3, scene 1, of *Wilhelm Tell* with a short poem—"Das Jägerliedchen"—the last line of which reads: *Was da kreucht und fleugt.*

resulting in such spellings as *czeytten* (*Zeiten*) and *fünffczig*. In the four-teenth century the *ß*-ligature appears as a substitute for an older *sz*, and from the same century arose the practice of indicating an umlauted vowel by means of the familiar suprascribed dots or ticks. When the umlauted diphthong came to be pronounced as the single vowel-sound *ü*, the *e* was then written *over* the *u* by many scribes in order to indicate the proper pronunciation of what had become a monophthong. This practice of indicating umlaut by means of a suprascript *e* soon spread to the vowels *a* and *o*, the superior letter in the course of time being reduced to its two upright strokes.[6]

Likewise in matters pertaining to interpunctuation there was great disparity, though some degree of conformity prevailed in the Prague and Vienna chanceries. Beginning in the thirteenth century, in addition to the use of a period or, more rarely, a comma to mark the end of a sentence or of a phrase, scribes began using a short slanting stroke known as a *virgula*. The use of the question mark also stems from the thirteenth century, though it did not become standard practice until the sixteenth century. The scribal tradition of using a capital letter or "majuscule" for the introductory word of a sentence or of a main clause is fairly standard procedure in ENHG times.

Major Dialects of Early New High German

By ENHG times the German speech area had reached approximately its modern proportions (pre-World War II). A comparison of Map 4 with Map 2 (Appendix 2) will show that the most obvious expansion beyond the older boundaries had been to the east. Beginning in the twelfth century, the provinces of Upper Saxony and Silesia were gradually settled by Germans from various parts of the *Altland*. Dialectologists distinguish three "waves" of migration to these colonial territories: a northern one from Lower Saxony (which exerted only a limited influence upon the East Middle German dialects), a central one from Thuringia and parts of Rhenish Franconia, and a southern one from East Franconia and Bavaria. In an oversimplified and not entirely accurate way, we can say that these

---

[6] The scripts used in many chanceries and *scriptoria* from about 1200 to 1500 are differentiated forms of what is generally known as "Gothic," a style of writing in which the formation of the letters is characterized by angular rather than by rounded strokes; the term *Gitterschrift* is especially descriptive. The so-called *Fraktur* still in limited use today—as well as the style of handwriting known as *Kurrentschrift* or *deutsche Schreibschrift*—reflects the angular, "broken" strokes of the old Gothic. Our "umlaut marks" are simply the vestiges of the two broken strokes of the Gothic-script *e*. For a short history of German writing, see R. Priebsch and W. E. Collinson, *The German Language* (5th ed.; London, 1962), chap. 9.

three routes met in Upper Saxony, then continued on into Silesia in a sporadic and diffused fashion. The population of Silesia east of the Oder-Neiße line remained essentially Slavic until much later. As a result of these migrations, what is labeled "East Middle German" on Map 2 in time came to be divided into three distinct dialects: Thuringian,[7] Upper Saxon, and Silesian, though the latter two do not emerge as discrete *Schriftdialekte* until well into the ENHG era.[8]

There are, of course, other differences in the dialect boundaries of approximately 1400 as compared with those of the older eras, though they cannot easily be shown on a single map scaled to the entire area. Most obvious is that certain of the major dialects (in addition to East Middle German) developed subgroups; furthermore, the dividing line separating Middle German from Low German had shifted slightly to the north along much of its east–west axis.

[7] Until the middle of the thirteenth century much of Thuringia used Low German, especially in the north. High German influence came chiefly from the southwest (West Middle German), via Erfurt. Though the Thuringians constitute one of the *Altstämme*, their language does not emerge as a literary vehicle until MHG times.

[8] Map 2 shows a small East Middle German enclave in what—prior to 1945—was East Prussia, reflecting the once widespread use of this dialect by the original colonizers of Prussia, the Teutonic Knights.

The Order of the Teutonic Knights (*der deutsche Orden, die Deutschherren, die Kreuzritter*), founded during the Third Crusade (1189–92), was granted the status of a principality of the empire by Frederick II. In 1229, at the invitation of Conrad of Masovia, Duke of Poland, the Knights, under the command of their dedicated *Hochmeister* Hermann von Salza (1210–39), mounted a successful crusade against the still un-Christianized Prussians—a Baltic people—and went on to conquer and colonize an area that came to include not only West and East Prussia, but Lithuania, Estonia, and other Baltic lands. For the next two hundred years, many Germans, from Lower Saxony, especially, migrated to this northeastern territory. In 1309 the seat of government—the residence of the *Hochmeister*—was moved to Marienburg (south of Elbing in East Prussia), where the Order continued to rule its vast holdings until, in the fifteenth century, the combined forces of the Lithuanians and Poles brought about its political downfall.

The official language of the Order was an East Middle German dialect (Thuringian-Saxon), for it was in the old *Mark Meißen* of the Wettin princes that the Teutonic Knights had established some of their earliest colonies. Later on, even though deep in Low German and Slavic territory, they continued to use East Middle German (it was also the language in which they conducted all official correspondence). By the fifteenth century, the area in which this dialect was spoken had been reduced to a small arc around Marienburg, though in the preceding two centuries its sphere of dominance had penetrated much farther south.

There is also a literature, largely religious, written by members of the Order; it, too, is in the Thuringian-Saxon dialect. Probably the best-known work of this sort is the *Theologia Deutsch* from the mid-fourteenth century. Martin Luther thought enough of this devotional treatise to have it printed in 1518 under the title *Eyn Deutsch Theologia*.

Arranged in outline form, we may list the principal dialects of Early New High German as follows:

(I. Low German)
  A. Low Franconian
  B. Low Saxon

II. Middle German
  A. Middle Franconian
    1. Ripuarian
    2. Moselle Franconian
  B. Rhenish Franconian
  C. East Middle German
    1. Thuringian
    2. Upper Saxon ⎱ *Schriftdialekte* from about 1400
    3. Silesian ⎰

III. Upper German
  A. East Franconian
  B. Swabian-Alemannic
  C. Bavarian

In tracing the rise of standard High German—*die Hochsprache*—it is most important to realize that by 1300 the normalizing linguistic tendencies of the High Medieval era had ended. Even at that time, however, all attempts to develop a standard language had been limited for practical purposes to the one social class, and with its passing, the first major effort to develop a common written form of the language that rose above local and regional differences died, almost aborning. In this phase of its development, German stands alone among the major modern languages of western Europe, for the history of the literary languages of English, French, Italian, and Spanish is unbroken in its progression from medieval to modern times. But the first Golden Age of literary German ended abruptly in the mid-thirteenth century, and the written forms of Late Middle High and Early New High German were again reduced to the status of regional dialects. In a sense, therefore, the beginnings of the NHG *Hochsprache* date no earlier than the era we are now considering. A few supra-territorial varieties of written German emerged out of the abundance of these regional *Schreibmundarten*, but not until the close of the seventeenth century did a generally acceptable literary standard develop.

Although not yet clearly differentiated in the literature, the distinctions between the dialects of the major "territories"[9] were established and well-known by the fourteenth century. The East Franconian poet, Hugo von Trimberg, writing around the year 1300, briefly described what to him were the most striking phonetic characteristics of twelve different dialects of High German. A few lines later he asks his readers' indulgence for the traits which he knows characterize his own language:

> ein ieglich mensche sprichet gern
> die sprâch bî der ez ist erzogen.
> sint mîniu wort ein teil gebogen
> gein Franken, nieman sî daz zorn,
> wan ich von Franken bin geborn.
> (*Der Renner*, lines 22,306 ff.)

Of the several efforts to overcome these dialectal differences and again to reach some sort of common literary medium, one of the most important was that exerted by the imperial and territorial chanceries—later to be joined by those of the cities—when they began issuing their *Urkunden*[10] in German.

Die Kanzleisprachen

Though the language of the *Urkunden* was traditionally Latin, the use of German increased markedly during the thirteenth and fourteenth centuries, a convention apparently traceable to the rise in both number and influence of the lesser nobility (*der niedere Adel*) in late medieval society. The social origins of this new class were humble and far removed from the Latin-monastic tradition of education—an education based of course upon literacy in Latin. Whereas *der Dienstadel*, members of the lesser nobility who served their lords in an administrative capacity, knew Latin (the chief clerk or "prime minister" of the chancery, for example), the knights trained for and dedicated to a career as professional soldiers—*der Schwertadel*—were not usually encumbered with such learning. In one

---

[9] In German history, the term *Territorium* (*Landesherrschaft*) has a specialized meaning somewhat analogous to our word "state" in its political sense. Corresponding roughly to the old grand duchies (their boundaries in turn reflecting in a general way the geographical disposition of the ancient German tribal groups, *die Altstämme*), the "territories" were established under the Hohenstaufen emperors as major administrative subdivisions of the *Reich*. These were the *Großterritorien*, to which various *Kleinterritorien* were later added.

[10] Though a brief definition cannot be completely satisfactory, *Urkunden* are legal instruments—edicts, charters, and the like—in epistolary form drawn up in a chancery (*Kanzlei*) and issued over the seal of a sovereign, a court, or a judicial officer.

of his courtly epics (*Gregorius auf dem Steine*, lines 1547–53), Hartmann von Aue has the abbot warn young Gregorius that any youth who is still in school at the age of twelve might just as well become a priest, since he will never acquire true proficiency as a knight. The warrior caste, made up primarily of the lesser nobles, had little patience with book learning.

Another factor which led to the greater use of German in the chanceries was the disintegration during the thirteenth century of the centralized power of the emperor. Even under Frederick II the bonds of émpire had been loosened. Then came the Great Interregnum (1256–73), after which all efforts to rebuild the empire or to form a united Germany served only to strengthen centrifugal tendencies. During these years the nobles became more and more a law unto themselves. Quite naturally, countless disputes arose among them, disputes involving rights of way, boundary lines, and the like. In fact, as a result of their many altercations, two new types of legal writs emerged: the *Sühne* (reconciliation) and the *Schiedsspruch* (arbitration). The very nature of such documents precluded the use of a standardized Latin formulary. Each dispute was different, and each instrument had to be tailored to fit its unique purpose. Furthermore, every safeguard had to be taken to insure that those affected understood the decisions. Tradition had it that Latin was the proper language for legal pronouncements, but this custom worked an intolerable hardship on the lesser nobles. Eventually they broke with protocol and began writing in their native German. Many of them, of course, could not afford to maintain a chancery staffed with Latin-writing scribes.

Approximately twenty-five hundred legal documents dated prior to 1299 are composed in German. Significantly, almost all of them are from the pens of lesser nobles. The geographical distribution of these German *Urkunden* is also interesting: over twenty-two hundred of them are from the territory along the middle and lower Rhine, land that early had been parceled out to smaller landowners. Some of the oldest of these documents—from about 1250—are found in Swabia and Austria, similarly long divided among the lesser nobles. Thuringia, on the other hand, was governed until late by a few great rulers: rich and powerful princes who maintained excellent chanceries. Latin prevailed in their realms until the last decade of the thirteenth century.

German had become commonplace as the language of the *Stadturkunden* —legal writs prepared in the chanceries of the burgeoning cities of medieval Germany—by the fourteenth century, although there are instances (especially in Switzerland) of its infrequent and isolated occurrence from about 1250. The city council of Munich first ordered a document written in German on June 15, 1300. Nürnberg, too, took the turn of the century as a starting point for converting from Latin to German. The records of Vienna are incomplete, but there are German *Urkunden* from 1280. Cologne employed Latin, with few exceptions, until 1325, and the ancient cities of the Middle Rhine held to Latin until after 1300. In Low German territory, Hildesheim issued a writ in German for the first time in 1302, Göttingen in 1325, and Hanover in 1329. The Hanseatic cities were easily the most conservative: the use of German in their chanceries did not become common until almost 1400.[11]

Evidence of this sort, incidentally, scotches the popular belief that the first triumphs of German over Latin in the everyday world of public affairs should be attributed to the burghers' need for a means of written communication other than Latin. As a matter of fact, the cities clung to the writing of Latin on the average of a half century longer than any other lay element of medieval Germany. It was the petty noblemen, and not the members of the newly emerged third estate, who first wrote in German.

The use of German for official purposes was given high-placed sanction when the imperial chanceries began issuing their writs in the vernacular, a practice that had its beginnings with the *Reichslandfriede* of 1235, was continued in a modest way under Rudolf von Hapsburg (1273–91), and became standard procedure under Ludwig the Bavarian (1314–47) of the House of Wittelsbach. After his break with the papacy in the latter part of his reign, Ludwig used German for almost all chancery matters.

Even though the vernacular under Ludwig enjoyed the status of an official language, however, no particular effort was made to standardize either its orthography or its usage. Chancery procedures of the time even encouraged diversity, for it was the accepted practice of those who were directing routine petitions to the Crown to include a properly worded and formulated *Urkunde*, needing only the signature and seal of the appropriate chancery official in order to validate it. Such documents were written in the dialect of the petitioner, so that the imperial archives from this era present a bewildering confusion of dialects and scribal practices.

Of special historical importance is the imperial chancery under the Luxemburgers: Charles IV (1347–78) and his sons Wenceslas (1378–1400) and Sigismund (1410–37). Located at Prague in Bohemia, their chancery employed a language that, in its phonetic structure, presented in several significant ways a compromise between the adjoining Upper German and East Middle German dialect areas. While exhibiting the MG monophthongs *î, û, iu* (< MHG *ie, uo, üe*), it had, however, adopted the UG

---

[11] See Felix Merkel, *Das Aufkommen der deutschen Sprache in den städtischen Kanzleien des ausgehenden Mittelalters* (Leipzig and Berlin, 1930), pp. 64–72.

diphthongs *au, ei, eu*. MG influence is evident in the frequent occurrences of *b* and *k* rather than the once-dominant UG forms, *p* and *ch* (UG *perch, chint*–MG *berg, kind*), as well as in the scribes' tendency to write unstressed *e* as *i*, and to retain *final* unstressed *e*. Furthermore, the spelling of the Prague chancery often lengthens etymologically short vowels standing in open syllables.

Obviously, the points of similarity between this written dialect and the modern *Hochsprache* are many. Also, by the end of the fifteenth century a variety of German similar to that of the imperial chancery was common to the territorial chanceries throughout Upper Saxony, Thuringia, and Silesia; indeed, it was used even in the Upper Saxon courts of law and in the universities of Leipzig and Wittenberg (to the extent that German was employed at all).

The degree to which the chancery language of the colonial territories reflected the linguistic practices of the imperial court is a much debated subject. An older generation of scholars, influenced primarily by the medievalist Konrad Burdach, believed that the Bohemian chancery was an immediate model for all the neighboring territorial chanceries. This viewpoint is now subject to modification, for according to the researches of such dialectologists as Theodor Frings, Ernst Schwarz, and Ludwig Erich Schmitt, the language of the imperial chancery under the Luxemburgers was modeled after the local dialects spoken in Prague and in certain other cities of Bohemia: dialects which, because of their relatively central location, exhibited features of both Upper and East Middle German. And according to the dialectologists, the literary dialects that developed in the eastern colonial territories, far from being a conscious imitation of the language of the Bohemian chancery, were modeled after the speech of the local settlers, whose ancestors at different times in the past had emigrated from the *Altland* and whose sundry dialects of UG and MG provenience had given way to a language which in its several features was a compromise between these various inherited speech-patterns.

Although the role played by the Bohemian chancery in the rise of the *Hochsprache* has in the past probably been too highly rated, to deny it a place of considerable importance would be inaccurate. The prestige of the imperial chancery cannot be discounted. Nor can the relevancy of linguistic features *other* than the phonology be ignored. Largely due to the efforts of Charles' gifted *Reichskanzler* Johann von Neumarkt, later Bishop of Olmütz, the language of the Prague chancery achieved a rhetorical elegance and flexibility that lent added luster to its already high status. Both Charles and his chancellor were attracted to the writings and the style of the Italian Humanists. As a result of the influence exerted by such writers as Boccaccio, Petrarch, and Rienzo, a major literary renaissance took place in Bohemia, a movement that achieved its most eloquent expression in a classic of early German literature, *Der Ackermann aus Böhmen,* written in 1401 by Johann von Tepl.

Stemming as it did from a center of literary as well as political importance, the polished language of Neumarkt's chancery must surely have exerted tremendous influence. In matters of style and syntax it would be pointless to dispute its importance in the over-all development of standard German. Such features as the neatly balanced compound-complex sentence, the use of juxtaposed synonyms, and the rhetorical question, are all examples of the style cultivated by the Italian Humanists. And these devices characterize not only the style of their Bohemian followers, but also that of the Prague chancery.

Beginning with the long reign of Frederick III (1440–93) of the Hapsburg dynasty, the imperial chancery was moved to Vienna. As a result, certain Upper German characteristics were again reflected in the orthography: *p* for *b; kch, ckh, kh* for *k,* and so forth. Even so, however, the imperial *Schreibidiom* remained essentially a blend of the UG and MG regional variants.

It was during the reign of Frederick's son, the gifted and humanistically oriented Emperor Maximilian I (1493–1519), that the first concerted and successful efforts were made to adopt a uniform written language in all the chanceries of the empire. Largely through the efforts of Maximilian's able chancellor, Niclas Ziegler, the more pronounced Upper German features of the Austrian *Kanzleisprache* were modified in favor of Middle German standards. And the chanceries in Saxony and Silesia adopted the most distinctive and widespread feature of Austro-Bavarian, namely, the diphthongization of the old long vowels ($\hat{\imath},\ \hat{u},\ \hat{u} > ei,\ au,\ eu$). These changes, coupled with certain spelling reforms, brought about a previously unrealized degree of uniformity in the written language used by the imperial chancery. From the reign of Maximilian on, all documents bearing the emperor's seal were composed in approximately the same language, regardless of which of the chanceries throughout the empire they may have been written in.

Of pivotal importance in the rise of standard High German is the development of the language used in the chancery of the electorate of Saxony in Wittenberg during the coregency of Ernst and Albrecht (1464–86) and, from 1486 to 1525, during the reign of Ernst's eldest son, Frederick the Wise, for Martin Luther claimed to have modeled his *Bibeldeutsch* in its image. Until their coregency was terminated in 1486, both Ernst and

Albrecht maintained their court in Dresden, a city which, though still in East Middle German linguistic territory, bordered on Bohemia. For many reasons, their chancery employed a variety of German that was basically close to that used in Prague: the dialects spoken in both cities had their origins in the linguistic blendings effected by previous migrations to the eastern colonies; many Bohemians had fled to Saxony at the time of the Hussite wars (1420–33), thus reinforcing certain features held more or less in common by all the colonial dialects; and the geographical proximity of the culturally superior city of Prague.

The sphere of influence exerted by the Saxon *Kanzleisprache* was extended when, in 1484, Ernst took up residence in Thuringia. And also of some linguistic significance was the election in 1480 of Ernst's younger son, Albrecht, to be Archbishop of Mainz. Under the direction of Albrecht's chancellor, Dr. Spigel, a written language in the style of that employed in the Saxon electorate was introduced into the episcopal chancery. This move enhanced the fortune and prestige of what was basically the *Kursächsische Kanzleisprache*, because many of the imperial diets were held in Mainz, and Dr. Spigel's scribes were entrusted with the task of composing the *Reichstagsabschiede*—the official accounts of the diets' deliberations and decisions. The language of these documents (printed and distributed throughout the empire) came to be held in high esteem as a model of elegant prose.

In summary, it is important to remember that the chancery languages are reflections of the dialects *spoken* in their respective areas. After the Interregnum the seat of empire had moved eastward, finally advancing into colonial territory. However, although their roots were in the spoken idiom, the chancery languages were being shaped into more flexible and adequate instruments of written communication, until in the late fifteenth century they had reached a passable degree of standardization. Their common phonetic basis had been determined largely by chance historical and political factors; in matters pertaining to syntax and style, however, their similarities resulted from the deliberate attempts of the chancellors to cultivate a more elegant and precise manner of expression. And in this area the efforts of Charles IV and Johann von Neumarkt were especially successful: the rhetorical flourishes characterizing the literary style of the Italian Renaissance are also hallmarks of the prose used by the early Bohemian Humanists. The workaday language of the chancery was seldom fashioned into prose of lasting beauty, but even so, its patterns of sentence construction, its reduplication and balancing of phrases, its use of synonyms and metaphors, are all reflections of what, in literary circles, also describes the cultivated style of the finest authors of the period.

We close our discussion of the *Kanzleisprachen* with two specimen texts: the one, a short passage from the most celebrated literary master-piece of the era, *Der Ackermann aus Böhmen*; the other, a few sentences of an *Urkunde* from the Prague chancery. The former, of course, is not an example of chancery German, but it will demonstrate the influence of the Humanistic style upon the written language of the time. Of special interest is a comparison of the sentence structure, for both selections exhibit the so-called "periodic" style (*die mehrgliedrige Periode*)—that is, carefully balanced compound-complex sentences.

Selection from Der Ackermann aus Böhmen

Merke, wie die leuchtigen rosen und die starkriechenden lilien in den gerten, wie die kreftigen würze und die lustgebenden blumen in den auen, wie die feststeenden steine und die hochwachsenden baume in wildem gefilde, wie die krafthabenden beren und die starkwaltigen lewen in entrischen [= *grausigen*] wustungen, wie die hochmachtigen starken recken, wie die behenden, abenteuerlichen, hochgelerten und allerlei meisterschaft woll vermügenden leute und wie alle irdische creatüre, wie künstig, wie listig, wie stark sie sein, wie lange sie sich enthalten, wie lange sie es treiben, müssen zu nichte werden und ver-fallen allenthalben. Und wann nu alle menschgeslechte, die gewesen sint, sint oder noch werden, müssen von wesen zu nichtwesen komen, wes solte die gelobte, die du beweinest, genießen, das ir nicht geschehe als andern allen und allen andern als ir?

(Chapter X, *Der Tod*)

Selection from an Urkunde; Prague, March 4, 1437

Sigmund von gots gnaden Romischer keyser zu allen czijten merer des reychs und zu Ungeren zu Behem etc. kunig. Lieben getruwen. wann wir manigfeldiclichen vernomen han, wie in dem heyligen reyche und nemlich Deutschen landen grosse und swere leuffe uferstanden sein, dadurch kriege und widerwertickeit in den landen teglichen ye me und mee wachssen, also das des reichs strasse zu wasser und zu lande nider-gelegt und schedlichen verhindert werden, das man der ane grosse sorge und arbeyd nicht gebruchen muge; so werden auch unsere und des reichs achte und aberachte versmehet, und vil fursten graven herren und stete tun dawider offentlichen den ungehorsamen rat und hulffe; so sin auch sußt [= *schon*] an offenen und hemelichen gerichten soliche gebrechen, als wir teglich vernemen, die da notdurftiglich zu besseren weren; deslichen von der muncze wegen, die auch den landen schaden bringet; und wann nu soliche vorberurte sachen und gebrechen unser keyserliche gemute zuvor besunder beweget hant und noch bewegen, und wir alleczijt gerne darczu wolten getan han und noch tun mit rate

und beystant unserr kurfursten und auch anderer fursten graven herren
und stete, damit soliche sache und gebrechen versehen und nach not-
durft gesatzt und geordnet weren worden und noch werden mochten:
und darumb so hann wir ytzund denselben unsern kurfursten fursten
graven herren und steten ernstlich geschreben zu uns gen Eger, zu
komen uff den heiligen phingstag schierest folgende, darynn wir sie, als
wir nicht zweyfelen, willig fynden.

When measured by the standards of contemporary prose, with its
preference for short sentences and economy of description, the luxuriance
of the periodic construction does not strike us as a model of good writing.
But in the hands of a literary craftsman skilled in the techniques of
classical rhetoric, such a *Schachtelsatz* ("encapsulated sentence" or "box-
within-a-box") could achieve considerable elegance of a sort, coupling
formal complexity with neatness and precision of articulation in a manner
reminiscent of a musical fugue. This style of writing was much abused,
however, and soon degenerated into the awkward, meandering, and florid
"officialese" referred to as *Amtsstil* or *Kurialstil*, further characterized by
its tiresome use of synonymous expressions and formula-like locutions.
Examples of this language are with us today in the set wordings of legal
documents, diplomas (*hiermit geben wir kund und zu wissen*), and the like.
Unfortunately, since the Crown was involved in regulating the far-flung
activities of Germany's merchants and tradesmen, the language of commerce also came to reflect in a high degree the terminology and the stilted
syntax commonly used by the secretaries of the imperial and royal
chanceries—a situation long deplored by teachers of rhetoric and composition, for the style of much business correspondence (in almost any
language, apparently) lags only slightly behind that of legal prose in
triteness, wordiness, and artificiality.

DAS GEMEINE DEUTSCH—OSTMITTELDEUTSCH

Largely as a result of attempts to standardize the principal *Kanzleisprachen*, two generalized and widely used varieties of High German came
into prominence during the ENHG era. Of these, the so-called *Gemeines*
(= *allgemeines*) *Deutsch*, an essentially Upper German dialect which had
first been fashioned into a literary instrument in the imperial chancery of
the Hapsburgs, came to serve as the standard written language of Austria
and southern Germany. It held this position until the eighteenth century,
only gradually giving way to the increasing popularity of a literary idiom
of East Middle German provenience, the language of Prague and of the
Saxon electorate. This *Ostmitteldeutsch* was to serve as the basis for
Luther's German and, ultimately, for the New High German *Hochsprache*.

Whereas High German literary languages of more than local or regional currency arose primarily through the efforts of the imperial and royal chanceries, a similar standardization of the many written dialects of Low German was effected by another force, the unifying influences of the Hanseatic League—the medieval federation of northern German cities bound together for purposes of mutual trade and protection.

Not only because of its importance in things commercial, but also because of its leadership in matters of law and civic administration, the city of Lübeck came to enjoy a position of eminence in northern Germany. Many younger or lesser cities copied its statutes, legal codes, and written language, so that by the mid-fourteenth century a more or less standardized Low German, patterned on the dialect of Lübeck, was used as a language of commerce, law, and literature, not only throughout northern Germany but as far away as the Hanseatic settlements in England, Scandinavia, the Baltic countries, and Russia. In fact, at no time either before or since has the German language exerted such a strong influence beyond its own borders. Actually, there was a brief period when it was the dominant commercial language throughout much of Scandinavia, especially Denmark.

However far-flung its adoption may once have been, this Low German *Geschäftssprache* was destined to lose out to the overriding influence and gradual spread of High German. The Hanseatic cities of West and East Prussia—under the flag of the Teutonic knights—had continued to use East Middle German for most of their correspondence. And as of approximately 1350 the chanceries of such Low German cities as Göttingen, Magdeburg, and Northeim were also using High German to an ever increasing degree. The trend continued, so that although this supraterritorial Middle Low German *Schriftsprache* left its mark on the language of commerce and jurisprudence, it had died out by the end of the fourteenth century.

The following specimen of Middle Low German is an excerpt from the statutes of the city of Lübeck (*Das alte Lübische Recht*) from the year 1294:

We ratmen [*Ratsherren*] van Lubeke prouet [*erfahren*] in maneghen saken, de vor vs komet, dat bewilen [*bisweilen*] eteleke vormunden nicht des an sic hebbet, dat se nutte [*nützliche*] vormunde wesen kunnen; bewilen sint se nicht so vlitich [*fleißig*] unde so weruesam [*tätig*] ofte [*oder*] so truwe, also dar to boret [*gebühret*], vnde bewilen scheppet [*schaffen*] se dar under eres silues nut [*ihres eigenen Nutzens*] vnde nicht uan rechte des nut, des vormunde se sin gheworden. Oc

beuinde we des uele [*vielmals*], dat iunghelinge, de comen sint to eren
achtein iaren, wan se de uormunden en [*ihnen*] antwordet ere ghut, dat
se den [*dann*] noch der wisheit vnde der clocheit nicht an sic hebbet, dat
se ere ghut nutteleken uorstan moghen, vnde dar uan is manech
mundich iunghelinc gàn uan ghude [*deswegen hat mancher junge
Mündiger sein Erbgut vergeudet*], hedde he bisorghere [*Nebensorger*] hat,
dat he sin gut lichte [*vielleicht*] nicht unbilleke vnde dumlike to bracht
hedde.

MITTELNIEDERLÄNDISCH

The Franconian dialects of the Low Countries had also, during the
thirteenth and fourteenth centuries, been subjected to various normalizing
tendencies, resulting in a standardized literary dialect. Broadly speaking,
this form of *Mittelniederländisch* served as the basis for today's Dutch and
Flemish.

YIDDISH

Also from this era we can trace the emergence and dispersion of Yiddish,
as a written language. Originating apparently as a modified form of the
German spoken by Jews in the Rhenish Palatinate, it later took on many
characteristics of the East Middle German dialects, since there had been
considerable Jewish migration to the colonial territories. Conventionally
written in a Rabbinical Hebrew script, the earliest documents in Yiddish
are from the last years of the fourteenth century. Although basically
German, it has been influenced by such languages as Hebrew, Polish, and
Russian. Of the many Yiddish dialects, the two main subdivisions are
West Yiddish, once spoken primarily in Germany, and East Yiddish, used
by Jews in the Slavic countries, especially Poland. It is chiefly the eastern
dialect that was brought to the United States by Jewish emigrations from
Central and Eastern Europe.

PENNSYLVANIA GERMAN

Seeking a new life more in consonance with their religious convictions,
a group of immigrants from the city and vicinity of Frankfurt-am-Main,
reaching the colony of Pennsylvania in 1683, founded there the first
German settlement in North America, which was later named "Germantown." These people spoke a Rhenish Franconian dialect. *Not Dutch.*
Attracted by the prosperity and the religious freedom enjoyed by the
colonists in Germantown, newcomers from Germany continued to arrive
for years to come, many of them also from the Rhenish Palatinate.

Because of the reluctance of the residents to mix with the outside world, this rural society has been able to preserve its speech and customs even to the present day, though the linguistic and social inroads have been considerable. Their language is a curious blend of English and Franconian dialect, much of it as incomprehensible to the native German as it is to the American "outsider." It has often attracted the interest of scholars.[12]

FOREIGN INFLUENCES

LATIN

From about 1450 to 1600, Latin exerted a greater influence upon German than did any other language. In the first German dictionary of foreign words (*Fremdwörterbuch*)—compiled by Simon Roth in 1571— there are some two thousand entries, almost all of them Latin. Indeed, the bulk of Latin loanwords still to be found in Modern German entered the language at this time.

The Roman Catholic church had continued to use Latin for all liturgical purposes and for its official correspondences, abetted substantially by an edict from Charles IV in 1369 decreeing it illegal to write on religious topics in German. And the Archbishop of Mainz in 1486 proclaimed that the Latin Vulgate was not to be translated into German for use by the laity.

However much the official language of the Church may have eventually infiltrated German, there was another force that accounted in still greater degree for the Latin influence of the fifteenth and sixteenth centuries— the Renaissance with its passionate dedication to the literary and philosophical ideals of Classical Humanism. The common language of learned men had long been Latin, but hardly that of Cicero. The disciples of the Renaissance sought to emulate the idiom of Rome's Golden Age, and they were inordinately successful. The vocabulary of German scholarship is still studded with the Latinisms inherited from this era. We list only a few of the thousands of such terms that make up the technical language of theology, law, medicine, philosophy, and all the other disciplines associated with higher learning. Such words as the following have in general passed into the vocabulary of the average educated person:

Absolution	*Kathedrale*
Advokat	*Medizin*

[12] See especially Carroll E. Reed and Lester W. Seifert, *A Linguistic Atlas of Pennsylvania German* (Marburg, 1954); also Ralph C. Wood, "Pennsilfaanisch oder Pennsylvaniendeutsch," *Deutsche Philologie im Aufriß* (Berlin, 1952), I, cols. 785–808.

Amnestie	*Metaphysik*
Apotheke	*Rezept*
Arterie	*Sekte*
Doktor	*Student*
Fakultät	*Takt*
Filter	*Tenor*
Fuge	*Text*
Hypothek	*Tinktur*
Inquisition	*Zirkel*

Latin also exerted an abiding influence on German syntax. As in Old High German times, authors imitated Latin grammatical constructions. Perhaps the most notorious of Latin syntactic borrowings from this era is reflected in the practice of transposing the verb to the end of a clause introduced by a subordinating conjunction or by a relative pronoun. And the use of participles in various types of absolute constructions became quite acceptable—a stylistic device still found in Modern German: *Einen Sturm fürchtend, kehrten wir nach dem Lande* and *Diese Arbeit vollendet, ging ich zu Bett.*[13]

As an example of the flagrant and excessive use of Latin in the prose of the day—a practice not limited only to learned discourse—we quote a paragraph from one of the most popular chapbooks of all time: *Historia von D. Johann Fausten, dem weitbeschreyten Zauberer und Schwartz-künstler* (1587), not intended as a scholarly work, but a *Volksbuch* in the fullest sense of the word.

Als D. Faust eins gantz gelernigen vnd geschwinden Kopffs, zum studiern qualificiert vnd geneigt war, ist er hernach in seinem *Examine* von den *Rectoribus* so weit kommen, daß man jn in dem Magistrat examiniert vnnd neben jm auch 16. *Magistros*, denen ist er im Gehôre, Fragen vnnd Geschickligkeit obgelegen vnd gesieget, Also, daß er seinen Theil gnugsam studiert hat, war also *Doctor Theologiæ*. Daneben hat er auch einen thummen, vnsinnigen vnnd hoffertigen Kopff gehabt, wie man jn denn allezeit den Speculierer genennet hat, Ist zur bôsen Gesellschafft gerahten, hat die H. Schrifft ein weil hinder die Thûr vnnd vnter die Banck gelegt, ruch vnd Gottloß gelebt, Zu dem fand D. Faustus seines gleichen, die giengen mit Chaldeischen, Persischen, Arabischen, vnd Griechischen Worten, *figuris, characteribus, coniura-tionibus, incantationibus*, vnnd wie solche Namen der Beschwerung vnd Zauberey môgen genennet werden. . . . Das gefiel D. Fausto wol, speculiert vnd studiert Nacht vnd Tag darinnen, wolte sich hernacher keinen *Theologum* mehr nennen lassen, ward ein Weltmensch.

---

[13] Quoted from George O. Curme, *A Grammar of the German Language* (2nd rev. ed.; New York, 1952), pp. 263, 267.

As a result of eastward expansions into the colonial territories, a limited number of foreign words—especially Slavic and Hungarian—were borrowed into the German vocabulary.[14] Mention has already been made of the term *Grenze. Knute*, borrowed from Russ. *knut*, first occurs in the sixteenth century in the compound *Knottpeitsche*. The word *Peitsche* itself is a fourteenth-century borrowing from the Slavic, probably from the Czech *bič*. Other borrowings from the Slavic are:

Graupe	*Pistole*
Gurke	*Popanz*
Halunke	*Quark*
Haubitze	*Zobel*[15]
Petschaft (a neuter noun < Czech *peček*)	

Contributions from the Hungarian (there are not many) include *Dolmetsch* (itself a loanword in Hungarian), *Heiduck, Husar,* and *Kutsche* (named after the Hungarian village of Kocs).

Contact with the Mediterranean world—especially in its eastern and southeastern reaches—introduced the Germans to many exotic foods, spices, and goods of all sorts. Even if the words for many of these items tended to enter the language by way of the Italian (and with an Italianized spelling), their derivations for the most part go back to Arabic or Persian, although they had often passed through several intermediate cultures before reaching the northern Mediterranean lands. Here is a brief list of words of this sort:

Alkohol	Arab. *alkoḥl*
Atlas	Arab. *aṭlas*
Barchent	Arab. *barrakân*
Borax	Pers. *bûräh*
Kaffee	Arab. *qahwa*
Kaper	Pers. *käbär*
Kattun	Arab. *quṭn*
Limone	Pers. *lîmûn*
Marzipan	Arab. *mautabân*
Orange	Pers. *nâräng*

[14] The reverse influence was much greater, that is, the influence of German upon the various languages of eastern Europe with which it came in contact.

[15] The history of most of these words, which are of Slavic etymology, is usually complex. This makes it difficult to specify from which of the Slavic languages the word was borrowed. The student should consult an etymological dictionary for details.

Scharlach	Arab. *siqillâṭ*
Sirup	Arab. *sarâb*
Zibebe	Arab. *zabîb*

NORTHERN EUROPE

The Germanic languages lying north of the High German dialect boundaries contributed few terms during this period (except to the speech of the sailor—*Seemannssprache*—a topic which we will take up separately in the section devoted to specialized dialects). Low German gave such words as:

Fracht	*Linnen*	*Qualm*
Gilde	*Makler*	*Rätsel*
Gerücht	*Prasser*	*Stapel*

Borrowings from Dutch included *Auster, Düne, Römer* (an ornate green wineglass; < Du. *roemen* *"rühmen"*), and *Süden*. The Scandinavian languages are represented by only a few words, most common of which include *Daune, Kiel, Hummer,* and *Renntier*.

SPECIALIZED DIALECTS (*Sondersprachen*)

The rise in ENHG times of what in German are called *Sondersprachen* (Fr. *langues spéciales*) reflects a society that had grown more stratified, specialized, and complex. In a sense, though, both Old High German and Middle High German, as we know them, are *Sondersprachen*, yielding only a limited account of the culture of their times. The Old High German of the manuscripts is largely the language of the Church; Middle High German has come down to us chiefly in the specialized idiom of courtly society. If written records of the earlier epochs were more substantial, they would mirror a world in which the transition from medieval to early modern times was not as abrupt or revolutionary as it might appear.

TRADE AND COMMERCE

Especially during the fifteenth and sixteenth centuries, the merchants of southern Germany began carrying on a brisk trade in the cities and ports of northern Italy, a circumstance which caused many Italian words to find their way into the specialized language of commerce. Some of these expressions have by now passed into the general vocabulary; for example:

Bank	*Kredit*
Bankerott	*Porto*
Bilanz	*Posten*
Kassa	*Risiko*
Konto	

Many others, however, are still felt to be limited to the special language of the bookkeeper or accountant:

a conto "on account"
blanko "unfilled, blank [as, for instance, an order]"
brutto "gross"
Faktur "invoice"
Kollo "bale, package"
netto "net"
Primo "first of the month"
Medio "middle of the month"
Obligo "liability"
Saldo "balance of an account"
Skonto (now usually *Diskont*) "discount, rebate"
Strazze "daybook, ledger"
Tara (borrowed originally from the Arabic) "deduction for the weight of a container"
Tratte "a check or draft drawn on a commercial account"
Ultimo "last of the month"

Certain expressions that were in fact borrowed from the Italian would now appear to have come from the French. A word like *Journal* (in the sense of "daybook" or "ledger") is a case in point. First taken into German as *zornal* < Ital. *giornale*, it was refashioned in the French manner during the sixteenth century, when Gallic influence was once again making itself felt in Germany. This trend continued, so that many French commercial terms were absorbed into German; for instance:

Acquit "receipt"
Allonge "an addendum [to an invoice, etc.]"
Avis (*Avisierung*) "advice"
Emballage "packing"
fallieren "default [in payments]"; also "to go bankrupt"
retournieren "return [merchandise]"
stornieren "to transfer from one account to another"

The language of the North German merchant was far less amenable to foreign influences than that of his counterpart in the South. When the prestige of the Hanseatic League had begun to wane, there was a sprinkling of loanwords, and then not from France or Italy, but from Holland. In the seventeenth century a few Dutch commercial terms entered the language: *Aktie, Dividende, Lotterie, Preiskurant* (= *Preisliste*). Terms such as these are not ultimately native to the Dutch language—except the word *Lotterie*—but were fashioned from Latin. They are nevertheless of a more indigenous nature than, say, a word such as Du. *bai* "bay," taken into

German (*Bai*) via the Netherlands in the fifteenth century, but before that
—by way of the French *baie*—deriving from Spanish *bahía*.

Loanwords from English were all but nonexistent in ENHG times. Not
until late in the eighteenth century do the merchants in northern Germany
start using such terms as *Banknote, Jobber, Partner,* and *Scheck.*

THE LANGUAGE OF THE SEAMAN

Just as contact with southern Europe had enriched the language of
commerce, so did it contribute to the vocabulary of seafaring men whose
ships dropped anchor in Mediterranean ports. Though it is not always
possible to trace the borrowing directly, Romance origins of terms such as
the following are obvious:

> *Barke* (Ital., Span. *barca*)
> *Besan* "mizzenmast" (Ital. *mezzana*)
> *Flotte* (Ital. *flotta,* Fr. *flotte*)
> *Fregatte* (Ital. *fregata*)
> *Golf* (Ital. *golfo*)
> *Galeere* (Ital. *galera*)
> *Kompaß* (Ital. *compasco*)
> *Marine* (Fr. *marine*)
> *Pinasse* "a light sailing ship" (Fr. *pinasse* "a boat made of spruce")
> *Port* (Fr. *port*)

The language of the sailors whose crafts sailed the waters of the North
Sea and the Baltic also contributed many nautical terms to standard
German, some of them now used in a general, nontechnical sense, such as
Abstecher, Flagge, and *scheitern;* others—still restricted in meaning—
include words such as *Klüver* "jib [sail]," *Kombüse* "ship's galley," *Maat*
"mate," and *Matrose* "sailor." Most of these expressions are common to
both Low German and Dutch, so that it is sometimes impossible to say
who borrowed from whom.

THE LANGUAGE OF THE SOLDIER

Military German as a specialized language does not really come into its
own until the time of the Thirty Years' War (1618–48), but a good
beginning was made a century earlier with the increasing use of mercenary
soldiers. Although this specialized idiom of the German military consisted
in the main of French accretions, the words were borrowed in a helter-
skelter fashion from all the Romance languages. From an almost endless
list, we select a few examples:

Armee	*Kanone*
Artillerie	*Kaserne*
Bajonett	*Kommiß*
Bataille	*Korps*
Chef	*Major*
Deserteur	*Offizier*
Etappe	*Parole*
Füsilier	*Sergeant*
Garde	*Soldat*
General	*Spion*

THE LANGUAGE OF THE MINER

Unique among the specialized dialects of the emerging modern era, that of the miner exhibits almost no foreign influences. Several words in common use today—most of them with transferred, nontechnical meanings —came into the language as technical mining expressions:

Ausbeute	*Klafter*
Einbuße	*Schacht*
Fundgrube	*Schicht*
Haspel	*Stichprobe*

One of the few loanwords in the *Bergmannssprache* is *Kux* "a share in a mine," a word of Late Latin origin that quite likely came into German via the Czech language (*kusek*).

THE LANGUAGE OF THE HUNTER

We have already referred to some of the terms of the chase that came into the language during the days of knighthood, most of them from France. However, much of the terminology peculiar to the hunt (*die Weidmannssprache*) is of ancient Germanic heritage, even though it does not occur in print until ENHG times. Examples are the words *Fähe* "bitch" and *Welpe* "young dog [whelp]," or the use of the term *Schweiß* in its specialized meaning of "blood [of the fallen prey]."

Of a somewhat different nature are those words that in the hunter's idiom had—and still have—a meaning other than the one commonly associated with the term. This situation applies especially to expressions for the body parts of birds and beasts of prey. In the following examples we list only the restricted meaning of the hunt: *Arm* "foreleg of an animal," *Lauf* "leg or foot of quadrupeds," *Lauscher* (pl.) "ears of deer, foxes, wolves, etc.," *Löffel* "ear of a rabbit," *Ständer* "foot of a fowl or water bird."

The *Weidmannssprache* has contributed several colorful words to the modern language, usually employed now in a figurative sense. Examples are *bärbeißig*, once used of a courageous or vicious hunting dog, now meaning simply "quarrelsome"; *naseweis*, originally "to point [*weisen*] with the nose"—"a pointer"—now meaning "saucy, impertinent, know-it-all"; *vorlaut*, once limited in meaning to a hunting dog that would give voice too soon, now generalized to mean "forward, noisy, hasty." These three words, once applied only to dogs, are now most often used with reference to people.

Numerous figures of speech were once specialized hunting terms; some of the more common expressions were:

> *auf den Busch klopfen*
> *auf falscher Fährte sein*
> *ins Gehege kommen*
> *jemand zur Strecke bringen*
> *jemand Fallstricke legen*
> *jemand ins Garn locken*
> *mit allen Hunden gehetzt werden*

THE INVENTION OF PRINTING

In our review of the various forces and factors that led to the emergence of a standard German language, we must mention the invention of printing with movable type. With the appearance of Johann Gutenberg's forty-two-line Latin Bibles from about 1455 on (see Plate 6), a new age was ushered in: the age of mass communication via the printed page. What had been the exclusive property of a select few, now became widely available in relatively cheap printed editions.

For a long time the volume of books printed in Latin was much greater than that in German. As of 1570, for instance, 70 per cent of the works printed in Germany were in Latin. Not until 1681 did German publications for the first time outnumber those in Latin. As might be expected, academic and professional interests clung longest to the use of Latin, though even in the field of literature German publications lagged behind those in Latin until late in the seventeenth century.[16]

In determining which dialect of German to use, the early printers customarily adopted that form of the language employed by the local chancery, though they soon strove for broader acceptance by following the practices of the imperial chancery. Since printing developed in

---

[16] As a matter of antiquarian interest, the mathematician Karl Friedrich Gauß (1777–1855) published his definitive work on the theory of numbers in Latin— *Disquisitiones arithmeticæ* (1801)—though by this time the writing of books in Latin was otherwise restricted to an ever dwindling number of classicists and churchmen.

southern Germany, the fifteenth-century *Offizinen* (as the early print shops were called; < Lat. *officîna*) in a general way championed *das Gemeine Deutsch*, which had spread from the imperial chancery of the Hapsburgs to become the standard written language of Upper Germany. All fourteen of the pre-Luther German Bibles were printed in this dialect, as was *Der Ackermann aus Böhmen*, from which we quoted earlier. With the coming of the Protestant Reformation (as we shall presently discuss in greater detail) this South German standard began to lose out to *Ostmitteldeutsch*, the other High German written dialect which had been fashioned largely in the chancery of the Saxon electorate and accepted in much of eastern and central Germany as standard.

The printers, however, did not slavishly follow the practices of even the royal and imperial chanceries, but tended to exercise a wide freedom of choice based in the final analysis upon their own dialectal preference. As a result there arose what are known as *Druckersprachen*. These "printers' languages" are of considerable importance in the history of standard High German.

During the sixteenth century in High German territory, four distinctive Upper German *Druckersprachen* developed: (1) Austro-Bavarian (Ingolstadt, Munich, Vienna); (2) Swabian (Augsburg, Tübingen, Ulm); (3) Upper Rhenish (Basel, Straßburg); and (4) Zürich Swiss. Middle German was represented by two general types: Upper Saxon (Leipzig, Wittenberg), and West Middle German (Frankfurt, Mainz, Worms). Yet another variety of printer's German—the East Franconian (Bamberg, Nürnberg)—occupied an intermediate position between Upper German and Middle German. First one and then another of these styles achieved a temporary superiority, until in the mid-sixteenth century the *officînae* in Wittenberg and Frankfurt, through their unprecedented successes as publishers of Luther's translation of the Bible, succeeded in taking a substantial lead.

We shall postpone any further discussion of the struggles to achieve a generally acceptable *Hochsprache* until we have had a chance to study the contributions made by the most important single figure in the history of the Modern High German language, Martin Luther (1483–1546).

Martin Luther

Previous generations often referred to Luther as the "creator" of New High German. Though he did not "create" the modern German language, he nevertheless did contribute enormously to its development and refinement as a literary instrument. Furthermore, because his translation of the

Bible had such wide distribution and acceptance, that dialect of German in which it was written did indeed come to serve as the authoritative basis for the modern *Hochsprache*.

Ich habe keine gewisse, sonderliche, eigene sprach im teutschen, sondern brauche der gemeinen teutschen sprach, daß mich beide Ober- und Niderländer verstehen mögen. Ich red nach der sächsischen cantzeley, welcher nachfolgen alle fürsten und könige im teutsch lande, alle reichstätte, fürstenhöfe schreiben nach der sächsischen und unsers fürsten cantzeley, darumb ists auch die gemeinste teutsche sprach. Kaiser Maximilian und Churfürst Friderich hertzog von Sachsen haben im römischen reiche die deutschen sprachen also in eine gewisse sprach zusammengezogen.

As this well-known quotation from his *Tischreden* proves, Luther deliberately adopted what he held to be *die gemeine teutsche sprach* as used by the royal Saxon chancery. And the sometimes niggling objections of contemporary dialectologists notwithstanding, this is what he did, though in later years he modified his language slightly in favor of other—chiefly southern and western—dialects of High German. His statement that the imperial and royal chanceries both used the same kind of written German cannot be accepted without qualification, but, as was pointed out earlier, they had by this time reached a fair degree of mutual uniformity. Of course, there were still differences. Luther's *Bibeldeutsch*, however, definitely favors East Middle German usage, though occasionally it follows Upper German norms.[17] Determining the precise nature of his earlier language is not always so easy, for prior to about 1524 Luther paid little attention to what he considered the relatively unimportant matter of

---

[17] To list a few orthographic and grammatical characteristics of Luther's German: in common with the Upper German dialects, he uses the new diphthongs *ei, au, eu*, but holds to the East Middle German monophthongization of MHG *ie, uo, üe*. The MHG diphthong *ei* is retained in that spelling by Luther, whereas *das Gemeine Deutsch* has *ai* (*Bein–Bain*). The voiced stops *b, d, g* seldom shift to their voiceless counterparts *p, t, k*—a prominent feature of Upper German. In his early writings especially, Luther uses preterite forms of the strong verb that in his day still distinguished the vowel of the singular from that of the plural (see p. 105), such as *treib, schrei*, which by that time in Upper German documents were usually given as *trîb, schrî*. In marked contrast to Upper German practices, Luther regularly retained final unstressed *e* (*Name, Leute–Nam, Leut*), as well as the *e* of prefixes and suffixes (*beschreiben, genommen, kleines–bschreiben, gnommen, kleins*). He also prefers *gehen* and *stehen* rather than the widespread (especially Alemannic) *gân, stân*.

Luther's vocabulary shows a decided East Middle German influence; so much so that southern German and Swiss printers frequently added a glossary to his works, giving the Upper German equivalents of words foreign to *Gemeines Deutsch*. In one edition of the Bible, for instance, Luther's *beben, fühlen, Lippe, Qual, täuschen*, are glossed as *bidmen, empfinden, Lefze, Pein, betrügen*.

orthography. In 1520 he wrote: ". . . ich fur war der zeyt nit hab, das ich müge sehen was der drucker fur bild buchstaben, tindten odder papyr nympt." As of approximately 1524, however, he began proofreading his material and issuing specific instructions to the typesetters and editors of his Wittenberg publisher, Hans Lufft. The complete translation of his New Testament appeared in 1522. The first printing of the entire Bible—both Testaments and the Apocrypha—appeared in 1534 (see Plates 7 and 8), and in 1545 Luther himself supervised the printing of the last edition to appear during his lifetime, *die Ausgabe letzter Hand*. Throughout this twenty-year period he made countless changes in the text, always striving to effect a standard and acceptable orthography, grammatical consistency, and utmost clarity of expression.

The *Lutherbibel* still stands as the most magnificent literary monument in the German language. Though its orthography and grammar are based to a large extent upon chancery practices in the Saxon electorate, its *style* certainly is not. Luther's great genius lay in his uncanny and inspired ability to forge a language that was idiomatic and natural. His was not the first German Bible; there had been fourteen such translations into High German, four into Low German. The first of these—that of Johann Mentel in 1461 (written in *das Gemeine Deutsch*)—had gone through seventeen editions. But it was Luther's translation that was destined to become *the* German Bible. As evidence of its unprecedented popularity, it is estimated that the printing house of Hans Lufft in Wittenberg sold something over one hundred thousand copies during the years 1534 to 1584, an extraordinarily high figure for that time.

As an example of Luther's unsurpassed skill in translating, we quote from the second chapter of the Epistle to the Philippians, verses 5–11, as they appear in Mentel's High German version of 1466 and as printed in Luther's 1545 edition:

Mentel	*Luther*
Wann ditz entphint in euch: das auch in ihesu cristo. Wie das er was in dem bilde gotz er masst nit den raube wesent sich geleich got: wann er verüppigt sich selber er nam an sich das bilde des knechts er ist gemacht in die geleichsam der mann; und ist funden in der wandelung als ein man. er gedemtiügt sich selber er ist gemacht gehorsam got dem vatter untz an den tod:	Ein jeglicher sei gesinnet, wie Ihesus Christus auch war. Welcher, ob er wol in göttlicher gestalt war, hielt ers nicht fur einen raub, Gotte gleich sein. Sondern aüssert sich selbs, und nam Knechtsgestalt an, ward gleich wie ein ander Mensch, und an geberden als ein Mensch erfunden. Ernidriget sich selbs, und ward gehorsam bis zum Tode, ja zum tode

wann untz an den tode des kreutzes.
Dorumb gott erhöch in. und gab
im einen namen der do ist uber ein
ieglichen namen: das in dem namen
ihesu cristi würd genaigt alles knye
der himelischen und der irdischen
und der hellischen: und ein ieglich
zunge begeche das der herre ihesus
cristus ist in der wunniglich gotts
des vatters.

am Creutz. Darumb hat jn auch
Gott erhöhet und hat jm einen
Namen gegeben, der uber alle
namen ist. Das in dem namen
Ihesu sich beugen sollen alle der
knie, die im Himel und auf Erden
und unter der Erden sind, und
alle Zungen bekennen sollen, das
Ihesus Christus der Herr sei, zur
ehre Gottes des Vaters.[18]

As was to be expected, not all of Luther's contemporaries were equally pleased with his efforts; the Roman Catholic theologians, especially, took him severely to task for what they considered to be certain willful and heretical distortions of the text. Luther answered his critics in the famous *Sendschreiben vom Dolmetschen*, written in 1530 as an open letter to his friend Wenzeslaus Link of Nürnberg. The letter should be read in its entirety by every student of the German language. We limit ourselves here to his defense of the translation of Luke 1:28—the words of greeting addressed to Mary by the Angel Gabriel: "Hail, thou that art highly esteemed, the Lord is with thee: blessed art thou among women." The Vulgate has: "Ave gratia plena: Dominus tecum: Benedicta tu in mulieribus," which Mentel had rendered as "Gegrússt seistu vol der genaden: der herr ist mit dir: du bist gesegent vnter den weibern." Luther's version reads: "Gegrüsset seistu Holdselige, der Herr ist mit dir, du Gebenedeite unter den Weiben." Now to the words of the *Sendschreiben*:

[18] Mentel's translation is based upon the Latin Vulgate. Luther, though giving priority to the Greek text, was strongly influenced by the Latin version with which he was so familiar. As far as this particular passage is concerned, there are no substantial discrepancies between the two sources. The wording of the Vulgate is as follows:

"Hoc enim sentite in vobis, quod et in Christo Iesu: qui cum in forma Dei esset, non rapinam arbitratus est esse se aequalem Deo: sed semetipsum exinanivit formam servi accipiens, in similitudinem hominum factus, et habitu inventus ut homo. Humiliavit semetipsum factus obediens usque ad mortem, mortem autem crucis. Propter quod et Deus exaltavit illum, et donavit illi nomen, quod est super omne nomen: ut in nomine Iesu omne genu flectatur caelestium, terrestrium, et infernorum, et omnis lingua confiteatur quia Dominus Iesus Christus in gloria est Dei Patris."

In the King James version of the Bible we read: "Let this mind be in you, which was also in Christ Jesus: Who, being in the form of God, thought it not robbery to be equal with God: But made himself of no reputation, and took upon him the form of a servant, and was made in the likeness of men: And being found in fashion as a man, he humbled himself, and became obedient unto death, even the death of the cross. Wherefore God also hath highly exalted him, and given him a name which is above every name: That at the name of Jesus every knee should bow, of things in heaven, and things in earth, and things under the earth; And that every tongue should confess that Jesus Christ is Lord, to the glory of God the Father."

Item, da der Engel Mariam grüsset und spricht: "Gegrüsset seistu
Maria vol Gnaden, der Herr mit dir." Wolan, so ists bisher schlecht den
lateinischen Buchstaben nach verdeudscht; sage mir aber, ob solchs
auch gut deudsch sei. Wo redet der deudsche Man also: Du bist vol
Gnaden? Und welcher Deudscher verstehet, was gesagt sei "vol
Gnaden"? Er mus denken an ein Fass vol Bier oder Beutel vol Geldes.
Darümb hab ichs verdeudscht: "Du Holdselige", damit doch ein
Deudscher desto mehr hinzu künne denken, was der Engel meinet mit
seinem Grus. . . . Wiewol ich dennoch damit noch nicht das beste
Deudsch hab troffen. Und hätte ich das beste Deudsch hie sollen nemen,
so hätte ich den Grus also verdeudschen müssen: "Gott grüsse dich, du
liebe Maria"; denn so viel wil der Engel sagen, und so würde er geredt
haben, wenn er hätte wöllen sie deudsch grüssen. . . . Wer Deudsch kan,
der weis wol, welch ein herzlich fein Wort das ist: Die liebe Maria, der
liebe Gott, der liebe Keiser, der liebe Fürst, der liebe Man, das liebe
Kind. Und ich weis nicht, ob man das Wort *"liebe"* auch so herzlich
und gnugsam in lateinischer oder andern Sprachen reden müge, das also
dringe und klinge ins Herz durch alle Sinne, wie es thut in unser Sprache.

Luther's German Bible is a translation from the Greek and Hebrew, but
because he consciously fashioned it after the language of the folk in the
first place, much of its vocabulary and phrasing have been adopted into
the everyday speech of the people. As he so aptly puts it in the *Sendschreiben vom Dolmetschen*:

Denn man mus nicht die Buchstaben in der lateinischen Sprache
fragen, wie man sol deudsch reden . . . sondern man mus die Mutter im
Hause, die Kinder auf der Gassen, den gemeinen Mann auf dem Markt
drümb fragen, und denselbigen auf das Maul sehen, wie sie reden, und
darnach dolmetschen. So verstehen sie es denn, und merken, das man
deudsch mit ihn redet.

The German language abounds in expressions taken from the Holy
Scriptures, a fact less well known to present-day generations than to their
more *bibelfest* forefathers. That this heritage still exists in the living
language, even though the speakers may be unaware of its origins, is in
itself proof of the purely linguistic influence of Luther's translation. On
almost any page of the Bible the reader can come across an expression or a
metaphor still used in the spoken language. To cite just a few examples:
"Er behütete ihn wie seinen Augapfel" (Deut. 32:10); "Der Herr merkt's
. . . und ist von ihm ein Denkzettel geschrieben . . ." (Mal. 3:16); "Und wo
das Volk im Lande durch die Finger sehen würde . . ." (Lev. 20:4); "Der
wird euch mit Feuer taufen" (Matt. 3:11); "Wer eine Grube macht, der
wird drein fallen" (Prov. 26:27); "Und da der Geist an mir vorüberging,
stunden mir die Haare zu Berge . . ." (Job 4:15); ". . . die da saßen am Ort
und Schatten des Todes, denen ist ein Licht aufgegangen" (Matt. 4:16);

"Bleibe im Lande, und nähre dich redlich" (Ps. 37:3); "Man zündet auch nicht ein Licht an, und setzt es unter einen Scheffel . . ." (Matt. 5:15); ". . . euere Perlen sollt ihr nicht vor die Säue werfen . . ." (Matt. 7:6); "Und er wird sie voneinander scheiden, gleich als ein Hirte die Schafe von den Böcken scheidet" (Matt. 25:32); "Im Schweiß deines Angesichts sollst du dein Brot essen" (Gen. 3:19); "So wird er . . . ein Stein des Anstoßes [sein] . . ." (Isa. 8:14). And, without giving the full wording or the location, we add the following terms:

> *ein Buch mit sieben Siegeln*
> *herrlich und in Freuden leben*
> *Gewissensbisse, Hiobspost, Krethi und Plethi*
> *ein Linsengericht*
> *ein verirrtes Schaf sein*
> *sein Scherflein beitragen*
> *wider den Strom schwimmen*
> *ein Wolf im Schafspelz sein*
> *in den Wind reden*

THE SPREAD OF LUTHER'S GERMAN

Luther's German was freely accepted throughout the East Middle German area, for in all essential features it was native to those parts. Its general adoption in western Germany (except in the Rhineland) was also soon accomplished, certainly in those regions favorable to the Reformation, such as Hesse. For the rest, however—North Germany, South Germany, and Switzerland—the new *Lutherdeutsch* was at first either rejected out of hand or allowed to make only tentative and superficial inroads against the various regional standards of written German.

Though the Reformer's teachings won wide and immediate acceptance throughout much of northern Germany, the adoption of his language as a literary vehicle was at first restricted. Luther's New Testament was translated into Low German in 1522, the year in which the High German original was first published, going through fifteen printings within a decade. All told, there were twenty-four Low German editions of the full Bible, the last one dated 1621. However, by the end of the sixteenth century, High German (specifically, Middle German) had been accepted as the dominant literary language of northern Germany—with the important exceptions of certain of the Hanseatic cities, Schleswig-Holstein, and the coastal and island lands of East Frisia, all of which continued to write in Low German for varying lengths of time (some, indeed, into the nineteenth century). *Plattdeutsch* also lived on in the theater as the principal language of the *Zwischenspiele*, between-act farces featuring the coarse antics of a clownish peasant. Such entr'actes occur in the otherwise High German dramas of Herzog Heinrich Julius von Braunschweig, in Georg Rollenhagen's *Die Froschmeuseler* (1595), and in his son Gabriel's *Amantes amentes* (1609).

Catholic Bavaria made few concessions to the "Protestant dialect" during the sixteenth and seventeenth centuries. Even within evangelical[19] circles in southern Germany, *Gemeines Deutsch* continued to be the preferred idiom of such leading literary figures as Hans Sachs (1494–1576), Johann Fischart (*ca.* 1545–90), and Jörg Wickram (*ca.* 1500–62). As for Catholic translations of the Bible into German, these were not long in coming. Most notable was the translation of the New Testament by Hieronymus Emser (1527), and the translations of the complete Bible made by Johann Dietenberger (1534) and Johann Eck (1537). Of these, Dietenberger's work—especially in a revised edition of 1662—became for some time the most widely used Catholic version of the Scriptures in German. Emser and Dietenberger based much of their translations upon Luther's Bible. Eck, on the other hand, specifically adopted the orthography of the imperial chancery. In all other respects he followed Emser's translation of the New Testament, but turned to the pre-Lutheran text of Mentel for his rendition of the Old Testament. Chiefly because of the artificial and wooden quality of its style, his work met with only limited success.

German-speaking Switzerland rejected not only Luther's German, but also that of the imperial chancery; the former on religious grounds—since the Swiss were followers of Calvin and Zwingli—the latter on political grounds. Even so, however, Swiss printers soon began making certain concessions toward Upper German (not Lutheran) literary usage. The most obvious innovation was to replace the old long vowels $\hat{i}$, $\hat{u}$, $\hat{u}$ with the diphthongs *ei*, *au*, *eu*. Their primary reason for introducing this change, however, was to give their books, especially the Zwingli Bible of 1527, a broader circulation.

In addition to the prestige and authority lent it by Holy Scripture, Luther's German received additional support—in evangelical circles, obviously—as the principal language of the pulpit, the church hymn, and of religious instruction. Its status was further enhanced when, in 1578,

---

[19] The term *evangelisch*—in use since about 1520—replaced the older *lutherisch*, and is the preferred synonym in Germany. The more general term *Protestant, protestantisch*—apparently coined in 1529—includes both the "evangelical" and the "reformed" churches, the latter word referring to those religious bodies that adopted the teachings of John Calvin and Ulrich Zwingli.

Johann Claius published one of the most distinguished and successful of the early grammars of German (written in Latin, however), choosing—as the title specifies—Luther's language as his standard: *Grammatica Germanicæ Linguæ ex bibliis Lutheri Germanicis et aliis eius libris collecta.* The eleventh and final edition of this important work is dated 1720. Claius' grammar did not sweep the field uncontested. *Das Gemeine Deutsch* found a protagonist in the Swabian grammarian Hieronymus Wolf—a follower of Luther—whose edition of Johann Rivius' *Institutiones grammaticæ* (to which was appended a short treatise on German orthography by Wolf) likewise appeared in 1578. Also championing Upper German usage is the historically significant grammar of the Rothenburg schoolmaster Valentin Ickelsamer: *Ein teütsche Grammatica*, published in approximately 1533. And Swiss German, too, was endorsed as the most acceptable form in which to write; prominent among its defenders was the Basel schoolteacher and poet, Johann Kolroß, whose *Enchiridion*[20] appeared in 1530.[21]

Obviously, the struggle to achieve a standard High German language was still unresolved at the close of the ENHG period. Luther's language had spread far beyond Wittenberg; indeed, it was probably read and understood by educated speakers of German everywhere, but it had by no means won universal acceptance. As of the year 1600 there were still three major literary dialects of High German: *Mitteldeutsch, Oberdeutsch,* and *Schweizerdeutsch.* Or, to use the terms proposed by Sebastian Helber in his *Syllabierbüchlein* of 1593: *die Mitter Teütsche, die Donawische,* and *die Höchst Reinische.*

THE NATURE AND CHARACTER OF EARLY NEW HIGH GERMAN

The language of the ENHG period is in many ways a study in contrasts, ranging from the elegant rhetoric of the early Humanists and the simple majesty of the Bible to the awkward verbosity of the chancery writ and the unadorned prose of the folk literature. Most notably, however, when measured by the standards of the High Medieval era, the dominant esthetic tone of the fifteenth and sixteenth centuries is almost unbelievably crude and vulgar. Indeed, a special "patron saint" of vulgarity, St.

---

[20] Kolroß' grammar was intended for advanced study. As he puts it: ". . . da mit die jhenigen so ettlicher maß schryben vnd läßen ergriffen, daruß was jnen noch manglet, auch in kurtzem erlernen mögen" (quoted from Max Hermann Jellinek, *Geschichte der neuhochdeutschen Grammatik* [Heidelberg, 1913], I, 53).

[21] The earliest German dictionaries also stem from this era, notably those compiled by Erasmus Alberus (1540), Josua Maaler (1561), and Nicodemus Frischlin (1586). We have already mentioned Simon Roth's *Teutscher Dictionarius* of 1571, the first *Fremdwörterbuch* in the German language.

Grobianus, was invented as a symbol characteristic of the times. His protection was frequently invoked in the contemporary literature, as in Sebastian Brant's *Narrenschiff* (1494), a popular and widely read didactic poem. Whereas Wolfram von Eschenbach in his *Willehalm* (*ca.* 1215) could not bring himself to translate *putaine* literally as *Hure*, referring to it obliquely as the word used of women who "die Minne feilhalten," the ENHG authors labored under no such restraint, sprinkling their dialogue liberally with such expressions as *Hurenjäger, Hurensohn, Hurentreiber*, and the like. Nor were the theologians of the time reticent about abusing one another in language that we now associate only with the barnyard or the gutter. They were especially fond of distorting one another's names: Luther was called *Luder* by his Catholic adversaries. He in turn converted the title and name of one of his most nettling opponents, Dr. Eck, into simply *Dreck*. The Jesuits were nicknamed the *Jesuwider*, and both Protestants and Catholics took turns calling each other names like *Teufelsgeschmeiß, Teufelskinder, Teufelsmäuler, Schlangenbrut*, and similar terms of forbearance and charity.

Whatever its esthetic shortcomings, the preferred language of the Lutheran Reformation was German, not Latin. While still using Latin for much of their correspondence and in many of their debates, the followers of Luther tended to equate the Roman tongue with the Roman church, so that to favor their native language as a matter of principle was in a sense but another expression of their precarious and embattled independence. The ill-fated Ulrich von Hutten (1488–1523), for instance, made a point of changing his Latin motto *alea jacta est* to the German *ich hab's gewagt*. And Luther, still using Latin when necessary or expedient, had the strongest sense of devotion to his *Muttersprache*—a term, incidentally, that first became current during his time.

As a result of these various forces and tendencies, the written medium that emerged had its roots deep in the language of the people: a language that was simple, earthy, rich in proverbial expressions and folklore. It was the idiom of everyday life—of the marketplace, the guild hall, the hearth and home.

CHAPTER SIX

The New High German Period

From 1600 to 1800

Renewed French Influence

IN SPITE of the considerable progress made throughout the sixteenth and seventeenth centuries toward the development and adoption of a standardized *Nationalsprache*, there was one influential area which tended to remain aloof, namely, the court. The language of royal society was seldom German. Indeed, since the days of Charles V (1519–56), the Hapsburg rulers of the *Reich* had usually preferred one of the Romance tongues. Commenting upon the linguistic choices at the imperial court, the Prussian monarch Frederick the Great (1740–86) wrote—in French!—as follows: "Under the reign of Emperor Joseph [I, 1705–11] only Italian was spoken at the Vienna court; Spanish prevailed under Charles VI [1711–40], and during the rule of Francis I [1745–65], born Lorrain, French was more commonly spoken than German. The same held true in the Electorates."[1]

Especially under France's "sun king," Louis XIV (1643–1715), did French culture come to exert an overwhelming influence in Germany, ushering in the so-called alamode era, during which time not only the French language, but almost anything French—clothing, foods, social customs and conventions—was adopted wholesale by the upper and middle classes. To cite one well-known instance: while a guest at the court of Frederick the Great, the celebrated Voltaire (1694–1778) wrote to the Marquis de Thibouville that he hardly realized he was in a foreign country,

---

[1] Translated from a quotation in Adolf Bach's *Geschichte der deutschen Sprache* (6th ed.; Heidelberg: Quelle & Meyer, 1956), p. 269.

and that a knowledge of German was needed only when traveling: "Je me trouve ici en France. On ne parle que notre langue. L'allemand est pour les soldats et pour les chevaux; il n'est nécessaire que pour la route."[2]

In past chapters we have more than once had occasion to mention the influences exerted by French upon the German language. In the seventeenth century, however, it was not so much a matter of *influence* as it was of possible *displacement*, for a knowledge of French was no longer limited to the aristocracy but was shared to an unprecedented degree by members of the middle class, many of whom used French in their homes in preference to German. The Leipzig professor of law, Christian Thomasius (1655–1728), who—after Paracelsus[3]—was the first to give his university lectures in German (1687), probably was not exaggerating when he wrote: "Bey uns Teutschen ist die französische Sprache so gemein worden, daß an vielen Orten bereits Schuster und Schneider, Kinder und Gesinde dieselbige gut genug reden. . . ."[4] Nor was the use of French limited to the intercourse of polite society; it also soon vied with Latin as the language of scholarship. The transactions of the distinguished Berlin Academy of Sciences, founded in 1700, were conducted in French until 1812, and some of Germany's most renowned men of learning, such as Gottfried Wilhelm von Leibniz (1646–1716), employed French for much of their correspondence and scholarly writing.[5]

There had always been some Germans who deplored what they considered to be excessive foreign influences. Nor was such opposition to the rampant and extravagant use of French lacking in the seventeenth and eighteenth centuries. For the first time, however, we find this resistance expressed in a concerted and organized fashion, for during this era there arose a number of societies specifically dedicated to the preservation and purification of the German mother tongue.

---

[2] *Voltaire's Correspondence*, ed. Theodore Besterman (Genève: Institut et Musée Voltaire, 1953——), XVIII, 188.

[3] In 1526–27 the Swiss physician and natural scientist Paracelsus (1493–1541) lectured in German at the University of Basel.

[4] As quoted by Hans Sperber and Wolfgang Fleischhauer, *Geschichte der deutschen Sprache* (3rd ed.; Berlin, 1958), p. 101.

[5] Though Leibniz' published works—that is, those published within his lifetime— were written in either French or Latin, he was nevertheless much concerned that his native language, too, should become a literary vehicle of comparable rank. He wrote two essays in German (both published posthumously) in which he expressed his views on this subject: "Ermahnung an die Teutsche, ihren Verstand und ihre Sprache besser zu üben" (written *ca.* 1680) and his more widely known "Unvorgreifliche Gedanken betreffend die Ausübung und Verbesserung der deutschen Sprache," written sometime around 1697.

DIE SPRACHGESELLSCHAFTEN

Modeled after the Florentine *Accademia della Crusca*, the German language societies numbered among their members most of the prominent authors and grammarians of the time. The first and most illustrious of these organizations, founded in Weimar in 1617 by Prince Ludwig von Anhalt-Köthen, was *die fruchtbringende Gesellschaft oder der Palmenorden*. Its membership included such prominent seventeenth-century men of letters as Andreas Gryphius, Friedrich von Logau, Johann Michael Moscherosch, Martin Opitz, and Philipp von Zesen.

Reflecting the enthusiastic response of patriotically inspired men who wished to purge their national language of foreign influences, other such societies were founded, usually by people who were already members of the Weimar *Palmenorden*. In 1643 Philipp von Zesen organized *die teutsch-gesinnte Genossenschaft* in Hamburg. The city of Nürnberg was the home of *der Pegnesische Blumenorden*, founded by the poets Sigmund von Birken, Georg Philipp Harsdörffer, and Johann Klaj. The old Hanseatic city of Lübeck was the seat of yet another influential language society, *der Elbschwanenorden*, formed in 1660 by Johann Rist. And there were others.

Although it is impossible to measure exactly, the influence exerted by the *Sprachgesellschaften* upon the language of the chancery, the court, and polite society in general was certainly minimal. With respect to the literary (specifically belletristic) language, however, their efforts met with considerable success, primarily because almost all the grammarians and writers (whom we shall discuss in the following two sections) were members of one or more of the societies. As a result, the creative literature of the seventeenth century is remarkably free of foreign linguistic influences.[6] In fact, the vocabulary of Modern German contains many words that were either coined or revived at that time to be used as substitutes for the borrowed terms then current. Especially to Harsdörffer and von Zesen must be credited the successful introduction of several native German words. As is apparent from the following list, the loanword did not necessarily disappear from the language, but at least an acceptable native synonym became available:

---

[6] Except in those instances where the aping of things French is held up to ridicule, as for instance in certain passages of Michael Moscherosch's *Gesichten Philanders von Sittewald* (1640), Hans Jakob Christoffel von Grimmelshausen's *Simplizissimi Prahlerei und Gepräng mit seinem teutschen Michel* (1673), Andreas Gryphius' *Horribilicribrifax* (1663), and Johann Lauremberg's *Veer Schertz Gedichte* (1652; in Low German).

Native German	Loanword
Anschrift	*Adresse*
Aufzug (of a drama)	*Akt*
Augenblick	*Moment*
Briefwechsel	*Korrespondenz*
Bücherei	*Bibliothek*
Fernglas	*Teleskop*
Gesichtskreis	*Horizont*
Grundstein	*Fundament*
Mundart	*Dialekt*
Nachruf	*Nekrolog*
Sinngedicht	*Epigramm*
Trauerspiel	*Tragödie*
Verfasser	*Author*
Vollmacht	*Plenipotenz*

Not all the attempts to replace foreign elements in the language were equally successful; indeed, some of the suggested substitutes were singularly inappropriate, ranging from merely humorous to downright grotesque. For instance, *Entknötelung* was proposed in lieu of *Interpretation, Gesichtserker* for *Nase, Jungfernzwinger* for *Nonnenkloster, Leichentopf* for *Urne,* and *Zitterweh* for *Fieber.* Words like *Fieber* and *Nase,* though originally borrowed from Latin, were scarcely "foreign" in any practical sense, having been in the language since Old High German times.

THE GRAMMARIANS

Concurrent with the founding in 1617 of *die fruchtbringende Gesellschaft,* Martin Opitz (1597–1639) wrote his historically important essay, *Aristarchus sive dê contemptû linguæ Germanicæ,* scoring his countrymen for neglecting their mother tongue and for the lack of esteem in which they held it. Convinced of the high destiny of the German language, he set himself the task of shaping it into an instrument capable of the full range of poetic expression, in no way inferior to Latin or French. The epochal work in which he laid down his principles appeared in 1624 under the title *Buch von der deutschen Poeterey.* Not a grammar in the formal sense of the word, this treatise on poetic theory and practice nevertheless exerted a great influence upon the literary idiom. In this book Opitz opposed the use of foreign, archaic, or dialectal terms. He established rules for the use of final *e,* urged poets to avoid meaningless "fillers," and gave preference to certain syntactic constructions which he felt should distinguish poetry from prose.

While Opitz was championing German as a poetic medium, the schoolmaster Wolfgang Ratichius (1571–1635) was conducting a campaign to have the study of German grammar included in the curriculum of the elementary schools. In 1612 he was invited to present his views to the Imperial Diet convening in Frankfurt. He was convinced that the early study of German grammar would accomplish two things: (1) it would serve as a reasonable and common foundation for the formal study of foreign languages later on, and (2) it would be the surest way to realize the dream of a standard national language: ". . . ein eintrechtige sprache im Reich bequemlich einzuführen, das ist, wie Sachsen, Francken, Schwaben, Düringer etc. der Hochdeutschen Sprachen gewehnen, vnd nachmahls derselben sich einmütigh gebrauchen mügen."[7] Ratichius won the support of several influential people, not the least of whom was Prince Ludwig von Anhalt-Köthen. As a direct result of the schoolmaster's efforts, German grammar was added to the curriculum of the elementary schools in Hesse, Weimar, and Köthen.

One highly regarded early grammar was written by Christian Gueintz (1592–1650), superintendent of schools in Halle, who, in his early years, had assisted Ratichius. Commissioned by Prince Ludwig von Anhalt in the name of *die fruchtbringende Gesellschaft*, Gueintz wrote a grammar entitled *Deutscher Sprachlehre Entwurf* (1641). This work, which was marred by a pedantic and belabored attempt to give a logical classification of the parts of speech, served one unanticipated but obliquely significant purpose: it prompted the most well-known of the seventeenth-century grammarians —Justus Georg Schottel (1612–76)—to try to compensate for what he considered certain weaknesses and shortcomings in Gueintz's work. Schottel's two most important grammatical studies are his *Teutsche Sprachkunst* of 1641 and the more renowned *Ausführliche Arbeit Von der Teutschen Haubt-Sprache* of 1663.

In these works Schottel stressed the importance of *normative* grammar, deeming it the special province and obligation of the grammarian to arbitrate and decide all matters of linguistic usage, to make an end to uncertainty in things linguistic.[8] His goal was to establish a rule for everything, even if the "rule" was sometimes nothing more than a statement of exceptions. This he accomplished by liberal recourse to analogy ("if this is so, then that is so") and by a cautious evaluation of the language used in print by men of learning. To Schottel the "best" language was the

[7] As quoted by Max Hermann Jellinek, *Geschichte der neuhochdeutschen Grammatik* (Heidelberg: Carl Winter's Universitätsbuchhandlung, 1913), I, 88–89.

[8] *Ibid.*, p. 134: "Aufgabe des Grammatikers ist der Ungewißheit ein Ende zu machen. '*Rationem reddere*' schwebt auch dem Schottelius als Ideal vor. Der einzelne Fall muß unter einen allgemeinen Satz gebracht werden, enthalte dieser auch nur das Eingeständnis der Regellosigkeit."

written language; indeed, only in this medium did he consider it worthy of investigation, for the spoken variety—unless based upon the literary norm —was nothing but unregulated dialect: "Ungewiß, gestückelt, unerkant und nur aus dem Maule des Pöbels genommen. . . ."[9] He made a point of asserting that the *Hochdeutsch* of his grammar was not patterned after any dialect—not even that of Meißen[10]—but reflected rather the written language of learned, wise, and experienced men (*virî, doctî, sapientês et perîtî*): a language that did not come naturally to anyone, but one which had to be acquired through "Fleiß und Arbeit." Children, of course, were able to use this idiom properly only after they had mastered its grammar in school.

Schottel's teachings prevailed throughout the second half of the seventeenth century. Not until 1690 did a work appear which in any serious sense vied with his, namely, the *Grundsätze der Deutschen Sprache* by the Berlin pedagogue, Johann Bödiker (1641–95). Bödiker made some abiding contributions, especially in the areas of syntax and orthography, though these were in part offset by his attempts to have accepted into the High German literary language certain features of his native Low German.

In 1723 Bödiker's grammar appeared in a new edition prepared by Johann Leonhard Frisch (1666–1743), one of the leading philologists of the day. In his edition of the *Grundsätze*, Frisch advised his readers to let their pronunciation of German be determined by their spelling of it ("sprich, wie du schreibst!"). Two years prior to this, the Hamburg poet Barthold Heinrich Brockes (1680–1747), in an essay on poetics, had already enunciated the same principle: "Man muß sprechen, wie man schreibet."[11]

Considerably more useful than the *Grundsätze* was the *Anweisungen zur teutschen Orthographie* by Hieronymus Freyer (1675–1747), a work that first appeared in 1721. Though containing little or nothing new, Freyer's exposition was a model of orderly and logical arrangement. The grammars of Bödiker and Freyer did much toward regulating the orthography as well as the pronunciation of the emerging High German standard. Both

[9] *Ibid.*, p. 136. This is a quotation from another of Schottel's works—in poetic form—*Der Teutschen Spracheinleitung* (1643).

[10] To the extent that he concerned himself with the spoken language, however, he advocated the dialect of Meißen (and Leipzig) as the most acceptable variety of German speech.

[11] Because the North Germans—many of whom spoke *Plattdeutsch* natively— often acquired a knowledge of High German via the printed page, this injunction to speak as one spelled (that is, to assign a fixed and distinctive pronunciation to each orthographic symbol) has often been held accountable for the "purer" pronunciation of High German in the north. Though this is by no means a full answer, the efforts to standardize pronunciation by relating it to a—by this time—stable orthography was indeed a major factor in favoring the spread of the *Hochsprache*.

works served as the basis for elementary school grammars, especially Freyer's *Anweisungen*, since it had been published by the *Waisenhaus* in Halle, one of the foremost purveyors of school texts at that time.

By far the most widely-known and influential grammar of the eighteenth century was written by the eminent Leipzig professor and—for at least two decades—undisputed czar of the world of German letters, Johann Christoph Gottsched (1700–66). His grammar bears the title, *Grundlegung einer Deutschen Sprachkunst, Nach den Mustern der besten Schriftsteller des vorigen und jetzigen Jahrhunderts*. This historically important work, first published in 1748, underwent six editions, the last in 1776. It was translated into Dutch, French, Hungarian, Latin, and Russian.

In his prestigious but technically rather slapdash treatise,[12] Gottsched's principal aim was to bring the rules of grammar into harmony with the precepts of reason and logic. The eighteenth century was the century of the Enlightenment, and from roughly 1725 to 1745 Gottsched was the acknowledged leader and oracle of this movement in German literary circles.

Although poorly organized and fraught with inconsistencies and irrelevancies, Gottsched's grammar—even more than Schottel's—was largely responsible for securing and enhancing the status of the Upper Saxon (Leipzig and Meißen) dialect as the most appropriate and acceptable variety of written *as well as spoken* German. Of further significance was his championing of usage as the ultimate authority in things linguistic.[13] He

---

[12] For a devastating but scholarly critique of Gottsched's *Sprachkunst*, see Jellinek, *Geschichte der neuhochdeutschen Grammatik*, I, 227–45. The following paragraph is typical: "Überhaupt sind Gottscheds Regeln nur zu oft praktisch wertlos. Was soll man mit einem Satz anfangen, wie S. 90: 'Man setze das *h* zu denen Selbstlautern, die einer Verlängerung bedörfen; bey denen aber nicht, die solche nicht nötig haben?' Oder was hat man von einer Anleitung, wie sie die X. Regel S. 92 gibt: 'Das *th* muß man in allen deutschen Wörtern, wo es gewöhnlich ist, behalten, wenn es im Plattdeutschen das *d* ausdrücken muß', wo doch gleich der Zusatz folgt, daß man *th* nicht in alle Wörter einführen solle, wo im Plattdeutschen *d* entspricht? Mußte wirklich in einer besondern Regel (S. 478) gesagt werden, 'daß bisweilen das lateinische Praeteritum imperfectum im Deutschen mit der völlig vergangenen Zeit ausgedrücket werden kann?' Statt das 'bisweilen' näher zu bestimmen, gibt Gottsched einfach ein paar Beispiele und schließt mit den Worten: 'Doch muß man sich nicht allemal so zwingen. Es kommt viel auf ein gutes Ohr an.' "

[13] *Ibid.*, pp. 238–39: "Das Verhältnis der Sprachregeln zum Gebrauch wird vollkommen klar und deutlich dargelegt. Da die Regeln aus der Sprache selbst genommen werden, unterwerfe man die Sprache nicht eigenmächtigen Gesetzen eines Sprachlehrers, 'sondern wenige von der Analogie abweichende Redensarten werden der Uebereinstimmung der meisten Exempel unterworfen. Man setzt also auch nicht das Ansehen eines Sprachkundigen der Gewohnheit; sondern eine allgemeinere Gewohnheit einer eingeschränktern entgegen.' Aber Ausnahmslosigkeit der Regeln sei unmöglich; die Regeln müssen nachgeben, wo der durchgängige Gebrauch aller Provinzen und

recommends "das fleißige Lesen guter Bücher" as the best way to achieve an elegant and effective command of German. Grammar to Gottsched was a useful but somewhat elementary tool for recognizing the more obvious features of a linguistic system. He saw no virtue in studying grammar for its own sake, but rather encouraged getting on to the language itself as soon as possible. Later grammarians of a traditional persuasion have never quite forgiven him this unorthodox posture.[14]

The last, and in many ways the greatest, of the grammarians of this era was Johann Christoph Adelung (1732–1806), whose numerous scholarly publications covered a diversified range. The work in which we are immediately interested—his two-volume grammar—appeared in 1782 under the title *Umständliches Lehrgebäude der Deutschen Sprache, zur Erläuterung der Deutschen Sprachlehre für Schulen.* The second half of this title refers to a book published a year earlier, his *Deutsche Sprachlehre. Zum Gebrauche der Schulen in den Königlichen Preußischen Landen*, a grammar that, coupled with his *Vollständige Anweisung zur Deutschen Orthographie* of 1788, enjoyed a long tenure in many of Germany's elementary and secondary schools.

In common with Gottsched, Adelung emphasized the importance of usage in determining the grammatical canon. And he believed, as did Schottel and Gottsched, that the language cultivated by the upper classes of the Saxon electorate was the most worthy of imitation.[15]

In one important respect, however, Adelung's theoretical premises

Mundarten widerspricht. 'Nur, wo der Gebrauch ungewiß, oder verschieden ist, da kann ein guter Sprachlehrer, durch die Aehnlichkeit der meisten Exempel oder durch die daraus entstandenen Regeln, entscheiden, welcher Gebrauch dem andern vorzuziehen sey.' "

[14] As, for instance, Jellinek's rather waspish judgment (*ibid.*, I, 229): "Aber Gottsched ist kein Grammatiker. Es fehlt ihm das grammatische Talent und die Lust am Handwerk. Für ihn ist die Sprachlehre nichts als ein Mittel zum Zweck, sie soll wirklich nur richtig sprechen und schreiben lehren. Das Buch ist liederlich gearbeitet, im kleinen wie im großen."

[15] "In Deutschland ist es seit der Reformation die Mundart der südlichern Chursächsischen Lande, welche damahls und noch lange hernach die blühendste und cultivierteste Provinz in dem ganzen Deutschlande war, und in Ansehung des in ihr so allgemein verbreiteten Geschmackes noch jetzt vor allen andern den Vorzug behauptet, obgleich manche ihr in den Wissenschaften glücklich nachgeeifert haben. Diese unter dem Nahmen des *Hochdeutschen* bekannte Mundart wird in den südlichen Chursächsischen Provinzen am allgemeinsten und zugleich am reinsten gesprochen, und hat sich aus ihrer Mitte durch Geschmack, Künste und Wissenschaften über einen großen Theil des übrigen Deutschlandes verbreitet, wo sie die Schrift- und Gesellschafts-Sprache des gesittetsten Theiles der Nation geworden ist, nur daß sich immer mehr gemeine Landessprache mit ihr vermenget, je weiter sie sich von ihrer Quelle entfernet, die noch jetzt eben so rein und lauter fließet als je." As quoted by Jellinek, *ibid.*, I, 361.

differed from those which characterized the works of his immediate pre-
decessors. Schottel, for instance, was much concerned with establishing
the principles of "philosophical" grammar, that is, attempting to find for
linguistic phenomena a reasonable explanation primarily in terms of logic.
Adelung, too, tried to determine the reasons why a language should
behave in a given way, but he preferred a *psychological* to a *philosophical*
explanation. This approach marks the beginning of a new era in the study
of language, an era that was to achieve its full expression in the second
half of the nineteenth century.

Adelung made an abiding contribution in one other capacity, namely,
as a lexicographer. In common with so many scholars of his day, he was
vitally concerned with establishing and maintaining the "purity" of the
language. Toward this end he compiled and published (during the years
from 1774 to 1786) the first substantial dictionary of German: *Versuch
eines vollständigen grammatisch-kritischen Wörterbuches Der Hochdeutschen
Mundart, mit beständiger Vergleichung der übrigen Mundarten, besonders
aber der oberdeutschen.* In this monumental work, which Adelung hoped
would become as definitive for German as the dictionary of the French
Academy was for French, he gave for each entry its spelling, pronunciation, grammatical classification, and meaning. In determining the meaning
of a term, he quoted from the works of the leading authors, especially
those of Upper Saxon provenience or residence. The era from approximately 1740 to 1760 Adelung considered "classic" in the development of
the standard literary language.[16]

Spread and Acceptance of a Standard Literary Language

Toward the close of the time span we are now considering—the seventeenth and eighteenth centuries—a more or less standardized *Schriftsprache* was adopted throughout the German-speaking lands. It was also a

---

[16] Mention should be made of three other dictionaries of historical importance that
were compiled during the era now under consideration. In 1691 appeared Kaspar von
Stieler's *Der deutschen Sprache Stammbaum und Fortwachs oder deutscher Sprachschatz.* And in 1801, Joachim Heinrich Campe, striving to rid German of its many
loanwords and foreign expressions, brought out his *Wörterbuch zur Erklärung und
Verdeutschung der unserer Sprache aufgedrungenen fremden Ausdrücke,* the standard
Fremdwörterbuch of the nineteenth century. Over the years 1807–11 Campe published
another valuable lexicon: *Ein Wörterbuch der deutschen Sprache.*

Although occasionally held up to bemused ridicule by certain of his contemporaries
(Schiller satirized him in his *Musenalmanach auf das Jahr 1797*), Campe had a genuine
talent for coining words. Many of his *Verdeutschungen* have found their way into the
standard language. To mention but a few: *Beweggrund (Motiv), Eilbote (Kurier),
Fallbeil (Guillotine), Festland (Kontinent), Stelldichein (Rendezvous), Zerrbild
(Karikatur).*

spoken language, but limited in currency to the educated classes. The speech of the average person continued, then as now, to be marked by features of local and regional dialects.

Although all the grammarians and rhetoricians mentioned in the foregoing section accepted *Lutherdeutsch* as a definitive expression of literary High German, few were willing to let it serve as the sole arbiter in things linguistic. There were at least two other authorities to which most of them appealed: the language of the more important chanceries, and the works of prominent contemporary authors. Especially the *Reichstagsabschiede* as composed in such chanceries as those at Mainz, Regensburg, and Speyer were held up as models of good writing, although certain of the grammarians—notably Bödiker, Frisch, and Gottsched—did not consider them worthy of unqualified imitation. As for the principal authors of the seventeenth century (we shall refer to the chief literary figures of the eighteenth century in the next section), either they represented the East Middle German dialect areas, or they were North Germans whose literary medium was essentially *Lutherdeutsch*.[17]

Protestant Swabia had generally adopted the emerging literary standard by the mid-seventeenth century. By 1700 such literary centers of German-speaking Switzerland as Bern and Zürich had also converted to the new *Schriftsprache*. Bavaria and Austria (and the Catholic Rhineland), however, were much slower to accept the change, in part for religious reasons certainly, but primarily because the East Middle German variant differed in so many ways from their own dialects as well as from the literary model to which they were accustomed, namely, *das Gemeine Deutsch*. By 1750, however, Gottsched's *Sprachkunst* was the recognized grammatical authority in the old imperial capital of Vienna; indeed, there were even plans to establish a chair of German at the University of Vienna and to call none other than Professor Gottsched to occupy it.

But Bavaria was not so easily won over. As late as 1779 the Bishop of

---

[17] These included such names as Jakob Böhme, Paul Fleming, Paul Gerhardt, Andreas Gryphius, Christian von Hofmannswaldau, Hans Michael Moscherosch, Martin Opitz, Johann Rist, Friedrich von Spee, and Philipp von Zesen. Only two prominent literary figures of the seventeenth century wrote in *das Gemeine Deutsch* (or in a close variant of it): the Nürnberger Jakob Ayrer and the immensely popular preacher Abraham a Santa Clara (Ulrich Megerle), an Augustinian friar, born in Swabia but for most of his adult life active as chaplain to the imperial court in Vienna. Other South German authors of some repute, such as Georg Philipp Harsdörffer of Nürnberg—as well as the artistically inferior but prolific *Meistersänger*—used a language that was closer to East Middle German than to Upper German. Much of the literary output of the Catholic South, incidentally, was at this time in Latin.

Regensburg—at the insistence of the Jesuits—rebuked a priest of his diocese, Heinrich Braun, for introducing "Lutheran" orthography in certain texts used in the public schools of Bavaria. However, another Jesuit—Ignaz Weitenauer, professor of Semitic languages at the University of Innsbruck—wrote a spirited rejoinder in Father Braun's defense, reminding the reverend clergy that changes in the spelling of German in no wise endangered the Church's doctrinal position.

Chief among the objections to the new orthography was its retention of final *e. Das Gemeine Deutsch* did not often indicate this vowel in conventional spelling, because it had been generally elided in the Upper German dialects. Prejudice in Catholic Bavaria against the "Lutheran *e*"— and against other features of the imported *Schriftsprache*—continued for a long time. However, even as in Austria, resistance was overcome, so that by the end of the eighteenth century a standard literary language common to all the German-speaking lands was a reality.

As we have seen, this new literary standard was a compromise made up of many elements and modified by many forces. In a very real sense its roots were in the language of Luther. But Luther did not create a new language: his avowed intention was to use the language of the *kursächsische Kanzlei*, which was based upon the dialects native to the southern half of the Saxon electorate, somewhat modified in favor of the Upper German of the imperial chanceries at Prague and, later, Vienna. As time went on, these two major literary dialects, though vying with one another for supremacy, were nevertheless influenced by each other. And there were other leveling forces: the city of Frankfurt, for instance, gradually overtook Wittenberg and competed with Leipzig in importance as a publishing center. Therefore, in the course of time, several features characteristic of West Middle German further modified the old *Lutherdeutsch*, thus making it more acceptable throughout Hesse and in the Rhineland.

In their efforts to strike an acceptable medium between the somewhat old-fashioned but still viable language of Luther and the more modern but technical and often belabored language of the chanceries, the grammarians and lexicographers appealed to yet a third authority, which was to become the most decisive of all, namely, the existing body of contemporary German literature.

LITERARY INFLUENCES

The literary language of the sixteenth century parallels the spoken idiom. The printed page reflects the simple vocabulary, the uncomplicated syntax, and the homely metaphors of colloquial speech.[18] But not so the *Schriftsprache* of the seventeenth century. One of the most significant events in the history of the modern *literary* language was the publication in 1624 of Opitz' *Buch von der deutschen Poeterey,* for in this treatise the twenty-seven-year-old poet laureate from Silesia laid down the principle that the language of poetry—like any work of art—should be above the mundane, elegantly fashioned and artistically contrived. He advocated the language of Luther as the most appropriate dialect of German, but the literary style which he championed was far removed from the straight-forward, unadorned prose of the Reformer. Opitz stands at the threshold of a new era in the history of the standard literary language, an era during which a specialized artistic idiom—a *Kunstsprache*—was consciously fashioned.

BAROQUE

In histories of German literature, the period from roughly 1600 to almost 1700 is often called "baroque" (< Portuguese *barocco* "an irregularly shaped pearl"). The term—first applied to a kind of architecture —refers in a literary sense to the ornate, metaphorical, bombastic style that characterizes much of the language of the so-called "Second Silesian *Dichterschule,*"[19] whose chief representatives included Andreas Gryphius (1616–64), Christian Hofmann von Hofmannswaldau (1618–79), and Daniel Caspar von Lohenstein (1635–83).

At its best the baroque style could be most effective, its structure marked by striking parallelisms, its vocabulary by rich and ingenious imagery. The following poem by Lohenstein is fairly typical:

Aufschrift eines Sarges

Irdisches und sterblich Volk, lebend-tote Erdengäste,
Ihr Verwerflinge des Himmels, ihr Gespenste dieser Welt,
Denen nichts als falsche Ware, nichts als Rauch und Wind gefällt,
Närr'sche: klettert und besteigt die bepalmten Ehrenäste,
Setzt euch Säulen von Porphyr, mauert euch aus Gold Paläste,
Festigt Tempel euch aus Marmor, der der Zeit die Waage hält,
Rafft zu euch mit gichtgen Klauen den verdammten Klumpen Geld,

---

[18] It would be easy to find exceptions to this statement in the literature of the sixteenth century, but as a generalization about the written language of the period, the sentence may stand.

[19] A style that found its counterparts in all the major contemporary literatures of western Europe. In Italy it was called *Marinism* after the poet Giambattista Marini (1569–1625); in Spain, *Gongorism* (Luis de Gongora, 1561–1627); in England, *euphuism,* after a character in the novels of John Lyly (1554?–1606); and *preciosity* in France, a term adapted from the title of a comedy by Molière (1622–73).

Macht euch euer stolzes Lob durch gelehrte Schriften feste;
Aber wißt: wann das Verhängnis euer Lebensgarn reißt ab,
Schwindet Wissenschaft und Kunst, Schätze, Reichtum, Ehr und Titel,
Und ihr nehmet nichts mit euch, als den nackten Sterbekittel,
Wo ihr anders aus dem allen noch erschwitzet Sarg und Grab.
Tausend, tausend sind gewest, die mich nicht erlangt noch haben,
Die die Lüfte, die die Glut, die der blaue Schaum begraben.

At its worst, however, the language of the baroque was unadulterated *Schwulst*: bombastic, precious, and often grotesque. Quoting from a contemporary novel which satirized this high-flown, artificial style, Sperber and Fleischhauer offer the following, admittedly somewhat exaggerated, example of *Schwulst* in its extreme form. They cite the first sentence of a letter: "Schönste Gebieterin, Glückselig ist der Tag, welcher durch das glutbeflammte Carfunckel Rad der hellen Sonnen mich mit tausend süßen Strahlen begossen hat, als ich in dem tiefen Meere meiner Unwürdigkeit die köstliche Perle Ihrer Tugend in der Muschel Ihrer Bekanntschaft gefunden habe."[20]

As is obvious from these two samples, the language of the poets of the Second Silesian School is especially rich in metaphors; in fact, one may speak of an "embarrassment of riches," for they went to great lengths in order to avoid everyday words and expressions. The moon was "der Sonne Kammermagd," the pearl a "Muschelkind," and the breast they called "das Zeughaus süßer Lust." In their efforts to intensify the descriptive power of their language, these poets used a sensuous vocabulary, studding their works with terms such as: *Aloe, Ambra, Bisam, Granit, Jasmin, Koralle, Marmor, Nektar, Porphyr, Purpur, Rose, Rubin*. They delighted in coining new and unusual nominal compounds: *Augenstrahl, Freudenrosen, Lilienbrüste, Nektarlippen, Wollustgluten, Zinnobermund*. Especially popular was the practice of joining adjectives into novel and striking combinations: *grimmgraus, loderndhell, rasendtoll, schimmerndlicht, schneegebirgt*. Some of the earlier occurrences of a participle-like form of certain adjectives, such as *bepalmt, bepurpurt, beschaumt*, date from this time.

The excessive and uncontrolled use of such florid language as this was bound to bring about a sharp reaction. And it did. Nevertheless, the Age of the Baroque—even in its decadent phase—forced the German language to take on new dimensions and to demonstrate latent potentials, necessary steps in the development of a flexible and versatile *Kunstsprache*.

---

[20] *Geschichte der deutschen Sprache* (3rd ed.; Berlin, 1958), pp. 102–3; the quotation is from Christian Weise's *Die drei ärgsten Erznarren in der ganzen Welt* (1672).

PIETISM

The seventeenth century in Germany, blighted as it was by the scathing devastations of the Thirty Years' War (1618–48), is a study in extremes and contrasts. On the one hand, the almost desperate longing for luxury, opulence, and voluptuousness; on the other, asceticism, mysticism, and pietism. Of the latter persuasion was one of the earlier forerunners of the pietistic movement, Jakob Böhme (1575–1624). In his *Aurora oder Morgenröte im Aufgang* (1612), he resumes the search of the medieval mystics for the *unio mystica*. Even more influential in later pietistic circles was Johann Arnd (1555–1621), a prominent preacher and the author of numerous devotional works, by far the best-known of which is his *Vier Bücher vom wahren Christentum* (1605). The essence of Arnd's "geläuterte Mystik" is his emphasis upon the importance of spiritual sensitivity and Christ-like charity as opposed to a coldly intellectual preoccupation with rite and dogma.

Though but a continuation of these earlier trends, the movement known as Pietism—by definition a conscious and purposeful reaction to the rigid and literalistic orthodoxy of seventeenth-century Lutheranism—first took definitive proportions under the leadership of Jakob Spener (1635–1705) and August Hermann Francke (1663–1727). In their prose and poetry the Pietists remind us of the medieval mystics: the same striving to "express the inexpressible," the same attempt to lend spiritual connotations to the language of the physical world, the same effective use of nominal and verbal affixes. Their vocabulary is rich in compounds containing *ein-* (*Eindruck, einleuchten*), *Wesen*, and *Licht*.

Although the language of Pietism is but an adaptation and reworking of the idiom fashioned by the earlier mystics, its recurrence at this time was of considerable moment, for these efforts to verbalize both the most delicate as well as the most overpowering of spiritual emotions placed additional demands upon the New High German language, extending and strengthening its resources and capacities.

Two of the most prolific and able poets among the Pietists were Gottfried Arnold (1666–1714) and Gerhard Tersteegen (1697–1769). An example of Arnold's style is the little poem, "An Christus":

Gott, den Brunnquell alles Guten, kann man ohne dich nicht schauen,
Christe, o du Licht der Wahrheit, meines Lebens sichre Bahn;
Kraft und Herz und Hand des Vaters, die die Welt ins Licht konnt bauen,
Sonne des gerechten Sinnes, Brunn des Lichtes, strahl mich an.

Much the same imagery is found in this excerpt from Tersteegen's "Gott ist gegenwärtig":

Du durchdringest alles:
Laß dein schönstes Lichte,
Herr, erleuchten mein Gesichte.
Wie die zarten Blumen
willig sich entfalten
und der Sonne stille halten,
laß mich so still und froh
deine Strahlen fassen.

Not a Pietist (Pietism was a Protestant movement), but sharing essentially the same spiritual heritage, was the Catholic convert, Angelus Silesius (Johann Scheffler, 1624–77), whose collection of epigrams and sonnets titled *Der cherubinische Wandersmann* (1657) shows the same struggle to reflect in language the ecstacies and visions of the spirit. The following lines are typical:

Mensch, werde wesentlich! Denn wann die Welt vergeht,
So fällt der Zufall weg: das Wesen, das besteht.

Ich weiß nicht, was ich bin; ich bin nicht, was ich weiß:
Ein Ding und nicht ein Ding, ein Pünktchen und ein Kreis.

Freund, so du etwas bist, so bleib doch ja nicht stehn:
Man muß aus einem Licht fort in das andre gehn.

The differences between this language and that of the later Baroque poets is at once apparent. Though a closer inspection would reveal certain mutual influences—especially with respect to word formation—the over-all contrasts are nevertheless striking. Indeed, in the last quarter of the seventeenth century when a reaction to Baroque life and letters set in, the simpler and in general better disciplined language of Pietism[21] continued to be held in high regard.

Earlier we quoted a passage from a novel in which the gaudy language of the later Baroque period is held up to caricature and ridicule. The author of this satire was Christian Weise (1624–1708), rector of the *Gymnasium* in Zittau (Saxony), and the most prominent literary figure of the time to crusade against the "gestirnte, balsamierte und vergüldte Redensart" of the Silesian poets. Weise strenuously opposed the notion that the language of poetry should be set apart from and above the language of prose. Advocating the principles of the influential French critic Nicolas Boileau, as set forth in his *L'Art poétique* (1674), Weise insisted that the chief purpose of the written word was to communicate

[21] This description would not apply much beyond about 1740. Especially in the works of Count Nicolaus Ludwig von Zinzendorf (1700–1760), founder of the strongly pietistic *Herrnhuter Gemeinde* (later the Moravian Brethren), did the language become maudlin and even fulsome.

as clearly and precisely as possible, regardless of the literary medium employed. In its spoken form, too, he stressed the importance of language as an instrument whereby a social group interacts, thus highlighting the wisdom and necessity of encouraging easy and effectual communication.[22]

There were many who shared Weise's views. They were the precursors of a new movement that was to dominate much of the eighteenth century, the Enlightenment.

THE ENLIGHTENMENT

As a cultural movement, the European Enlightenment may be described as an effort to make reason the guiding principle of life, and to permit the dictates of reason—clarified and strengthened by knowledge—to determine the moral and ethical code of both the individual and society.

Under strong influences from England, France, and Holland, the Enlightenment was first proclaimed in Germany by two professors at the University of Halle in Saxony: the jurist Thomasius and the philosopher Christian Wolff (1679–1754). Wolff was more responsible for developing the new tenets into a philosophical system (Rationalism). However, both scholars owed much to the teachings of Leibniz and to the system of "natural law" advocated by one of the greatest legal minds of the age, Samuel Pufendorf (1632–94).

As it applied to aesthetics and literature, the foremost interpreter of Wolff's philosophy was Johann Christoph Gottsched, who in his *Ausführliche Redekunst* of 1728 and in the *Versuch einer kritischen Dichtkunst vor die Deutschen* (1730) not only called for an end to the Baroque fashion in letters, but proposed an approach to stylistics and rhetoric that was to become dogma in many circles for the next two decades.[23] Gottsched's famous statement on style appears in the *Redekunst*:

> Denn überhaupt ist dieses die Regel im guten Schreiben, daß man seine Sache recht verstehen, hernach aber die Gedanken davon so aufsetzen muß, wie sie einem beyfallen; ohne daran zu denken, ob man es mit einfachen oder zusammengesetzten Perioden verrichtet. . . . Es ist nichts lächerlicher als wenn sich einfältige Stilisten immer mit ihrem

---

[22] It was during this time that many of the flowery formulas used in polite conversation were dropped in favor of less conspicuous expressions. The use of *Sie* as a pronoun of direct address to replace the elaborate *Euer Gnaden* dates from this era.

[23] For an excellent study of this period, see Eric A. Blackall's *The Emergence of German as a Literary Language: 1700–1755* (Cambridge: At the University Press, 1959).

obwohl, jedoch; gleichwie, also; nachdem, als; alldieweil, daher; sintemal und allermaßen behelfen: gerade als ob man nicht ohne diese Umschweife seine Gedanken ausdrücken könnte. . . . Man wird auch dergestalt [by avoiding such unwieldy conjunctions] viel deutlicher reden und schreiben, als wenn man immer eine Menge von Gedanken in einem weitläuftigen Satz zusammen bindet (Blackall, p. 175).

Directed primarily against the involved periodic sentences of the chancery style, these remarks also applied to the excessive use of parallelism and antithesis which characterized much of the Baroque writing.

In matters pertaining to the vocabulary, too, Gottsched pronounced judgment. In his *Beobachtungen über den Gebrauch und Misbrauch vieler deutscher Wörter und Redensarten* (1758), he warned his readers that the uncritical and wholesale use of metaphors—"wo man deutlich und verständlich reden soll"—had gradually corrupted all languages and would also hasten the decline of German. His admonition was: "Man denke nicht: Es klingt doch hübsch, oder neu, oder hoch! Was nicht vernünftig ist, das taugt gar nicht" (*Redekunst*).[24]

Gottsched's theories and principles certainly had a salutary effect upon the *Hochsprache* of the eighteenth century. A corrective was needed to offset the convoluted style of the chanceries and the verbal pyrotechnics of the Late Baroque. But "reasonable" as his teachings were, they lacked life and warmth. The creative spirit neither could nor would always pause to reflect upon the *bon sens* of its outpourings. His feelings held in check by a cold and sterile intellect, the poet was sorely hampered in his approach to the irrational, the sublime, the marvelous. Although the Enlightenment was to have yet another and even more effective champion, the predictable revolt against Gottsched was not long in coming.

BODMER AND BREITINGER

In 1740 two works were published in Zürich that were destined to exert a powerful influence upon the German literary language: *Kritische Abhandlung von dem Wunderbaren in der Poesie* by Johann Jakob Bodmer (1698–1783) and *Kritische Dichtkunst* by Johann Jakob Breitinger (1701–76).

These two polemics against Gottsched's rationalistic and French-inspired Classicism resulted from a long series of disagreements over the nature and function of poetry. Taking as their ideals the German literature

---

[24] *Ibid.*, p. 172.

of the Middle Ages[25] and the English writings of John Milton (1608–74),[26] the Zürich professors—though agreeing with Gottsched that poetry should be an imitation of nature ("Nachahmung der Natur")—insisted that the poet not be held to the observance of man-made rules in his efforts to fathom the grandeur and the wondrous (even irrational) mysteries of Nature. He should be free to give his imagination full play as long as he did not exceed the limits of probability ("Das Wunderbare braucht in der Poesie keine Wahrheit, sondern Wahrscheinlichkeit"). As long as the principle of verisimilitude was observed, it made not the slightest difference whether a given interpretation of nature was demonstrably "true" in any philosophical sense.

Bodmer and Breitinger also rebelled against the Gottschedian injunction which prohibited, or at least severely limited, the use of metaphors, pointing to the figurative, picturesque language of medieval German literature, so rich in imagery and forceful *Machtwörter* (a term coined by Luther), and to English—an impressive example of a free, unfettered language capable of strong and vivid expression, qualities which they felt were lacking in the vapid and bland German recommended by Gottsched.

English, thought Bodmer, had preserved many features which he admired in Middle High German. He liked the monosyllabic nature of its verbs, the way it had sloughed off its inflectional endings, the freedom of its word-order. It is full of features, he says, which give light, life and strength to style. It is rich in participial constructions. It has a great facility for using intransitive verbs with transitive force and transitive verbs with intransitive or passive meaning. It has valuable gerunds and gerundial expressions whereas German now has none although it had them in the fourteenth century. . . . Bodmer and Breitinger made two important contributions to the development of the German language: they advocated strong, metaphorical expression and they pointed to the Middle Ages as an example.[27]

ROCOCO AND EMPFINDSAMKEIT

In his feud with the Swiss, Gottsched emerged the loser. After 1740 his position became ever more vulnerable. Even in Leipzig his authority no

---

[25] In 1748 Bodmer published the first of several historically important anthologies of Middle High German poetry under the title *Proben der alten schwäbischen Poesie des dreyzehnten Jahrhunderts*. He also brought out an edition of Ulrich Boner's *Edelstein* (*ca.* 1350; in its day a widely read collection of proverbs, folk tales, and fables, which in 1461 enjoyed the distinction of becoming the first printed German book). Of more importance in the history of literature, in 1757 Bodmer published the first printed version of the greatest of the MHG folk epics, the *Nibelungenlied*; see Mary Thorp, *The Study of the Nibelungenlied* (Oxford: At the Clarendon Press, 1940), pp. 115ff.

[26] Bodmer's prose translation of *Paradise Lost* appeared in 1732.

[27] Blackall, *Emergence of German*, p. 313.

longer went unchallenged. In 1744 a number of young writers, who until then had been active followers of Gottsched, renounced his leadership in favor of the stand taken by Bodmer and Breitinger and founded a new journal. This renegade group's publication was entitled *Neue Beiträge zum Vergnügen des Verstandes und Witzes* (usually referred to as the *Bremer Beiträge*), and it stood in direct opposition to the orthodox *Belustigungen des Verstandes und Witzes*, edited by Johann Joachim Schwabe (1714–84), one of Gottsched's more prominent academic supporters. Numbered among the rebels were Christian Fürchtegott Gellert (1715–69), Friedrich von Hagedorn (1708–54), Gottlieb Wilhelm Rabener (1714–71), and Johann Elias Schlegel (1719–49).

The major objection to the teachings of their erstwhile *cher maître* was his reluctance to countenance any style couched in emotional, figurative, or "irrational" language. So, forming their own society—*Der Leipziger Dichterverein*—the young poets attempted in their compositions to strike a compromise between the two extremes: the lucid but often dry and pedantic style of the rationalistic school, and the lively but overly flamboyant manner of the Baroque writers. The literary style resulting from this compromise is usually called "Rococo." The German word that best describes it is *anmutig*: delicate, airy, and charming—like the architectural style after which it is named.

An intermediate stage between the Baroque and the Classic, the Rococo can lay no special claim to literary or linguistic distinction. A small group of minor poets—the Anacreontics (Wilhelm Ludwig Gleim, 1719–1803; Johann Nikolaus Götz, 1721–81; Johann Peter Uz, 1720–96)—wrote playfully and prettily about the sweet pleasures of wine and dalliance, delighting in words such as *Amor, artig, Entzücken, Elysium, golden, schalkhaft*.

The movement's most effective representative was Christian Fürchtegott Gellert, a member of the *Leipziger Dichterverein* and, at the time of his death, professor of philosophy at the University of Leipzig. He is remembered for his fables, for the novel *Das Leben der schwedischen Gräfin von G***, and for his extensive personal correspondence. It is in this last-mentioned genre that his pleasing, witty, and warmhearted language is set off to its best advantage. In fact, the Rococo found its fullest expression in the informal, urbane, epistolary style so highly regarded in polite society of eighteenth-century Germany.[28]

Another significant factor that caused the *Leipziger Dichterverein* to

---

[28] Numbered among Gellert's publications is a manual on letter writing, *Praktische Abhandlung von dem guten Geschmack in Briefen* (1751).

break with Gottsched was the English influence: the novels of Samuel Richardson (1689–1761)—*Pamela, Clarissa Harlowe, Sir Charles Grandison*; Lawrence Sterne (1713–68)—*Tristram Shandy* and *Sentimental Journey through France and Italy*; Oliver Goldsmith (1730–74)—*The Vicar of Wakefield*; and Edward Young (1683–1765)—*Night Thoughts on Death and Immortality*. These works exerted a strong influence upon the Leipzig group (among others), turning its members more and more in the direction of an artistic trend that was to play a major role in the shaping of the language and literature of the eighteenth and early nineteenth centuries. The name for this particular orientation (the terms "school" or "movement" are not quite appropriate) is *Empfindsamkeit*: essentially an appreciative and responsive awareness of feelings, sensibilities, and moods (Lessing had proposed *empfindsam* as a translation of "sentimental"). Though its most soaring expression is Klopstock's *Messias*, a similar emotional conditioning is characteristic of much of the Pietistic literature, and is also found in the writings of the somewhat later Storm and Stress authors, including those of the young Schiller and Goethe.

KLOPSTOCK

The fourth volume (1748) of the *Bremer Beiträge* contained the first three cantos of a poem that was to make a greater contribution to the modern German *Schriftsprache* than any work since Luther's translation of the Bible, namely, *Der Messias* by Friedrich Gottlieb Klopstock (1724–1803). The majestic and powerful language of this greatest of Christian epics in the German tongue created an immediate sensation. Bodmer and Breitinger were jubilant: German literature now had its Milton. And Gottsched's prestige went rapidly waning.

Even in the first few hexameters of the opening canto, one can perceive the vital and "seraphic" grandeur of its language:

> Sing, unsterbliche Seele, der sündigen Menschheit Erlösung,
> Die der Messias auf Erden in seiner Menschheit vollendet,
> Und durch die er Adams Geschlechte die Liebe der Gottheit
> Mit dem Blute des heiligen Bundes von neuem geschenkt hat.
> Also geschah des Ewigen Wille. Vergebens erhub sich
> Satan wider den göttlichen Sohn; umsonst stand Juda
> Wider ihn auf: er tats, und vollbrachte die große Versöhnung.
> Aber, o Tat, die allein der Allbarmherzige kennet,
> Darf aus dunkler Ferne sich auch dir nahen die Dichtkunst?
> Weihe sie, Geist Schöpfer, vor dem ich hier still anbete,

Führe sie mir, als deine Nachahmerin, voller Entzückung,
Voll unsterblicher Kraft, in verklärter Schönheit entgegen.

Much has been written on Klopstock's contribution to the literary standard.[29] We shall here limit ourselves to a review of some of the more obvious linguistic features of his poetry. The dynamism of Klopstock's language may in large part be attributed to its essentially verbal rather than nominal character. Not only did he create verbal forms from existing nouns and adjectives—*äugeln, kleineln, kunstwörteln*—but he employed direction-giving prefixes with verbs whose meanings did not otherwise involve the idea of motion: *aufweinen, entgegenjauchzen, entgegenlächeln.* In order to strengthen the semantic impact of a verb, he frequently dropped its conventional prefix, thereby focusing attention upon the root itself: *(be)decken, (ver)dorren, (ver)fertigen, (um)schatten, (er)schrecken.* Most distinctive of all, perhaps, is Klopstock's versatile use of participles compounded with nouns and adverbs:[30] *bangzerrungen, blütenumduftet, himmelfliegend, sanftleuchtend, tiefauftönend, wahnsinnbetrunken.* Even in his choice of nouns, he was fond of coining compounds in *-er* (a suffix indicating the agent or doer of an action)—*Allvollender, Zukunftswisser*—and of employing the present participle in its nominal capacity—*die Auferstehenden, der Erlösende.*

Klopstock especially favored certain words, many of them common to the language of the Pietists:

ätherisch	*Schöpfung*
brünstig	*seelenvoll*
donnern	*seraphisch*
Heil (and the greeting *Heil dir!*)	*strömen*
heilig	*wehmütig*
hingegossen	*zärtlich*
Myriade	*zerfließen*

Of towering importance in the history of Modern High German, Klopstock's contribution to the development of the literary standard was enormous. He freed the language from the countless restrictions of syntax dictated by the grammarians, rhetoricians, and philosophers. By exploiting the rich word-forming genius of German, he demonstrated its ability to generate a vast and flexible vocabulary.

[29] For a brief bibliography of the especially pertinent studies, see Blackall, *Emergence of German*, p. 319, n. 2.

[30] Showing the influence of Milton's language: "earthborne," "ivy-covered," "heaven-warring," "night-warbling."

WIELAND AND LESSING[31]

The language of Klopstock's epic is sublime and noble, but far too intense, overpowering, and poetic for anything but the highest forms of dramatic expression. It served magnificently as a counterbalance to the insipid and unimaginative language of the Gottschedian era; but a compromise was necessary. The writer who first succeeded in merging the two stylistic extremes into a felicitous and graceful instrument for both prose and poetry was Christoph Martin Wieland (1733–1813).

In his early works Wieland was much under the spell of Klopstock. The first edition of his famous *Bildungsroman, Agathon* (1766–67), is heavily tinged with sentimentalism, though not in the seraphic manner so characteristic of the *Messias*. His is rather a kind of secular *Empfindsamkeit* which lays more stress upon a pleasure-seeking sensuousness, reminiscent of the Anacreontic spirit. Blackall's choice of a quotation to illustrate this point is quite appropriate:

> Die allgemeine Stille, der Mondschein, die rührende Schönheit der schlummernden Natur, die mit den Ausdünstungen der Blumen durchwürzte Nachtluft, tausend angenehme Empfindungen, deren liebliche Verwirrung meine Seele trunken machte, sezte sie in eine Art von Entzükung, worinnen ein andrer Schauplaz von unbekannten Schönheiten sich vor mir aufthat; es war nur ein Augenblik, aber ein Augenblik, den ich um eines von den Jahren des Königs von Persien nicht vertauschen wollte.[32]

"A beautiful balance between wit and feeling," Wieland's language is infinitely graceful and civilized. Because it so harmoniously blends the sentimental and the rational, his style exhibits no strongly distinctive traits, yet achieves "eine von bis dahin ungekannter Leichtigkeit und Frische." Wieland's stylistic genius was recognized by so eminent a critic as Goethe, who, in a conversation with Eckermann dated January 18, 1825, paid him this rare tribute: "Wielanden verdankt das ganze obere Deutschland seinen Stil."

Much of Wieland's writing originally appeared in a journal which he founded and edited: *Der Teutsche Merkur* (1773–89), the first general belletristic periodical in the German language, modeled after a French

[31] Because I consider Blackall's discussion of the style and language of these two authors so superior and well-presented, I gratefully acknowledge my indebtedness to him in this section—a skimpy synopsis of chapters XI and XII of his *Emergence of German.*

[32] This is a quotation from the now-rare first edition of *Agathon*; in this case a most desirable source, since Wieland made extensive revisions in the text of the second edition, revisions which toned down the sentimental style of the novel.

prototype, *Mercure de france.* Wieland's admiration for the French language and literature is perceptible in his style, as well as his sometimes excessive use of French loanwords (for which he was criticized by several of his contemporaries).

In his later years, Wieland outgrew to an extent his admiration for Klopstock and for the soaring metaphors and emotional language of the *Messias.* But even though his mature style is a model of urbane wit and civilized restraint, there always remained in his language a certain affinity for the *Empfindsamkeit* of his earlier years.

We stated previously that the Enlightenment was to have yet another and even more effective champion than Gottsched. The reference was to Gotthold Ephraim Lessing (1729–81). Known to students of literature as the reformer of the German theater, a brilliant and perceptive writer on almost all phases of esthetics, and a dramatist of considerable stature, Lessing was also interested in problems relating to the history, structure, and usage of language. He was well acquainted with Dr. Johnson's dictionary of English. He wrote a critical review of Gottsched's grammar, a work of which he generally approved. Lessing reputedly gathered material over a fifteen-year period for a proposed dictionary which he hoped one day to publish, though he is said to have abandoned the project after the first volume of Campe's work appeared.

Etymological studies always fascinated him. This antiquarian curiosity is especially evident in his edition of Logau's poetry, wherein Lessing noted with approval the occurrence of many words which—by his time— had become either archaic or obsolete. He contended that some of the old words were in fact more effective than their modern, more complexly structured variants. Logau used *Drang, plotz, verkünden,* and *Blick,* where the contemporary idiom would require *Drangsal, plötzlich, verkündigen,* and *Augenblick.* Lessing urged that a word such as Logau's *vervielen* should not be allowed to die, pointing to the neat semantic distinctions inherent in such related groupings as *vermchren, vervielen,* and *vervielfältigen*: "Das Wasser vermehrt sich; alle Blumen vervielen sich; einige Blumen vervielfältigen sich" (Blackall, p. 355).

Especially attracted to these archaic words, Lessing believed them to be somehow "stronger" than their successors. As examples he cites *gumpen* (= *hüpfen*), *kosen* (= *reden*), and *Thurst* (= *Mut*). His fondness for the older stages of the language also fostered a lively interest in German dialects, though his concern was limited to terms of provincial or regional currency that occurred in literature. In a review of a lexicon of the dialect spoken in Hamburg, Lessing stated with rare insight that no adequate etymological dictionary of the German language could be compiled until similar lexica of all the major dialects had been provided.

As might be expected, Lessing did not favor the indiscriminate use of loanwords. At one time he criticized Wieland for employing French borrowings for which there were good native equivalents.

Almost untouched by the language of Klopstock and the other sentimentalists, Lessing took as his stylistic model the clear and concise writing of Voltaire. From roughly 1750 to 1770, Lessing was the most dominant and influential voice of the Enlightenment in Germany, successfully challenging Gottsched's once unquestioned authority in matters of literary and dramatic import. The three opening paragraphs of his famous *17ter Literaturbrief*, which dealt the aging Leipzig *Literaturpapst* a blow from which he never recovered, may serve as examples of the prose style which Heinrich Heine (1797–1856) likened to the architectural style of the Romans: ". . . höchste Solidität bei der höchsten Einfachheit":

> "Niemand," sagen die Verfasser der Bibliothek, "wird leugnen, daß die deutsche Schaubühne einen großen Teil ihrer ersten Verbesserung dem Herrn Professor *Gottsched* zu danken habe."
> Ich bin dieser Niemand; ich leugne es geradezu. Es wäre zu wünschen, daß sich Herr Gottsched niemals mit dem Theater vermengt hätte. Seine vermeinten Verbesserungen betreffen entweder entbehrliche Kleinigkeiten oder sind wahre Verschlimmerungen.
> Als die *Neuberin* [prominent theatrical figure of the time] blühte und so mancher den Beruf fühlte, sich um sie und die Bühne verdient zu machen, sahe es freilich mit unserer dramatischen Poesie sehr elend aus. Man kannte keine Regeln; man bekümmerte sich um keine Muster. Unsre *Staats- und Heldenaktionen* [a hopelessly mediocre and banal kind of tragedy] waren voller Unsinn, Bombast, Schmutz und Pöbelwitz. Unsre *Lustspiele* bestanden in Verkleidungen und Zaubereien; und Prügel waren die witzigsten Einfälle derselben. Dieses Verderbnis einzusehen, brauchte man eben nicht der feinste und größte Geist zu sein. Auch war Herr Gottsched nicht der erste, der es einsahe; er war nur der erste, der sich Kräfte genug zutraute, ihm abzuhelfen. Und wie ging er damit zu Werke? Er verstand ein wenig Französisch und fing an zu übersetzen; er ermunterte alles, was reimen und "Oui Monsieur" verstehen konnte, gleichfalls zu übersetzen; . . . kurz, er wollte nicht sowohl unser altes Theater verbessern als der Schöpfer eines ganz neuen sein. Und was für eines neuen? Eines französierenden; ohne zu untersuchen, ob dieses französierende Theater der deutschen Denkungsart angemessen sei oder nicht.

Lessing's vocabulary contains many words reflecting the philosophical, esthetic, and broadly humanitarian ideals of the Enlightenment, some of them native to German, others borrowed or translated from English and French:

Aufklärung	*Menschenliebe*
Bildung	*rührend*
bemitleiden	*Tatsache*
Denkfreiheit	*Toleranz*
Dilettant	*weinerlich*
Freidenker	*Weltbürger*
Humanität	*Weltgeist*
Ideal	

STORM AND STRESS

In 1767–68 Johann Gottfried Herder (1744–1803) published *Fragmente über die neuere deutsche Literatur*.[33] Demanding a return to a natural language unencumbered by man-made rules, foreign influences, and philosophical systems, he urged his fellow Germans to look to their own past, folklore, and environment for poetic and linguistic inspiration. He held up the ancient Greeks as the model of a civilization built upon its own inner and native resources.

Herder's words fell upon fertile soil. A restless, dissident, postwar generation[34] of literary hotspurs was already in open revolt against the entire social order which had been established by adherents of the Enlightenment. Jean Jacques Rousseau's (1712–78) call "Back to Nature!" became their own battle cry. Their literary ideal was the *Originalgenie*, the poet who recognized no rules and no restrictions, giving full rein to his creative genius.

The language of the Storm and Stress writers is explosive, elliptical, parenthetical. They omit definite articles and personal pronouns, trying by this and other techniques to mirror the abrupt, unstudied manner of the emotional and sometimes violent outbursts of unrestrained speech so typical of the *Machtkerls* whom they admired so much. A good example of the style is the following passage in a drama by Friedrich Maximilian Klinger (1752–1831), the revised title of which—*Sturm und Drang*—was subsequently applied to the whole of this unruly and revolutionary period in German letters. The speaker is the young Lord Bushy, who, with two companions as erratic as himself, had left Scotland for America in order to take part in the Wars of Independence against the English. Lord Bushy speaks about himself in the following words:

[33] Herder also wrote a treatise on the origin and nature of language that had an abiding influence upon nineteenth-century linguistic theory: *Abhandlung über den Ursprung der Sprache* (1770).

[34] This period marked the end of the Seven Years' War (1756–63), a conflict which had pitted the eventually victorious forces of Prussia under Frederick the Great against the combined might of Austria, France, and Russia.

Bin alles gewesen. Ward Handlanger, um was zu sein. Lebte auf den Alpen, weidete die Ziegen, lag Tag und Nacht unter dem unendlichen Gewölbe des Himmels, von den Winden gekühlt und von innerem Feuer gebrannt. Nirgends Ruh, nirgends Rast. —Seht, so strotze ich voll Kraft und Gesundheit und kann mich nicht aufreiben. Ich will die Campagne hier mitmachen als Volontär, da kann sich meine Seele ausrecken, und tun sie mir den Dienst und schießen mich nieder, gut dann! Ihr nehmt meine Barschaft und zieht!

The language of the Storm and Stress was too violent, too confused, and too much a jumble of various linguistic trends to have more than a transitory effect upon the literary standard. Its influence ended with the advent of the Classical period in German literature, a period identified above all by the mature works of Goethe and Schiller.

SUMMARY

As is evident from the foregoing pages, the history of the German language during the seventeenth and eighteenth centuries is essentially a history of the development of the *Schriftsprache*. Although it was a highly complex era from a literary point of view, during this time the language underwent none of the profound changes in phonology and morphology that had marked its evolution in the fifteenth and sixteenth centuries.

To what extent the spoken language had been standardized during the period from 1600 to 1800 cannot be stated with any precision: probably not much. Among literate circles, something approaching a common idiom was used—the Meißen dialect—though a close study of the spelling practices, as well as the printed comments, reveals that dialectisms and regional pronunciations flavored the speech of even the most literate elements of society. The realization of a standard High German spoken language was not to come about until well into the nineteenth century, and even then its acceptance would be subject to many qualifications.

CHAPTER SEVEN

The New High German Period

From 1800

LITERARY INFLUENCES

CLASSICISM (*Goethe and Schiller*)

IN ATTEMPTING to characterize that which is essentially "classic" in Greek art, the historian and archeologist Johann Joachim Winckelmann (1717–68), in a work which was to have a profound influence upon German Classicism—*Geschichte der Kunst des Altertums* (1764)—had used the phrase "edle Einfalt und stille Größe." These two qualities of noble simplicity and quiet grandeur later came to be distinguishing features of the literature produced during the period in German letters referred to either as "Classicism" or as "The Age of Goethe and Schiller."

Emulating the Greek ideals, the language of German Classicism—as exemplified above all in the mature works of Johann Wolfgang von Goethe (1749–1832) and Johann Christoph Friedrich Schiller (1759–1805)—shows, as Adolf Bach puts it,

> . . . edles Maßhalten und Klarheit, Verinnerlichung und Wärme des Gefühls, Kühnheit der Gedanken in vollendeter Ausdrucksfähigkeit auch sprachlich in eins gebildet. Hier ist alles Gewaltsame und Ungeordnete überwunden in der Wortwahl, der Wortbildung wie im Satzbau, die unter dem Gesetz der gliedhaften Einordnung jedes Teils in ein Ganzes stehen" (*Geschichte der deutschen Sprache*, 8th ed., p. 382).

However, although one can point to certain features of word formation and syntax which have their parallel in either Homeric or Classical Greek, the influence of the ancient Greek language upon late-eighteenth-century literary German was at best only superficial. As did Klopstock, Goethe and Schiller make abundant use of adjectival compounds of all kinds[1]—of which ancient Greek had a lavish abundance—though it should be borne in mind that none of these constructions, no matter how Greek-like in flavor, goes beyond the word-forming capacities native to the German language.

Their use of the syntactic device, which occurs commonly in Greek, of placing an adjective after the noun and repeating the definite article also lends an air of classical antiquity to their writings; for example, *die Tränen, die unendlichen*. However reminiscent of Greek usage, structures of this sort were not alien to the older stages of literary German. Although not common, examples such as MHG *tier diu wilden, gewalt den meisten, sîn jaget daz rîche* were admissible.

By their choice of vocabulary, too, the German Classicists sought to recreate the Greek esthetic ideal. Especially in the later works of Goethe, we notice an obvious attempt to employ words, usually modifiers, intended to elicit this mood of "noble simplicity and quiet grandeur." His language, in fact, reflects three major steps in his literary development. His earliest writings, revealing the influence of the Anacreontic poets, show a preference for such terms as *Bach, Busen, Lust, munter, rosenfarbig, seufzen, zärtlich*. Next came the Storm and Stress era and a fondness for emotive language suggestive of inner conflict: *dumpf, düster, schrecklich, stürmisch, verworren*. And finally his Classical period, in which he favors words denoting the uncomplicated and usually constructive emotions: *behaglich, edel, groß, gut, heiter, rein, trefflich, tüchtig, würdig*.

The language of Classicism often displays a measured, epic quality reminding us of Homer, as exemplified in the following passage from Goethe's drama, *Hermann und Dorothea*. Notice the mood of simple dignity and unfeigned naturalness. The selection is taken from the scene in which Hermann, escorting his bride home to his parents, is leading her down the steep path of a terraced vineyard hill:

Und so leitet' er sie die vielen Platten hinunter,
die, unbehauen gelegt, als Stufen dienten im Laubgang.
Langsam schritt sie hinab, auf seinen Schultern die Hände;
und mit schwankenden Lichtern, durchs Laub, überblickte der Mond sie,

---

[1] These include compounds in which the last element is a present or past participle —*allbezwingend, hochgetürmt, langerfleht, schönheitliebend*—as well as those characterized by the linking together of adverb and adjective or adjective and adjective, to mention only the more frequently occurring types.

eh' er, von Wetterwolken umhüllt, im Dunkeln das Paar ließ.
Sorglich stützte der Starke das Mädchen, das über ihn herging;
aber sie, unkundig des Steigs und der roheren Stufen,
fehlte tretend; es knackte der Fuß, sie drohte zu fallen.
Eilig streckte gewandt der sinnige Jüngling den Arm aus,
hielt empor die Geliebte; sie sank ihm leis auf die Schulter,
Brust war gesenkt an Brust, und Wang' an Wang. So stand er,
starr wie ein Marmorbild, vom ernsten Willen gebändigt,
drückte nicht fester sie an, er stemmte sich gegen die Schwere.
Und so fühlt' er die herrliche Last, die Wärme des Herzens
und den Balsam des Atems, an seinen Lippen verhauchet,
trug mit Mannesgefühl die Heldengröße des Weibes.

In a somewhat different vein, but still characteristic of the period, are
these lines from another of Goethe's dramas, *Iphigenie,* so reminiscent of
the closely mitered and stately language of the Classical Greek tragedy:

Heraus in eure Schatten, rege Wipfel
des alten, heil'gen, dichtbelaubten Haines,
wie in der Göttin stilles Heiligtum,
tret' ich noch jetzt mit schauderndem Gefühl,
als wenn ich sie zum erstenmal beträte,
und es gewöhnt sich nicht mein Geist hierher.
So manches Jahr bewahrt mich hier verborgen
ein hoher Wille, dem ich mich ergebe;
doch immer bin ich, wie im ersten, fremd.
Denn ach! mich trennt das Meer von den Geliebten,
und an dem Ufer steh' ich lange Tage,
das Land der Griechen mit der Seele suchend;
und gegen meine Seufzer bringt die Welle
nur dumpfe Töne brausend mir herüber.

Much more could be said concerning the style and vocabulary of
Classicism. From the historical point of view, however, there are few
structural differences setting off the literary language of this period from
that of the immediately preceding half-century. The language of Gellert
and Wieland, for instance, is in its form much like that of Goethe and
Schiller. The differences—of great importance to the rhetorician and
student of literature—are rather those of creative ability and poetic
purpose. Goethe and Schiller were literary geniuses of the highest order,
and both saw in the art of ancient Greece what seemed to them the most
sublime expression of the human heart and mind. This spirit they sought
to recapture in their own inspired creations, striving after the balanced
and harmoniously articulated sentence, all the while choosing a vocabulary
to enhance and enforce the esthetic effect of their meticulously contoured
language.

ROMANTICISM

Probably of more linguistic interest is that period in German literature, contemporary with Classicism (running approximately from 1800 to about 1840), which is known as "Romanticism"[2]—a movement by no means limited to Germany.

Consciously opposed to the balanced and restrained literary style of the Classicists, the German Romanticists deliberately sought to force the language to its outer limits of expressiveness. They stressed the emotive qualities of the words themselves, called attention to the affinities between poetry and music, and in their writing tended to concentrate upon mood more than upon clarity and precision of lexical meaning.

An absorbing interest in olden times and in the folklore and folksongs of their own culture are other marks of the Romanticists. They revived many archaic words. The following nouns—all very much alive today— were listed as archaic or obsolescent in dictionaries of the eighteenth century:

Ahn	*Heim*
Aue	*Sippe*
Fehde	*Ungestüm*
Gau	*Weidwerk*
Hain	*Wonne*

They also reveled in terms that smacked of mystery and magic:

fatal	*magisch*
feenhaft	*schauerlich*
geheimnisvoll	*verhängnisvoll*
gespensterhaft	*wunderbar*
grauenhaft	*zauberhaft*

And the Romanticists were fascinated by the night, as illustrated by the famous motto of the Prelude to Ludwig Tieck's (1773–1853) drama, *Kaiser Octavianus*:

> Mondbeglänzte Zaubernacht,
> die den Sinn gefangen hält,
> wundervolle Märchenwelt,
> steig' auf in der alten Pracht!

[2] The Late Latin adjective *romanticus* meant simply "written in a Romance language" (as distinguished from Latin), just as the French noun *roman* referred originally to a narrative composed in one of the Romance vulgates. Used in the sense of "prose fiction," the word was borrowed into German during the seventeenth century. *Die Romantik*, as a term for a literary genre or movement, was apparently coined as an antonym of *Klassik* by the poet Novalis (pen name of Friedrich von Hardenberg, 1772–1801).

Typical in its imagery and symbolism, the following poem by one of the movement's most prominent figures, Baron Joseph von Eichendorff (1788–1857), is a good example of the language of Romanticism:

Sehnsucht

Es schienen so golden die Sterne;
Am Fenster ich einsam stand
Und hörte aus weiter Ferne
Ein Posthorn im stillen Land.
Das Herz mir im Leib entbrennte,
Da hab' ich mir heimlich gedacht:
Ach, wer da mitreisen könnte
In der herrlichen Sommernacht!

Zwei junge Gesellen gingen
Vorüber am Bergeshang,
Ich hörte im Wandern sie singen,
Die stille Gegend entlang,
Von schwindelnden Felsenschlüften,
Wo die Wälder rauschen so sacht,
Von Quellen, die von den Klüften
Sich stürzen in Waldesnacht.

Sie sangen von Marmorbildern,
Von Gärten, die überm Gestein
In dämmernden Lauben verwildern,
Palästen im Mondenschein,
Wo die Mädchen am Fenster lauschen,
Wenn der Lauten Klang erwacht,
Und die Brunnen verschlafen rauschen
In der prächtigen Sommernacht.

ROMANTICISM AND THE BEGINNINGS OF GERMAN PHILOLOGY

The Romantic movement is important to us for yet another reason, for during its tenure interest in the older stages of the German language and its literature was first systematically cultivated. Primarily because of their enthusiasm for Germanic folklore and antiquity, several of the Romanticists are numbered among the founders of what later became the academic discipline known as "Germanic philology" (*germanische Sprachwissenschaft*).

Although claim to world fame rests on their collection of folk tales (*Kinder- und Hausmärchen*, 1812–15), the brothers Jacob (1785–1863) and Wilhelm (1786–1859) Grimm were also interested in the history of their mother tongue. With typical Romantic enthusiasm for the natural and the unsophisticated, Jacob Grimm in the preface to the first edition of his grammar, calls upon every native-born German to forsake the pedantry of schoolmasters' rules and speak the language as he learned it at his mother's knee. He emphasizes his wish to *describe* rather than *prescribe*—an approach which has since then been considered basic to the scientific investigation of languages.

Our earliest comparative Germanic grammar is by Jacob Grimm: his *Deutsche Grammatik,* the first edition of which appeared in 1818. Though both brothers also edited a number of Old German literary documents, their most enduring philological achievement is the monumental *Deutsches Wörterbuch,* a project which, though too far-reaching to be completed within their lives, claimed much of their time and devotion. This many-volumed and definitive work started appearing in 1854; it was completed in 1960.

Two other brothers, who were more directly concerned with Romanticism as a literary movement (both men were influential as teachers and critics), also contributed much to Germanic philology in its broader, comparative aspects: August Wilhelm (1767–1845) and Friedrich (1772–1829) Schlegel. Friedrich's book, *Über die Sprache und Weisheit der Indier* (1808), did much to awaken interest in the comparative study of the ancient Indic language. August Wilhelm, a leading Orientalist of his time, was appointed to the first chair for Sanskrit to be established at a German university (Bonn). They also wrote and lectured on the philosophy of language, and both took an avid interest in the editing and translating of medieval texts. August's unpublished notes and commentary on the Middle High German epic, *Das Nibelungenlied,* compiled over a thirty-year period, fill three large folio volumes.[3]

The poet and scholar Ludwig Tieck, already mentioned, brought out in 1803 a modernized version of several of the Middle High German courtly love poems, using Bodmer's and Breitinger's edition of the original verses (*Sammlung von Minnesingern aus dem schwäbischen Zeitpuncte,* 1758–59). These were followed by other translations of consistently high quality.[4]

[3] For a brief and readable survey of the beginnings of Germanic philology, the student should read Martin Joos and Frederick R. Whitesell, *Middle High German Courtly Reader* (Madison: University of Wisconsin Press, 1951), pp. 252–72.

[4] Tieck is also famous as a translator of Shakespeare. Assisted by his daughter, Dorothea, and Count Wolf Baudissin, he spent fifteen years translating Shakespeare's works, completing his portion in 1840. August Wilhelm Schlegel had begun the task, translating seventeen of the Englishman's dramas over the years 1797–1810. The "Tieck-Schlegel" translation, as it is referred to, is unsurpassed, remaining to this day the standard version of Shakespeare (though not the only one). It is one of the most successful translations of modern times.

Tieck also translated Miguel Cervantes' classic, *Don Quixote de la Mancha,* as well as several selections from Old Spanish and Old English literature.

Schlegel, too, translated from the Spanish, publishing a volume of Calderón's

BEYOND ROMANTICISM

Beyond Romanticism lies the era which, from a linguistic point of view, we call "modern." Each subsequent literary movement—Realism, Naturalism, Expressionism, Impressionism, and so forth—is of course characterized by its language. Still, these distinctions are chiefly stylistic. There have been many lexical changes and innovations, the orthography has undergone revisions, and rhetorical styles have varied from one movement to another. But the structure of the language—what Hans Glinz calls "die innere Form"—has suffered few modifications. At least so it seems to us, for linguistic change can seldom be observed directly. Alterations take place so slowly as to go undetected within the lifetime of sometimes even several generations of speakers of the language. True, we notice trends that seem to be taking a language in one direction or another, but whether such tendencies will one day assume the proportion of actual systemic changes, only a future generation will be able to say.

A tendency of this sort is the alleged "nominalization" of the language, one example of which is the substituting of a noun phrase for a single verb: *eine Anordnung erlassen* instead of simply *anordnen*; *ein Urteil fällen* rather than *beurteilen*; *unter Beweis stellen* in preference to *beweisen*. Though admittedly wordier, such periphrases do have the advantage—as Hugo Moser points out (*Deutsche Sprachgeschichte*, 4th ed., p. 175)—of anticipating the message of the normally last-place verb, thus offsetting to some extent what has long been considered the clumsiest feature of German word order. Other evidence of a trend toward nominalization is seen in the ease and frequency with which new abstract nouns in *-heit*, *-keit*, *-tum*, *-ung*, and so forth are added to the vocabulary.

This increase in the use of nominals is considered by some stylists to reveal an ominous weakening of linguistic vitality. Rhetoricians point out that a verb-rich style is "dynamic," whereas a noun-heavy style tends to be "static." However, accurate as such an observation may be, it is essentially an esthetic judgment; there would seem to be little reason to attach any particular structural merit to either style. While there can be no doubt but that the number of derivative nouns in the German vocabulary has increased over the past century or so, probably the only valid comment is that the word-forming genius of the language continues to be a major force in its growth and development.

The last hundred years have also witnessed several modifications

---

dramas in 1803, followed the next year by a collection of poems translated from the Spanish, Italian, and Portuguese: *Blumensträuße italienischer, spanischer und portugiesischer Poesie.*

centering on the formation and function of the cases. As an example, the *s*-ending of the masculine and neuter genitive singular is used less frequently than it once was. Now acceptable even in the written language are constructions such as the following: *die Wirtschaft des heutigen Deutschland(s)*; *die Bilder des jüngeren Holbein(s)*; *die hellen Tage des schönen Mai(s)*; *ein Lehrbuch des Latein(s)*.

The genitive has undergone drastic restrictions in its function as the required case for the object of many verbs, for most of these verbs are now construed either with the object in the accusative case or else with a prepositional object (see Curme, *A Grammar of the German Language*, 2nd ed., pp. 509–14, for additional examples of earlier and modern usage):

Er achtet nicht des Vorteils–Er achtet nicht den [or auf den] Vorteil.
Er bedarf des Trostes–Er bedarf den Trost.
Er begehrt des Reichtums–Er begehrt den [or nach dem] Reichtum.

The use of the dative case, too, has undergone restrictions. It was once favored as a formal device for signaling the indirect object of a verb, but this function is now more often assumed by a preposition. A construction such as *er schreibt an seinen Vater* probably occurs with greater frequency than *er schreibt seinem Vater*. And, though of less import, the use of the *e*-ending to mark the dative singular of monosyllabic masculine and neuter nouns (*dem Manne*) is now—except for a few fixed expressions—a matter of stylistic preference.

Modern usage also tolerates certain verbal constructions which until now were generally condemned. For instance, though the grammars still call for subjunctive II forms (that is, the subjunctive based upon the past tense of the indicative: *kam–käme*) in the *wenn*-clause of contrary-to-fact conditional sentences, the colloquial language today tolerates the use of *würden* and the infinitive: *wenn er kommen würde* instead of *wenn er käme*.

Another such instance is to be found in the formation of the imperative. The second person singular imperative of strong verbs whose stem-vowel is *e* (*essen, lesen*) sometimes occurs as *esse, lese* rather than as *iß, lies*.

Other differences, of course, set off the contemporary language from that of 1850 or 1900, but from the historical point of view even the sum total of these changes or trends is not impressive, yet. If German should one day exhibit only two cases—the subjective and objective—then what we can now only call "trends" or "tendencies" will be referred to as "beginnings" or "early occurrences."

However, if we cannot with any certainty predict the future, we can in retrospect see that during the first half of the nineteenth century the German language achieved its full range of literary expression, its rich natural resources at last graced with the stylistic versatility and suppleness required by the creative artist. The German-speaking people now had a *Schriftsprache* equal to that of the other great cultures of Europe.

TOWARD A STANDARD ORTHOGRAPHY

The twentieth century had begun before a standardized spelling finally prevailed throughout Germany, Austria, and Switzerland. Resistance to the several attempts at regulation or reform was considerable; some of it was reasonable, some stemmed from petty or provincial attitudes.

The basic issue was whether to spell etymologically or phonetically. Jacob Grimm came out in favor of an orthography that would relate a word to its etymon. Thus, even though in Middle High German the plurals of *gast* and *hand* were spelled *geste* and *hende*, he advocated *gäste* and *hände*.[5] Just how far to carry this practice was never decided. *Eltern* is related to *alt*, just as is *fertig* to *fahren*, yet not even Grimm proposed the spellings **Ältern* and **färtig*.

Most of those who had an interest in the problem, however, favored a phonetically oriented orthography. One of its most influential advocates was Rudolf von Raumer, himself once a student of Jacob Grimm.[6] In 1854 von Raumer published a book (*Über deutsche Rechtschreibung*) which helped clarify the problems attending orthographic reform and suggested solutions. In 1876 the Prussian government asked von Raumer to prepare an agenda for a conference which was commissioned with the task of preparing a reasonable and generally acceptable spelling reform.

This conference, "zur Herstellung größerer Einigung in der deutschen Rechtschreibung," held in Berlin the following year, bore fruit, for not long thereafter the states of Prussia and Bavaria adopted official spelling manuals which incorporated many of the proposals made at its sessions. Not everyone was happy with the results, especially Chancellor von Bismarck of Prussia, who permitted their adoption by the public schools, but would not allow the government ministries to change over to the

[5] In Upper German texts especially, perhaps in an effort to distinguish its pronunciation from that accorded the *e* of "primary umlaut," the vowel resulting from the later mutation known technically as "secondary umlaut" was often rendered in writing by a small *e* placed directly over the *a*. This diacritic, together with the letter *a*, eventually developed into what we now refer to as the "*a*-umlaut sign" (*ä*), e.g., MHG *mähte* and *nähte*.

[6] Rudolf von Raumer (1815–76) held the University of Erlangen's first chair for Germanic philology. Of interest to students of the German language, he wrote the first history of Germanic philology: *Geschichte der germanischen Philologie, vorzugsweise in Deutschland* (1870).

so-called "Puttkamersche Rechtschreibung."[7] However, in spite of such formidable opposition, the new orthography was soon adopted by most of the German states, though several prominent educators openly resented what they considered unwarranted governmental interference in their personal and civic liberties.[8]

In 1901 another conference on orthography was called, again in Berlin, this time including representatives not only of the German *Reich*, but also of Austria and Switzerland. The reforms proposed by the members of this commission were incorporated into a book entitled *Amtliches Wörter-verzeichnis für die deutsche Rechtschreibung zum Gebrauch an den preußischen Kanzleien*. Within the next few years this manual, or close versions of it, was adopted by almost all the German-speaking lands, including Austria and Switzerland.

The present-day standard reference work on German orthography, based upon the Prussian model, is *Dudens Rechtschreibung der deutschen Sprache und der Fremdwörter*,[9] now in its seventeenth edition (1973).

Although modern German spelling is a definite improvement over the English, it is not fully phonemic, that is, it does not have a separate symbol for each structurally significant class of sounds in the language. Accepting the stage pronunciation (to be discussed in the next section) as standard, a few of the discrepancies between letter and sound are: (1) there is no distinction in pronunciation between *ai* and *ei*, or between *e* and *ä*; (2) the letter *g*, ordinarily pronounced [g], is pronounced [ç] when occurring finally after *i (König, ledig)*; (3) *v* is pronounced now [f] as in *Vers*, now [v] as in *Violine*; (4) the letters *y* and *ü* are usually pronounced alike—as in *Mystik, müßten*;[10] (5) the digraph *ie* is not usually pronounced diphthong-

---

[7] Robert von Puttkamer (1828–1900), Prussian statesman. It was during his tenure of office as Minister of Education (1879–81) that the new Prussian *Regelbuch* on orthography was introduced.

[8] Prominent in this group was Rudolf Hildebrand (1824–94), a professor of Germanic philology at the University of Leipzig and for several years editor-in-chief of the *Deutsches Wörterbuch*. A book he wrote on the principles and methods of the teaching of German had a profound influence upon his generation. In this book— *Vom deutschen Sprachunterricht in der Schule*—he stressed the validity of the spoken language, pointing out that pedagogues had no right to tamper with the historically derived idiom of the people.

[9] Konrad Duden (1829–1911), German educator. He brought out the first edition of the *Rechtschreibung* in 1880. There are now two such "Dudens": one for West Germany, one for East Germany. The one used in the East bears the title *Duden Wörterbuch und Leitfaden der deutschen Rechtschreibung*.

[10] The letter *y*, when standing for the semivowel [j], occurs only in loanwords from English: *Yawl*, *Yard*, and so forth. It occurs in a few other English loanwords (*Story*, *Teddybär*), where it is pronounced [i].

ally, as the spelling would indicate, but as [î], a pronunciation also accorded the letter *i* in certain words (*Liter, Wisent,* etc.). Though this tally is not at all complete, it demonstrates that German spelling could profit from still further reform.[11]

An orthographic feature that has come in for considerable criticism is the capitalization of substantives, a practice that Jacob Grimm considered to be an unnecessary nuisance. There have been periodic attempts to do away with the convention, the latest one still in doubt (1974), but to date its proponents have outnumbered its opponents. With the exception of a few specialized journals, German publications continue to capitalize all nominals.

A final note on a topic more or less related to orthography—the printing and writing of German. Reference has already been made to the historical development of the style of type previously much used for the printing of German. Since the end of World War II, however, the occurrence of this "Gothic" script (*Fraktur, Eckenschrift*) has become quite restricted. Although employed for newspaper headlines, lead paragraphs, placards, and occasionally as an artistic device in other situations, it has in general been replaced by the Roman script (*Antiqua, Rundschrift*). In like manner the old *Kurrentschrift* or *deutsche Schreibschrift*, once standard for written German, has given way to the *Lateinschrift* (*Normalschrift*): postwar generations of German school children use only the latter.

Toward a Standard Pronunciation

Successful efforts to standardize the pronunciation of German have lagged behind the normalization of its orthography. Reformers such as Gottsched and Adelung had urged upon all literate Germans the adoption of that pronunciation used by the educated classes of Meißen, Leipzig, and Dresden, even though their proposals were generally received with something less than enthusiasm by those living beyond the borders of the Saxon electorate. The language societies of the eighteenth century, too, had in principle supported efforts to regulate the pronunciation, but the problem of finding a commonly acceptable standard proved too difficult.

Dialectal pronunciation was (and is) in itself not necessarily associated with lack of learning or cultural attainment. The speech of both Goethe and Schiller, for instance, reflected their geographic origins. In their verses,

---

[11] One rather drastic effort at reform was attempted in 1876 with the organization of *der allgemeine ferein für fereinfachte rechtschreibung*. Never large in membership, neither popular nor successful, this society passed out of existence sometime prior to World War II.

too, they occasionally reveal their native dialects. One example is Goethe's rhyming of *neige* and *-reiche* in the sequence "Ach neige, du Schmerzensreiche . . . ," thus confirming his spirantal and voiceless articulation of intervocalic *g*. Schiller avoided reciting his poetry in public, since his Swabian accent sometimes caused him difficulties and embarrassment.

Although the goal of a standardized pronunciation was never pursued with the same sense of urgency as was that attending orthographic reform, there was reason enough to strive for some acceptable standard that could be taught in the schools, used in the pulpit and on the stage, and in general serve as a verbal counterpart to the stabilized and regulated written language. However, it was not until the last decade of the nineteenth century that the pronunciation of the *Schriftsprache* achieved widespread standardization. As a result of a conference (again held in Berlin) of phoneticians, stage directors, and public school educators, one of the participants, the Breslau professor Theodor Siebs (1862–1941), was able to publish the first edition of his *Deutsche Bühnenaussprache* (1898). As the title indicates, the book was intended to apply to the language used upon the stage. However, its precepts were soon extended to help regularize the pronunciation of the written language in all formal situations, so that in 1922 the title was amended to read *Deutsche Bühnensprache—Hochsprache*. The present title of the work (19th rev. ed., 1971) is simply *Deutsche Aussprache*.

As proposed by the reform commission, the normalized pronunciation incorporated many Low German phonetic characteristics, most obvious of which were the voiced stops [b], [d], [g], and the voiced sibilant [z], sounds generally lacking in the Upper German dialects. The stage pronunciation, in fact, did much to confirm the widely held notion that the *Hochsprache* as used in the North was "purer" than that heard in the South. A more accurate explanation, however, is that the High German literary standard was a foreign language to the native Low German speaker, who usually wrote and spoke it according to rules laid down in textbooks. The Middle and South German, on the other hand, tended to strike a compromise between his native dialect of High German and any prescribed or suggested pronunciation of the *Hochsprache*.

The student should realize that the *Bühnenaussprache* is a contrived pronunciation, which does not coincide completely with any living dialect. It must be learned. True, its authority and prestige, confirmed by the support given it in the schools, is great, so that most speakers who lay claim to a higher education adhere to its norms—at least on those occasions when they are on their linguistic good behavior. But such conformity has its limits. Siebs's *Deutsche Hochsprache,* for instance, still recommends that *r* be pronounced as an apical trill (*Zungenspitzen-r*), advising against the uvular pronunciation (*Zäpfchen-r*). The majority of native speakers, however, have for many decades employed only the uvular variety. A recent textbook of German phonetics has this to say:

> Diese alte deutsche r-Lautung [the apical trill] ist stark im Schwinden. In hochdeutscher Umgangssprache fällt heute geradezu auf, wer sie bildet. SIEBS scheint mit seiner Empfehlung . . . eine´auf die Dauer aussichtslose Position zu halten. Auch auf der Bühne hört man es kaum noch, den jungen Eleven wird es weder planmäßig beigebracht noch in der Prüfung abverlangt.[12]

The influence of such normalizing forces as compulsory education and radio and television has done much to popularize a modified version of the stage pronunciation. Nevertheless, the living language has its roots in the native soil, and the listener can usually detect traces of regional dialect in the speech of even the most sophisticated speaker. And there should be no objection to this. We disparage someone who "talks like a book"; and we object to a stilted, unnatural pronunciation, of the sort that is sometimes affected, unfortunately also off-stage, by poorly trained actors and actresses (to name the worst offenders).

Regulating the pronunciation of a language, even to the extent that it is desirable, is infinitely more difficult than controlling the orthography of whatever system of writing is used to record it, perhaps because we are not normally disturbed by differences of pronunciation as such (that is, as long as communication is not impaired). We tend to accept such variations simply as evidence of different geographical provenience or cultural background. Of course, if a given pronunciation or dialect is alleged to be socially inferior, critics will attach varying degrees of prejudice to it. But we are usually neutral in our attitude toward an accent that does nothing more than identify the speaker as a New Englander, a Westerner, or a Southerner. So it is in German, too. And there would seem to be no gain in trying to erase from the pronunciation of the standard national language those overtones which identify the speaker as a Bavarian, a Rhinelander, or a Low Saxon.

FOREIGN INFLUENCES

FRENCH

The enthusiasm with which the French Revolution (1789–1802) was greeted by many Germans accounted for a new influx of French words, most of them from the political arena. To mention but a few:

---

[12] Hans-Heinrich Wängler, *Grundriß einer Phonetik des Deutschen* (Marburg an der Lahn: N. G. Elwert Verlag, 1960), p. 88. In the second edition of 1967, Prof. Wängler changes the wording of this passage somewhat, but the sense of the quotation stands.

Brüderlichkeit (fraternité)
Freiheit (liberté)
Gleichheit (égalité)
Hochverrat (haute trahison)
Menschenrechte (droits de l'homme)
Staatsbürger (citoyen)

Other terms—some of them already in the language but now invested with new meaning—include:

Agitator
Emigrant
Emporkömmling (parvenu)
Guillotine (named after its designer, Joseph Guillotine)
liberal
Propaganda
reaktionär
Revolution
Royalist
Sanskulotte (literally, "without knee-breeches," a revolutionary
      extremist)

Many French words—outright loans as well as loan-translations—contributed to the new and ever expanding vocabulary of the German parliamentary system (itself an adaptation of the English and French models):

Abgeordneter (député)
Fraktion
Kandidat
Linke (la gauche)
Majorität
Minorität
Rechte (la droite)
Tagesordnung (ordre du jour)
Veto

Modern German, however, has not been too hospitable to its recent French loanwords. As early as 1848 a Roman Catholic priest, Father J. G. C. Brugger, directing his protests against the French elements in the German vocabulary, had founded *Der Verein für deutsche Sprachreinheit*. This particular movement met with scant success. In the summer of 1885, however, Professor Hermann Riegel, a museum director in Braunschweig, organized a society destined to exert an abiding influence: *Der allgemeine deutsche Sprachverein* (now *Die Gesellschaft für deutsche Sprache*). Though its program was broader, more realistic and conciliatory than that proposed by Father Riegel, it still actively encouraged the elimination of French loans.

An important step in this direction was taken in 1874 when the post-master-general, Heinrich von Stephan (1831–97), issued a series of directives deleting more than seven hundred French terms used in the postal and telephone services of Germany. At that time such loanwords as *Korrespondenzkarte, Kuvert, poste restante,* and *Telefon* were replaced by *Postkarte, Umschlag, postlagernd,* and *Fernsprecher,* respectively. The members of the new *Sprachverein* were so pleased with Postmaster von Stephan's reforms that they conferred upon him the society's first honorary membership.

In the twentieth century the National Socialists led the fight against foreign elements (especially French) in the vocabulary. The national railroad had early Germanized many heretofore French terms: *Billet, Coupé, Perron, Wagon-lit, Wagon-restaurant,* for example, were changed to *Fahrkarte, Abteil, Bahnsteig, Schlafwagen, Speisewagen.*

Military terminology had long been predominantly French, though the hostilities of 1914–18 wrought many changes. Almost total purging of what remained of the French heritage was effected under the Nazis, who introduced a new and thoroughly "Germanic" military nomenclature, much of which was later dropped.

ENGLISH

Prior to the nineteenth century, English influence upon the German vocabulary was limited to that exerted by literary movements and by the English parliamentary system of government. Borrowings from the latter field include:

> *Adresse*
> *Bill*
> *ein Gesetz lesen* "to read a bill"
> *ein Gesetz einbringen* "to introduce a bill"
> *Sprecher*
> *zur Ordnung rufen* "to call to order"
> *zur Sache!* "the question!"

The nineteenth century, however, witnessed a major influx of English words from many fields, especially those of commerce, fashion, foods, and sports. As might be expected, the Anglo-Saxon influence has always been stronger in northern Germany, especially in the great commercial centers along the Baltic. A representative list of loanwords would include such items as the following:

Banknote
Beefsteak
Bonds
Buchmacher "booky"
Champion
Derby
Export
fashionable
Fußball
Gentleman
Pantry
Partner
Plaid (a shawl or lap rug made of plaid)
Pullover
Pump (high-heeled shoe)
Rekord
Roastbeef
Scheck
Slipper
Smoking (dinner jacket)
Sport
Start
Sweater
Tennis
Tip
Trainer
Trust
Ulster (a long loose overcoat)

AMERICAN

The influence of American English upon German is, with few exceptions, a twentieth-century phenomenon; in fact, one might almost say a post-World War II phenomenon. From about 1945 to the present, the number of American words and phrases taken over into German has reached astounding proportions. There is no accurate way of judging how many of these can be considered "borrowed"; some have been translated, but most of them are probably *Gastwörter* that will one day wear out their welcome. Much of the English used by the communications media to advertise the wares of their clients is lost upon many Germans, except to the extent that they may consider such language chic and sophisticated. Many young Germans, who glibly parrot words and expressions related to the American entertainment world, use them in a way that reveals their uncertainty as to what they actually mean. Sometimes, on the other hand, an American term will be invested with a new, and presumably, specifically German meaning. For example, the word "hot" is listed in the 1968 edition of Gerhard Wahrig's *Deutsches Wörterbuch* (Gütersloh: Bertelsmann-Lexikon Verlag) as a masculine noun with the meaning "leidenschaftlich bewegte Improvisation und Synkopierung einer Jazzmelodie." Whereas the jargon of American musicians contains such expressions as a "hot break" or a "hot lick," the use of the word "hot" as a noun in this sense is foreign to the American idiom.

Even now, a full generation after World War II, the inundation continues; the number of American words and expressions that has since entered the German language must run into the hundreds of thousands. Some of them by now can no doubt be considered "eingedeutscht," that is, German for all practical purposes. The following brief list was compiled at random from the Wahrig dictionary. Not one of these words occurs in the 1939 edition of *Heath's New German and English Dictionary*, ed. Karl Breul, revised and enlarged by J. Heron Lepper and Rudolf Kotterhahn (Funk & Wagnalls Company; New York):[13]

Babysitter
Band (feminine; pronounced as in English "dance band")
Bestseller
Blizzard
Bluejeans
Blues (music)
Boß
Break (music)
Coca-Cola
Computer
Creek (in its American usage as a stream of water smaller than a river)
Crew
Cross-Country (used as a noun: "a cross-country race")
Date (appointment)
Drift (and *driften*)
Drink
Drive-in-Kino
Jet
Job
Jury (especially a committee of judges for art shows, sporting events, etc.)
Killer (and *killen*)
Layout (and *Layouter*)

[13] Whether one or the other of these terms may actually have been borrowed from British English, I cannot say.

Lunch (and *lunchen*)
Make-up
Manager (and *managen*)
Mixer (and *mixen*) (not only in the sense of "mixing drinks" but also
   to mean "mixing" sound channels when recording music)
News
Non-stop-Flug
Quiz (and *Quizmeister*)
Rock'n'Roll
Striptease
Swing (and *swingen*) (dance)
Target
Teenager[14]
Travellerscheck
Trend

There is increasing evidence that American English is beginning to exert
an influence upon German that goes beyond mere vocabulary borrowing.
For instance, the number of loan translations (see p. 69, n. 20) is slowly
growing. Examples of this can be illustrated by such phrases as: *die Schau
stehlen*, "to steal the show"; *einmal mehr*, "once more" or "[play it] one
more time"; *herumhängen*, "to hang around [a person or place]"; and
überlappen, "to overlap."

American influence is also obvious in those cases where German has
adopted the English version of two "false cognates": words similar in form
but with different meanings (compare the French expression for such
wordpairs: *faux amis* or "false friends"). Thomas Mann wrote this sentence: "Es ist ein Glück, daß er das alles so recht wohl nicht mehr realisiert
hat." *Realisieren* has long been part of the German vocabulary, but with
meanings other than "to understand fully." Another such "false friend"
is the word *Hintergrund*, originally a loan translation from British English
in the sense of "background of a painting, of a theatrical scene, or of a
picture." The term now occurs frequently with the heretofore un-German
meaning: "the totality of a person's experience, knowledge, and education," as in the sentence "Herr Schmidt verfügte über einen liberalen
Hintergrund."

Other examples of this kind are *kontrollieren*, "to supervise, inspect,"
used in the sense of English *control*: "Er kann sich überhaupt nicht mehr
kontrollieren"; or *spenden*, "to donate, give generously," now occasionally

[14] Also modeled after Eng. *-teen* is the German *Twen*, "a person in his twenties."
To my knowledge this analogical formation does not occur in English.

employed with the English meaning "to expend funds": "Sie spenden mehr [Geld] als früher." And in casual, spoken German there is the marked tendency to overwork the adjective-adverb *wirklich*, "true, genuine, real," as the equivalent of the noncommittal English conversational rejoinder "really" ("Oh, really?"). Although German *wirklich* does include this meaning (*meinst Du wirklich?* "Do you really think so?"), the more frequently occurring responses (polite, but usually indifferent) are expressions such as *so, tatsächlich, was Sie nicht sagen*, and the like.

American influence is also noticeable in the choice of prepositions used by some Germans. The following Americanisms are now fairly commonplace: *in 1972* rather than *im Jahre 1972; in anderen Worten* rather than *mit anderen Worten; in Deutsch* rather than *auf Deutsch* ("Say it *in German*"); *Mitleid für ihn haben* instead of *Mitleid mit ihm haben* ("to have sympathy *for him*"); *für drei Monate* instead of *drei Monate* or *drei Monate lang* ("*for* three months").

Finally, the doubling of an adverb or adjective in English to lend an iterative effect to the simplex is being carried over into German: *wieder und wieder* (instead of *immer wieder*) "again and again"; *dunkler und dunkler* (instead of *immer dunkler*) "darker and darker."[15]

RUSSIAN

Obviously of greater influence in the German Democratic Republic (DDR), Russian and the politically oriented idiom of Communism are also leaving their mark upon German. However, the number of Russian loan words in the language is still quite modest. The following list contains some of the more frequently occurring borrowings. Those words marked with an asterisk are also now commonly used in the Federal Republic (BDR):[16]

Apparatschik "party functionary"

*Exponat "article for display at expositions, in museums, etc."

*Kombinat "two or more industrial plants contributing to a common production program"

---

[15] All these Americanisms have been recorded in the speech and writing of native Germans living in Germany, and are neither isolated occurrences, nor, as one might well imagine, instances of an English speaker's faulty command of the German idiom. The examples were culled from two sources: Gustav Korlén, "Führt die Teilung Deutschlands zur Sprachspaltung?" *Der Deutschunterricht* 21, no. 5 (October 1969): 5–23, *passim*; and Hugo Moser, *Sprachliche Folgen der politischen Teilung Deutschlands* (Düsseldorf: Pädagogischer Verlag Schwann, 1962), p. 10.

[16] These examples are taken from Hugo Moser, *Sprachliche Folgen*, pp. 11–30, *passim*; and Ernst G. Riemschneider, *Veränderungen der deutschen Sprache in der sowjetisch besetzten Zone Deutschlands seit 1945* (Düsseldorf: Pädagogischer Verlag Schwann, 1963), pp. 14–32, *passim*.

Komsomol "Communist youth organization"
Kursant "one who is taking a training course of some kind"
Natschalnik "a superior [*Vorgesetzter*] (at work)"
Novator "one who devises and/or introduces new and more productive working methods"
Spartakiade "an international sports tournament"
Sputnik (literally, "companion") "man-made earth satellite"
Subotnik "a worker who donates his services voluntarily to the State"
Towaritsch "comrade"

To this list may be added a somewhat larger inventory of loan translations, such as:

Aktivist "an exemplary and politically committed worker"
Brigade "smallest organizational unit of workers, technicians, etc." (from French *brigade*)
Held der Arbeit "honorary title conferred upon outstanding workers"
Kader "highly trained and politically reliable key personnel" (from French *cadre*)
Kollektiv "collective farm" (translates Russ. *Kolxoz*; now usually referred to as an LPG: *Landwirtschaftliche Produktionsgenossenschaft*)
Kulturhaus (also *Kulturpalast*) "recreational hall, town hall"
Praktizismus "emphasis upon practical problems to the neglect of ideology and political theory"
Neuerer (translates Russ. *novator*; see under "borrowings" above for definition)
Verdienter (*Arzt, Lehrer*, etc.) *des Volkes* "honorary title for distinguished and outstanding service by a professional"

Interesting, too, is the choice of prefixes and suffixes whereby new noun-compounds are formed. Here the difference is only one of degree, since similar examples (though usually not so many) can be found in the German of the BRD. Compounds in which the first element is *neu-* are common: *Neubürger, Neulehrer, Neusiedler*. Also popular are compounds involving *best-* : *Bestarbeiter, Beststudent*. Quite distinctive are the compounds with *nur-* : *Nurfachleute, Nurgelehrtentum, Nurkünstlertum*. And exhibiting direct Russian influence are the formations with *-ant: Kapitulant, Kursant*.

The fact that there have been two editions—one for the West and one for the East—of the popular and authoritative *Duden* dictionary (see p. 172, no. 9 for more information) for over twenty years, is in itself evidence of substantial semantic differences between the German spoken and written in the BRD and the DDR. A few examples, extreme enough to be illustrative, will suffice:

West-Duden (BRD)	*East-Duden* (DDR)
Aktiv: "Grammar: action word, verb"	"1. Workers' group that collectively strives for the fulfillment of social, political, economic, and cultural goals; 2. Grammar: verb"
Blasphemie: "reviling God: insulting remarks about something sacred"	"reviling, insulting remarks about something of deep significance"
Kapitalismus: "individualistic economic and social order, whose driving force is the individual's desire to succeed"	"economic and social order that rests upon private ownership of means of production and upon exploitation of the worker"
Verelendung: (no entry)	"legally sanctioned and consistent worsening of workers' living conditions in a capitalistic state"

The influence of the *Russian language* upon German then, as compared with that exerted by American English, is still indeed minimal; however, the *semantic* influence of Communist political ideology is considerable. This sort of influence may well turn out to be the more pervasive and enduring, because it derives its strength and authority from the German language itself; even the neologisms are, with rare exceptions, of native German stock. For the rest, the old familiar words are simply given new or modified meanings which can easily be given the status of dictionary definitions that meet with official approval. The schools will carry on from there.

POLITICAL, INDUSTRIAL, AND MILITARY INFLUENCES

During the nineteenth century Germany emerged as a modern industrialized nation and as a major political and military power. The language mirrors all these changes and developments, some of which we shall now mention.

The turbulent political struggles of the last century either introduced or gave expanded meanings to expressions such as these:

Attentäter	*maßregeln*
Brandredner	*Mußpreuße*

freisinnig	*Polizeistadt*
gesinnungstüchtig	*radikal*
großdeutsch	*Säbelregiment*
Klassenkampf	*Sozialdemokrat*
kleindeutsch	*Streik*
Kommunismus	*Streikbrecher*
Krach	*Zivilcourage*
Kulturkampf	*Zukunftsstaat*

The extent to which the mixture of slang, jargon, and "officialese" known as *Nazideutsch* will leave its traces in the language cannot yet be determined. Much of it was a stylistic and esthetic atrocity—a characteristic which seems to mark the bureaucrat's use of language the world over. Terms that smack too strongly of the Hitler era, though in themselves innocent, tend to be avoided by many speakers and writers: *Bewährung, Gleichschaltung, Rasse, Reich* (with reference to Germany), and many compounds of *Volk, such as völkisch, volksfeind, volksfremd.*[17] (The one happy exception is *Volkswagen,* which has become almost a household word in the United States.)

The recent technological advances and discoveries which have created Germany's modern industrialized society resulted in new words such as *Atom(-kern, -kraft), Benzin, Dampfheizung, Dynamo, Eisenbahn, Fernsehen, Flugzeug, Hochspannung, Kraftwagen, Kunststoff, Lokomotive, Raketen (-antrieb, -flugzeug), Rundfunk.* And the surnames of many people who in one way or another were involved in the design or manufacture of some well-known product have now become designations for the products themselves: *Hohner* (harmonicas), *Junghans* (watches), *Luger* (pistols), *Pfaff* (sewing machines), *Porsche* (automobiles), *Zeiß* (lenses), and so forth.

The two great wars of the twentieth century left their mark on the German language. From World War I stem such words as *Abwehrschlacht, Bomber, Bunker, Flak* (abbreviated from *F Lieger Abwehr Kanone*),[18] *Niemandsland, Schützengraben, Trommelfeuer, U[ntersee]boot.*

We are too close to the Second World War to evaluate its linguistic impact. The everyday speech of the men and women who saw military service during those years will always be colored by expressions from that era, but we cannot yet say how much of this language will be accepted into

---

[17] An intriguing account of the language of National Socialism is contained in the book by Viktor Kemperer, *LTI: Die unbewältigte Sprache. Aus dem Notizbuch eines Philologen* (Munich, 1969). The letters, which served as the cryptic title of the journal he kept during the war years, stand for *Lingua Tertii Imperii,* "Language of the Third Reich."

[18] Neologisms constructed in this way are called "blends" or "portmanteau words."

the speech of later generations. Probably very little of it, if we can judge from the past. A few of the words born of World War II are: *Blitzkrieg, Bodenmannschaft, Bombenteppich, Leuchtfallschirm, Luftschutzkeller, Panzer(-division, -schiff, -wagen), Sirene, Stuka* (abbreviated from *STUrzKAmpfflugzeug*), *Sturmtruppen, verdunkeln* (and *entdunkeln*), *warnen* (and *entwarnen*),[19] *Wuwa* (abbreviated from *WUnderW Affe*).

Inherited from the early postwar days of privation and hunger—and now apparently fixed in the contemporary language—are words such as *hamstern*, "to horde (food, money, etc.)"; *schieben*, "to engage in smuggling or profiteering"; *Schlange stehen*, "to stand in line"; *strecken* "to 'stretch' foodstuffs by adding some other, usually more available, ingredient (potatoes to bread dough, e.g.)." From the same era stem *Ersatz, Kriegsgewinnler, Rationierung, Schleichhandel.*

DIE UMGANGSSPRACHE

That form of the language which is characterized in speech by a pronunciation and vocabulary containing local and regional elements is referred to as the *Umgangssprache,* though the term is not absolute. There is no precise dividing line separating either *Hochsprache* from *Umgangssprache,* or *Umgangssprache* from *Mundart;* the one merges almost imperceptibly into the other.

Because there is no single, commonly accepted term for that variety of the *written* language which also avails itself of an easy, often informal, even colloquial style, we shall let the word *Umgangssprache* serve for both, though the student should be aware that the expression usually refers only to the spoken idiom.

Writers for the daily press, especially those reporting on the happenings of the hour, could spend little time polishing their prose. Circumstances forced them to develop a straightforward, uncomplicated style that in many ways approached the structure of everyday speech, with its easy syntactic transitions, its colloquialisms, and its clichés. But this was, after all, the language of the people, and the newspapers were printed for them. The philosopher Arthur Schopenhauer (1788–1860) considered journalism to be the lowest form of literary activity, and from his point of view such

---

[19] *Verdunkeln* and *warnen* are by no means of recent origin. *Entdunkeln* and *entwarnen*, though of later coinage, are likewise not new: *entdunkeln*, for instance, occurs around 1800 in the sense of "clear up, brighten up." *Entwarnen* is used about fifty years later with the meaning "to warn someone of something." However, as used during World War II to signal an air raid "alert" (*warnen*), and to "black out" all sources of light (*verdunkeln*), and then to sound the "all clear" (*entwarnen*), and raise the blackout shades (*entdunkeln*), these words took on what must be considered new meanings.

condemnation may have seemed deserved.[20] Nevertheless, the journalistic style was much copied: it was easy to read and "modern."

As its name indicates, the literary movement known as "Naturalism" (approximately 1880 to 1900) was primarily concerned with analyzing life as the dramatist thought it really was—especially those aspects which, because of their harshness and ugliness, were seldom touched upon by the artist and not discussed in polite society. Naturalism was much concerned with problems of social injustices and prejudices.

The most famous representative of the movement in Germany was the Silesian dramatist, Gerhart Hauptmann (1862–1946). From a linguistic standpoint, Hauptmann was one of the first High German playwrights of the modern era to employ dialect as a medium for serious dramatic dialogue.[21] His first work to be performed, *Vor Sonnenaufgang* (1889), contains passages in the Silesian dialect. Another of his major dramas, *Die Weber* (1892), was first written entirely in that dialect, even to its title, *De Waber*. But even when written in standard High German, the language of the dramas of Naturalism was that of the *Umgangssprache*, a drastic departure from the Classical norm. From that day on, dramatists could let their characters use the easy cadences and the popular vocabulary of everyday speech, even if the theme were one of high tragedy.

The third impetus to the rise of the colloquial languages was two speech societies (none of the *Sprachgesellschaften* of the seventeenth century still existed by this time). The major goal of Father J. G. C. Brugger's *Verein für deutsche Sprachreinheit* was to purge all foreign elements (especially French) from the vocabulary. However, the literary and cultural fashion of the day was such that responsible people in high places were not particularly scandalized by French influences upon the language,[22] and Father Brugger's movement came to naught.

The second and by far more important of the nineteenth-century language societies was Hermann Riegel's *Allgemeiner deutscher Sprach-*

---

[20] See the chapter "Über Schriftstellerei und Stil" in *Arthur Schopenhauers Sämtliche Werke*, ed. Arthur Hübscher (2nd ed.; Wiesbaden: F. A. Brockhaus, 1946–50), VI, 532–87 (in Vol. II of "Parerga und Paralipomena").

[21] German has a rich and venerable tradition of dialect literature (see Alfred Lowack, *Die Mundarten im hochdeutschen Drama* [Leipzig, 1905]). In Hauptmann's time, however, dialect had long been discarded as the conventional vehicle for serious High German theater. The Naturalistic dramatists' use of dialect, moreover, was not at all intended to evoke humor or folksiness, but was meant to heighten and intensify the stark dramatic effects for which they were striving.

[22] As late as 1862, Prince Otto von Bismarck (1815-98), while serving as ambassador to the court of Alexander II of Russia, made his official reports to the Prussian Foreign Office in French.

verein. Though it, too, encouraged the elimination of French loanwords (but not out of prejudice, its members insisted), the society's program included several other objectives, the most far-reaching of which was "die Pflege und die Hebung der deutschen Sprache." Notice that the reference is not to the already established literary medium of the Classical Age— which could only be imitated and preserved, not cultivated and elevated— but that the object of their concern was simply "the German language"; in other words, the *Umgangssprache*. They considered it their duty to keep that language in a state of optimum efficiency, pruning away any features or accretions which might weaken or mar it, striving always to increase its capabilities and prestige. And, in spite of certain excesses, the society has done much good.

These three forces—the popular press, the theater of Naturalism, and the *Allgemeiner deutscher Sprachverein*—worked together to enhance the status of the colloquial standard language, so that today the so-called "gebildete Umgangssprache" in its various regional manifestations is probably as highly regarded, and certainly as widely used, as the bookish and sometimes rather remote *Hochsprache*.

The colloquial standard is another step toward a true *Einheitssprache*: a uniform language, both written and spoken, for all German-speaking people. Whether this goal will—or should—be realized is another matter. But the local dialects seem headed for ultimate extinction. On the other hand, few people want the pronunciation and use of their native language arbitrarily decided and enforced by an academy, a commission, or a Ministry of Education. Living languages cannot be controlled in this way, as has been amply demonstrated by the limited effectiveness of the French and Spanish Academies, even when they restrict their purview, as they actually do, to the written language. Perhaps a cultivated colloquial standard, differing in details but agreeing in essentials, is the closest approximation to an acceptable yet workable *Einheitssprache*. If so, then Germany is on its way toward realizing this goal.

PRINCIPAL HIGH GERMAN DIALECTS

To describe the High German dialects in more than a few pages would go beyond the scope of this book.[23] Dialectology is an involved study at best. Even the basic question of how to establish a dialect boundary must be given an arbitrary answer, depending upon one's point of view and the

---

[23] The best general study in English is R. E. Keller's *German Dialects* (Manchester: The University Press, 1961). The following discussion owes much to Keller's presentation.

purpose of the work at hand. Summaries consisting of selected illustrations can have only a restricted validity, for dialects, unless impeded by some natural barrier, have no sharp boundaries, but rather so-called "Rand-gebiete," which are transition zones linking together neighboring dialects. Furthermore, individual differences—age, social background, educational level—affect the language of any given area.

Since the emphasis in this book has been on the historical development of the language, our usual reference for purposes of comparison will be either to the phonology reconstructed for Proto-Germanic or to Middle High German. If the reference is to "High German," it is the standard *Hochsprache* which is meant.

For citing phonemes or words from an earlier linguistic period (even if reconstructed, as in the case of Proto-Germanic), normal orthography set in italics is used. Examples from the modern dialects are placed within square brackets and written in phonetic transcription (see Chapter VIII for the phonetic alphabet). Following the words given in phonetic transcription is the standard High German form.

The geographical location of the Modern High German dialects is given in Map 4 (Appendix 2).

LOW GERMAN

Linguistically, the Low German dialect area is divided into Low Saxon and Low Franconian; of these, only Low Saxon is geographically "German."[24] They have in common the feature that sets them apart from the High German dialects—they have undergone none of the consonant changes associated with the High German consonant shift.

MIDDLE GERMAN

Of the three western Franconian dialects, the Mosel and Rhenish subdivisions may be grouped under the rubric "Middle Franconian." Ripuarian, though sharing most of the features of the other two, is in some respects different.

General characteristics (Middle Franconian).

1. MHG *p, t, k* and *b, d, g* tend to coalesce into a single class of voiceless lenis stops:

    [b̥lɒːd̥s] "Platz," [d̥uːn] "tun," [grɑŋg] "krank"

2. PGmc. *t* in final position remains unshifted in several common words:

    [ɒləd̥] "alles," [d̥ɒd̥] "das," [d̥ɪd̥] "dies," [vɒd̥] "was"

---

[24] The Low German and Low Franconian dialects are not described. The student is referred to the standard handbooks listed in the bibliography.

3. PGmc. *p* in initial position, medially when doubled, and finally, remains unshifted:

[pʻɒːḍ] "Pfad," [æḇəl] "Apfel," [uḇ] "auf"

4. MHG [ç] occurs as [š]:

[laɪš] "Leiche," [gəfɛlɪš] "gefällig"

5. MHG *b* intervocalically occurs as [v] (there is also a bilabial variant):

[ɒːvə] "aber"

6. MHG *t, d* occur intervocalically as [r] or [R]:

[muːrə] "Mutter," [fɒːrə] "Vater"

7. MHG *en* in final unstressed position occurs as [ə]:

[hɑvə] "haben"

8. MHG *â* occurs as [ɒ] and [o]:

[šḇrɒːχ] "Sprache," [noːχ] "nach"

9. PGmc. *p*, when preceded by *l* or *r*, remains unshifted in Ripuarian, a characteristic which sets off Ripuarian from Mosel and Rhenish Franconian:

[vɛəḇə] "werfen," [hɛlḇə] "helfen"

Thuringian, Upper Saxon, and Silesian constitute the East Middle German dialects. As shown on the map, a small area in East Prussia was, as late as the 1930's, still inhabited by speakers of a Middle German dialect (see p. 108, n. 8, for explanation), though the rest of East Prussia, to the extent that its inhabitants use dialect, belongs to the Low German speech area. Southwestern and southern Thuringia are transition zones (*Übergangszonen*), the dialects of the former sharing many features with Middle Franconian (especially with the Rhenish or Hessian variety), the latter having much in common with East Franconian.

General characteristics.

1. MHG *p, t, k* and *b, d, g* are kept apart in Silesian, but tend to merge into a single series of voiceless lenis stops in Thuringian and Upper Saxon (as in the Middle Franconian examples under 1).

2. (a) PGmc. *p* in initial position occurs as [f]:

[fɛəḍ] "Pferd"

(b) PGmc. *p*, when preceded by *m*, remains unshifted:

[šḍumḇ] "stumpf"

3. MHG *en* in final unstressed position is either elided or occurs as [ə]; in southern Silesia a low central vowel occurs in this position:

[hɛlfa] "helfen"

4. MHG *ei* and *au* occur as [e] and [o]:

[ḇeːn] "Bein," [ḇoːm] "Baum"

5. MHG *ü* and *ö* occur without labialization:
   [b̥iːnə] "Bühne," [šeːn] "schön"
6. MHG *ě* occurs as [a] in Thuringian and Upper Saxon:
   [fə̥gasə] "vergessen"
7. MHG *ê* and *ô* occur in Silesian as [i] and [u]:
   [šniː] "Schnee," [ruːt] "rot"
8. MHG *ǒ* occurs in Silesian as [u]:
   [zulə] "sollen"

UPPER GERMAN

Though historically a Middle German dialect, East Franconian—also known as *Hochfränkisch* and *Oberfränkisch* is now more appropriately discussed under the heading of Upper German. Of all the High German dialects, its sound system most nearly agrees with that of the *Hochsprache*. The reason is not hard to determine: East Franconia is centrally located. Whenever compromises between Middle and Upper German were made, the results tended to approximate the phonology native to East Franconian. Of course, many differences distinguish the regional dialect from the standard language, but by comparison to the diversities of the Alemannic and Bavarian dialects, East Franconian presents few problems. We shall, therefore, in this brief survey, limit our observations to Alemannic and Bavarian.

General characteristics (Alemannic).

1. MHG *ie, uo, üe* are generally preserved:
   [liə̯b̥] "lieb," [b̥uə̯b̥] "Bube," [fyəs] "Füße"
2. MHG *î, û, iu* (= [y]) are generally preserved:
   [tsiːt] "Zeit," [uːf] "auf," [tyːtš] "deutsch"
3. MHG *e* resulting from secondary umlaut (see p. 85, n. 3)—as well as certain other MHG *e*-sounds—tends to be pronounced [æ]:
   [b̥æːχ] "Bäche"
4. MHG *en* in final unstressed position occurs as [ə]:
   [fɒːrə] "fahren"
5. PGmc. *k* in most positions is shifted to the corresponding spirant, occurring as [χ], whether in the environment of front or back vowels:
   [χɪnt] "Kind," [χaštə] "Kasten"
6. PGmc. *k*, when followed by *n*, when doubled, or when preceded by the prefix *ge-*, is shifted in the Upper Alemannic (as well as in some of the Upper Bavarian) dialects to the affricate [kχ]:
   [d̥æŋkχə] "denken," [d̥ɪkχ] "dick," [kχænə] "gekennen" (dialect)

7. MHG *p* and *t* tend to occur as unaspirated fortis stops, especially in the Upper Alemannic dialects:

    [plɒts] "Platz," [trɛtə] "treten"

8. MHG *b*, *d*, *g* tend to occur as unaspirated lenis stops, especially in the Lower Alemannic dialects:[25]

    [b̥uəb̥] "Bube," [lɛːd̥ə] "Leder," [æɪg̥ə] "eigen"

9. MHG *sp* and *st* occur as [šp] and [št] in all positions:

    [g̥šlɒg̥ə] "geschlagen," [ɪšt] "ist"

10. The MHG prefixes *be-* and *ge-* occur usually without the vowel:

    [b̥šæftɪχt] "beschäftigt," [gvɒχsə] "gewachsen"

11. MHG *n*, when immediately followed by *s* or *f*, is usually elided:

    [føɪf] "fünf," [øɪs] "uns"

12. HG *gehen* and *stehen* occur as [gɒːn] and [štɒːn]

13. The HG diminutive suffix *-lein* occurs as [lə], [li], [la]:

    [mæɪdlə] "Mädlein" (*Mädchen*)

14. In Alsatian, MHG *û*, *uo*, and *ou* are usually palatalized to [y], [yə], [øɪ]:

    [hyːs] "Haus," [g̥yəd̥] "gut," [g̥øɪfə] "kaufen"

15. Swabian diphthongizes MHG *î*, *û*, *û* to [əɪ], [əu], [øʊ]:

    [b̥ləɪvə] "bleiben," [həus] "Haus," [møʊlə] "Mühle"

16. Swabian elides MHG *n* when followed immediately by *s*, and nasalizes the preceding vowel:

    [gãs] "Gans"

General characteristics (Bavarian). Dialectologists recognize three major dialect areas: north, middle, and south. Each of these includes many sub-groups. The dialect spoken north of the Danube and from the Lech River in the west to the Czechoslovakian border in the east is called *North Bavarian* (or sometimes *Lower Bavarian*). Just to the south, in an area encompassing much of the provinces of Lower Bavaria, Upper Bavaria, and Lower Austria, lies *Middle Bavarian* (which includes the dialects native to Munich and Vienna). *South Bavarian*, which has about the same east–west boundaries, is located for the most part in the Bavarian and Austrian Alps. It includes the dialects spoken in the Austrian provinces of Kärnten, Tyrol, Salzburg, and Steiermark (the dialect of Vorarlberg is not

---

[25] Determining the precise phonetic quality and the distribution patterns of the labial, alveolar, and velar stops in the various Alemannic dialects is a complicated task. As a rule of thumb one may say that, though these sounds are unaspirated and voiceless (at least relatively so) throughout the entire Alemannic area, their pronunciation in the upper (southern) dialects tends to be decidedly fortis, whereas the lower (northern) dialects employ mainly, sometimes exclusively, a lenis articulation.

Bavarian, but rather Low Alemannic). We shall restrict our discussion largely to the characteristics of *Middle Bavarian*:

1. MHG *ie*, *uo*, *üe* in general remain, though *üe* is now pronounced without lip-rounding:

    [liɒb̥] "lieb." [bluɒd̥] "Blut." [briɒda] "Brüder"

2. MHG *î*, *û*, *iu* (= *û*) occur as [aɛ], [ao], [aɛ]:

    [dzaɛd̥] "Zeit." [haos] "Haus." [haɛza] "Häuser"

3. MHG *ö* and *ü* occur as [ɛ] and [ɪ]:

    [meçd̥] "möchte." [hɪb̥š] "hübsch"

4. MHG *ei* occurs as [ɒ]

    [lɒɒb̥] "Leib"

5. MHG *e*, which arose by secondary umlaut (sometimes recorded as *ä*; see p. 171, note 5), occurs as [a] or, less often, as [æ]:

    [maχd] "Mächte"

6. MHG final *e* is dropped (see example just cited under 5).

7. MHG *p*, *t*, *k* and *b*, *d*, *g* do not contrast initially, but occur as a single series of voiceless, semifortis stops:

    [d̥ɔg] "Tag." [b̥ɛng] "Berg." [guɒd̥] "gut"

8. MHG *p*, *t*, *k* and *b*, *d*, *g* tend to occur medially and finally as a single series of voiceless, lenis stops:

    [liɒb̥] "lieb." [d̥saɛd̥] "Zeit." [d̥ɔg] "Tag"

9. HG *gehen* and *stehen* are pronounced [ge̥ː]. [šd̥ẽː]

10. The HG diminutive suffix -*lein* occurs as [əl]:

    [mʊd̥əl] "Mädchen" (the exact HG equivalent would be *Mädlein*).

THE GERMAN SPEECH ATLAS

We shall close our discussion of the German dialects with a few remarks about the most ambitious modern attempt to record the spoken varieties of the language: a project which resulted in the publication of the monumental *Deutscher Sprachatlas* (DSA).

In 1876 the librarian of the University of Marburg, Georg Wenker (1852–1911), began a survey, first of the dialects spoken in the Rhineland around Düsseldorf, but later including all of central and northern Germany. He prepared a questionnaire consisting of forty sentences composed in the literary standard, sending copies to about forty thousand schools. The teachers were asked to reproduce as best they could in conventional script the local dialectal equivalents of the printed sentences. In 1881 Wenker published the first six maps of his *Sprachatlas von Nord- und Mitteldeutschland*, but this was just the beginning. Aided by government funds, he expanded his investigation to include the entire *Reich*. Eventually, more than 350,000 replies to his questionnaire were received, and the arduous task of recording the data on maps was started. Under Wenker's successor, Ferdinand Wrede (1863–1934), publication of the *Deutscher Sprachatlas* started in 1926; it was finally completed in 1956.

The DSA provides little information about either morphology or vocabulary, however, since it was primarily designed to record only the phonology. To help overcome this deficiency, Walther Mitzka, one of Wrede's successors, sent out in 1938 another questionnaire designed to elicit everyday vocabulary. The results of this project are being published in another atlas, the *Deutscher Wortatlas* (1951ff.), under the editorship of Mitzka and Ludwig Erich Schmitt.

A somewhat different undertaking of great promise is that of the *Deutsches Spracharchiv* in Münster, founded and directed by Eberhardt Zwirner, which contains a library of taped recordings (*Lautbibliothek der deutschen Mundarten*) made in over two thousand localities in West Germany. Studies based upon this material are being published from time to time.

In addition to the resources just mentioned, there are many other atlases, dictionaries, and grammars devoted to a single dialect or group of closely related dialects. Information about them can be found in the standard bibliographical handbooks. There are also two journals devoted to research in dialectology: *Zeitschrift für deutsche Sprache* (formerly *Zeitschrift für Mundartforschung*) and *Zeitschrift für Dialektologie und Linguistik* (formerly *Zeitschrift für deutsche Wortforschung*).

New Directions in German Grammar

The past twenty-five years have seen the first fundamental changes in theoretical and applied German grammar since the eighteenth century. And these changes are reflected to a surprising degree in the grammars currently being used in most primary and secondary school systems of the two Germanies, Austria, and Switzerland, as well as in the courses of instruction offered by the colleges of education in those countries.

The impetus was provided in 1949–50, when Leo Weisgerber published a four-volume work bearing the title *Von den Kräften der deutschen Sprache* (in the third edition of 1962, the four volumes were reduced to two: *Grundzüge der inhaltbezogenen Grammatik* and *Die sprachliche Gestaltung der Welt*). As early as the 1920's, Weisgerber was already developing a fresh approach to language analysis (his *Muttersprache und Geistesbildung* was published in 1929), influenced to a considerable extent by Wilhelm von Humboldt's (1767–1835) "relativity principle": the idea that our view of life and of our environment is largely conditioned by the language we speak; our minds are cast in a certain linguistic mold which predetermines our interpretation of the world about us ("sprachbedingte Weltanschauung").

Weisgerber's works are highly theoretical and make for difficult reading; his basic premise, however, is clear: German should be analyzed on its own terms, not according to a grammatical system inherited from Latin, Greek, or any other language. Holding the noun to be the nucleus of the sentence, he suggested techniques whereby this syntactic unit could be analyzed into its discrete elements. These procedures depended largely upon semantic distinctions for their validity: they were "meaning oriented" (*inhaltbezogen*) rather than "structurally oriented" (*formbezogen* or *lautbezogen*). Weisgerber's theories, interpreted and enthusiastically applied by many young grammarians during the 1950's, broke dramatically with traditional German grammar as presented in the last prewar edition (1935) of the prestigious and conservative *Duden: Grammatik der deutschen Sprache*, itself largely an orthodox restatement of a long-standing classic first published in 1850: Friedrich Bauer's *Grundzüge der neuhochdeutschen Grammatik für die unteren und mittleren Klassen höherer Bildungsanstalten*, a treatise uncompromisingly committed to the age-old principles of "philosophical" or "logical" grammar as handed down by such authorities as Schottel and Gottsched (see pp. 140–45).

Hardly had Weisgerber's *inhaltbezogene Grammatik* had time to start giving new direction to the study of grammar in West Germany (we shall discuss the situation in East Germany a bit later on), when a new and fundamentally different approach to grammatical analysis attracted the attention of linguists and grammarians alike. Reference is made to the first edition (1952) of Hans Glinz's epochal work, *Die innere Form des Deutschen*. In order to appreciate the significance and impact of this grammar, we must briefly review the development of a new school of linguistics which took shape in the 1930's and 1940's.

During these years a new and controversial, but highly productive approach to linguistic analysis, now usually referred to as "structuralism," had arisen, largely outside Germany. The groundwork underlying this method for investigating and describing language had been laid for the most part by such scholars as the Pole, J. Baudouin de Courtenay (1845–1929)—christened Jan Ignacy Niecislaw—and the Swiss, Ferdinand de Saussure (1857–1913). Until the war put a stop to most theoretical research throughout Europe, there were several groups of scholars working on and contributing to this new "structural" linguistics. One of the most creative and seminal groups was the so-called "Prague Circle," perhaps most frequently identified with the name of one of its several brilliant theoreticians, Count Nikolas Trubetzkoy (1880–1938).

During the troubled and chaotic decade of the 1940's, the United States became one of the few places where linguistic research could still be conducted on a significant scale. Two names most intimately associated with the new discipline during its formative years in this country are those of the Americans, Edward Sapir (1884–1939) and Leonard Bloomfield (1887–1949). They advocated a kind of structuralism which attempted to analyze language primarily, if not exclusively, in terms of form and of formal relationships, rather than by techniques which relied for their validity upon semantics and logic. "Meaning" to them was to be established solely by *structural* facts, not by information from the nonlinguistic world, that is, the world outside of and largely beyond language ("mentalism").

Unfortunately, Glinz, who had prepared his manuscript during the 1940's, was almost totally unaware of the intensive and fruitful investigations being carried on by American linguists (and by many European refugees who had fled to our shores) over these same years. It stands as a major tribute to him, that, working in near isolation from other structuralists, he was able to develop a system of analysis very close to that arrived at by some of the most brilliant scholars in the United States, all having free and easy access to one another's findings, for the most part as printed in the distinguished journal of the American Linguistic Society, *Language*, and the journal of the Linguistic Circle of New York, *Word* (now no longer published).

Glinz's announced purpose in writing *Die innere Form des Deutschen* was, in his own words, "die Struktur unseres Deutsch so objektiv wie möglich zu erkennen und zu beschreiben" (1st ed., p. 11). In order to accomplish this goal, he devised three discovery-procedures for establishing the syntactic constituents of German; to these procedures he gave the names *Verschiebeprobe*, *Ersatzprobe*, and *Weglaßbarkeit*. Rudimentary as these tools were, Glinz applied them with such skill and with such decisive results, that simplified versions of his new grammar were soon being used in many schools. The ultimate tribute was paid him in 1959, when the first postwar *Duden: Grammatik der deutschen Gegenwartssprache* came out in a completely revised edition, employing his basic techniques and adopting much of his terminology.

By 1964, thanks to the selfless dedication of such scholars as Hans Glinz, Hugo Moser, Walter Porzig, Leo Weisgerber, and many others, West

German linguists were able to organize their efforts and to begin working once again as a community of scholars. This aim was realized primarily by the founding in that year of the *Institut für deutsche Sprache* (IDS) in Mannheim as a center for the study of contemporary German. Its announced purpose was the study of the German *Standartsprache* (note spelling) since 1945, and its goal was to compile an authoritative descriptive grammar of this language.[26] Hugo Moser, of the University of Bonn, has been the institute's president since its inception.

The institute is divided into sections—each section devoted to a specific research theme—and it draws upon the counsel and services of distinguished Germanists from all over the world. Not committed to any particular "school" of linguistics (although in practice favoring the structural), the IDS serves both as a research center and as a clearing house for contemporary language study in the Federal Republic of Germany.

Its grammar is far from completed, though much has already been accomplished. Starting in 1967 with a series of preliminary studies entitled *Sprache der Gegenwart*, the IDS, joined in the venture by the *Goethe-Institut*,[27] was able to publish in 1971 the first three volumes of its projected grammar, *Heutiges Deutsch: Linguistische und didaktische Beiträge für den deutschen Sprachunterricht*. This grammar will eventually consist of three series (*Reihen*): (1) *Linguistische Grundlagen*, more commonly known as *Forschungsberichte*; (2) *Texte*; and (3) *Didaktische Auswertungen*. There are currently (1974) two volumes of Series 1 and one volume of Series 2 available.[28]

[26] For a more detailed account of the IDS and of its publications, see Byron J. Koekkoek, "Collective Review," *German Quarterly* 46, no. 2 (March 1973): 240–49.

[27] Reestablished in 1951 as *Das Goethe-Institut zur Pflege deutscher Sprache und Kultur im Ausland*, one of its first moves was to introduce summer courses in Germany for foreign teachers of the language. These courses are now conducted throughout the Federal Republic and in West Berlin, and are attended annually by thousands of students. In addition to its basic goal of teaching German at all levels for students and teachers from abroad, the *Goethe-Institut*, working mainly through the Federal Ministry of Foreign Affairs (*Das auswärtige Amt*), has also established cultural centers in almost all countries maintaining diplomatic relations with the BRD. In addition to arranging presentations of all sorts for touring German writers, actors, and musicians (to name the more obvious categories), the institutes maintain carefully stocked libraries (books, films, slides, tapes, etc.) for the use of all those interested in some phase of German culture.

[28] Series 1: Siegfried Jäger, *Der Konjunktiv in der deutschen Sprache der Gegenwart: Untersuchungen an ausgewählten Texten;* Klaus Brinker, *Das Passiv im heutigen Deutsch; Form und Funktion*; and Series 2: *Texte gesprochener Standartsprache I*. Erarbeitet im Institut für deutsche Sprache, Forschungsstelle Freiburg im Breisgau. All three were published under the auspices of *das Institut für deutsche Sprache* and of *das Goethe-Institut* by the Max Hueber Verlag in Munich and by the Pädagogischer Verlag Schwamm in Düsseldorf.

Series 2—*Texte*—consists of analyses and evaluations of contemporary German based upon the so-called "Mannheimer Korpus" and "Freiburger Korpus." The former comprises more than 1,500,000 words of running text selected from several cultural levels of contemporary prose; the latter, including some 600,000 words of continuous discourse, was also chosen to represent all major levels of usage.[29]

The East German counterpart of the *Institut für deutsche Sprache* is the *Zentralinstitut für Sprachwissenschaft* of the Academy of Sciences in Berlin, long known as *die Arbeitsstelle für strukturelle Grammatik*. The word *"strukturell"* in the old title caused some confusion, since the methodological orientation of the Berlin research center has from its beginnings (late 1950's) been dominated by transformational-generative theory. To the early, postwar, East German linguists, "structural" meant "transformational-generative," though with the passage of time and the broadening of avenues of communication, it became obvious that the term was frequently misinterpreted by others. The new title also better reflects the primary commitment of the organization, namely, a commitment to the development of universal linguistic theory, with only a peripheral interest in the application of its findings to the classroom teaching of German. The *Zentralinstitut* concentrates on the German language for the same reason that most of our transformationalists usually limit their attention to English: it is the only language for which they themselves as native speakers have built-in controls for testing the "well-formedness" of a clause or sentence. Since their goal is to identify and isolate features of universal grammar, it should in theory matter little which language is involved (although the heresy still persists—especially among older scholars—that the more languages one knows, the better equipped he is as a linguist). Another feature which distinguishes the two research organizations is that the IDS is obliged to tolerate a diversity of theoretical perspectives, whereas the *Zentralinstitut* has declared transformational theory to be the only orthodox approach to linguistic analysis, although "orthodoxy" is still subject to conflicting definitions.

[29] As an historical aside it should be mentioned that in 1966, when the research leading to these first volumes of *Heutiges Deutsch* was begun, the IDS and the *Goethe-Institut*, supported in part by funds from the *Stiftung Volkswagenwerk*, set as their goal the identification of what they called the "Grundstrukturen der deutschen Sprache." They also occasionally used the term "Grunddeutsch" as a synonym for "Grundstrukturen." However, the expression "Grunddeutsch" had already been preempted in 1960 by the American Germanist, J. Alan Pfeffer, whose own *Institut für Grunddeutsch* has since provided us with several excellent studies of contemporary German.

By and large, the theoretical positions of the *Zentralinstitut* are the ones set forth by Noam Chomsky in his *Aspects of the Theory of Syntax* (1965), although the premises and procedures of the institute's pre-1965 publications are of course based upon Chomsky's first book on transformational-generative grammar, *Syntactic Structures* (1957). The theme basic to both these books and to all transformational research is *"how to account for a native speaker's competence."* According to Chomsky, linguistic competence is reached when the speaker has somehow mastered the system of rules by which he generates language. We learn a language by acquiring a set of rules and these rules generate the language. Any language supposedly has a finite set of elementary syntactic structures or basic sentence-patterns. By applying another set of rules—called "transformations"—these "kernel sentences" can be expanded by the native speaker, presumably indefinitely.

Since the ultimate objective of transformational research is to identify the features of universal grammar which lie hidden beneath the superficial differences distinguishing one language from another, it is, according to orthodox transformational doctrine, not especially profitable to spend time on "taxonomic" studies (read "structural"), which do little more than describe the surface structures of language (*Oberflächenstrukturen*). Nor does it actually matter that the linguist restrict his investigations to only one language (usually his native tongue) since the "rules," if correctly derived and applied, will reveal the "deep structures" (*Tiefenstrukturen*) which are presumably much the same for all languages. Certainly only the latter are of any abiding concern to the transformational linguist; anything else is regarded as "trivial."

The publications of the *Zentralinstitut* bear the generic title *Studia Grammatica*.[30] Three of the first four (there are now about a dozen) are monographs, each written by a prominent East German linguist: *Studia Grammatica II: Grammatik des deutschen Verbs* (1963) is authored by Martin Bierwisch, best-known of the *Zentralinstitut's* theoreticians and one of the major forces in the organization;[31] *Studia Grammatica III: Syntax des deutschen Adjektivs* is by Wolfgang Motsch, and *Studia Grammatica IV: Die zusammengesetzten Sätze des Deutschen* (1964) is from the

[30] For a mercifully nontechnical, but excellent review of the *Studia Grammatica*, vols. I–VII, see Byron J. Koekkoek, "Collective Review," *German Quarterly* 43, no. 1 (January 1970): 84–91.

[31] *Studia Grammatica I* (1962) contains contributions by Bierwisch, Hartung, and Motsch, in addition to several unsigned outlines of proposed research themes. Hartung's article, "Die Passiv-transformationen im Deutschen" (pp. 90–114), is especially interesting.

pen of Wolfdietrich Hartung. Most of the post–1965 volumes consist of papers on a given theme, written by several contributors (all the *Studia* are published by the Akademie Verlag in Berlin).

The *Zentralinstitut* has not limited itself to the study of German. There are investigations, both finished and still "forthcoming," of Albanian, Russian, and Spanish. There are also plans for a multiauthored transformational grammar of German (much like the *Heutiges Deutsch* of the IDS), although this is a long-range project which may take years to be completed, if indeed it ever is.

The transformationalists of the Berlin Academy share certain characteristics with their colleagues in the United States and elsewhere. For instance, they are but little concerned with the pragmatic side of their work. This in itself is no cause for censure, since theoretical linguists and grammarians are seldom interested in the practicality of their research. In the case of the transformationalists, however, each new development seems to move them another step away from the position of traditional linguistics, namely, that the study of *language* should be based upon the study of *languages*. This is not to deny that the transformationalists have discovered some interesting and occasionally important facts about living languages, or that some of their terminology has proved to be more apt and descriptive than either that of the structuralists or of the traditionalists. But all these "spin-offs" are of scant concern to them. Indeed, as the formulas become ever more complex and abstract, and as the examples become ever more strained and unreal, it seems to many that transformational grammar is rapidly becoming more properly the domain of the mathematician and the symbolic logician rather than that of the student of language.

A comparison of the impact which the two institutes are exerting upon the school grammars of their respective countries, reveals that the West German *Institut für deutsche Sprache* has certainly been the more effective. In addition to its own research programs, it is formally or informally affiliated not only with almost every organization in the BRD engaged in language study, but with all the West German universities as well. The East German *Zentralinstitut,* on the other hand, is purely a research institute. Although it has loose ties to certain organizations interested in applied linguistics and language teaching—such as the *Herder-Institut* in Leipzig (with goals similar to those of the *Goethe-Institut* in Munich)—it is primarily dedicated to the abstract study of language. Furthermore, its theoretical orientation is monolithic: all of its members presumably accept transformational grammar as orthodox dogma, and everyone works within this framework. The IDS, conversely, reflects all hues of linguistic theory. Although the older generation tends to veer away from transformational studies, some of the younger members are enthusiastic about its tenets and techniques. However, so far the structural approach has proved to be more pliable, practical, and effective when applied to a language-teaching situation (with a few notable exceptions). The outcome is still far from clear. Whichever side prevails, or even if the outcome is more or less a draw, German grammar will never again be the same.[32]

---

[32] Two informative articles, in addition to those mentioned in notes 29 and 30, also containing pertinent and useful bibliographies, should be mentioned: R. R. K. Hartmann, "Recent Trends in German Linguistics," *Die Unterrichtspraxis* 6, no. 1 (Spring, 1973): 92–105; and Randall L. Jones, "German Language Research in East and West Germany," *Die Unterrichtspraxis* 3, no. 2 (Fall, 1970): 96–100.

CHAPTER EIGHT

A Brief Description of the Sounds of German

ARTICULATORY or physiological (anatomical) phonetics describes the movements and positions of the vocal apparatus during the speech act (phonation).

Consonants are differentiated by noting which movable part or "articulator" (lips, tongue, uvula) makes full contact (stop), near contact (spirant), or multiple contact (trill) along the upper surfaces of the oral or "buccal" cavity (labial, dental, alveolar, palatal, velar).[1]

---

[1] The region immediately posterior to the fauces (the aperture leading from the mouth to the throat) is named the "pharynx." That portion of it which connects with the posterior nares (interior nostrils) may be called the "naso-pharynx." Though constriction of the pharyngeal muscles plays a part in the production of certain sounds, these are not phonemic in English or German.

Inferior or "ventral" (toward the belly) to the pharynx is the larynx, a musculo-cartilaginous structure lying between the pharynx and the trachea or windpipe (the larynx is the upper extension of the trachea). It contains the cartilages, both fixed and movable, to which are affixed the tiny muscles called the "vocal cords." The air space between the cords is the "glottis" (see Fig. 3). These cords, or more properly "bands" (Stimmbänder), can be brought tightly together, thus occluding the air passage (as they do whenever we exert pressure against the musculature of the diaphragm). By quickly releasing this occlusion and concurrently expelling the pent-up breath, we produce a sound which phoneticians call a "glottal stop," written in phonetic transcription as [ʔ]. This "catch" in the voice is usually heard at the beginning of the second utterance in the exclamation "Oh, oh!" as in the sentence: "Oh, oh! I didn't see that puddle!" The glottal stop is not phonemic in either English or German, though it is a characteristic feature of the North German dialects, as for instance in the pronunciation of Verein [fɛɐʔaɪn] or Achtung [ʔaxtuŋ].

Differences in the acoustic and auditory quality of vowels are effected by modifying the shape and size of the oral cavity. We therefore note which part of the tongue acts as articulator: the tip (apex), the blade, or the back (dorsum); and the height to which it is raised toward the concave surface extending from the alveolar ridge (formed by the sockets of the upper teeth and the tissues covering them) to the soft palate or "velum." By applying these criteria, we arrive at a basic classification which describes a

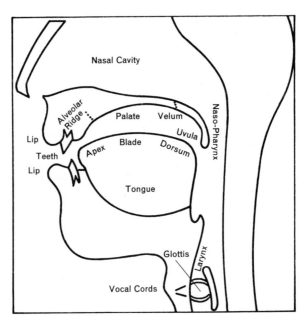

Figure 3. Diagram of the Vocal Tract.

vowel as front, central, or back, and—on the perpendicular axis—as high, mid, or low. As can be seen from the vowel chart, several intermediate degrees of tongue height must be established in actual practice.

The phonetician must also note whether the production of a given sound is characterized by features of "co-articulation," such as lip-rounding (labialization) or a puff of air following the release of an occluded sound (aspiration). The absence of aspiration may also be an important part of a phonetic description. If a sound is articulated with tenseness and force, it may be described as "fortis"; conversely, a sound articulated with weak force and tension may be called "lenis."

It is also necessary to establish whether or not the column of air extending from the base of the lungs to the oral or nasal exits has been set in motion by the oscillations of the vocal bands (cords) attached to the cartilages located in the larynx. If these delicate folds of tissue vibrate during phonation, the speech sounds are described as "voiced"; if there is no vibration, the sounds are said to be "voiceless."

The breath is expelled either through the mouth or through the nose, depending upon whether the velum is raised or lowered. If the velum—an intricate complex of muscle tissue—is raised, thus shutting off the nasal exit, the sounds of speech are described as "oral." If the velum is lowered, thereby diverting the flow of air through the nostrils, speech sounds are classified as "nasal." Sometimes the position of the velum allows air to escape through both the mouth and the nose. Sounds produced under these conditions are said to be "nasalized."

CONSONANTS

A. Stops (occlusives, explosives)

1. Bilabial
   (a) Voiceless: [p] "Platz."
   (b) Voiceless lenis: [b̥] Rhen. Franc. [b̥lɒːd̥s] "Platz."
   (c) Voiced: [b] "Ball."

In standard English and German, the unvoiced stops [p], [t], [k] are usually aspirated, as in *pay, ten,* and *cat.* However, in the consonant cluster [sp] (German [šp]), the second element is pronounced without aspiration, as in Eng. *spin,* Ger. *Spinne.* The voiced stops [b], [d], [g] are pronounced without aspiration in both standard English and German. The voiceless lenis stops [b̥], [d̥], [g̥]—rarely heard in American English (the *p* of *Baptist* and *báptize* is often given a voiceless lenis pronunciation in southern and midwestern speech) —occur in most of the Middle and Upper German dialects. The phonetically untrained speaker of English usually cannot distinguish this series from the voiced lenis series.

2. Alveolar
   (a) Voiceless: [t] "tun."
   (b) Voiceless lenis: [d̥] Rhen. Franc. [d̥uːn] "tun."
   (c) Voiced: [d] "danken."

3. Velar
   (a) Voiceless: [k] "Kind."
   (b) Voiceless lenis: [g̥] Rhen. Franc. [g̥ɪnd̥] "Kind."
   (c) Voiced: [g] "geben."

    4. Glottal

       Voiceless: [ʔ] "Achtung," "Verein."

  B. Spirants (fricatives)

    1. Bilabial

      (a) Voiceless: [φ]. The bilabial voiceless spirant does not have phonemic status in either standard English or German, yet it occurs as a positional variant of other sounds. It is heard in

FIGURE 4.

Phonetic Chart : Consonants

	LABIAL vcls voiced			ALVEOLAR vcls voiced		PALATAL vcls voiced		VELAR vcls voiced			GLOTTAL voiceless
STOPS	p		b	t	d			k		g	?
SPIRANTS	φ	f	ƀ v	s	z	š	ž	ç χ		g̣	h
AFFRICATES	pf			ts		tš		kχ			
NASALS			m		n					ŋ	
LATERALS					l					L	
TRILLS					r					R	

    f, v : labiodental spirants
      ç : a pre-velar spirant
      r :   an apical trill
     R :   a uvular trill

    Additional symbols :
      ° : lenis pronunciation
      ʽ : aspiration

Note : For an explanation of the symbols *þ* and *đ* (see p. 195, n. 2).

      German in lax pronunciations of a word like *Quelle*, in which [kφɛlə] will alternate with [kfɛlə]. In English, the initial segment of *when* in the speech of most people may be classified as a lax bilabial voiceless spirant (this sound is variously analyzed by phoneticians).

      (b) Voiced: [ƀ]. The voiced bilabial spirant is likewise lacking in the phonemic inventory of standard English and German. However, it is heard in the German dialects, where it alternates intervocalically with the voiced labiodental spirant [v], as for instance in the pronunciation of *aber* in Middle Franconian: [ɒƀə] or [ɒvə]. This is the sound given to the letters *b* and *v* when they occur intervocalically in Spanish: [saƀér] *saber* "to know."

2. Labiodental
    (a) Voiceless: [f] "fein."
    (b) Voiced: [v] "Wein."

3. Alveolar[2]
    (a) Voiceless: [s] "bis."
    (b) Voiced: [z] "so."

4. Palatal
    (a) Voiceless: [š] "Schule."
    (b) Voiced: [ž] "Blamage," "Journalist." This sound is rare in the dialects. Unless they have acquired it as a foreign pronunciation, Germans tend to replace it with the voiceless counterpart.

5. Velar
    (a) Voiceless: The stage pronunciation recognizes a prevelar spirant [ç]—used in the presence of front vowels, as in "ich" —and a central velar [χ], to be heard in other surroundings: "Achtung," "Loch." The High Alemannic dialects use a distinctive postvelar pronunciation in all positions.
    (b) Voiced: The standard language does not recognize a voiced velar spirant [g], though in certain of the Upper German dialects it is frequently heard as a positional variant for the velar spirant in voiced surroundings: High Alemannic [uːrgig] "genuine."

6. Glottal
    There is only the voiceless, laxly articulated "breath sound" (*Hauchlaut*): [h] "Hauch."

C. Affricates
    Affricates consist of a stop followed immediately by a homorganic (of the same class) spirant. In articulating these sounds, the tongue hesitates between the occlusion and the complete release.

---

[2] German has only the "sibilants" or "groove" spirants. The others, the "slit" spirants (so called because of the way the tongue flattens out against the roof of the mouth rather than forming a groove), are heard as the initial sound of *thing* and *this* recorded phonetically as [þ] and [đ].

1. Bilabial: [pf] "Pferd."

2. Alveolar: [ts] "Zeit."

3. Palatal: [tš] "Patsch." Under the influence of the following sibilant, the alveolar stop is strongly palatalized, as can be demonstrated by comparing its point of articulation in the words *Zeit* and *Patsch*.

4. Velar: [kχ] High Alemannic [tæŋkχə] "denken." This affricate is the most distinguishing feature of the High Alemannic or Swiss dialects, though it also occurs in some of the Bavarian dialects.

D. Laterals[3] (liquids)

1. Alveolar: [l] "Lippe."

2. Velar (or dorsal): [L]. This is a positional variant of the alveolar lateral and is heard in the speech of many Germans, occurring usually in the vicinity of low back vowels. The velar [L] is frequently heard in the dialects and the *Umgangssprachen*, though not recognized by the stage pronunciation. Many speakers of English—especially of British English—use it in words such as *Paul* and *all*. The second *l* of *little* is often accorded a velar pronunciation.

E. Nasals

1. Bilabial: [m] "mein."

2. Alveolar: [n] "Nase."

3. Velar: [ŋ] "singen."

F. Trills[4]

1. Apical: [r] "recht." Though recognized as "correct" in the stage pronunciation, this sound is of limited occurrence in the living language.

2. Uvular: [R] "recht." This is the most frequently used trill in German. It alternates with a weakly articulated, voiceless velar spirant.

---

[3] So called because the air escapes "laterally," the tongue maintaining contact medially along the roof of the mouth.

[4] Trills are best described by naming them after the articulating organ, in this case either the apex (tip) of the tongue, or the fleshy pendant that forms part of the posterior border of the velum, the uvula (Lat. "little grape").

Vowels

A. Front Vowels
  1a. High unrounded: [i] "Biene."
  1b. High rounded: [y] "Bühne."
  2a. Lower-high unrounded: [ɪ] "dick."
  2b. Lower-high rounded: [ʏ] "dünn."
  3a. Higher-mid unrounded: [e] "Sehne."
  3b. Higher-mid rounded: [ø] "Söhne."
  4a. Lower-mid unrounded: [ɛ] "Bett."
  4b. Lower-mid rounded: [œ] "Böttcher," "Löffel."
  5. Higher-low unrounded: [æ] Middle Bav. [ænlig] "ähnlich."

B. Central Vowels
  1. Lower-mid unrounded: [ə] "Gabe" (last sound).
  2. Low unrounded:[5] [a] "Vater."

C. Back Vowels (note: all back vowels but 5a are rounded)
  1. High: [u] "Buch."
  2. Lower-high: [ʊ] "Bucht."
  3. Higher-mid: [o] "Sohn."
  4. Lower-mid: [ɔ] "Tochter."
  5a. Low unrounded: [ɑ] Middle Bav. [hɑos] "Haus"; also heard in some American pronunciations of words such as *law* and *paw*.
  5b. Low rounded: [ɒ] Middle Franc. [ɒvə] "aber"; compare British Eng. pronunciation of *not, lot*.

Semivowels

Semivowels are phonemes which can function either as vowels or as consonants, depending upon their distribution. When fully voiced, they are recorded as vowels—[i], [u]—when voiceless, or relatively so, they are accorded consonantal (nonsyllabic) status and may be transcribed [i̯] and [u̯] or [j] and [w]. In this book a special symbol is used only for the high-front semivowel: [j].

Diphthongs

A syllable pronounced without hiatus (pause), in which one element is more sonorous (voiced) than the other, is called a "diphthong." For our

---

[5] Siebs's *Hochsprache* cautions against making too great a distinction between [a] and [ɑ]. There is scant differentiation in the North, many speakers using only the central vowel. But the Middle and Upper German dialects observe a marked difference in the pronunciation between, say, *lassen* and *Vater*, employing the low central vowel for the former sound but using a low back vowel in the pronunciation of *Vater*.

purposes we may use a somewhat restricted definition, and say that a diphthong is a combination of vowel plus semivowel. All such diphthongs in standard English and German are classed as "falling," that is, the principal stress falls at the beginning of the syllable. There are only three of these compound sounds in the *Hochsprache*: [aɪ] "Bein," [aʊ] "Baum", and [øɪ] "Leute." However, as is evident from a survey of the dialects, several other varieties also occur.

Some Features of Coarticulation

Labialization. Theoretically, any vowel may be pronounced with lip-rounding or labialization. In German all the back vowels but one are

Figure 5.
Phonetic Chart : Vowels

	FRONT		CENTRAL		BACK	
	unrd	rounded	unrd	rounded	unrd	rounded
High	i	y				u
Lower-high	ɪ	ʏ				ʊ
Higher-mid	e	ø				o
Lower-mid	ɛ	œ	ə			ɔ
Higher-low	æ					
Low			a		ɑ	ɒ

Additional symbols :
ˆ or : = long vowel.
˘ = short vowel.
˜ = nasalization.

commonly rounded; there is also a series of rounded front vowels, popularly called the "umlaut" vowels. These sounds are simply front vowels pronounced with rounded or pursed lips.

Tenseness. Many languages distinguish between the tense (fortis) and lax (lenis) pronunciation of a consonant. In standard English and German, for instance, the voiceless stops [p], [t], [k] are pronounced with much more muscular tension than are the corresponding voiced stops: [b], [d],

[g]. Several of the High German dialects, however, merge these two classes of sounds into a single series of voiceless unaspirated *lenis* stops, recorded in phonetic script as [b̥], [d̥], [g̊]. These sounds are difficult for the phonetically untrained speaker of English to distinguish. He will accuse the German of "mixing up his *p*'s and *b*'s."

Aspiration. Any one of the stops may be articulated in such a way that a little puff of air accompanies their release. This is the usual pronunciation of [p], [t], [k] in standard English and German. An important exception occurs when these sounds are immediately preceded by a sibilant ([s] in English, [š] in German). By contrasting the pronunciations of *pin* and *spin*, the speaker will notice that the bilabial stop of the second word is articulated without a noticeable puff of breath (unaspirated). In phonetic transcription aspiration may be indicated, if necessary, by placing the diacritic ' after the symbol for the stop: [p'].

Nasalization. All voiced sounds may be nasalized by letting part of the breath stream escape through the nose. Neither standard English nor German accords phonemic status to such sounds, though both languages have them as dialectal variants. The speech of many Midwesterners is often said to have a "nasal twang." Of the High German dialects, both Swabian and Bavarian have marked nasalization. German phoneticians refer to "die schwäbische Näselung." Nasalized vowels are indicated in phonetic transcription by placing a tilde over the vowel symbol, e.g., [ã].

Appendix I

PLATES

The Golden Horn of Gallehus. A golden drinking horn from about 400 A.D., found near Gallehus in Jutland. Note runic inscription carved just below lip of horn (see p. 22 ff.). **Actual length of horn approximately 24 inches.**

An early Germanic runic alphabet or "futhark" (named after the first six runes: *f-u-th-a-r-k*; cf. Eng. "Abc's").

PLATE I

ïΨïsΛNƆhΛ̵ϚΛNƆ͚ϹΛΨ
Ɔnïн· ΨΛΤΕΙΥΛΙΛΛπΚΛΠϜΕΤΙƆΛ
ΕSΛïΛSΒïïΖΥΙSΨΛNSΛΙΠΤΛNS
SΥΕΓΛΜΕΛΙΨïST· SꝶНΛΝΓΕΙ
ΥΛΙΚΙΛꝶННΙΚSΥΕΚΛΙΨ· ïΨнΛΙΚ
ΤꝶïΖΕϜΛΙΚΚΛнΛΒΛΙΨSΙΚНΙS.ïΨ
SΥΛΚΕΜΙΚΒΛꝶΤΛNƆ· ΛΛΙSϚΛNƆΛS

Two verses from the Gothic Bible (see pp. 6 and 61ff.). A black and white reproduction of a few lines of the beautiful Codex Argenteus (silver and gold ink on purple parchment), an early sixth-century manuscript now in the University library at Uppsala, Sweden.

The Gothic text—Mark 7:6–7—in conventional transliteration is as follows: "iþ is andhafjands qaþ du im þatei waila praufetida Esaïas bi izwis þans liutans, swe gameliþ ist: so managei wairilom mik sweraiþ, iþ hairto ize fairra habaiþ sik mis. (7) iþ sware mik blotand, laisjandans. . . ."

The King James version has: "He answered and said unto them, Well hath Esaias prophesied of you hypocrites, as it is written, This people honoureth me with their lips, but their heart is far from me. (7) Howbeit in vain do they worship me, teaching. . . ."

Note: the symbol þ is to be pronounced as *th* in Eng. *thing*.

PLATE II

PLATE III

The beginning of the *Hildebrandslied* (see p. 75, note 26), sole representative in German of heroic poetry from the pre-Christian era. Although essentially High German, the language of the manuscript is a curious and unexplained mixture of Old High German and Old Saxon. Both external and internal evidence suggests that the manuscript was written at the monastery of Fulda in the first years of the ninth century. In the following transliteration and translation of the first two lines, notice the unshifted consonants in forms like *ik, đat,* and *tuem* (dative plural of *twê* "zwei"):

Ik gihorta đat seggen đat sih urhettun aenon muotin Hiltibraht enti Hadubrant untar heriun tuem. . . .

Ich hörte das sagen, daß sich ausforderten einzeln bei der Begegnung Hildebrand und Hadubrand zwischen den Heeren beiden. . . .

Note: the symbol đ is to be pronounced as *th* in Eng. *this.*

Ik gihorta ðat seggen ðat sih urhettun ænon muo
tin · Hiltibraht enti Haðubrant untar heriun tuem ·
sunu fatarungo iro saro rihtun garutun se iro
guðhamun gurtun sih iro suert ana helidos
ubar ringa do sie to dero hiltiu ritun · Hiltibraht
gimahalta heribrantes sunu · her uuas heroro
man ferahes frotoro · her fragen gistuont fohem
uuortum · hwer sin fater wari fireo in folche · eddo
welihhes cnuosles du sis · ibu du mi enan sages ik
mi de odre weit chind in chunincriche · chud ist
min al irmindeot · Hadubraht gimahalta hiltI
brantes sunu dat sagetun mi usere liuti alte anti
frote dea erhina warun · dat hiltibrant hætti
min fater ih heittu hadubrant forn her ostar
giweit floh her otachres nid hina miti theotrihhe
enti sinero degano filu · her furlaet in lante luttila
sitten prut in bure barn unwahsan arbeo laosa
her raet ostar hina det sid detrihhe darba gistuontun
fateres mines dat uuas so friuntlaos man
her was otachre ummet tirri degano dechisto
unti deotrihhe darba gistuontun her was eo folches at ente imo was eo fehta ti leop
chud was her chonnem mannum ni waniu ih iu
lib habbe

A page from the Hohenems-Laßberg manuscript (C) of the Middle High German folk-epic, *Das Nibelungenlied*. The manuscript is from the early thirteenth century. Its script is a good example of the so-called "Gothic book-script" (see p. 107, note 6). The transliteration begins with the last word of the first line—the capitalized *Nu*—and ends in the middle of the fourth line.

Nu lat iuch unbilden, sprach do Hagene, niht mine rede darumbe: swie halt iu geschiht, ich rat iu an den triuvan, welt ir iuch wol bewarn, so sult ir zuo den Hiunen vil gewaerliche varn.

Nun laßt euch verdrießen, sprach da Hagen, und nicht wegen meiner Rede: wie es euch auch immer geschieht, ich rate euch aufrichtig, wollt Ihr euch gut bewahren, so sollt Ihr zu den Hunnen gut gerüstet fahren.

wir mvzen an die vart. ez walder gvter knte. d' sich alle zite bewart.
lat vch vnbilden. sp̄ch do Hagene niht. mine rede darvmbe. swie halt iv
geschiht. ich rat w anden triwen. welt ir vch wol bewarn. so svlt ir zv
den Hvnen. vn gewerliche varn. Sewir niht welt erwinden. so besen
det nv man. die besten die ir vinden. od' mo̊ge̊ han. so wel ich vz in al
len. vsent rit gvt. so ne chan vns niht gewerren. d' argen Chriemh niue
Del wil ich gerne volgen. sprach d' knnte rchant. do hiez er boten riten. wi
ten in sin lant. do brahte man d' beide. driv tvsunt vn mer. si wanden niho
erwerben also gremelichiv ser. Sirten willechliche. in Gunthers lant.
man hiez in gebn allen. rosse vn ovch gewant. die mit in varn wolden.
zv den Hvnen dan. d' kunte in gvtem willen. d' vil manigen gewan. Do
hiez von Tronege Hagene. Danchwart den brv̊d' sin. ir beid'rechen sehrach.
bringen an den Rin. die chomen ritrliche. harnasch vn gewant. des brah
ten vil die degene. in daz Gunthers lant. Do chom d' herre Volker. ein
kvne spileman. hin ze hove nach eren. mit drizech siner man. die heren
solch genurte. ez moht ein kunic tragen. daz er zen Hvnin wolde. dar hiez
er dem chvnige sagen. Wer d' volker were. daz wil ich wizzen lan. er
was ein edel herre. im was ovch vnd'tan. vil d' gvten rechen. in Burgon
den lant. durch daz er videln kunde. was er d' spileman genant. Tvsent
welt Hagene. die het er wol bechant. vn was in starchen stvrmen. het e
gestvnnt ir hant. vn swaz si ze begengen. des het er vil geschen. in chunde
ovch and's nemen. niwan frv̊mcheit reim. Die boten von den Hv
nen. vil sere da vorot. wande ir vorht zir herren. diu was harte grot.
si gerten tageliche. vrlovbes von dan. des engunde niht Hagene. daz was
dvrch list getan. Er sp̄ch zv sime herren. wir svln daz wol bewarn. daz
wir si noch lazen riten. e daz wir selbe varn. dar nach in tagen sibenen wi'
in ir lant. trev vns iemen argen mv̊t. daz wirt vns deste baz bechant.
Sone chan ovch sich vro Chriemh. bereiten niht dar zv. daz vns durch ir
rete. iemen schaden tv. hat ab' si den willen. ez mag ir leide ergan. wande
wir fvren in inen. manigen vz erwelten man. Schilt vn schilde. vn
and'ir gewant. daz si fvren solden. in Etelen lant. daz was nv gar be
reiter. vil manigem chvnem man. die Etelen videlere hiez man do ze
hove gan. Do si die forsten sahen. do sp̄ch Gernot. d'chvnic wil nv lei

PLATE V

The beginning of the Middle High German court-epic *Der arme Heinrich* by Hartmann von Aue (see p. 95). The manuscript is from the late thirteenth or early fourteenth century. A transcription of the first seven lines follows:

Ditz [Dies] ist der arme heinrich
Got mach uns im [ihm] gelich [gleich].
Ein Ritter so geleret was,
daz er an den buchen las,
was er dar an geschriben vant:
der was Hartman genant
unde was ein dinsteman [Dienstman] von Owe [Aue].

Ditz ist der arme heinrich
Gott mach vns im gelich
Ein Ritter so geleret was
Daz er an den buchen las
Was er dar an geschriben vant
Der was hartman genant
Vn was ein dinstman von owe
Der nam im eine schowe
An einem ieslichen buche
Dar an begond er fuche
Ob er iht des vunde
Da mit er swere stunde
Senfter mochte machen
Mit so geweren sachen
Daz zv gotes eren tohte
Da mit er sich mochte
Gelieben den leuten
hie besinnet er vns deuten
Ein rede die er geschriben vant
Dar vmbe hat er sich genant
Daz er siner arebeit
Die er an ditz buch hat geleit
Ane lon iht belibe

PLATE V

A page from one of Gutenberg's early Latin Bibles of approximately 1460. Thirty years later portions of the text and margins were illuminated by hand. The capital *B* is the first letter of line 10—the beginning of the first Psalm:

Beatus vir qui non abiit in consilio impiorum: et in via peccatorum non stetit: et in cathedra pestilentie non sedit.

(King James version) Blessed is the man that walketh not in the counsel of the ungodly, nor standeth in the way of sinners, nor sitteth in the seat of the scornful.

plicitate sermonis a septuaginta inter=
pretibus non discordat. Hec ergo et vo=
bis et studioso cuiq; fecisse me sciens.
non ambigo multos fore· qui vel inui=
dia vel supercilio malent contempnere
et videre predara quam discere:et de
turbulento magis riuo quam de pu=
rissimo fonte potare. Explicit prolog'
Incipit liber hympnozu vel soliloquozu

Eatus vir qui non
abijt in consilio im=
piozu: et in via pec
catorum non stetit :
et in cathedra pesti=
lentie non sedit. Sed
in lege domini volutas eius : ᴣ in lege
eius meditabit die ac nocte. Et erit
tamᵹ lignu quod platatum est secus
decursus aquaru : qd fructu suu dabit
in tpe suo. Et foliu eius non defluet : ᴣ
omnia quecuᵹ faciet prosperabutur.
Non sic impij non sic : sed tamᵹ pul=
uis que proicit ventus a facie terre. I=
deo non resurgut impij in iudicio : neqᴣ
peccatores in consilio iustorum. Quoni=
am nouit dominus via iustoᴣ: ᴣ iter
impiorum peribit. Psalmus dauid
uare fremuerut getes : et ppli me=
ditati sunt inania? Astiterut
reges terre et principes conuenerunt in
unu : aduersus dnm ᴣ aduersus cristu ei°.
Dirumpamᵒ vincla eoᴣ : ᴣ piciamᵒ
a nobis iugu ipoᴣ. Qui habitat in ce=
lis irridebit eos: ᴣ dns subsanabit eos⸱
Tunc loquet ad eos in ira sua: ᴣ in
furore suo coturbabit eos. Ego au

Title page of the first printing of the entire Bible in Luther's translation (1534).

PLATE VII

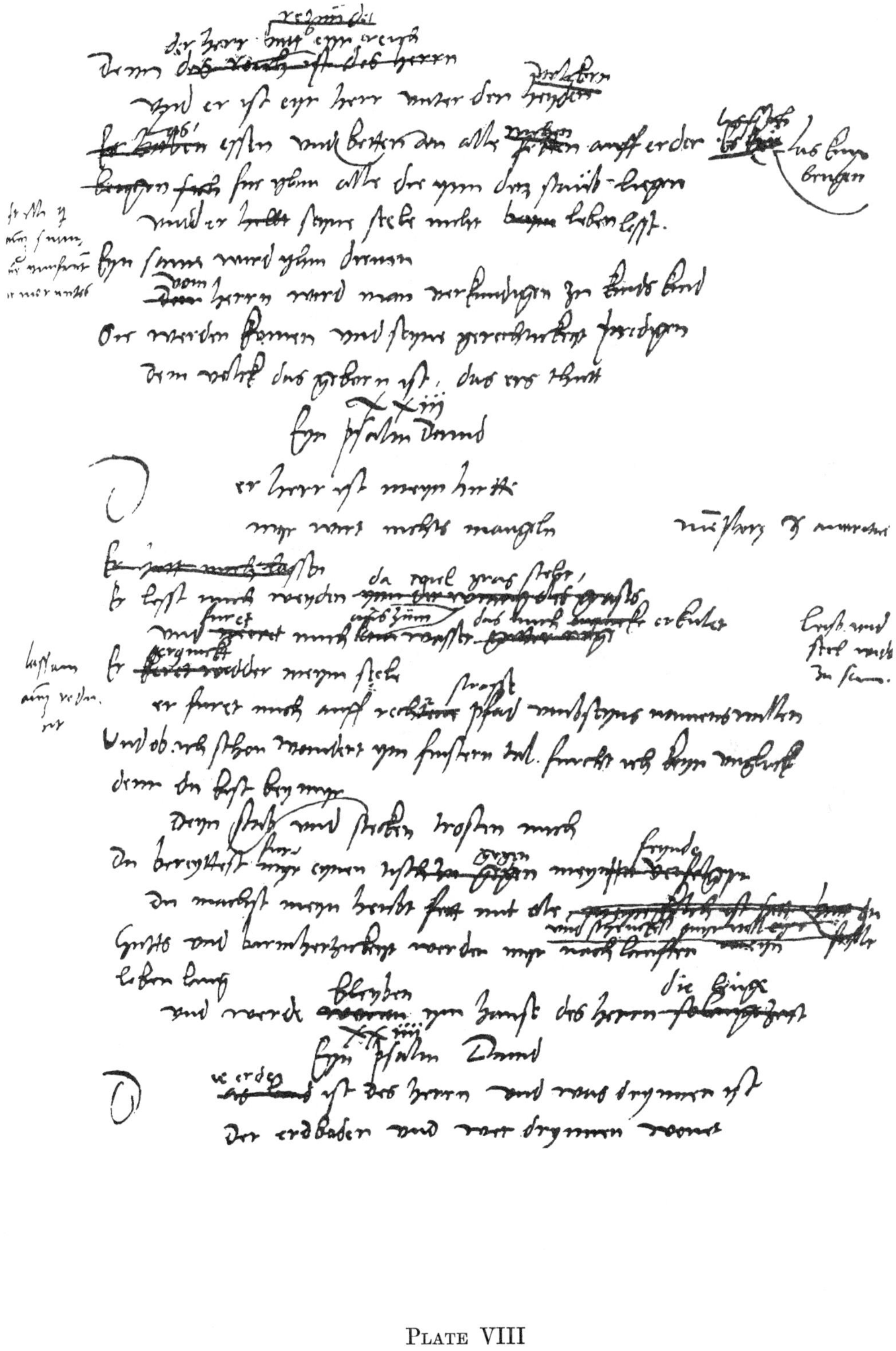

PLATE VIII

PLATE VIII

The Twenty-third Psalm (lower two-thirds of page, excluding last three lines) in Luther's own handwriting. Corrections in the original are made in red ink. The first letter of the first word (*Der*) is at the left-hand margin, approximately one-half inch removed from the -*er* (see p. 130).

Der herr ist meyn hirtte
myr wirt nichts mangeln
Er lesst mich weyden da viel gras steht,
und furet mich zum wasser das mich erkulet
Er erquickt meyne seele
Und er furet mich auff rechter strasse umb seyns
namens willen
Und ob ich schon wandert ym finstern tal. furcht ich
keyn ungluck
denn du bist bey myr. . . .

Der Herr ist mein Hirte; mir wird nichts mangeln.
Er weidet mich auf einer grünen Aue,
und führet mich zum frischen Wasser;
Er erquicket meine Seele; er führet
mich auf rechter Straße um seines Namens willen.
Und ob ich schon wanderte im finstern Tal, fürchte
ich kein Unglück; denn du bist bei mir. . . .

Appendix II

MAPS

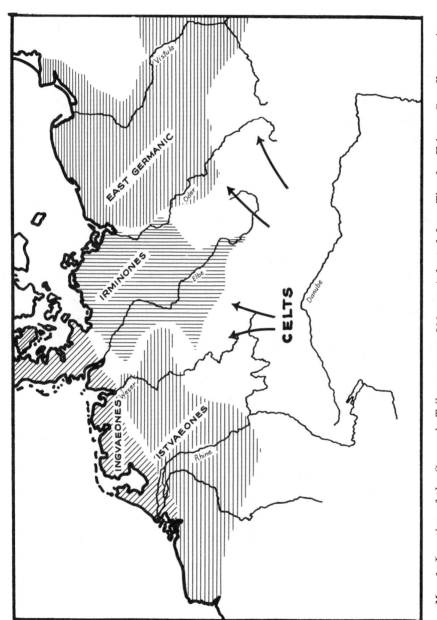

MAP 1. Location of the Germanic Tribes approx. 300 B.C. (adapted from Theodor Frings, *Grundlegung einer Geschichte der deutschen Sprache* [2nd ed.; Halle: Max Niemeyer Verlag, 1950])

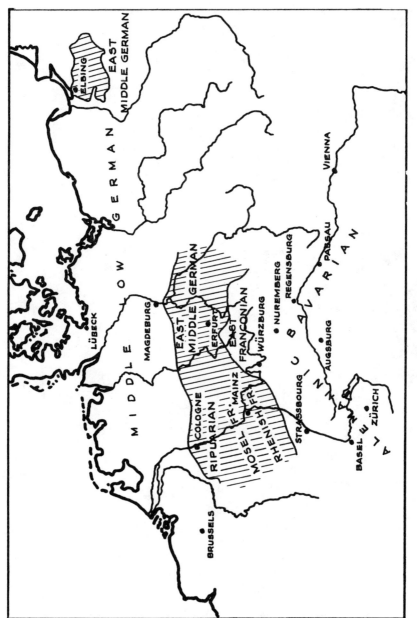

Map 2. Middle High German Literary Dialects

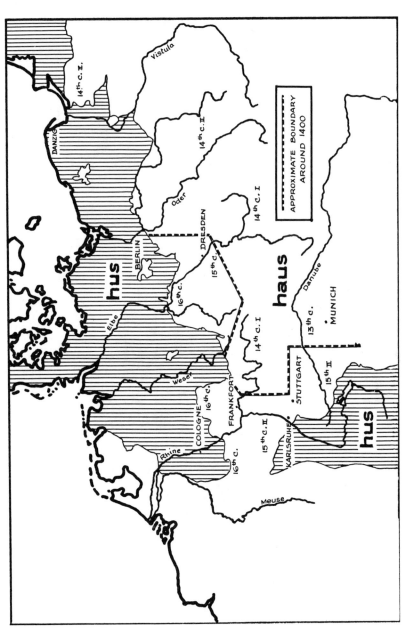

MAP 3. Chronological Progression of New High German Diphthongization: $u > au$. Leaf 24 of the *Deutscher Sprachatlas* (redrawn from Adolf Bach, *Deutsche Mundartforschung* [2nd ed.; Heidelberg: Carl Winter Universitäts-verlag, 1950], p. 205). *Note:* I = first half of century; II = second half of century

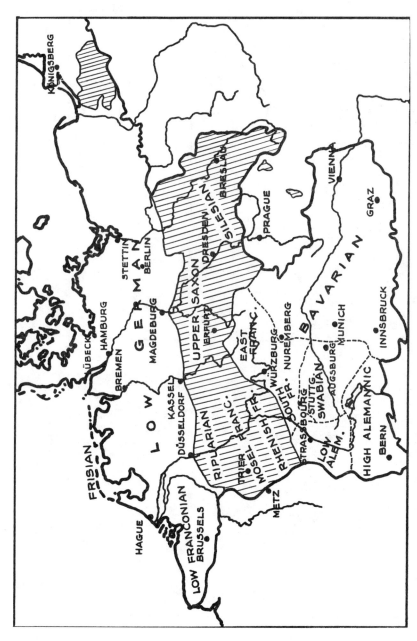

MAP 4. The Principal German Dialect Areas as of Approximately 1930 (slightly modified from Adolf Bach, *Geschichte der deutschen Sprache* [8th ed.; Heidelberg: Quelle & Meyer, 1965], p. 102)

DEUTSCHLAND

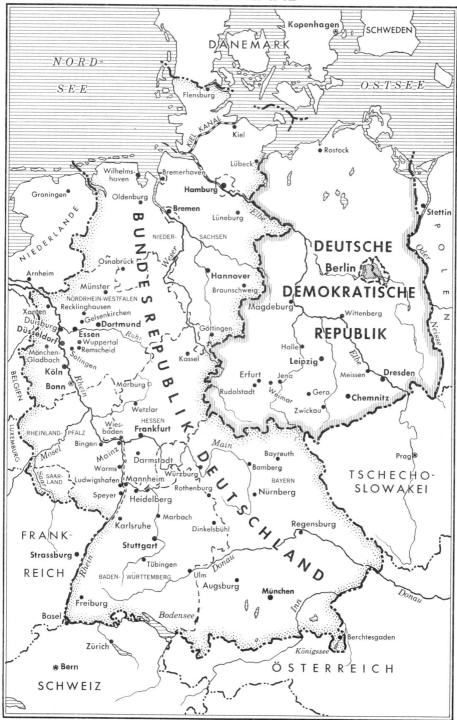

MAP 5. Postwar Germany Showing the Political Boundaries of the Federal Republic (BRD) and of the Democratic Republic (DDR) (reprinted from Harry Steinhauer, *Kulturlesebuch für Anfänger* [2nd ed.; New York: Macmillan, 1967])

Selected Bibliography

In common with all selected bibliographies, this one reflects its compiler's personal—and sometimes seemingly arbitrary—choices. However, a special word of explanation about the selection of articles from the periodical literature seems called for.

Two general criteria are observed: (1) with certain exceptions, most of the entries are dated after 1920; (2) items from journals printed in the United States are given preference wherever feasible.

While reference to the periodical literature prior to approximately 1920 is still required of the scholar, most of the pertinent research findings from those years have long since been incorporated into the standard handbooks, so that the nonspecialist is seldom required to consult the older numbers of the journals for factual information. As for giving preference to articles appearing in United States journals, and especially to those contributions written in English, the explanation is simply that one of the chief purposes of this bibliography is to provide English-speaking students with as much reading material as possible. Another reason for favoring journals printed in this country is that any college library will have them, whereas only those libraries with more substantial holdings can be assumed to have fairly complete runs of the German periodicals.

These criteria have caused some of the classic articles from an older era to be omitted, as well as some superior studies printed in German publications of recent decades. The reader is therefore warned that he must complement this bibliography with those contained in the standard German works on the history of the language. Most of these compilations are quite good, though none of them gives adequate coverage to the journals printed in the United States.

Many distinguished studies were regretfully omitted solely because they were felt to be too specialized or too difficult for inclusion in a general, introductory text. To the instructor who wonders why certain choices were made at all, the only excuse offered is that these entries have proved themselves appropriate—at least in the compiler's judgment—for outside reading assignments in classes in the history of the German language.

Histories of the Language

Bach, Adolf. *Geschichte der deutschen Sprache.* 9th ed. Heidelberg, 1971.

Behaghel, Otto. *Geschichte der deutschen Sprache.* 5th ed. Berlin and Leipzig, 1928.

Chambers, William Walker, and John R. Wilkie. *A Short History of the German Language.* London, 1970.

Frings, Theodor. *Grundlegung einer Geschichte der deutschen Sprache.* 3rd ed. Halle, 1957.

Hirt, Herman. *Geschichte der deutschen Sprache.* 2nd ed. Munich, 1925.

Kirk, Arthur. *An Introduction to the Historical Study of New High German.* Manchester, 1923.

Kluge, Friedrich. *Unser Deutsch: Einführung in die Muttersprache.* Revised by Lutz Mackensen, 6th ed. Heidelberg, 1958.

Mackensen, Lutz. *Die deutsche Sprache unserer Zeit.* 2nd rev. ed. Heidelberg, 1971.

Moser, Hugo. *Annalen der deutschen Sprache.* 4th rev. ed. (Sammlung Metzler, No. 5) Stuttgart, 1972.

———. *Deutsche Sprachgeschichte: Mit einer Einführung in die Fragen der Sprachbetrachtung.* 6th ed. Tübingen, 1969.

Polenz, Peter von. *Geschichte der deutschen Sprache.* (Sammlung Göschen, nos. 915, 915a) 7th rev. ed. Berlin, 1970.

Priebsch, Robert, and William E. Collinson. *The German Language.* 6th rev. ed. London, 1966.

Rooth, Erich. *Saxonica: Beiträge zur niedersächsischen Sprachgeschichte.* Lund, 1949.

Tschirch, Fritz. *Geschichte der deutschen Sprache.* Vol. 1. 2nd rev. ed. Berlin, 1972; Vol. II. Berlin, 1969.

Weisgerber, Johann Leo. *Von den Kräften der deutschen Sprache.* (See particularly, Vol. I, *Grundzüge der inhaltbezogenen Grammatik*; and Vol. IV, *Die geschichtliche Kraft der deutschen Sprache.*) 3rd rev. ed. Düsseldorf, 1962.

Historical Grammars

Behaghel, Otto. *Deutsche Syntax.* Heidelberg, 1923–32.

Curme, George O. *A Grammar of the German Language.* 2nd ed. New York, 1922.

Grimm, Jacob. *Deutsche Grammatik.* Vols. I and II revised by Wilhelm Scherer. Berlin, 1870–78; Vols. III and IV revised by Gustav Roethe and Edward Schroeder. Gütersloh, 1890–98 (reprinted in Hildesheim, 1967).

Karstien, Carl. *Historische deutsche Grammatik.* Vol. I. Heidelberg, 1939.

Meisen, Karl. *Altdeutsche Grammatik.* 2nd ed. (Sammlung Metzler Nos. 2, 3.) Stuttgart, 1968.

Paul, Hermann. *Deutsche Grammatik.* 4th/6th ed. Halle, 1959.

Stolte, Heinz. *Kurze deutsche Grammatik.* 3rd ed. Halle, 1962. A condensation of Paul's five-volume work cited above.

DICTIONARIES

Deutsches Wörterbuch, eds. Jacob and Wilhelm Grimm *et al.* Berlin, 1859–1960. (2nd ed. in progress; letters A-F, 1962ff.)

Deutsches Wörterbuch, eds. Gerhard Wahrig *et al.* Gütersloh, 1970.

Dornseiff, Franz. *Der deutsche Wortschatz nach Sachgruppen.* 7th ed. Berlin, 1970.

Duden: *Rechtschreibung der deutschen Sprache und der Fremdwörter*, 17th ed. Mannheim, 1973.

Heyse, Johann. *Allgemeines verdeutschendes und erklärendes Fremdwörterbuch.* 21st ed. Hanover, 1922.

Kluge, Friedrich. *Etymologisches Wörterbuch der deutschen Sprache.* Revised by Walther Mitzka. 20th ed. Berlin, 1967.

Küpper, Heinz. *Wörterbuch der deutschen Umgangssprache.* Hamburg, 1955–70.

Lipperheide, Franz von. *Spruchwörterbuch.* 3rd ed. Leipzig, 1935.

Paul, Hermann. *Deutsches Wörterbuch.* Revised by Werner Betz. 5th ed. Tübingen, 1966 (6th ed. [= 5th ed.] Studienausgabe, 1968.)

Schulz, Hans, and Otto Basler. *Deutsches Fremdwörterbuch.* Strasbourg and Berlin. Vol. I, 1913; Vol. 2, 1942; Vol. 3, in preparation.

Der Sprach-Brockhaus. 7th rev. ed. Wiesbaden, 1968.

Trübners Deutsches Wörterbuch, eds. Alfred Götze and Walther Mitzka. Berlin, 1939–57.

BILINGUAL DICTIONARIES

Cassell's German Dictionary. Revised ed. New York, 1971.

Engeroff, Karl, and Cicely Lovelace-Käufer. *An English-German Dictionary of Idioms.* 2nd enlarged ed. Munich, 1967.

Farrell, Ralph Barstow. *A Dictionary of German Synonyms*, 2nd ed. Cambridge, Eng., 1971.

Langenscheidt's Concise German Dictionary. New York, 1969.

Langenscheidt's Muret-Sanders Encyclopedic Dictionary of the English and German Languages, ed. Otto Springer. New York, 1969.

Langenscheidt's New College German Dictionary. German-English/English-German. Berlin, Munich, Zurich, 1973.

Taylor, Ronald, and Walter Gottschalk. *A German–English Dictionary of Idioms.* 2nd corrected ed. Munich, 1966.

PHONETICS

Dieth, Eugen. *Vademekum der Phonetik.* 2nd ed. Bern, 1968.

Essen, Otto von. *Allegemeine und angewandte Phonetik.* 4th ed. Berlin, 1966.

Moulton, William G. *The Sounds of English and German.* (Contrastive Structure Series of the Modern Language Association's Center for Applied Linguistics, No. 1.) Chicago, 1962.

Siebs, Theodor. *Deutsche Aussprache*, eds. Helmut de Boor, Hugo Moser, and Christian Winkler. 19th rev. ed. Berlin, 1971.

Wängler, Hans Heinrich. *Grundriß einer Phonetik des Deutschen mit einer allgemeinen Einführung in die Phonetik.* 2nd rev. ed. Marburg, 1967.

DIALECTOLOGY

Bach, Adolf. *Deutsche Mundartforschung.* 3rd ed. Heidelberg, 1969.

Deutscher Sprachatlas, eds. Ferdinand Wrede, Bernard Martin, and Walther Mitzka. Marburg, 1927–56.

Deutscher Wortatlas, eds. Walther Mitzka and Ludwig Erich Schmitt. Gießen, 1951–71.

Grimme, Hubert. *Plattdeutsche Mundarten.* (Sammlung Göschen, No. 461) 2nd ed. Berlin and Leipzig, 1922.

Keller, Rudolf Ernst. *German Dialects.* Manchester, 1961.

Lautbibliothek der deutschen Mundarten, eds. Eberhard Zwirner *et al.* Göttingen, 1958ff.

Martin, Bernard. *Die deutschen Mundarten.* 2nd ed. Heidelberg, 1959.

Mitzka, Walther. *Deutsche Mundarten.* Heidelberg, 1943.

———. *Handbuch zum Deutschen Sprachatlas.* Marburg, 1952.

Sarauw, Christian. *Niederdeutsche Forschungen.* Copenhagen, 1921–24.

Schmitt, Ludwig Erich. *Deutsche Wortforschung in europäischen Bezügen: Untersuchungen zum Deutschen Wortatlas.* Gießen, 1958ff.

Schwarz, Ernst. *Die deutschen Mundarten.* Göttingen, 1950.

ONOMASTICS (WORT- UND NAMENKUNDE)

Bach, Adolf. *Deutsche Namenkunde.* 2nd ed. Heidelberg, 1952–56.

Deutsche Wortgeschichte, eds. Friedrich Maurer and Friedrich Stroh. 2nd ed. Berlin, 1959.

Gottschald, Max. *Die deutschen Personennamen.* Revised by E. Brodführer. (Sammlung Göschen, No. 422). 2nd ed. Berlin, 1955.

Schirmer, Alfred. *Deutsche Wortkunde.* Revised by Walther Mitzka. (Sammlung Göschen, No. 929.) 6th ed. Berlin, 1969.

Schwarz, Ernst. *Deutsche Namenforschung.* Göttingen, 1949–50.

Seiler, Friedrich. *Deutsche Sprichwörterkunde.* Munich, 1922.

Trier, Jost. *Der deutsche Wortschatz im Sinnbezirk des Verstandes.* Heidelberg, 1931.

PERIODICALS

This partial listing of journals devoted to or at least containing occasional contributions to the field of Germanic or German philology is limited to those periodicals currently being published. No attempt is made to give the various titles under which a given journal may have appeared in the past. The date refers to the first year of publication, though few of the older European journals have had an uninterrupted run.

Acta philologica Scandinavica. Copenhagen, 1962——.
Archiv für das Studium der neueren Sprachen. Braunschweig, 1846——.
Beiträge zur Geschichte der deutschen Sprache und Literatur. Tübingen,
    1874——. (The title of this important journal is sometimes abbreviated
    to *Beiträge*—as it is in this book—or is given as *PBB*, the letters
    standing for *Paul-Braune Beiträge.* Hermann Paul and Wilhelm Braune
    were the founders and first editors of the periodical.)
Beiträge zur Namenforschung. Heidelberg, 1949——.
Der Deutschunterricht. Stuttgart, 1949——.
Études germaniques. Paris, 1946——.
Germanic Review (GR). New York, 1926——.
Germanisch-Romanische Monatsschrift (GRM). Heidelberg, 1909——.
German Quarterly (GQ). Appleton, Wisconsin, 1928——.
IRAL (= International Review of Applied Linguistics in Language
    Teaching. The abbreviation, however, is the actual title). Heidelberg,
    1963——.
Journal of English and Germanic Philology (JEGP). Urbana, Illinois,
    1897——.
Korrespondenzblatt des Vereins für niederdeutsche Sprachforschung. Neu-
    münster, 1875——.
Modern Language Journal (MLJ). Ann Arbor, Mich., 1916——.
Modern Language Notes (MLN). Baltimore, Md., 1886——.
Modern Language Quarterly (MLQ). Seattle, Wash., 1939——.
Modern Language Review (MLR). Cambridge, Eng., 1905——.
Monatshefte. Madison. Wis., 1899——.
Muttersprache. Lüneburg, 1958——.
Neuphilologische Mitteilungen. Helsinki, 1899——.
Niederdeutsche Mitteilungen. Lund, 1945——.
Niederdeutsches Jahrbuch. Neumünster, 1877——.
Philological Quarterly (PQ). Iowa City, Iowa, 1922——.
Publications of the Modern Language Association of America (PMLA).
    Menasha, Wis., 1884——.
Unterrichtspraxis (UP). Philadelphia, Pa., 1968——.
Wirkendes Wort. Düsseldorf, 1950——.
Yearbook of the German Society of Pennsylvania. Philadelphia, Pa.,
    1950——.
Zeitschrift für deutsche Philologie (ZfdPh). Berlin, 1868——.
Zeitschrift für deutsches Altertum und deutsche Literatur (ZfdA). Wies-
    baden, 1841——.
Zeitschrift für deutsche Sprache (ZfdS). Berlin, 1964——.
Zeitschrift für deutsche Wortforschung (ZfdWf). Berlin, 1901——. Neue
    Folge 1, 1960 (= Vol. 46 in the old series that ran from 1900 to 1914).
Zeitschrift für Dialectologie und Linguistik (ZfDl). Wiesbaden, 1969——.
Zeitschrift für Mundartforschung (ZfMaf). Wiesbaden, 1935——.

CHAPTER ONE: INDO-EUROPEAN

*General Works on Language and on the Historico-comparative
Method in Linguistics*

Bloomfield, Leonard. *Language*. New York, 1933.

Gray, Louis H. *Foundations of Language*. Corrected ed. New York, 1958.

Lehmann, Winfred P. *Historical Linguistics*. 2nd ed. New York, 1973.

Meillet, Antoine. *La méthode comparative en linguistique historique*. Oslo,
1925. (English translation by Gordon B. Ford, Jr., *The Comparative
Method in Historical Linguistics*. Paris, 1967).

Porzig, Walter. *Das Wunder der Sprache*. 4th ed. Bern, 1967.

Saussure, Ferdinand de. *Cours de linguistique générale*. Paris, 1916. (This
work has been widely translated. The English version is by Wade
Baskin, *Course in General Linguistics*. New York, 1959).

Vendryes, Joseph. *Le langage: introduction linguistique à l'histoire*. 2nd ed.
Paris, 1959. (There is an English translation of the first edition of
1921: *Language: A Linguistic Introduction to History*. New York, 1925).

Wartburg, Walter von. *Einführung in Problematik und Methodik der
Sprachwissenschaft*. Revised by G. Ineichen. 3rd ed. Tübingen, 1970.
(There is a French translation: *Problèmes et méthodes de la linguistique*.
Paris, 1946).

Waterman, John T. *Perspectives in Linguistics*. 2nd ed. Chicago, 1970.

Weinreich, Uriel. *Languages in Contact*. New York, 1953.

Bibliographies

"Annual Bibliography," in *Publications of the Modern Language Association of America*. Menasha, Wis., 1921——. (See under "General
Language and Linguistics.")

Bibliographie linguistique. Utrecht, 1939——. (See under "General
Linguistics" and "Indo-European Languages.")

Indogermanisches Jahrbuch. Strasbourg and Berlin, 1914——.

Journals Devoted to General and Indo-European Linguistics

Archivum linguisticum. Glasgow, 1949——.

Bulletin de la société de linguistique de Paris. Paris, 1869——.

Indogermanische Forschungen. Strasbourg and Berlin, 1892——.

Journal of the American Oriental Society. New Haven, Conn., 1850——.

Kratylos. Wiesbaden, 1956——.

Language: Journal of the Linguistic Society of America. Baltimore, Md.,
1925——.

Lingua. Haarlem, 1952——.

Mémoires de la société de linguistique de Paris. Paris, 1868——.

Norsk Tidskrift for Sprogvidenskap. Oslo, 1928——.

Orbis, Louvain, 1952——.

Die Sprache: Zeitschrift für Sprachwissenschaft. Vienna, 1949——.

Voprosy jazykoznanija. Moscow, 1952——.

Word: Journal of the Linguistic Circle of New York. New York, 1947———.
Wörter und Sachen. Heidelberg, 1909———.
Zeitschrift für vergleichende Sprachforschung. Berlin and Göttingen, 1852———. (Sometimes referred to as "Kuhn's *Zeitschrift*" and abbreviated *KZ*).

Dictionaries

Buck, Carl D. *A Dictionary of Selected Synonyms in the Principal Indo-European Languages*. Chicago, 1949.
Pokorny, Julius. *Indogermanisches etymologisches Wörterbuch*. Bern/ Munich, 1959–69.
Walde, Alois, and Julius Pokorny. *Vergleichendes Wörterbuch der indogermanischen Sprachen*. Berlin and Leipzig, 1927–32.

Encyclopedias

Ebert, Max (ed.). *Reallexikon der Vorgeschichte*. Berlin, 1924–32.
Schrader, Otto, and Alfons Nehring (eds.). *Reallexikon der indogermanischen Altertumskunde*. 2nd ed. Berlin and Leipzig, 1917–29.

Grammars

Brugmann, Karl. *Grundriß der vergleichenden Grammatik der indogermanischen Sprachen*. 2nd ed. Strasbourg, 1897–1916. (reprinted in Berlin, 1967.) (English translation of 1st ed.: *Elements of the Comparative Grammar of the Indo-Germanic Languages*. New York, 1888–95.)
———. *Kurze vergleichende Grammatik der indogermanischen Sprachen*. Strasbourg, 1904. (reprinted in Berlin, 1970; there is a French translation: *Abrégé de grammaire comparée des langue indo-européennes*. Paris, 1905.)
Hirt, Herman. *Indogermanische Grammatik*. Heidelberg, 1921–37.
Hudson-Williams, Thomas. *A Short Introduction to the Study of Comparative Grammar (Indo-European)*. Cardiff, 1935.
Kieckers, Ernst. *Einführung in die indogermanische Sprachwissenschaft*. Munich, 1933.
Krahe, Hans. *Indogermanische Sprachwissenschaft*. 5th ed. Berlin, 1966–69. (Sammlung Göschen, Nos. 59, 64.)
Meillet, Antoine. *Introduction à l'étude comparative des langues indo-européennes*. 8th ed. Paris, 1937. (Available in a reprint by the University of Alabama Press.)

Monographs

Arntz, Helmut (ed.). *Germanen und Indogermanen: Festschrift für Herman Hirt*. Heidelberg, 1936.

Brandenstein, Wilhelm (ed.). *Studien zur indogermanischen Grundsprache.* Vienna, 1952.

Childe, Vere Gordon. *The Aryans: A Study of Indo-European Origins.* London, 1926.

Dauzat, Albert. *L'Europe linguistique.* 2nd ed. Paris, 1953.

Feist, Sigmund. *Kultur, Ausbreitung und Herkunft der Indogermanen.* Berlin, 1913.

Hencken, Hugh. *Indo-European Languages and Archeology.* (American Anthropologist, Memoir 84.) Menasha, Wis., 1955.

Hirt, Herman. *Die Indogermanen: Ihre Verbreitung, ihre Urheimat und ihre Kultur.* Strasbourg, 1905–17.

Krahe, Hans. *Sprache und Vorzeit.* Heidelberg, 1954.

———. *Sprachverwandtschaft im alten Europa.* Heidelberg, 1950.

Meillet, Antoine. *Les dialectes indoeuropéens.* 2nd ed. Paris, 1922. (English translation by Samuel N. Rosenberg. *The Indo-European Dialects.* University, Ala., 1967.)

———, and Marcel Cohen (eds.). *Les langues du monde.* 2nd ed. Paris, 1952.

Pisani, Vittore. *Le lingue indoeuropee.* 2nd ed. Brescia, 1964.

Porzig, Walter. *Die Gliederung des indogermanischen Sprachgebiets.* Heidelberg, 1954.

Schmidt, Wilhelm, S.V.D. *Die Sprachfamilien und Sprachenkreise der Erde.* Heidelberg, 1926.

Schrader, Otto, and Hans Krahe. *Die Indogermanen.* 4th ed. Leipzig, 1935.

Thieme, Paul. *Die Heimat der indogermanischen Gemeinsprache.* Wiesbaden, 1954.

Articles

Cardona, George. Review of Hans Krahe, *Indogermanische Sprachwissenschaft*, Vol. II, in *Language*, 36 (1960), 534–39.

Childe, V. Gordon. "Old World Prehistory: Neolithic," *Anthropology Today* (Chicago, 1953), pp. 193–210.

Clark, J. Grahame D. "Archeological Theories and Interpretation: Old World," *Anthropology Today* (Chicago, 1953), pp. 343–60.

Cowgill, Warren. Review of Hans Krahe, *Indogermanische Sprachwissenschaft*, Vol. I, in *Language*, 35 (1959), 90–94.

Diver, William. Review of Winfred P. Lehmann, *Historical Linguistics*, *Word*, 19 (1963), 100–106.

Dyen, Isidore. "Language Distribution and Migration Theory," *Language*, 32 (1959), 611–26.

Dyen, Isidore. "Reconstruction, the Comparative Method, and the Protolanguage Uniformity Assumption," *Language*, 45, no. 3 (1969), 499–518.

Greenberg, Joseph H. "Historical Linguistics and Unwritten Languages," *Anthropology Today* (Chicago, 1953), pp. 265–86.

Gudschinsky, Sarah C. "The ABC's of Lexicostatistics (Glottochronology)," *Word* 12 (1956), 175–210.

Heizer, Robert F. "Long-Range Dating in Archeology," *Anthropology Today* (Chicago, 1953), pp. 3–42.

Hoenigswald, Henry M. "The Principal Step in Comparative Grammar," *Language*, 26 (1950), 357–64.

———. Review of Paul Thieme, *Die Heimat der indogermanischen Gemeinsprache*, *Language*, 32 (1956), 313–16.

Höfler, Otto. "Stammbaumtheorie, Wellentheorie, Entfaltungstheorie," *Beiträge*, 77 (1955), 30–55, 424–76; 78 (1956), 1–44.

Hoijer, Harry. "The Relation of Language to Culture," *Anthropology Today* (Chicago, 1953), pp. 554–73.

"Indo-Europeans," in *The Encyclopedia Britannica*, 12th ed. (Chicago, 1961), pp. 265–67.

Krahe, Hans. "Was ist vergleichende Sprachwissenschaft?" *Gymnasium*, 56 (1949), 23–33.

Lane, George S. "On the Present State of Indo-European Linguistics," *Language*, 25 (1949), 333–42.

———. Review of Otto Höfler, "Stammbaumtheorie . . . [see above]," *Language*, 35 (1959), 315–21.

Lees, Robert B. "The Basis of Glottochronology," *Language*, 29 (1953), 113–27.

Marchand, James W. "Was There Ever a Uniform Proto-Indo-European?" *Orbis*, 4 (1955), 428ff.

Maurer, Fritz. "Zur vor- und frühdeutschen Sprachgeschichte," *Der Deutschunterricht*, 3 (1951), 5–20.

Movius, Hallam L., Jr. "Old World Prehistory: Paleolithic," *Anthropology Today* (Chicago, 1953), pp. 163–92.

Oakley, Kenneth P. "Dating Fossil Human Remains," *Anthropology Today* (Chicago, 1953), pp. 43–56.

Philippson, Ernst A. "Der Stand der Indogermanenfrage und der Ursprung der Germanen, *GQ*, 14 (1941), 143–54.

Pulgram, Ernst. "Family Tree, Wave Theory and Dialectology," *Orbis*, 2 (1953), 67–72.

———. "Proto-Indo-European Reality and Reconstruction," *Language*, 35 (1959), 421–26.

Rouse, Irving. "The Strategy of Culture History," *Anthropology Today* (Chicago, 1953), pp. 57–76.

Schapiro, Meyer. "Style," *Anthropology Today* (Chicago, 1953), pp. 287–312.

Stevick, Robert D. "The Biological Model and Historical Linguistics," *Language*, 39 (1963), 159–69.

Sturtevant, Edgar H. "The Prehistory of Indo-European: A Summary," *Language*, 28 (1952), 177–81.

Teeter, Karl V. "Lexicostatistics and Genetic Relationship," *Language*, 39 (1963), 638–48.

Teilhard de Chardin, Pierre. "The Idea of Fossil Man," *Anthropology Today* (Chicago, 1953), pp. 93–100.

Tovar, Antonio. "Linguistics and Prehistory," *Word*, 10 (1954), 333–50.

Trubetzkoy, Nikolaus S. "Gedanken über das Indogermanenproblem," *Acta linguistica*, 1 (1939), 81–89.

Vallois, Henri V. "Race", *Anthropology Today* (Chicago, 1953), pp. 145–62.

Weinert, Hans. "Der fossile Mensch," *Anthropology Today* (Chicago, 1953), pp. 101–19.

Chapter Two: Germanic

Many of the items listed in this section contain material pertinent to subsequent chapters as well. The student is therefore advised to pay special attention to the entries given under Bibliographies, Dictionaries, and Encyclopedias.

Bibliographies

"Annual Bibliography." *Publications of the Modern Language Association of America*. Menasha, Wis., 1921——. (See under "Germanic languages and literatures.")

Bibliographie linguistique. Utrecht, 1939——. (See under "Langues germaniques.") "Bibliographie zur deutschen Philologie," *Archiv für das Studium der neueren Sprachen*. Braunschweig, 1950——.

"Bibliography of Scandinavian Philology," *Acta Philologica Scandinavica*. Copenhagen, 1952——.

Deutsche Bibliographie: Zeitschriften 1945–1952. Frankfurt a.M., 1958.

Diesch, Carl H. *Bibliographie der germanistischen Zeitschriften*. Leipzig, 1927. (Bibliographical Publications of the Germanic Section, Modern Language Association of America, No. 1.)

Germanistik: Internationales Referatenorgan mit bibliographischen Hinweisen. Heidelberg, 1960——.

Hansel, Johannes. *Bücherkunde für Germanisten*. 6th ed. Berlin, 1972.

Indogermanisches Jahrbuch. Strasbourg and Berlin, 1914——. (See under "Germanisch.")

Jahresbericht für deutsche Sprache und Literatur. Berlin, 1959——. (This publication is the continuation of what were for many years the two principal annual bibliographies devoted to Germanic philology and German literature, respectively. Consult Hansel's *Bücherkunde*, III, par. 18a for details.)

Loewenthal, Fritz. *Bibliographisches Handbuch zur deutschen Philologie*. Halle, 1932.

Mossé, Ferdinand. "Bibliographica Gotica. A Bibliography of Writings on the Gothic Language to the End of 1949," *Medieval Studies*, 12 (1950), 237–324; "Supplement," 15 (1953), 169–83; Mossé, Ferdinand, and James W. Marchand. "Second Supplement," 19 (1957), 174–96.

Springer, Otto. "Germanic Bibliography 1940–1945," *JEGP*, 45 (1946), 251–326.

Union List of Periodicals Dealing with Germanic Languages and Literatures. London, 1956.

The Year's Work in Modern Language Studies. Oxford and Cambridge, 1929———. (See under "German language.")

Dictionaries (*Etymological*)

Falk, Hjalmar, and Alf Torp. *Norwegisch-dänisches etymologisches Wörterbuch,* trans. Hermann Davidsen. Heidelberg, 1910.

Feist, Sigmund. *Vergleichendes Wörterbuch der gotischen Sprache.* 3rd ed. Leiden, 1939.

Franck, Johannes. *Etymologisch Woordenboek der Nederlandsche taal.* 2nd ed. 's-Gravenhage, 1912.

Hellquist, Elof. *Svensk etymologisk ordbok.* 3rd ed. Lund., 1970.

Holthausen, Ferdinand. *Altenglisches etymologisches Wörterbuch.* 2nd ed. Heidelberg, 1963.

Jóhannesson, Alexander. *Isländisches etymologisches Wörterbuch.* Bern, 1951———.

Kluge, Friedrich. *Etymologisches Wörterbuch der deutschen Sprache,* ed. Walther Mitzka. 20th ed. Berlin, 1967.

Skeat, Walter W. *An Etymological Dictionary of the English Language.* 4th ed. Oxford, 1910. (Revised and enlarged ed., Oxford 1963.)

Torp, Alf, and Hjalmar Falk. *Wortschatz der germanischen Spracheinheit.* 4th ed. Göttingen, 1909.

Encyclopedias

Deutsche Philologie im Aufriß, eds. Wolfgang Stammler *et al.* 2nd ed. Berlin, 1957–1962. (reprinted in Berlin, 1966ff.)

Grundriß der germanischen Philologie, eds. Hermann Paul *et al.* 2nd ed. Strasbourg, 1900–1909. (A third edition, begun in 1911, is still appearing as a series of independent monographs. It lacks the continuity and articulation of the second edition.)

Hoops, Johannes. *Reallexikon der germanischen Altertumskunde.* 2nd rev. ed. Eds. H. Beck *et al.* Berlin, 1968ff.

Müllenhoff, Karl. *Deutsche Altertumskunde.* Berlin, 1890–1920. (reprinted in Amsterdam, 1970ff.)

Schwarz, Ernst. *Deutsche und germanische Philologie.* Heidelberg, 1951.

Stroh, Friedrich. *Handbuch der germanischen Philologie.* Berlin, 1952.

Grammars

Boer, Richard C. *Oorgermaansch handboek.* 2nd ed. Haarlem, 1924.

Delbrück, Berthold. *Germanische Syntax.* Leipzig, 1910–19.

Hirt, Herman, *Handbuch des Urgermanischen.* Heidelberg, 1931–34.

Kluge, Friedrich. *Nominale Stammbildungslehre der altgermanischen Dialekte.* 3rd ed. Freiburg i.B., 1926.

———. *Urgermanisch: Vorgeschichte der altgermanischen Dialekte.* 3rd ed. Strasbourg, 1913.

Krahe, Hans. *Germanische Sprachwissenchaft.* 7th ed. (Sammlung Göschen, Nos. 238, 780.) Berlin, 1969.
Prokosch, Eduard. *A Comparative Germanic Grammar.* Philadelphia, 1939. (An inexpensive paper-bound copy of this grammar may be ordered through the secretary of the Linguistic Society of America. See a recent number of the society's journal, *Language,* for the proper address.)
Streitberg, Wilhelm. *Urgermanische Grammatik.* 3rd ed. Heidelberg, 1963.

Monographs

Arntz, Helmut. "Gemeingermanisch," in *Germanen und Indo-Germanen,* ed. Hermann Arntz. Heidelberg, 1936. Vol. II, pp. 429ff.
———. *Handbuch der Runenkunde.* 2nd ed. Halle, 1944.
———. "Urgermanisch, Gotisch und Nordisch," in *Beiträge zur germanischen Sprachwissenschaft: Festschrift für Otto Behaghel.* Heidelberg, 1924.
———, and Hans Zeiss. *Die einheimischen Runendenkmäler des Festlandes.* Leipzig, 1939.
Elliot, Ralph. *Runes: An Introduction.* Cambridge, Eng., 1959.
Fischer, Hermann. *Deutsche Altertumskunde in Grundzügen.* 3rd ed. Leipzig, 1931.
Fourquet, Jean. *Les mutations consonantiques du germanique.* Paris, 1948.
Karsten, Torsten E. *Die Germanen: Eine Einführung in die Geschichte ihrer Sprache und Kultur.* Berlin, 1928.
Krause, Wolfgang. *Runeninschriften im älteren Futhark.* Halle, 1937.
———. *Runen* (Sammlung Göschen, No. 1244/1244a.) Berlin, 1970.
Maurer, Friedrich. *Nordgermanen und Alemannen.* 3rd ed. Strasbourg, 1952.
Meillet, Antoine. *Caractères généraux des langues germaniques.* 4th ed. Paris, 1930. (English translation by William P. Dismukes. *General Characteristics of the Germanic Languages.* Coral Gables, 1970.)
Much, Rudolph. *Deutsche Stammeskunde.* 3rd ed. Berlin and Leipzig, 1920.
———. *Der Eintritt der Germanen in die Weltgeschichte.* Vienna, 1925.
———. *Die Germania des Tacitus.* Revised and ed. by Wolfgang Lange. Heidelberg, 1967.
Müllenhoff, Karl. *Die Germania des Tacitus erläutert.* Berlin, 1920. (reprinted in Amsterdam, 1970.)
Neckel, Gustav. *Altgermanische Kultur.* Leipzig, 1925.
———. *Germanen und Kelten.* Heidelberg, 1929.
Norden, Eduard. *Die germanische Urgeschichte in Tacitus Germania.* Leipzig, 1923.
Schütte, Gudmund. *Our Forefathers, the Gothonic Nations.* Cambridge, Eng., 1933.
Schwarz, Ernst. *Goten, Nordgermanen, Angelsachsen.* Bern and Munich, 1951.
Tacitus on Britain and Germany: A New Translation of the "Agricola" and the "Germania," trans. H. Mattingly. (Penguin Books.) Middlesex, Eng., 1948.

Articles

Arndt, Walter W. "The Performance of Glottochronology in Germanic," *Language*, 35 (1959), 180–92.

Beck, Heinrich. "Sprachliche Argumente zum Problem des Runenaufkommens," *ZfdA*, 101, No. 1 (1972), 1–13.

Bennett, William H. "The Earliest Germanic Umlauts and the Gothic Migrations," *Language*, 28 (1952), 339–42.

———. "The Operation and Relative Chronology of Verner's Law," *Language*, 44, 2, pt. 1 (1968), 219–23.

Betz, Werner. "Die Lehnbildungen und der abendländische Sprachausgleich," *Beiträge*, 67 (1944), 275–302.

Biener, Clemens. "Steigerungsadverbia bei Adjektiven," *Beiträge*, 64 (1940), 165–204.

Carr, Charles T. "The Oldest Use of the Preposition *zu* in Germanic," *JEGP*, 33 (1934), 219–21.

Delbrück, Berthold. "Das schwache Adjektivum und der Artikel im Germanischen," *Indogermanische Forschungen*, 26 (1918), 187–99.

Dillon, Myles. "Germanic and Celtic," *JEGP*, 42 (1943), 492–98.

Feist, Sigmund. "Illyrisch-germanisches," *Beiträge*, 53 (1929), 397–401.

Fiedler, H. G. "The Oldest Study of Germanic Proper Names," *MLR*, 37 (1942), 185–92.

Fowkes, Robert A. "Germanic Etymologies," *JEGP*, 44 (1945), 208–28.

———. "Two Germanic Etymologies," *JEGP*, 42 (1943), 269–308.

Frings, Theodor. "Zur Grundlegung einer Geschichte der deutschen Sprache," *Beiträge*, 76 (1955), 401–534.

Fromm, Hans. "Die ältesten germanischen Lehnwörter im Finnischen," *ZfdA*, 88 (1957–58), 81–101, 211–40, 299–324.

Galton, Herbert. "Sound Shift and Diphthongization in Germanic," *JEGP*, 53 (1954), 585–600.

Gutenbrunner, Siegfried. "Vorindogermanisches bei den rheinischen Germanen?" *ZfdA*, 88 (1958), 241–49.

———. "Zum Namen Germanen," *Beiträge*, 65 (1942), 106–20.

Hammerich, Louis L. "Die germanische und die hochdeutsche Lautverschiebung. I. Wie entsteht die germanische Lautverschiebung?" *Beiträge*, 77 (1955), 1–29.

Hamp, Eric P. "Negau *harigasti*," *Language*, 31 (1955), 1–3.

Helm, Karl. "Zur vorgeschichtlichen Betonung des germanischen Substantivums," *Beiträge*, 71 (1961), 250–65.

Holmes, Urban T. "Germanic Influence on Old French Syntax," *Language*, 7 (1931), 194–99.

Hoops, Johannes. " 'Right' and 'Left' in the Germanic Languages," *Etudes germaniques*, 5 (1950), 81–96.

Jung, Edmund. "Chronologie relative des faits phonétiques en germanique commun," *Etudes germaniques*, 11 (1956), 294–320.

Kabell, Aage. "Münchner Runenfunde," *ZfdA*, 99, No. 2 (1970), 83–87.

Kahane, Henry R. and Renée T. "Germanic Derivatives of Romance Words," *JEGP*, 60 (1961), 460–76.

Karsten, Torsten E. "Die germanischen Lehnwörter im Finnischen," *GRM*, 6 (1914), 65ff.

Krogmann, Willy. "Der Ursprung der Germanen," *ZfdPh*, 60 (1935) 279–83.

Kuhn, Hans. "Gewässernamen in Siedlungs- und Bevölkerungsnamen," *ZfdA*, 98, No. 3 (1969), 161–70.

Kuhn, Hans. "Zur Gliederung der germanischen Sprachen," *ZfdA*, 86 (1955), 1–47.

Kurath, Hans. "Prokosch's Theory of the Germanic and the High German Consonant Shift: A Reply," *JEGP*, 39 (1940), 376–82. (See article by Strong and Willey below.)

Lane, George S. "The Germano-Celtic Vocabulary," *Language*, 9 (1933), 244–64.

———. "Some Semantic Borrowings in Wulfila," *PQ*, 12 (1933), 321–26.

———. "Two Germanic Etymologies," *JEGP*, 32 (1933), 293–95, 483–87.

Laur, Wolfgang. "Die germanischen Frauennamen auf- gard/gerðr und ihr Ursprung aus dem Bereich des Kultischen," *Beiträge*, 73 (1951), 321–46.

———. "Zur Herkunftsfrage der Nordfriesen," *GRM*, 4 (1954), 324–36.

Lehmann, Winfred P. "The Conservatism of Germanic Phonology," *JEGP*, 52 (1953), 140–52.

———. "A Definition of Proto-Germanic," *Language*, 37 (1961), 67–74.

———. "The Germanic Weak Preterite Endings," *Language*, 19 (1943), 313–19.

———. "Some Phonological Observations Based on Examination of the Germanic Consonant Shift," *Monatshefte*, 55 (1963), 229–35.

Lehmann, Winfred P., "The Proto-Germanic Words Inherited from Proto-Indo-European which Reflect the Social and Economic Status of the Speakers," *ZfMaf*, 35, No. 1 (1968), 1–25.

Lloyd, Albert L. "Is There an *a*-umlaut of *i* in Germanic?" *Language*, 42, No. 4 (1966), 738–45.

Lohse, Gustav. "Zur Frühgeschichte der Nordseegermanischen (Ingwäonischen) Dialekte," *GRM*, 28 (1940), 24–39.

Lotspeich, C. M. "Romance and Germanic Linguistic Tendencies," *JEGP*, 24 (1925), 325–34.

———. "A Theory of Ablaut," *JEGP*, 16 (1917), 173–86.

McClean, R. J. "Germanic Nursery Words," *MLR*, 42 (1947), 353–57.

Marchand, James W. "Notes on Gothic Manuscripts," *JEGP*, 56 (1957), 213–24.

Maurer, Friedrich. "Gemeingermanisch," *Der Deutschunterricht*, 1 (1949), 1ff.

———. "Zur vor- und frühdeutschen Sprachgeschichte," *Der Deutschunterricht*, 3 (1951), 5–21.

Mentz, Arthur. "Schrift und Sprache der Burgunder," *ZfdA*, 85 (1954), 1–17.

Metcalf, George J. "Konrad Gesner's Views on the Germanic Languages," *Monatshefte*, 55 (1963), 149–56.

Metlen, Michael. "Word Order," *JEGP*, 32 (1933), 531–33.

Mitzka, Walther. "Ostgermanische Lautverschiebung?" *ZfdA*, 96, No. 4 (1967), 247–59.

Moulton, William G. "The Stops and Spirants of Early Germanic," *Language*, 30 (1954), 1–42.

Mueller, Eugen H. "Theories Concerning the Origin of the Grammatical Gender in German," *GQ*, 16 (1943), 90–98.

Must, Gustav. "The Inscription of the Spearhead of Kovel," *Language*, 31 (1955), 493–98.

———. "The Origin of the Germanic Dental Preterit," *Language*, 27 (1951), 121–35.

Neckel, Gustav. "Die Verwandtschaft der germanischen Sprachen untereinander," *Beiträge*, 51 (1927), 1–17.

Nordmeyer, George. "Lautverschiebungserklärungen," *JEGP*, 35 (1936), 482–95.

Penzl, Herbert. "Orthography and Phonemes in Wulfila's Gothic," *JEGP*, 49 (1950), 217–30.

Pittioni, Richard. "Zur Frage nach der Herkunft der Runen und ihrer Verankerung in der Kultur der europäischen Bronzezeit," *Beiträge*, 65 (1941), 373–84.

Pokorny, Julius. "Germanen und Kelten," *ZfdPh*, 53 (1928), 383–85.

Prokosch, Eduard. "Die deutsche Lautverschiebung und die Völkerwanderung," *JEGP*, 16 (1917), 1–26.

———. "Hypothesis of a Pre-Germanic Substratum," *GR*, 1 (1926),47–71.

———. "Inflectional Contrasts in Germanic," *JEGP*, 20 (1921), 468–90.

———. "Lautverschiebung und Lenierung," *JEGP*, 21 (1922), 119–26.

Reichardt, Konstantin. "The Inscription on Helmet B of Negau," *Language*, 29 (1953), 306–16.

Rogge, Christian. "Entstehung des schwachen Praeteritums im Germanischen," *Beiträge*, 50 (1927), 321–36.

Rosenfeld, Helmut. "Die Inschrift des Helms von Negau," *ZfdA*, 86 (1955–56), 241–65.

———. "Name und Kult der Istvionen (Istwäonen)," *ZfdA*, 90 (1960), 161–81.

Senn, Alfred. "Verbal Aspects in Germanic, Slavic, and Baltic," *Language*, 35 (1949), 402–9.

Simon, Karl. "Die Runenbewegung und das Arianische Christentum," *ZfdPh*, 53 (1928), 41–48.

———. "Die vorgeschichtliche Besiedlung Deutschlands und das germanisch-deutsche Sprachproblem," *ZfdPh*, 55 (1930), 129–47.

Springer, Otto. "German and West Germanic," *GR*, 16 (1941), 3–20.

Strong, Leon H., and Norman L. Willey. "Dynamic Consonantal Permutation," *JEGP*, 39 (1940), 1–12.

Twaddell, W. Freeman. "The Inner Chronology of the Germanic Consonant Shift," *JEGP*, 38 (1939), 337–59.

Vayles, Joseph B. "Some Gothic Etymologies and the Theory of 'Restwörter'," *JEGP*, 66 (1967), 169–78.

Velten, Harry V. "A Note on the Sound-Shifts," *GR*, 7 (1932), 76–80.
———. "The Order of the Pre-Germanic Consonant Changes," *JEGP*, 43 (1944), 42–48.
Vendryes, Joseph, "Sur les plus anciens emprunts Germaniques en Latin," *Etudes germaniques*, 3 (1948), 131–37.
Walker, James A. "Gothic -leik- and German *lik- in the Light of Gothic Translations of Greek Originals," *PQ*, 28 (1949), 274–93.
Waterman, John T. "The Germanic Consonant Shift and the Theories of J. Fourquet: A Critique," *GQ*, 36 (1963), 165–70.
Wrede, Ferdinand. "Ingwäonen und Westgermanisch," *Zeitschrift für deutsche Mundarten*, 19 (1924), 270ff. (One of the previous titles of *Zeitschrift für Dialektologie und Linguistika*.)

CHAPTER THREE: THE OLD HIGH GERMAN PERIOD
(Old High German–Old Saxon)

Dictionaries

Graff, Eberhard G. *Althochdeutscher Sprachschatz oder Wörterbuch der althochdeutschen Sprache.* Berlin, 1834–46. (reprinted in Hildesheim, 1963.)
Holthausen, Ferdinand. *Altsächsisches Wörterbuch.* (Niederdeutsche Studien, Vol. 1) 2nd ed. Cologne, 1967.
Karg-Gasterstädt, Elisabeth, and Theodor Frings. *Althochdeutsches Wörterbuch.* Berlin, 1952——.
Schade, Oskar. *Altdeutsches Wörterbuch.* 2nd ed. Halle, 1872–82. (Reprinted in Hildesheim, 1969.)
Sehrt, Edward H. *Vollständiges Wörterbuch zum Heliand und zur altsächsischen Genesis.* 2nd ed. Göttingen, 1966.
Schützeichel, Rudolf. *Althochdeutsches Wörterbuch.* Tübingen, 1969.

Grammars

Baesecke, Georg. *Einführung in das Althochdeutsche.* Munich, 1918.
Basler, Otto. *Altsächsisch.* Freiburg i.B., 1923.
Braune, Wilhelm. *Althochdeutsche Grammatik.* Revised by Walther Mitzka. 12th ed. Tübingen, 1967.
Ellis, Jeffrey. *Elementary Old High German Grammar.* Corrected reprint. Oxford, 1966.
Gallée, Johann H. *Altsächsiche Grammatik.* 2nd ed. Halle, 1910.
Holthausen, Ferdinand. *Altsächsisches Elementarbuch.* 2nd ed. Heidelberg, 1921.
Naumann, Hans. *Althochdeutsches Elementarbuch.* Revised by Werner Betz. (Sammlung Göschen, No. 1111/1111a) 4th ed. Berlin, 1967.
Schatz, Josef. *Althochdeutsche Grammatik.* Göttingen, 1927.

Monographs

Aubin, Hermann. *Von Raum und Grenzen des deutschen Volkes.* Breslau, 1938.

Baesecke, Georg. *Der deutsche Abrogans und die Herkunft des deutschen Schrifttums.* Halle, 1930. (reprinted in Hildesheim, New York, 1970.)

———. *Der Vocabularius Sti. Galli in der angelsächsischen Mission.* Halle, 1933.

Betz, Werner. *Deutsch und Lateinisch. Die Lehnbildungen der althochdeutschen Benediktinerregel.* 2nd ed. Bonn, 1965.

———. *Der Einfluß des Lateinischen auf den althochdeutschen Sprachschatz: Der Abrogans.* Heidelberg, 1936.

Brinkmann, Hennig. *Sprachwandel und Sprachbewegung in althochdeutscher Zeit.* Jena, 1931.

Bruckner, Wilhelm. *Die Sprache der Langobarden.* Strasbourg, 1895. (reprinted in Berlin, 1969.)

Eis, Gerhard. *Altdeutsche Handschriften.* Munich, 1949.

Franz, Wilhelm. *Die lateinisch-romantischen Elemente im Althochdeutschen.* Strasbourg, 1884.

Frings, Theodor. *Antike und Christentum an der Wiege der deutschen Sprache.* Berlin, 1949.

———. *Sprache und Geschichte.* Halle, 1956.

Kirchner, Joachim. *Germanistische Handschriftenpraxis.* 2nd ed. Munich, 1967.

Maurer, Friedrich. *Leid: Studien zur Bedeutungs- und Problemgeschichte.* 3rd ed. Bern, 1964.

Penzl, Hermann. *Lautsystem und Lautwandel in den althochdeutschen Dialekten.* Munich, 1970.

Petri, Franz. *Germanisches Volkserbe in Wallonien und Frankreich.* Bonn, 1937.

———. *Zum Stand der Diskussion über die fränkische Landnahme und die Entstehung der germanisch-romanischen Sprachgrenze.* Bonn, 1954. (reprinted in Darmstadt, 1963.)

Rooth, Erich. *Saxonica: Beiträge zur niedersächsischen Sprachgeschichte.* Lund, 1949.

Simon, Werner. *Zur Sprachmischung im Heliand* (*Philologische Studien und Quellen,* Heft 27.) Berlin, 1965.

Steinbach, Franz. *Studien zur westdeutschen Stammes- und Volksgeschichte.* Jena, 1926. (reprinted in Darmstadt, 1962).

Trier, Jost. *Der deutsche Wortschatz im Sinnbezirk des Verstandes,* Vol. 1. Heidelberg, 1931.

Wagner, Kurt. *Die Gliederung der deutschen Mundarten.* (Abhandlungen der Mainzer Akademie, Geistes- und sozialwissenschaftliche Klasse, No. 12.) Mainz, 1954.

Wartburg, Walter von. *Umfang und Bedeutung der germanischen Siedlung in Nordgallien im 5. und 6. Jahrhundert im Spiegel der Sprache und der Ortsnamen.* Berlin, 1950.

Weisgerber, Leo. *Theudisk.* (Marburger Universitätsrede, No. 5.) Marburg, 1950.

Articles

Adolf, Helen. "OHG *wuntarôn* and the Verbs of Fear and Wonder (A Study in Onomasiology)," *JEGP*, 46 (1947), 395–406.

———. "Words, Objects, Ideas: OHG *gotawebbi*," *JEGP*, 58 (1959), 442–56.

Baesecke, Georg. "Das Althochdeutsche von Reichenau nach den Namen seiner Mönchslisten," *Beiträge*, 52 (1928), 92–148.

Betz, Werner. "Lateinisch und Deutsch," *Der Deutschunterricht*, 3 (1951), 21–36.

———. "Das gegenwärtige Bild des Althochdeutschen," *Der Deutschunterricht*, 5 (1953), 94–108.

Boor, Helmut de. "Zum althochdeutschen Wortschatz auf dem Gebiet der Weissagung," *Beiträge*, 67 (1944), 65–110.

Carr, Charles T. "Number in Old High German," *JEGP*, 35 (1936), 214–42.

———. "The Oldest Use of the Preposition *zu* in German," *JEGP*, 33 (1934), 219–21.

———. "Some Old High German Conjunctions," *JEGP*, 32 (1933), 488–503.

Galton, Herbert. "The Old High German Diphthongization and After," *JEGP*, 55 (1956), 8–12.

———. "The Old High German Epenthetic Vowel," *JEGP*, 55 (1956), 234–46.

Hammerich, Louis L. "Worin besteht die hochdeutsche Lautverschiebung?" *Beiträge*, 77 (1955), 165–203.

Heffner, R-M. S. "Zum Weissenburger Katechismus," *JEGP*, 40 (1941), 545–54, and 41 (1942), 194–200.

Höfler, Otto. "Die zweite Lautverschiebung bei Ostgermanen und Westgermanen," *Beiträge*, 79 (1957), 161–350.

Karg-Gasterstädt, Elisabeth. "Aus der Werkstatt des althochdeutschen Wörterbuches: Ehre und Ruhm im Althochdeutschen," *Beiträge*, 70 (1948), 305–31.

Kaspers, Wilhelm. "Germanische Götternamen," *ZfdA*, 83 (1951), 79–91.

———. "Wort- und Namenstudien zur Lex Salica," *ZfdA*, 82 (1950), 291–335.

Kufner, Herbert L. "History of the Middle Bavarian Vocalism," *Language*, 33 (1957), 519–29.

Lawson, Richard H. "The Alternation of First and Second Class Weak Verbs in *Otfried* and *Tatian*," *JEGP*, 60 (1961), 491–97.

———. "Old High German Past Tense as a Translation of Latin Present Tense in *Tatian*," *JEGP*, 58 (1959), 457–64.

———. "The Old High German Translations of Latin Future Active in *Tatian*," *JEGP*, 57 (1958), 64–71.

———. "The Prefix *gi-* as a Perfectivizing Future Significant in OHG *Tatian*," *JEGP*, 64 (1965), 90–97.

———. "The Verbal Prefix 'ge-' in the Old High German and Middle High German Benedictine Rules," *JEGP*, 67 (1968), 647–55.

Lindqvist, Axel. "Studien über Wortbildung und Wortwahl im Althochdeutschen mit besonderer Rücksicht auf die nomina actionis," *Beiträge*, 60 (1936), 1–133.

Lloyd, Albert L. "The Verbs of the Meaning Class 'Do or Make' in the Old High German of Notker Labeo," *GR*, 36 (1961), 245–56.

———. "Vowel Shortening and Stress in the Old High German of Notker Labeo," *JEGP*, 60 (1961), 79–101.

Loewe, Richard. "Die Dehnung von Vokalen einsilbiger Wörter im Althochdeutschen und Mittelhochdeutschen," *Beiträge*, 51 (1927), 271–87.

Mahlendorf Ursula R. "OS *Gêst*: OHG *Geist*," *JEGP*, 59 (1960), 480–90.

Marchand, James. "The Phonemic Status of OHG *E*," *Word*, 12 (1956), 82–90.

Maschke, Erich. "Studien zu Waffennamen der althochdeutschen Glossen," *ZfdPh*, 51 (1926), 137–99.

Mitzka, Walther. "Die althochdeutsche Lautverschiebung und der ungleiche fränkische Anteil," *ZfdA*, 83 (1951), 107–13.

———. "Hessen in althochdeutscher und mittelhochdeutscher Dialektgeographie," *Beiträge*, 75 (1953), 131–57.

———. "Das Langobardische und die althochdeutsche Dialektgeographie," *ZfMaf*, 20 (1951), 1ff.

Moser, Hugo, "Stamm und Mundart," *ZfMaf*, 20 (1952), 129ff.

Moser, Hugo. "Zu den Lautverschiebungen und ihrer methodischen Behandlung," *Der Deutschunterricht*, 6 (1954), 56–82.

Müller, Gertraud. "Aus der Werkstatt des althochdeutschen Wörterbuches: die althochdeutschen Partikelkomposita," *Beiträge*, 70 (1948), 332–50.

Orton, Graham. "The Predicate Adjective in Old High German," *JEGP*, 50 (1951), 332–48.

Penzl, Herbert. "The Development of Germanic *ai* and *au* in Old High German," *GR*, 22 (1947), 174–81.

———. "Old High German *r* and Its Phonetic Identification," *Language*, 37 (1961), 488–96.

———. "Scribal Practice, Phonological Change, and Biuniqueness," *GQ*, 44 (1971), 305–10.

———. "Umlaut and Secondary Umlaut in OHG," *Language*, 25 (1949), 223–40.

Raven, Fritjof A. "Flexibility in Old High German Weak Verbs," *GR*, 31–32 (1956–57), 66–74.

———. "Phasenaktionsarten im Althochdeutschen," *ZfdA*, 92 (1963), 165–83.

Rupp, Heinz. "Entstehung und Sinn des Wortes 'Deutsch', Ein Forschungsbericht," *Der Deutschunterricht*, 3 (1951), 74–79.

Scherer, Philip. "Aspect in the Old High German of Tatian," *Language*, 32 (1956), 423–34.

Schirokauer, Arno. "Die Wortgeschichte von *Herr*," *GR*, 21 (1946), 55–60.

Schreyer, Brigitte. "Eine althochdeutsche Schriftsprache," *Beiträge*, 73 (1951), 351–86.

Schröbler, Ingeborg. "Bemerkungen zur ahd. Syntax und Wortbedeutung," *ZfdA*, 82 (1950), 240–51.

Schröter, Ernst. "Die Sprache der deutschen Namen des bischöflichen Traditionsbuches von Passau," *Beiträge*, 62 (1938), 161–286.

Schwarz, Ernst. "Die althochdeutsche Lautverschiebung im Altbairischen (mit besonderer Heranziehung der Salzburger Güterverzeichnisse)," *Beiträge*, 50 (1927), 242–87.

———. "Die Ausweitung des deutschen Wortschatzes," *Der Deutschunterricht*, 3 (1951), 37–53.

———. "Zur deutschen Wortforschung," *Der Deutschunterricht*, 3 (1951), 37–52.

Schweikle, Günther. "Die Herkunft des ahd. Reimes; zu Otfrieds von Weißenburg formgeschichtlicher Stellung," *ZfdA*, 96, No. 3 (1967), 165–212.

Seymour, Richard K. "Old High German -*âta*,-*ât* in Middle High German and in Present-Day German Dialects," *Language*, 39 (1963), 235–41.

Steche, Theodor. "Die Entstehung der Spiranten in der hochdeutschen Lautverschiebung," *ZfdPh*, 64 (1939), 125–48.

———. "Zeit und Ursachen der hochdeutschen Lautverschiebung," *ZfdPh*, 62 (1937), 1–56.

Trier, Jost, "Spiel," *Beiträge*, 69 (1947), 419–62.

Twaddell, W. Freeman. "A Main Clause with 'Final' Verb in Notker's *Boethius*," *JEGP*, 31 (1932), 403–6.

———. "*Werden* und *Wesen* Again," *GR*, 7 (1932), 81–83.

———. "*Werden* und *Wesen* with the Passive in Notker," *GR*, 5 (1930), 288–93.

Velten, Harry V. "A Note on Semantic Borrowing in Old Saxon," *JEGP*, 30 (1931), 494–97.

Wagner, Kurt. "Hochsprache und Mundart in althochdeutscher Zeit," *Der Deutschunterricht*, 8 (1956), 14–24.

Woods, Frank L. "Nominal Compounds of the Old High German *Benedictine Rule*," *JEGP*, 56 (1957), 42–51.

Zieglschmid, A. J. Friedrich. "The Historical Development of the Past Subjunctive in German," *JEGP*, 29 (1930), 372–76.

CHAPTER FOUR: THE MIDDLE HIGH GERMAN PERIOD

Dictionaries

Benecke, Georg Friedrich, Wilhelm Müller, and Friedrich Zarncke. *Mittelhochdeutsches Wörterbuch*. Leipzig, 1854–66. (reprinted in Hildesheim, 1963.)

Der kleine Benecke, ed. Albert Leitzmann. Halle, 1934.

Lexer, Matthias. *Mittelhochdeutsches Handwörterbuch*. Leipzig, 1872–78. (reprinted in Stuttgart, 1970.)

———. *Mittelhochdeutsches Taschenwörterbuch*. 33rd ed. Stuttgart, 1969.

Grammars

Boor, Helmut de, and Roswitha Wisniewski. *Mittelhochdeutsche Grammatik.* (Sammlung Göschen, No. 1108.) 6th ed. Berlin, 1969.

Eis, Gerhard. *Historische Laut- und Formenlehre des Mittelhochdeutschen.* Halle, 1958.

Mausser, Otto. *Mittelhochdeutsche Grammatik auf vergleichender Grundlage.* Munich, 1932–33. (reprinted in Wiesbaden, 1971.)

Paul, Hermann. *Mittelhochdeutsche Grammatik.* Revised by Hugo Moser and Ingeborg Schröbler. 20th ed. Tübingen, 1969.

Senn, Alfred. *An Introduction to Middle High German.* New York, 1937.

Weinhold, Karl, Gustav Ehrismann, and Hugo Moser. *Kleine mittelhochdeutsche Grammatik.* 15th ed. Vienna, 1968.

Wright, Joseph. *A Middle High German Primer,* ed. M.O'C. Walshe. 5th ed. Oxford, 1955.

Zupitza, Julius, Franz Nobiling, and Fritz Tschirch. *Einführung in das Studium des Mittelhochdeutschen.* 3rd ed. Jena, 1963.

Articles

Banta, Frank G. "Tense and Aspect in the Middle High German of Berthold von Regensburg," *JEGP*, 59 (1960), 76–92.

Batts, Michael S. "Poetic Form and Medieval German Scribal Practice," *JEGP*, 62 (1963), 697–702.

Besch, Werner. "Schriftzeichen und Laut: Möglichkeiten der Lautwertbestimmungen an deutschen Handschriften des späten Mittelalters," *ZfdPh*, 80 (1961), 287–302.

Boor, Helmut de. "Frühmittelhochdeutscher Sprachstil," *ZfdPh*, 52 (1927), 31–76.

Brackett, Mary Williams. "Middle High German Loan Fields: *Intellectus— Verstan*," *JEGP*, 51 (1952), 571–79.

Church, Henry W. "The Compound Past Tenses in Middle High German," *JEGP*, 15 (1916), 1–22.

Fleischhauer, Wolfgang. "Zur Geschichte des Wortes 'Innig' und seiner Verwandten," *Monatshefte*, 37 (1945), 40–52.

Fourquet, Jean. "The Two E's of Middle High German: A Diachronic Phonemic Approach," *Word*, 8 (1952), 122–35.

Hasse, H. "Beiträge zur Stilanalyse der mhd. Predigt," *ZfdPh*, 44 (1912), 1–37, 169–98.

Hicks, Fred C. "Strengthening Modifiers of Adjectives and Adverbs in Middle High German," *JEGP*, 4 (1902), 267–347.

Hollander, Lee M. "Middle High German *Sch*," *JEGP*, 46 (1947), 82–91.

Jordan, Gilbert J. "MHG *ûf den plân treten* and NHG *auftreten*," *Monatshefte*, 37 (1945), 81–84.

Jungandreas, Wolfgang. "Die sprachliche Germanisierung des Mosellandes im frühen Mittelalter," *ZfdA*, 102 (1973), 67-81.

Kamihara, Kin'ichi. "Über die un-verba im Mittelhochdeutschen," *ZfdS*, 25, 1/2 (1969), 37–48.

Kammel, Willibald. "Modusgebrauch im Mittelhochdeutschen," *ZfdPh*, 36 (1904), 86–115.

Karg, Fritz. "Die Konstruktion *apo koinou* im Mittelhochdeutschen (Syntaktische Studien I)," *Beiträge*, 49 (1925), 1–63.

Karsten, Torsten E. "Zur Scheidung der kurzen *e*-Laute im Mittelhochdeutschen," *Beiträge*, 28 (1903), 254–59.

Kaufmann, Friedrich, "Behaghels Argumente für eine mittelhochdeutsche Schriftsprache," *Beiträge*, 13 (1888), 464–503.

Kayser, Rudolf. "Minne und Mystik im Werke Mechthilds von Magdeburg," *GR*, 19 (1944), 3–15.

Kettner, Emil. "Zu den Handschriftenverhältnissen des Nibelungenliedes," *ZfdPh*, 34 (1902), 311–64.

Mayer, Anton. "Zum Alter des Übergangs von *sk* zu *š*," *Beiträge*, 53 (1929), 286–90.

Moser, Hugo, "Schichten und Perioden des Mittelhochdeutschen," *Wirkendes Wort*, 2 (1951–52), 321–28.

Moser, Virgil. "Über den mhd. Diphthong *eü*," *Beiträge*, 51 (1927), 107–34.

———. "Zur frühmhd. Grammatik," *ZfdPh*, 44 (1912), 37–77.

Müller, Ernst Erhard. " 'Wachter blas uf, blas uf, es taget schon.' Eine Lücke im Wortfeld," *ZfdA*, 102 (1973), 250–82.

Neumann, Hans. "Problemata Mechtildiana," *ZfdA*, 82 (1948), 143–72.

Öhmann, Emil. "Der französische Einfluß auf die deutsche Sprache im Mittelalter," *Neuphilologische Mitteilungen*, 32 (1931), 195–220.

———. "Hochsprache und Mundarten im Mittelhochdeutschen," *Der Deutschunterricht*, 8 (1956), 24–36.

———. "Die romanischen Bestandteile im mittelhochdeutschen Wortschatz," *Beiträge*, 73 (1951), 273–83.

———. "Der romanische Einfluß auf das Deutsche bis zum Ausgang des Mittelalters," in *Deutsche Wortgeschichte* (2nd ed.; Strasbourg, 1959), I, 269ff.

———. "Zur Geschichte des deutschen Suffixes *-ieren*," *Neuphilologische Mitteilungen*, 54 (1953), 159ff.

Palander, Hugo (see also *Suolahti*, the Finnish form of the name). "Der französische Einfluß auf die deutsche Sprache im 12. Jahrhundert," *Mémoires de la société néo-philologique de Helsingfors*, No. 3 (Helsinki, 1901), pp. 77–204.

Pfeifer, Peter. "Die mittelhochdeutschen Umlauts-*e* der südbairischen Mundart des Reggelberges," *Beiträge*, 52 (1928), 72–92.

Prestel, Josef. "Beobachtungen zum Wortersatz im Mittelhochdeutschen," *Beiträge*, 52 (1928), 313–44.

Ritzert, A. "Die Dehnung der mhd. kurzen Stammsilbenvocale in den Volksmundarten des hochdeutschen Sprachgebiets auf Grund der vorhandenen Dialektliteratur," *Beiträge*, 23 (1898), 131–222.

Russ, Charles V. J. "Die Ausnahmen zur Dehnung der mhd. Kurzvokale in offener Silbe, "*ZDL*, 36 (1969), 82–88.

Schirokauer, Arno. "Studien zur mittelhochdeutschen Reimgrammatik," *Beiträge,* 47 (1922), 1–126.

Schmitt, Ludwig Erich. "Die sprachschöpferische Leistung der deutschen Stadt im Mittelalter," *Beiträge,* 66 (1942), 196–226.

Schmoldt, Benno. "Das Bedeutungslehnwort: Eine Einführung am Beispiel der deutschsprachigen Mystik des Mittelalters," *Der Deutschunterricht,* 15 (1963), 44–51.

Selmer, Carl. "Die spätmittelhochdeutschen Bestandteile der Universitätsbibliothek zu Yale und ihre Dialektbestimmung," *PMLA,* 57 (1936), 37–58.

———. "Standardized or Non-Standardized Old German Prose Texts?" *GR,* 10 (1935), 126–29.

Seward, Ora P. "The Strengthened Negative in Middle High German," *JEGP,* 3 (1900-1901), 277–333.

Sievers, Eduard. "Zum *apo koinou* im Mittelhochdeutschen," *Beiträge,* 50 (1927), 99–111.

———. "Zum Umlaut des *iu* im Mittelhochdeutschen," *Beiträge,* 20 (1895), 330–35.

Springer, Otto. "Etymologisches Spiel in Wolframs Parzival," *Beiträge,* 87 (1965), 166–81.

Suolahti, Hugo (see also under *Palander*). "Der französische Einfluß auf die deutsche Sprache im 13. Jahrhundert," *Mémoires de la société néophilologique de Helsingfors,* No. 8 (Helsinki, 1929), pp. 3–310.

Triwunatz, Milosch. "Zur Ausstoßung des schwachen *e* im Bairischen des 11. und 12. Jahrhunderts," *Beiträge,* 38 (1913), 358–70.

Vogt, Heinrich L. "Das mittelhochdeutsche Wörterbuch: Editionsgrundsätze und Probeartikel," *ZfdPh,* 80 (1961), 253–72.

Wendman, Robert W. "Nominal Compounds in Middle High German, based on Study of the Manesse Manuscript," *JEGP,* 40 (1941), 349–59.

Zieglschmid, A. J. Friedrich. "Zum mittelhochdeutschen Sprachstand der Vogtländischen Mundart," *PQ,* 9 (1930), 379–89.

CHAPTER FIVE: THE EARLY NEW HIGH GERMAN PERIOD
(Early New High German–Middle Low German)

Dictionaries

Götze, Alfred. *Frühneuhochdeutsches Glossar.* 7th ed. Berlin, 1967.

Lasch, Agathe, Conrad Borchling, and Gerhard Cordes. *Mittelniederdeutsches Handwörterbuch.* Neumünster, 1926ff.

Schiller, Karl, and August Lübben. *Mittelniederdeutsches Wörterbuch.* Bremen, 1875–82. (reprinted in Münster, Wiesbaden, 1969.)

Grammars

Brooke, Kenneth. *An Introduction to Early New High German.* Oxford, 1955.

Lasch, Agathe. *Mittelniederdeutsche Grammatik.* Berlin, 1914.

Lübben, August. *Mittelniederdeutsche Grammatik.* Leipzig, 1882. (reprinted in Osnabrück, 1970.)

Moser, Virgil. *Frühneuhochdeutsche Grammatik.* Vol. 1. Heidelberg, 1929–51.

Monographs

Bahder, Kurt von. *Grundlagen des neuhochdeutschen Lautsystems: Beiträge zur Geschichte der deutschen Schriftsprache im 15. und 16. Jahrhundert.* Strasbourg, 1890.

———. *Zur Wortwahl in der frühneuhochdeutschen Schriftsprache.* Heidelberg, 1925.

Besch, Werner. *Sprachlandschaften und Sprachausgleich.* Munich, 1967.

Bindewald, Helene. *Die Sprache der Reichskanzlei zur Zeit König Wenzels: Ein Beitrag zur Geschichte des Frühneuhochdeutschen.* Halle, 1928.

Brodführer, E. *Untersuchungen zur vorlutherischen Bibelübersetzung.* Halle, 1928.

Dietz, Philipp. *Wörterbuch zu Dr. Martin Luthers deutschen Schriften.* 2nd ed. Leipzig 1870–72. (reprinted in Hildesheim, 1961.)

Eis, Gerhard. *Mittelalterliche Fachliteratur.* 2nd rev. ed. (Sammlung Metzler, No. 14.) Stuttgart, 1967.

Francke, Carl. *Grundzüge der Schriftsprache Luthers.* 2nd ed. Halle, 1913ff.

Frings, Theodor. *Die Grundlagen des Meißnischen Deutsch: Ein Beitrag zur Entstehung der deutschen Hochsprache.* Halle, 1936.

Götze, Alfred. *Die hochdeutschen Drucker der Reformationszeit.* Strasbourg, 1905. (reprinted in Berlin, 1963.)

Gumbel, Hermann. *Deutsche Sonderrenaissance in deutscher Prosa: Strukturanalyse deutscher Prosa im 16. Jahrhundert.* Frankfurt am Main, 1930. (reprinted in Hildesheim, 1965.)

Jellinek, Max H. *Geschichte der neuhochdeutschen Grammatik von den Anfängen bis auf Adelung.* Heidelberg, 1913ff. (reprinted in Heidelberg, 1968ff.)

Kluge, Friedrich. *Von Luther bis Lessing.* 5th ed. Leipzig, 1918.

Lasch, Agathe. *Geschichte der Schriftsprache in Berlin bis zur Mitte des 16. Jahrhunderts.* Dortmund, 1910.

Lindmeyr, Bernhard. *Der Wortschatz in Luthers, Emsers und Ecks Übersetzung des Neuen Testamentes.* Strasbourg, 1899.

Leurs, Grete. *Die Sprache der deutschen Mystik des Mittelalters im Werke der Mechthild von Magdeburg.* Munich, 1926.

Maurer, Friedrich. *Studien zur mitteldeutschen Bibelübersetzung vor Luther.* Heidelberg, 1929.

———. *Untersuchungen über die deutsche Verbstellung in ihrer geschichtlichen Entwicklung.* Heidelberg, 1926.

Merkel, Felix. *Das Aufkommen der deutschen Sprache in den städtischen Kanzleien des ausgehenden Mittelalters.* Leipzig and Berlin, 1930.

Moser, Virgil. *Historisch-grammatische Einführung in die früneuhoch-deutschen Schriftdialekte.* Halle, 1909. (reprinted in Darmstadt, 1971.)

Pietsch, Paul. *Luther und die hochdeutsche Schriftsprache.* Breslau, 1883.

Rosenzweig, Franz. *Die Schrift und Luther.* Berlin, 1926.

Rückert, Heinrich Carl Albrecht. *Geschichte der neuhochdeutschen Schrift-sprache.* Leipzig, 1875.

Schmitt, Ludwig Erich. *Untersuchungen zu Entstehung und Struktur der "Neuhochdeutschen Schriftsprache."* Köln-Graz, 1966.

———. *Die deutsche Urkundensprache in der Kanzlei Kaiser Karls IV (1346–1378). (Zeitschrift für Mundartforschung,* Beiheft Nr. 15.) Halle, 1936.

Vancsa, Max. *Das erste Auftreten der deutschen Sprache in den Urkunden.* Leipzig, 1895. (reprinted in Leipzig, 1963.)

Zirker, Otto. *Die Bereicherung des deutschen Wortschatzes durch die spätmittelalterliche Mystik.* Jena, 1923.

Articles

Bayerschmidt, Carl F. "Johannes Veghe, A Low German Preacher of the Fifteenth Century," *GR,* 20 (1945), 3–20.

———. "The Low German of Lauremberg's *Scherzgedichte,*" *GR,* 21 (1946), 61–70.

———. "The Question of a Middle Low German *Schriftsprache,*" *GR,* 18 (1943), 3–10.

Bebermeyer, G. "Luthersprache und Lutherbibel: Ein Literatur- und Forschungsbericht," *Zeitschrift für deutsche Bildung,* 6 (1930), 537–44.

Berger, Arnold E. "Luther und die neuhochdeutsche Schriftsprache: Alte Probleme in neuer Sicht," in *Deutsche Wortgeschichte* (2nd ed.; Strasbourg, 1959), II, 37–132.

Besch, Werner. *Sprachlandschaften und Sprachausgleich im 15. Jahrhundert,* reviewed by John T. Waterman in *Language,* 46, No. 2, pt 1 (1970), 474–80.

———. "Zur Entstehung der neuhochdeutschen Schriftsprache," *ZfdPh,* 87 (1968), 405–26.

Biener, Clemens. "Veränderungen am deutschen Satzbau im humanist-ischen Zeitalter," *ZfdPh,* 78 (1959), 72–82.

Bischoff, Karl. "Hochsprache und Mundarten im mittelalterlichen Niederdeutschen," *Der Deutschunterricht,* 8 (1956), 73–86.

Bloomfield, Leonard. Review of Virgil Moser, *Frühneuhochdeutsche Grammatik, JEGP,* 30 (1931), 407–9.

Bluhm, Heinz. "The Evolution of Luther's Translation of the Twenty-Third Psalm," *GR,* 26 (1951), 251–58.

———. "Luther's Translation and Interpretation of the 'Ave Maria,'" *JEGP,* 51 (1952), 196–211.

———. "Recent American Research on Luther's German Bible," *GR,* 18 (1943), 161–71.

————. "The Rendering of Galatians 3:23–4:2 in the Printed High German *Plenaria* and in Luther's Christmas *Postil*," *JEGP*, 64 (1965), 213–31.

Eis, Gerhard. "Beiträge zur spätmittelalterlichen deutschen Prosa aus Handschriften und Frühdrucken," *JEGP*, 52 (1953), 76–89.

Erben, Johannes. "Die sprachgeschichtliche Stellung Luthers," *Beiträge*, 76 (1954), 166–79.

Florer, Warren W. "Gender-Change from MHG to Luther, as seen in 1545 Edition of the Bible," *PMLA*, 15 (1900), 442–49.

Franke, Carl. "Zu Luthers Schriftsprache," *ZfdPh*, 48 (1920), 450ff.

Frings, Theodor, and Ludwig Erich Schmitt. "Der Weg zur deutschen Hochsprache," in *Jahrbuch der deutschen Sprache* (Berlin, 1944), I, 67–121.

Grundmann, H. "Übersetzungsprobleme im Spätmittelalter," *ZfdPh*, 70 (1947–48), 113–45.

Gürtler, Hans. "Zur Geschichte der deutschen -er-Plurale, besonders im Frühneuhochdeutschen: I," *Beiträge*, 37 (1912), 492–543.

————. "Zur Geschichte der deutschen -er-Plurale, besonders im Frühneuhochdeutschen: II, III," *Beiträge*, 38 (1913), 67–224.

Kehlenbeck, Alfred P. "Die mittelniederdeutschen Laute im Williamsburger [Iowa] Platt," *JEGP*, 37 (1938), 382–95.

Lasch, Agathe. "Vom Werden und Wesen des Mittelniederdeutschen," *Niederdeutsches Jahrbuch*, 51 (1925), 55–76.

Lindner, Kurt. "Zur Sprache der Jäger," *ZfdPh*, 85–86 (1966–67), 407–31, 101–25.

Masarík, Zdenek. "Zur Spätmittelalterlichen Wortgeographie: Die Wochentagsnamen der deutschen Kanzleisprache des 14.–16. Jahrhunderts in Mähren," *ZfMaf*, 34 (1967), 281–89.

Maurer, Friedrich. "Zur Frage nach der Entstehung unserer Schriftsprache," *GRM*, 2 (1951), 108–15.

Mendels, Judy. "Jacob Böhme's *r*," *JEGP*, 52 (1953), 559–63.

Mensing, Otto. "Beiträge zur niederdeutschen Syntax," *ZfdPh*, 34 (1902), 505–15.

Merkel, Gottfried Felix. "Vom Fortleben der Lutherischen Bibelsprache in 16. und 17. Jahrhundert," *ZfdS*, 23 (1967), 3–12.

Mitzka, Walther. "Die Ostbewegung der deutschen Sprache," *ZfMaf*, 19 (1943–44), 81ff.

Molz, Hermann. "Die Substantivflexion seit mittelhochdeutscher Zeit; I. Teil: Masculina," *Beiträge*, 27 (1902), 209–343.

————. "Die Substantivflexion seit mittelhochdeutscher Zeit; II: Neutra," *Beiträge*, 31 (1906), 277–393.

Moser, Hugo. "Die Entstehung der neuhochdeutschen Einheitssprache," *Der Deutschunterricht*, 3 (1951), 58–74.

————. "Grundfragen der frühneuhochdeutschen Forschung," *GRM*, 14 (1926), 25–34.

————. " 'Fromm' bei Luther und Melanchthon: Ein Beitrag zur Wortgeschichte in der Reformationszeit," *ZfdPh*, 86 (1967), 161–82.

Moser, Virgil. "Das *e* bei Seb. Brant," *ZfdPh*, 44 (1912), 331–45.

——. "Die frühneuhochdeutsche Sprachforschung und Fischarts Stellung in ihren Rahmen," *JEGP*, 24 (1925), 163–83.

Moulton, William G. "Jacob Böhme's Uvular *r*," *JEGP*, 51 (1952), 83–89.

——. "Zur Geschichte des deutschen Vokalsystems," *Beiträge*, 83 (1961), 1–35.

Mutschmann, Heinrich. "Die Entwicklung von Nasal vor stimmloser Spirans im Niederdeutschen," *Beiträge*, 32 (1907), 544–50.

Nordlund, Sven. "Die Ausgleichung des Präteritalablauts bei Georg Rollenhagen," *Beiträge*, 55 (1931), 207–13.

Richter, Werner. "Wandlungen des Lutherbildes und der Lutherforschung," *GRM*, 38 (1946), 129–49.

Roemheld, Friedrich. "Die Längenbezeichnungen in der deutschen Rechtschreibung," *Der Deutschunterricht*, 7 (1955), 71–83.

Rosenfeld, H. F. "Humanistische Strömungen," in *Deutsche Wortgeschichte* (2nd ed.; Strasbourg, 1959), I, 329ff.

Schirokauer. Arno. "Frühneuhochdeutsch." in *Deutsche Philologie im Aufriß* (Berlin, 1952ff.), I, cols. 1013–76.

——. "Das Werden der Gemeinsprache im Wörterbuch des Dasypodius," *GR*, 18 (1943), 286–303.

——. "Die Wortbildung 'Zirlin-Mirlin' (Aufkommen, Verbreitung, Bedeutungs-Spielraum eines Modeworts)," *JEGP*, 47 (1948), 398–402.

Schmitt, Ludwig Erich. "Zur Entstehung und Erforschung der neuhochdeutschen Schriftsprache," *ZfMaf*, 12 (1936), 193ff.

——. "Die sprachschöpferische Leistung der deutschen Stadt im Mittelalter," *Beiträge*, 66 (1942), 196–226.

Schwarz, Ernst. "Die Grundlagen der neuhochdeutschen Schriftsprache," *ZfMaf*, 12 (1936), 1ff.

Senn, Alfred. "Ostpreußens Vorgeschichte sprachlich beleuchtet," *GR*, 15 (1940), 3–19.

Skála, Emil. "Das Prager Deutsch," *ZfdS*, 22 (1966–67), 84–91.

Sobel, Eli. *Sebastian Brant, Ovid, and Classical Allusions in the Narrenschiff* (University of California Publications in Modern Philology, Vol. 36, No. 12 [Berkeley, 1952]), pp. 429–40.

Stammler, Wolfgang. "Von mittelalterlicher deutscher Prosa, Rechenschaft und Aufgabe," *JEGP*, 48 (1949), 15–44.

——. "Zur Sprachgeschichte des 15. und 16. Jahrhunderts," in *Vom Werden des deutschen Geistes: Festgabe G. Ehrismann* (Berlin, 1925), pp. 171–89.

Thornton, Thomas P. "Die Schreibgewohnheiten Hans Rieds im Ambraser Heldenbuch," *ZfdPh*, 81 (1962), 52–82.

Waterman, John T. "The Influence of the Lesser Nobility on the Rise of Standard Literary German," *Monatshefte*, 58 (1956), 25–33.

Zimmermann, Walter. "Ergänzende Funde zum frühneuhochdeutschen Wortschatz," *ZfdPh*, 58 (1933), 49–61.

CHAPTER SIX: THE NEW HIGH GERMAN PERIOD
(See Chapter Seven for dictionaries and grammars.)

Monographs

Ganz, Peter F. *Der Einfluß des Englischen auf den deutschen Wortschatz 1640–1815.* Berlin, 1957.

Kaiser, Karl. *Mundart und Schriftsprache: Versuch einer Wesensbestimmung in der Zeit zwischen Leipniz und Gottsched.* Leipzig, 1930.

Konrad, Gustav. *Herders Sprachproblem im Zusammenhang der Geistesgeschichte: Eine Studie zur Entwiklung des sprachlichen Denkens der Goethezeit.* Berlin, 1937. (reprinted in Nedeln, Liechtenstein, 1967.)

Ladendorf, Otto. *Historisches Schlagwörterbuch.* Strasbourg, 1906. (reprinted in Hildesheim, 1968.)

Langen, August. *Der Wortschatz des deutschen Pietismus.* 2nd rev. ed. Tübingen, 1968.

Palmer, Philip Motley. *The Influence of English on the German Vocabulary to 1800: A Supplement.* Berkeley, 1960. (A supplement to *Der Einfluß des Englischen auf den deutschen Wortschatz, 1640–1815* by P. F. Ganz.)

Schönaich, Christof Otto von. *Neologisches Wörterbuch oder die ganze Ästhetik in einer Nuß* (1754), ed. Albrecht Köster. Leipzig, 1900.

Unger, Rudolf. *Hamann und die Aufklärung.* 2nd ed. Halle, 1925. (reprinted in Darmstadt, 1963.)

Weber, Hanna. *Herders Sprachphilosophie: Eine Interpretation in Hinblick auf die moderne Sprachphilosophie.* Berlin, 1939. (reprinted in Nedeln, Liechtenstein, 1967.)

Wendland, Ulrich. *Die Theoretiker und Theorien der sogenannten galanten Stilepoche und die deutsche Sprache: Ein Beitrag zur Erkenntnis der Sprachreformbestrebungen vor Gottsched.* Leipzig, 1930.

Articles

Alanne, Eero. "Das Eindringen der romanischen Sprache in den deutschen Wortschatz des Frühbarock," *ZfdS*, 21 (1964–65), 84–91.

Beißner, F. "Klopstock als Erneuerer der deutschen Dichtersprache," *Zeitschrift für Deutschkunde*, 56 (1942), 235ff.

———. "Studien zur Sprache des Sturms und Drangs," *GRM*, 22 (1934), 417–29.

Belaval, Yvon. "Leibniz et la langue allemande," *Etudes germaniques*, 2 (1947), 121–32.

Burdach, Konrad. "Universelle, nationale und landschaftliche Triebe der deutschen Schriftsprache im Zeitalter Gottscheds," in *Festschrift für August Sauer* (Stuttgart, 1925), pp. 12–71.

Carlson, Harold G. "Classical Pseudonyms of the Sixteenth and Seventeenth Centuries in Germany," *GQ*, 13 (1940), 15–18.

Daniels, Karlheinz. "Erfolg und Mißerfolg der Fremdwortverdeutschung: Schicksal der Verdeutschungen von J. H. Campe," *Muttersprache*, 69 (1959), 46–54, 105–14.

Feldmann, W. "Fremdwörter und Verdeutschungen des 18. Jahrhunderts," *Zeitschrift für Wortforschung*, 8 (1906–7), 49ff.

———. "Modewörter des 18. Jahrhunderts," *Zeitschrift für deutsche Wortforschung*, 6 (1904), 101ff.

Fleischhauer, Wolfgang. "Das Selbst," *ZfdS*, 22 (1966–67), 92–95.

Fleming, Willi. "Barock," in *Deutsche Wortgeschichte* (2nd ed.; Strasbourg, 1959), II, 1ff.

Friedrich, W. P. "Late Renaissance, Baroque or Counter-Reformation?" *JEGP*, 46 (1947), 132–43.

Funke, Erich. "Aussprache und 'Sprechung' bei Klopstock," *Monatshefte*, 48 (1956), 361–69.

Ganz, Peter F. "Seventeenth-Century Loan Words in German," *JEGP*, 54 (1955), 80–90.

Goldstein, L. "Beiträge zu lexikalischen Studien über die Schriftsprache der Lessingperiode," in *Festschrift für Oscar Schade* (n.p., 1896), pp. 51ff.

Hegeman, Daniel V. B. "Boswell's Interviews with Gottsched and Gellert," *JEGP*, 46 (1947), 260–63.

Henne, Helmut. "Das Problem des Meissnischen Deutsch oder 'was ist Hochdeutsch' im 18. Jahrhundert," *ZfMaf*, 35 (1968), 109–29.

———. "Zum deutschen Wortschatz des Frühbarock: Ein schlesisches Schulwörterbuch von 1620," *ZfMaf*, 33 (1966), 23–36.

King, Robert D. "In Defense of Klopstock as Spelling Reformer: A Linguistic Appraisal," *JEGP*, 66 (1967), 369–82.

Kurrelmeyer, W. "American and Other Loanwords in German," *JEGP*, 43 (1944), 286–301.

Langen, August. "Deutsche Sprachgeschichte vom Barock bis zur Gegenwart," in *Deutsche Philologie im Aufriß* (Berlin, 1952ff.) I, cols. 1077–1151.

———. "Klopstocks sprachgeschichtliche Bedeutung," *Wirkendes Wort*, 3 (1952–53), 330ff.

———. "Verbale Dynamik in der dichterischen Landschaftsschilderung des 18. Jahrhunderts," *ZfdPh*, 70 (1949), 249ff.

Legner, Wolfram K. "The Compound Nouns in the Works of Andreas Gryphius," *JEGP*, 44 (1945), 36–55.

Levie, Dagobert de. " 'Heilig,' 'Opfern,' und 'Unsterblichkeit': Eine geistesgeschichtlich orientierte Wortstudie," *Monatshefte*, 50 (1958), 337–47.

———. "Zum Begriff und Wort 'Menschenliebe,' " *Monatshefte*, 55 (1963), 301–11.

Loomis, C. Grant. "English Writers in Gottsched's *Handlexikon*," *JEGP*, 42 (1943), 96–103.

Metcalf, George J. "Latin and German Abstractions as Forms of Address," *GR*, 20 (1945), 218–31.

———. "The Origins of Modern German Polite *Sie*-Plurals with Particular Reference to the Works of Christian Weise," *PMLA*, 52 (1937), 1204–13.

———. "Schottel and Historical Linguistics," *GR*, 28 (1953), 113–25.

Moser, Virgil. "Beiträge zur Lautlehre Spees," *ZfdPh*, 46 (1915), 17–80.

———. "Deutsche Orthographiereformen des 17. Jahrhunderts," *Beiträge*, 70; 71 (1948–49), 467–96; 386–465.

———. "Deutsche Orthographiereformer des 17. Jahrhunderts," *Beiträge*, 60 (1936), 193–258.

———. "Zum bayrisch-österreichischen Schriftdialekt," *Beiträge*, 47 (1923), 364ff.

———. "Zur Sprache der Luther-Bibel im 17. Jahrhunderts," *Beiträge*, 47 (1923), 357ff.

Palmer, Philip M. "New World Words in German," *Monatshefte*, 37 (1945), 481–88.

Pfleiderer, W. "Die Sprache des jungen Schiller in ihrem Verhältnis zur neuhochdeutschen Schriftsprache," *Beiträge*, 28 (1903), 273ff.

Purdie, Edna. "Some Descriptive Compounds in Klopstock's Poetic Vocabulary," *GR*, 31 (1956), 88–96.

Schwentner, Ernst. "Zur Geschichte der älteren nhd. Lexikographie," *Beiträge*, 50 (1927), 149–52.

Shumway, D. B. "The Language of the Luther Bible of 1671," *GR*, 5; 6 (1930–31), 247–87; 345–77.

Spann, Meno. "Fremdwort und Fremdphrase," GQ, 9 (1936), 49–54.

Sperber, Hans. "Beiträge zur Geschichte der deutschen Sprache im achtzehnten Jahrhundert," *ZfdPh*, 52 (1927), 331–45.

———. "Der Einfluß des Pietismus auf die Sprache des 18. Jahrhunderts," *Deutsche Vierteljahrsschrift*, 8 (1930), 149ff.

———. "Die Sprache der Aufklärung," *Zeitschrift für Deutschkunde*, 43 (1929), 777ff.

———. "Die Sprache der Barockzeit," *Zeitschrift für Deutschkunde*, 43 (1929), 670ff.

———. "Zur Geschichte des Wortes 'Teilnahme' und seiner Verwandten," *Monatshefte*, 35 (1943), 241–54.

———."Zur Sprachgeschichte des 18. Jahrhunderts," *ZfdPh*, 54 (1929), 80–97.

Stoltenberg, H. L. "Vernunftsprachtum," in *Deutsche Wortgeschichte* (2nd ed.; Strasbourg, 1959), II, 157ff.

Thiele, Friedrich. "Durch Volksetymologie vermummte deutsch-englische Sprachgleichungen," *GQ*, 16 (1943), 183–87.

Voss, Ernst. "The Cradle of the Modern High German Literary Language," *GR*, 9 (1934), 266–71.

Walz, John A. "English Influence on the German Vocabulary of the Eighteenth Century," *Monatshefte*, 35 (1943), 156–64.

Waterman, John T. "Johann Clauberg's *Ars Etymologica Teutonum* (*1663*)," *JEGP*, 72 (1973), 390–402.

CHAPTER SEVEN: THE NEW HIGH GERMAN PERIOD

Dictionaries and Grammars

In addition to the titles listed on pp. 234–36, the following reference works dealing specifically with the contemporary language should be noted:

Brinkmann, Hennig. *Die deutsche Sprache.* 2nd ed. Düsseldorf, 1971.

Duden Grammatik der deutschen Gegenwartssprache. Revised by P. Grebe. 3rd ed. Mannheim, 1973.

Duden Stilwörterbuch der deutschen Sprache. Revised by G. Drosdowski *et al.* 6th ed. Mannheim, 1970.

Erben, Johannes. *Abriß der deutschen Grammatik.* 10th ed. Berlin, 1967.

Glinz, Hans. *Deutsche Grammatik.* Frankfurt, 1970ff.

———. *Die innere Form des Deutschen: Eine neue deutsche Grammatik.* 6th ed. Bern, 1973.

Schulz, Dora, and Heinz Griesbach. *Grammatik der deutschen Sprache.* 9th ed. Munich, 1972.

Monographs

Arens, Hans. *Analyse eines Satzes von Thomas Mann.* (*Wirkendes Wort,* Beiheft Nr. 10.) Düsseldorf, 1946.

Bartholmes, Herbert. *Tausend Worte Sowjetdeutsch.* Göteborg, 1956.

Brenner, Oscar. *Die lautlichen und geschichtlichen Grundlagen unserer Rechtschreibung.* 2nd ed. Munich, 1914.

Bues, Manfred. *Die Versportung der deutschen Sprache im 20. Jahrhundert.* Griefswald, 1937.

Dunger, Hermann. *Die deutsche Sprachbewegung und der Allgemeine Deutsche Sprachverein.* Berlin, 1910.

———. *Engländerei in der deutschen Sprache.* Berlin, 1909.

Fiesel, Eva Lehmann. *Die Sprachphilosophie der deutschen Romantik.* Tübingen, 1927.

Fischer, Paul. *Goethe-Wortschatz.* Leipzig, 1929. (reprinted in Cologne, 1968.)

Gipper, Helmut. *Bausteine zur Sprachinhaltsforschung.* 2nd ed. Düsseldorf, 1969.

Glinz, Hans. *Der deutsche Satz.* 6th ed. Düsseldorf, 1970.

Herrmann, Ferdinand. *Modische Erscheinungen im heutigen Deutsch.* Bielefeld, 1931.

Hübner, Arthur. *Goethe und die deutsche Sprache.* Langensalza, 1933.

Hunt, Robert Nigel. *A Guide to Communist Jargon.* London, New York, 1957.

Klemperer, Viktor. *LTI* (= Lingua Tertii Imperii [Language of the Third Reich]): *Die unbewältigte Sprache. Aus dem Notizbuch eines Philologen.* Munich, 1969.

Mackensen, Lutz. *Sprache und Technik.* Lüneberg, 1953.

Martini, Fritz. *Das Wagnis der Sprache: Interpretationen deutscher Prosa von Nietzsche bis Benn.* 5th ed. Stuttgart, 1964.

Matthias, Erich, and Hansjürgen Schierbaum. *Errungenschaften: Zur Geschichte eines Schlagwortes unserer Zeit.* Munich, 1961.

Moser, Hugo. *Sprache und Religion.* (*Wirkendes Wort*, Beiheft Nr. 7.) Düsseldorf, 1964.

——. *Sprachliche Folgen der politischen Teilung Deutschlands.* (*Wirkendes Wort*, Beiheft Nr. 3,) Düsseldorf, 1962.

Palmer, Lucille V. "The Language of German Expressionism." Ph.D. dissertation, University of Illinois, 1938.

Polenz Peter von. *Funktionsverben im heutigen Deutsch.* (*Wirkendes Wort*, Beiheft Nr. 5.) Düsseldorf, 1963.

Pranse, Karl. *Grußformeln in neuhochdeutscher Zeit.* Breslau, 1930.

Rausch, Georg. *Goethe und die deutsche Sprache.* Leipzig, 1909.

Reed, Carroll E. *The Pennsylvanian German Dialect Spoken in the Counties of Lehigh and Berks: Phonology and Morphology.* Seattle, Wash., 1949.

Riemschneider, Ernst G. *Veränderungen in der deutschen Sprache in der sowjetisch besetzten Zone Deutschlands seit 1945.* (*Wirkendes Wort*, Beiheft Nr. 4.) Düsseldorf, 1963.

Rodens, Franz. *Die Zeitungssprache.* Bonn, 1938.

Rohr, Ursula. *Der Theaterjargon.* Berlin, 1952.

Rühle, Jürgen. *Literatur und Revolution: Die Schriftsteller und der Kommunismus.* Cologne, 1960. (English translation by Jean Steinberg, *Literature and Revolution: A Critical Study of the Writer and Communism.* New York, 1969.)

Seidel, Eugen, and Ingeborg Seidel-Slotty. *Sprachwandel im Dritten Reich.* Halle, 1961.

Steuernagel, Otto. *Die Einwirkung des Deutschen Sprachvereins auf die deutsche Sprache.* Breslau, 1926.

Thomas, Robert. *Wandlungen der deutschen Sprache seit Goethe und Schiller.* Augsburg, 1922.

Thon, Luise. *Die Sprache des deutschen Impressionismus.* Munich, 1928.

Weisgerber, Leo. *Die ganzheitliche Behandlung eines Satzbauplanes.* (*Wirkendes Wort*, Beiheft Nr. 1.) Düsseldorf, 1962.

Zieglschmid, A. J. Friedrich. *Zur Entwicklung der Perfektumschreibung im Deutschen.* (Publications of the Linguistic Society of America, Language Dissertation No. 6.) Baltimore, Md., 1929.

Articles

Adler, H. G. "Zum Bedeutungswandel im Deutschen," *Muttersprache* (1961), pp. 144–80.

Admoni, W. G. "Zur deutschen Sprache der Gegenwart," *ZfdPh*, 89 (1970), 436–46.

Adolf, Helen. "Intonation and Word Order in German Narrative Style," *JEGP*, 43 (1944), 71–79.

Appelt, E. P. "Vom Wesen der deutschen Soldatensprache," *JEGP*, 37 (1938), 367–81.

Arndt, Walter. "Modal Particles in Russian and German," *Word*, 16 (1960), 323–36.

Bach, Adolf. "Deutsche Namen in historisch-geographischer Sicht," *Der Deutschunterricht*, 9 (1957), 5–32.

Bahder, Karl von. "Die neuhochdeutsche Sprachforschung, ihre Ergebnisse und Ziele," *PQ*, 4 (1925), 61–70.

Behaghel, Otto. "Zur Worstellung des Deutschen," in *Curme Volume of Linguistic Studies* (Philadelphia, 1930), pp. 29–33.

Berning, Cornelia. "Die Sprache des Nationalsozialismus," *ZfdWf*, 46 [N.F. 1] (1960), 71–118; 47 [N.F. 2] (1961), 178–88.

Betz, Werner. "Der zweigeteilte Duden," *Der Deutschunterricht*, 12 (1960), 82–99.

———. "Liberalisierung der Großschreibung," *ZfdS*, 20 (1964–65), 115–18.

Biener, C. "Die Stellung des Verbs im Deutschen," *ZfdA*, 63 (1926), 225–56.

Boesch, Bruno. "Die Eigennamen in ihrer geistigen und seelischen Bedeutung für den Menschen," *Der Deutschunterricht*, 9 (1957), 32–51.

Boeschenstein, Hermann. "Sprachstilistische Merkmale Hermann Stehrs," *GR*, 9 (1934), 130–39.

Bolz, Werner. "Neuere Literatur zu Hochsprache, Mundart und Umgangssprache: Ein Forschungsbericht," *Der Deutschunterricht*, 8 (1956), 86–92.

Bratu, Traian. "Die Stellung der Negation *nicht* im Neuhochdeutschen," *ZfdPh*, 65 (1940), 1–17.

Brinkmann, Hennig. "Satzprobleme," *Wirkendes Wort*, 8 (1957–58), 129–41.

———. "Der Umkreis des persönlichen Lebens im deutschen Dativ," *Muttersprache* (1953), pp. 104–11.

Bues, Manfred. "Der Sport und unsere Sprache," *Muttersprache* (1952), pp. 17–25.

Bungert, Hans. "Zum Einfluß des Englischen auf die deutsche Sprache seit dem Ende des zweiten Weltkrieges," *JEGP*, 62 (1963), 703–17.

Burkhard, Arthur. "The Beginnings of the New Poetic Language in Germany," *PQ*, 10 (1931), 138–50.

———. "The Language of Conrad Ferdinand Meyer's Lyric Poems," *JEGP*, 30 (1931), 531–55.

———. "The Language of Detlev von Liliencron's Lyrics and Ballads," *JEGP*, 30 (1931), 236–54.

Campbell, Thomas Moody. "Aspects of Nietzsche's Struggle with Philology to 1871," *GR*, 12 (1937), 251–66.

Carr, Charles T. "German Grammars in England in the 19th Century," *MLR*, 30 (1935), 481–501.

———. "The Position of the Genitive in German," *MLR*, 28 (1933), 465–79.

Chambers, W. W. "Language and Nationality in German Pre-Romantic and Romantic Thought," *MLR*, 41 (1946), 382-92.

Collinson, William E. "German War Words," *MLR*, 14 (1919), 87-93.

———. "The Irrational Negative in Concessive Sentences: A Study in German Syntax," *MLR*, 10 (1915), 349-65.

Collitz, Klara H. "The Suffix *-ei* in Modern German," *GR*, 3 (1928), 55-70.

Condoyannis, George E. "Word Order in Colloquial German," *Monatshefte*, 36 (1944), 371-77.

Dahlberg, Torsten. "Fremdwörter und Politik in Ostdeutschland," *Moderna Språk*, 54 (1960), 368-77.

Dangers, Robert. "Wilhelm Busch als Sprachschöpfer und Sprachforscher," *Muttersprache* (1953), pp. 11-15.

Dieckmann, Walther. "Kritische Bemerkungen zum sprachlichen Ost-West-Problem," *ZfdS*, 23 (1967), 136-65.

Duckworth, David, "Der Einfluß des Englischen auf den deutschen Wortschatz seit 1945," *ZfdS*, 26 (1970), 9-31.

Eggers, Hans. "Wandlungen im deutschen Satzbau," *Der Deutschunterricht*, 13 (1961), 47-62.

Erben, Johannes. "Gesetz und Freiheit in der deutschen Hochsprache der Gegenwart," *Der Deutschunterricht*, 12 (1960), 5-25.

Fiedler, H. G. "Two Problems of the German Preterite-Present Verbs," *MLR*, 23 (1928), 188-96.

Fleischhauer, Wolfgang. "Beitrag zur Entwicklungsgeschichte der Wortfamilie 'Innig' im Neuhochdeutschen," *Monatshefte*, 40 (1948), 89-100.

Fowkes, Robert A. "Friedrich Hebbel and Comparative Linguistics," *GR*, 30 (1955), 294-300.

Franck, Theodor. "Die Leistung der Abstrakta im Deutschen," *Muttersprache* (1962), pp. 97-102, 135-140.

Frey, John R. "The Historical Present in Narrative Literature, Particularly in Modern German Fiction," *JEGP*, 45 (1946), 43-67.

Funke, Erich. "Die Schallform des Expressionismus," *JEGP*, 34 (1935), 408-13.

Geyl, Ernst-Günther. "Versuch einer Klärung der in der strukturellen Linguistik und von Chomsky bevorzugten philosophischen Termini," *Muttersprache*, 82 (1972), 13-26.

Gilbert, Glenn G. "Dative *vs.* Accusative in the German Dialects of Central Texas," *ZfMaF*, 32 (1965), 288-95.

Gipper, Helmut. "Wilhelm von Humboldt als Begründer Moderner Sprachforschung," *Wirkendes Wort*, 15 (1965), 1-19.

Glinz, Hans. "Wortarten und Satzglieder im Deutschen, Französischen und Lateinischen," *Der Deutschunterricht*, 9 (1957), 13-29.

Goedsche, C. R. "Verbal Aspect in German," *JEGP*, 33 (1934), 506-19.

Grosse, Friedrich. "Durative Verben und präfigierte Perfektiva im Deutschen," *Der Deutschunterricht*, 15 (1963), 95-106.

Grosse, Siegfried. "Die deutsche Satzperiode," *Der Deutschunterricht*, 12 (1960), 66-82.

———. "Neuere Arbeiten zur deutschen Sprache der Gegenwart," *Der Deutschunterricht*, 12 (1960), 102–8.

———. "Reklamedeutsch," *Wirkendes Wort*, 16 (1966), 89–104.

Guentherdt, Ingrid. "A Prosodic Isogloss in German Dialects," *ZfDuL*, 40 (1973), 29–35.

Haile, H. G. "Thomas Mann und der 'Anglizismus,'" *Monatshefte*, 51 (1959), 263–69.

Heffner, R.-M. S. "Proposed Changes in the Rules for German Orthography," *Monatshefte*, 47 (1954), 175–79.

Hotzenköcherle, Rudolf. "Entwicklungsgeschichtliche Grundzüge des Neuhochdeutschen," *Wirkendes Wort*, 12 (1962), 321–31.

———. "Großschreibung oder Kleinschreibung?" *Der Deutschunterricht*, 7 (1955), 30–50.

Jurgensen, Manfred. "Die Sprache im zweigeteilten *Duden*," *ZfdS*, 26 (1970), 42–59.

Kaempfert, Manfred. "Germanistische Linguistik. Ein Überblick über die Entwicklung der letzten Jahre," *ZfdPh*, First Part, 91 (1972), 82–113; Second Part, 92 (1973), 87–115; Third Part, 92 (1973), 396–443.

Kainz, Friedrich. "Klassik und Romantik," *Deutsche Wortgeschichte* (2nd ed.; Strasbourg, 1959), II, 223ff.

Kaufmann, Eugen. "Der Fragenkreis ums Fremdwort," *JEGP*, 38 (1939), 42–63.

Kaufmann-Hillenkamp, Berta. "Kultur im Spiegel des Wortschatzes," *Der Deutschunterricht*, 7 (1955), 5–20.

Klappenbach, Ruth. "Gliederung des deutschen Wortschatzes der Gegenwart," *Der Deutschunterricht*, 12 (1960), 29–45.

———. "Die Silbentrennung," *Der Deutschunterricht*, 7 (1955), 93–103.

Klerber, Wolfgang. "Vom Sinn der Flurnamenforschung: Methoden und Ergebnisse," *Der Deutschunterricht*, 9 (1957), 91–102.

Koekkoek, Byron S. "The Impact of Transformational Linguistics on Language Teaching," *UP*, No. 3 (1970), 3–6.

Koerner, E. F. K. "Notes on the Semantics of Technical Terms in the Description of the Varieties of Contemporary German," *GQ*, 44 (1971), 1–23.

Kolb, Herbert. "Pluralisierung des Abstraktums. Über Rekonkretisierungstendenzen im Abstraktwortschatz des Deutschen, *ZfdS*, 25 (1969), 21–36.

Kracke, Arthur. "Das 'Zeit'-Wort: Tempus, Aktionsart, Aspekt," *Der Deutschunterricht*, 13 (1961), 10–40.

———. "Die Bauelemente der Sprache und ihre Funktionen im einfachen Satz," *Der Deutschunterricht*, 10 (1958), 19–47.

Kronasser, Heinz. "Kultur und Sprache," *Muttersprache* (1960), pp. 98–104.

Kurrelmeyer, W. "American and Other Loanwords in German," *JEGP*, 43 (1944), 286–301.

Kurth, R. "Über den Gebrauch der Bildungen auf *-ei, -erei, -elei*," *Beiträge*, 75 (1953), 442–51.

————. "Zum Gebrauch der sogenannten *ge-* Abstrakta," *Beiträge*, 75 (1953), 314–20.

Lang, Wilhelm. "Zur geschichtlichen Deutung der Konjunktive," *Der Deutschunterricht*, 15 (1963), 67–77.

Lehnemann, Widar. "Standessprache und Gemeinsprache," *Der Deutschunterricht*, 15 (1963), 51–63.

Leisli, Ernst. "Deutsch und Englisch," *Muttersprache* (1961), pp. 257–64.

Leopold, Werner F. "Recent Developments in the German Language," *JEGP*, 57 (1958), 232–69.

Lerch, Eugen. "Zwei Wortprägungen der deutschen Sprache der Gegenwart," *JEGP*, 39 (1940), 201–8.

Liedke, Herbert R. "Vom Wesen und Wortschatz der Autosprache," *Monatshefte*, 31 (1937), 285–93.

Linn, Rolf N. "The Role of *nicht ein* in German," *UP*, No. 2 (1972), 142–45.

Loose, Gerhard. "Zur deutschen Soldatensprache des zweiten Weltkrieges," *JEGP*, 46 (1947), 279–89.

McClean, R. J. "The Use of 'Ein' with Plurals in German," *MLR*, 48 (1953), 33–38.

McKay, John C. "Some generative rules for German time adverbials," *Language*, 44 (1968), 25–50.

McLintock, David R. "Die umgelauteten Praeterito-praesentia und der Synkretismus im deutschen Verbalsystem," *Beiträge*, 83 (1961), 271–77.

Mathieu, Gustave. "Was liest Hänschen in Ostdeutschland?" *GQ*, 30 (1957), 15–19.

Maurer, Friedrich, "Namenforschung," *Der Deutschunterricht*, 9 (1957), 102–8.

————. "Schriftsprache und Mundarten," *Der Deutschunterricht*, 8 (1956), 5–14.

————. "Sprachgebrauch und Sprachrichtigkeit," *Der Deutschunterricht*, 12 (1960), 99–102.

————. "Über Arten der deutschen Wortbildung besonders Wortkreuzungen," *ZfdPh*, 53 (1928), 167–83.

Mechow, Max. "Zur deutschen Soldatensprache des zweiten Weltkriegs," *ZfdS*, 27 (1971), 81–100.

Mehl, E. "Zur Fachsprache der Leibesübungen," *Muttersprache* (1954), pp. 204–42, 299–302.

Meisnest, Frederick W. "The Double Infinitive Construction in German," *GQ*, 5 (1932), 97–103.

Meyer, Herman C. "The Imperative in German Popular Plant Names," *JEGP*, 50 (1951), 509–16.

Moser, Hugo. "Die Entstehung der neuhochdeutschen Einheitssprache," *Der Deutschunterricht*, 3 (1951), 58–74.

————. "Entwicklungstendenzen des heutigen Deutsch," *Der Deutschunterricht*, 6 (1954), 87–107; also in *Moderna Språk*, 50 (1956), 213–35.

————. "Mundart und Hochsprache im neuzeitlichen Deutsch," *Der Deutschunterricht*, 8 (1956), 36–61.

————. "Namenfelder," *Der Deutschunterricht*, 9 (1957), 51–72.

————. "Neuere und neueste Zeit," in *Deutsche Wortgeschichte* (2nd ed.; Straßburg, 1959), III, 445ff.

————. "Rechtschreibung und Sprache: Von den Prinzipien der deutschen Orthographie," *Der Deutschunterricht*, 7 (1955), 5–30.

Moulton, William G. "Structural Dialectology," *Language*, 44 (1968), 451–66.

Müller, Eugen H. "The German Language of Today," *GQ*, 25 (1952), 35–41.

Must, Gustav. "English *holy*, German *heilig*," *JEGP*, 59 (1960), 184–89.

————. "The Marking of the F-Sound in German Orthography," *Monatshefte*, 58 (1966), 150–56.

————. "The Origin of the German Word *Ehre* 'Honor,' " *PMLA*, 76 (1961), 326–29.

Naumann, Walter. "Grillparzer: Der Dichter und die Sprache," *Monatshefte*, 45 (1953), 337–54.

Nock, Francis J. "Notes on E. T. A. Hoffmann's Linguistic Usage," *JEGP*, 55 (1956), 588–603.

Obenauer, Karl J. "Vom Abschwören großer Worte," *Muttersprache* (1952), pp. 75–79.

Öhmann, Emil. "Die Pluralformen auf -*s* in der deutschen Substantivflexion," *ZfdA*, 91 (1962), 228–36.

————. "Nochmals die Pluralisierung des Abstraktums," *ZfdS*, 26 (1970), 32–36.

————. "Über die Pluralbildung von abstrakten Substantiven im Deutschen" *Beiträge*, 65 (1942), 134–52.

Pfeffer, J. Alan "Die Relativpronomen *der* und *welcher* in Wort und Schrift," *UP*, 6, No. 2 (1973), 90–97.

Pfleiderer, Wolfgang. "Ablehnung der Kleinschreibung durch die schweizerische Orthographie Konferenz," *Wirkendes Wort*, 16 (1966), 18–23.

Pilch, Herbert. "Das Lautsystem der hochdeutschen Umgangssprache," *ZfdMaF*, 33 (1966), 247–66.

Pniower, O. "Goethe als Wortschöpfer," *Euphorion*, 32 (1931), 362–83.

Raabe, Paul. "Zum Suffix -*ler* in der Gegenwartssprache," *Beiträge*, 78 (1956), 45–56.

Rahn, Fritz. "Die geplanten Reform-Betrachtungen und Vorschläge," *Der Deutschunterricht*, 7 (1955), 108–25.

Renicke, Horst. "Deutsche Aspektpaare," *ZfdPh*, 80 (1961), 86–99.

Rositzke, Harry A. "Short and Long Stops in High German," *JEGP*, 43 (1944), 88–93.

Rupp, Heinz. "Einiges Grundsätzliche zur Wortforschung," *Der Deutschunterricht*, 3 (1951), 53–58.

Sachs, Emmy. "On *steinalt*, *stockstill*, and Similar Formations," *JEGP*, 62 (1963), 581–96.

Schmidt-Hidding, Wolfgang. "Das Verhältnis von Idiomatik und Grammatik," *Der Deutschunterricht*, 9 (1957), 43–59.

Schneider-Facius, F. "Der Funkschriftsteller," *Welt und Wort*, 9 (1954), 297ff.

Schobel, Herbert. "Alte and neue Münznamen," *Der Deutschunterricht*, 13 (1961), 63–78.

——. "Reste alten Sprachgebrauchs in neuerer Zeit," *Der Deutschunterricht*, 15 (1963), 77–95.

Schröder, Friedrich. "Zur Bedeutungsgeschichte von Gast," *ZfdPh*, 56 (1931), 384–94.

Schwanzer, Viliam. "Störungen in der deutschen Sprachstruktur durch Isolation und Einwirkungen des Slawischen," *ZfdPh*, 87 (1968), 86–96.

Shetter, William Z. "The Meaning of German *noch*," *Language*, 42 (1966), 42–66.

Spalding, K. "The Idiom of a Revolution: Berlin, 1848," *MLR*, 44 (1949), 60–74.

Sperber, Hans. "Im Spiegel der Sprache," *Monatshefte*, 31 (1939), 394–99.

Springer, Otto, "New High German *-el* in Nominal Compounds," *Language*, 25 (1949), 410–15.

Spuler, Linus. "Der Deutschschweizer und die deutsche Sprache," *GQ*, 39 (1966), 221–28.

Stegmann, Kurt von. "Der Artikel: Geschlechtswort oder Geleitwort?" *Der Deutschunterricht*, 9 (1957), 29–43.

——. "Die Pluralumwälzung im Deutschen," *Der Deutschunterricht*, 10 (1958), 75–84.

Steinhauser, Walter. "Slawisches im Wienerischen," *Muttersprache* (1958), pp. 133–42.

Sternberger, Dold, und Werner Betz. "Das heutige Deutsch—nachlässig, verräterisch oder einfach zeitgemäß?" *ZfdS*, 23 (1967), 129–35.

Stopp, F. J. "Indirectly Compounded Verbal Forms in Present-Day German," *MLR*, 52 (1957), 355–62.

Strothman, Friedrich W. "The Influence of Aspect on the Meaning of *Nomina Agentis* in Modern German," *JEGP*, 34 (1935), 188–200.

Suhl, Abraham. "Anglizismen in Thomas Manns 'Doktor Faustus,'" *Monatshefte*, 40 (1948), 391–95.

Swenson, Rodney. "A Vocabulary Frequency Count: Based on Three Leading West German Newspapers," *UP*, No. 3 (1970), 22–32.

Tschentscher, Christhild. "Geschichte der Silbe '*-tum*' im Deutschen," *Muttersprache* (1962), pp. 1–8, 39–47, 67–78.

Twaddell, W. Freeman. "Grammatical Notes: The Auxiliary *werden*; the Preposition *als*," in *Festschrift für Detlev W. Schumann*, ed. Albert R. Schmitt (München, 1970), 383–86.

Ulvestad, Bjarne. "Object Clauses Without *daß* Dependent on Negative Governing Verbs in Modern German," *Monatshefte*, 47 (1955), 329—38.

Valk, Melvin. "Die Entwicklung der deutschen Fußballsprache," *JEGP*, 34 (1935), 567–71.

Vater, Heinz. "Some New Words in the German Language," *UP*, No. 3 (1970), 8–11.

Wagner, Kurt. "Das 19. Jahrhundert," in *Deutsche Wortgeschichte* (2nd ed.; Strasbourg, 1959), II, 409ff.

Walz, John A. "Linguistic Notes on Goethe's *Faust*, Part I," *JEGP*, 29 (1930), 204–32.

Wandruszka, Mario. "Das Passivum in der romanischen Sprachen, im Englischen und Deutschen," *Der Deutschunterricht*, 13 (1961), 40–47.

Waterman, John T. "The Preterite and Perfect Tenses in German: A Study in Functional Determinants," *GR*, 31 (1956), 104–14.

Waterman, John T. "The Occurrence of 'Als' as a Preposition," *Monatshefte*, 64 (1972), 132–35.

Weiss, Gerhard. "The Dropping of the Genitive -*s* in Personal Names." *Monatshefte*, 47 (1955), 168–74.

Wessel, P. B. "Sprachzertrümmerung und Sprachschöpfung in der Lyrik Gottfried Benns," *ZfdPh*, 87 (1968), 457–69.

Winter, Werner. "Vom Genetiv im heutigen Deutsch," *ZfdS*, 22 (1966–67), 21–35.

Wittmer, Felix. "Stefan George als Übersetzer," *GR*, 3 (1928), 361–80.

Zender, Matthias. "Über Heiligennamen," *Der Deutschunterricht*, 9 (1957), 72–91.

Zieglschmid, A. J. Friedrich. "English-Amerikanischer Einfluß auf den Wortschatz der deutschen Sprache der Nachkriegszeit," *JEGP*, 34 (1935), 24–33.

Dialect Studies

Althaus, Hans Peter. "Wortgeographische und sprachsoziologische Studien zum jiddischen Lehnwortschatz im Deutschen," *ZfdS*, 21 (1964–65), 20–41.

Bayerschmidt, Carl F. "The Present Status of a Standard Low German Orthography," *JEGP*, 39 (1940), 494–502.

Beranek, Franz J. "Jiddisch," *Deutsche Philologie im Aufriß* (Berlin, 1952ff.), I, cols. 1551–90.

Beyer, Ernst. "A propos de l'*ü* alsacien en pays de Bade." *Etudes germaniques*, 11 (1956), 240–44.

Bohnenberger, K. "Über die Ortsgrenze des Alemannischen: Tatsächliches und Grundsätzliches," *Beiträge*, 52 (1928), 217–91.

Habersaat, Karl. "Zur Geschichte der jiddischen Grammatik: Eine bibliographische Studie," *ZfdPh*, 84 (1965), 419–35.

Kratz, H., and H. Milnes. "Kitchener German: A Pennsylvania German Dialect," *MLQ*, 14 (1953), 184–98, 274–83.

Langeweyde, Wolf S. von. "Das Ruhrgebiet und seine Sprache," *Muttersprache* (1958), pp. 1–4.

Leopold, Werner F. "The Decline of German Dialects," *Word*, 15 (1959), 130–53.

———. "Low German: A Receding Language," *GQ*, 34 (1961), 123–33.

———. "Die Mundart bei Flüchtlingen in Westdeutschland," *Language*, 37 (1961), 509–21.

Mitzka, Walther. "Hochdeutsche Mundarten," in *Deutsche Philologie im Aufriß* (Berlin, 1952ff.), I, cols. 655–768.

Moser, Hugo. "Die Sprache im geteilten Deutschland," *Wirkendes Wort,* 7 (1961), 1–21.

———. "Umsiedlung und Sprachwandel," *Festgabe für Theodor Bäuerle* (2nd ed.; Stuttgart, 1956), 121ff.

———. "Ursachen von Sprachgrenzen," *ZfMaf,* 22 (1954), 87ff.

Moulton, William G. "The Dialect Geography of *hast, hat* in Swiss German," *Language,* 37 (1961), 497–508.

———. "The Short Vowel Systems of Northern Switzerland," *Word,* 16 (1960), 155–82.

Müller, Ernst E. "Zur historischen Mundartforschung," *Beiträge,* 74 (1952), 454–85.

Penzl, Herbert. "Lehnwörter mit Mittelenglisch *a* vor *r* im Pennsylvanisch-Deutschen Dialekt," *JEGP,* 37 (1938), 396–402.

Reed, Carroll E. "Loan-Word Stratification in Pennsylvania German," *GQ,* 40 (1967), 83–86.

———. "The Question of Aspect in Pennsylvania German," *GR,* 22 (1947), 5–12.

———. "A Survey of Pennsylvania German Morphology," *MLQ,* 9 (1948), 322–42.

———. "A Survey of Pennsylvania German Phonology," *MLQ,* 8 (1947), 267–89.

Roedder, Edwin C. "Linguistic Geography," *GR,* 1 (1926), 281–308.

———. "Neue Schriften zur deutschen Mundartforschung," *JEGP,* 45 (1946), 380–410.

———. "Wortgeographie der hochdeutschen Umgangssprache," *JEGP,* 23 (1924), 422–30.

Schirmunski, Viktor. "Sprachgeschichte und Siedlungsmundarten." *GRM,* 18 (1930), 113–22, 171–88.

Schwarz, Ernst. "Ostmitteldeutsche Sprachprobleme," *Beiträge,* 52 (1928), 361–98.

Semler, Carl. "Die Herkunft der Palatisierung und Mouillierung des *l*-Lautes in deutschen Dialekten," *PMLA,* 50 (1935), 1200–22.

———. "Velarization and *u*-Vocalization of *l* in German Dialects," *PMLA,* 48 (1933), 220–44.

Senn, Alfred. "Verhältnis von Mundart und Schriftsprache in der deutschen Schweiz," *JEGP,* 34 (1935), 42–58.

Springer, Otto. "Dialektgeographie und Textkritik," *PMLA,* 56 (1941), 1163–78.

———. "The Study of the Pennsylvania German Dialect," *JEGP,* 42 (1943), 1–39.

Szadrowsky, M. "Zur hochalemannischen Syntax," *Beiträge,* 54 (1930), 65–137.

Tesnière, Lucien. "Le *ü* alsacien outre-Rhin," *Etudes germaniques,* 9 (1954), 153ff.

———. "Le *ü* du dialecte alsacien," *Etudes germaniques,* 3 (1948), 147–56.

Thierfelder, Franz. "Deutsche Sprache im Ausland," *Deutsche Philologie im Aufriß* (Berlin, 1952ff.), I, cols. 499–576.

Veith, Werner. "Pennsylvaniendeutsch: Ein Beitrag zur Entstehung von Siedlungsmundarten," *ZfMaf*, 35 (1968), 254–83.

Wood, Ralph C. "Pennsilfaanisch oder Pennsylvaniendeutsch," *Deutsche Philologie im Aufriß* (Berlin, 1952ff.), I, cols. 785–808.

———. "Pennsylvania 'High German,' " *GR*, 20 (1945), 299–314.

Zinsli, Paul, "Hochsprachen und Mundarten in der deutschen Schweiz," *Der Deutschunterricht*, 8 (1956), 61–73.

CHAPTER EIGHT: A BRIEF DESCRIPTION OF THE SOUNDS OF GERMAN

(See entries on p. 235 under the heading "Phonetics.")

Index

Ablaut: in German strong verg, 33-34; series, compared in OHG, MHG, 105-6

(Der) Abrogans, 74

(Der) Ackermann aus Böhmen, 114; selection from, 116

Adelung, Johann Christoph, 144, 173

Adjectival declension: origins of, 31-33

Admonitio generalis: significance for OHG, 74

Affixation: used by Mystics to increase vocabulary items, 101, 150

Affricates: defined, 205; inventory of, 205-6

Albanian, 4

Albéric de Piscaçon, 89

Albrecht von Halberstadt, 95

Alemanni *(Elb-Germanen):* migration of, 43

Alemannic: UG dialect, 127; phonetic characteristics of, 190-201

Alliteration: as a poetic device, 23, 73

Alpengermanen, 44

(Die) althochdeutschen Gespräche: significance of, 78

American English: loanwords in NHG, 179-80

American influence on NHG, 178-81

Anacreontics: poetry of, 155

Analogy: in development of ENHG, 103-6

Analytic structure: defined, 30

Angelus Silesius (Johann Scheffler), 151

Angles: emergence of, 44

Anlautsgesetz. See Notker Labeo

Apophony. *See* Ablaut

Arabic: influence on vocabulary of ENHG, 122-23

Archaeology: and chronology of German sound shift, 27; and location of German homeland, 39-42

Arianism: defined, 69*n*

Armenian, 4; sound shift compared to Gmc., 28-29

Arnd, Johann, 150

Arnold, Gottfried, 150

Aśoka, 9

Aspiration: feature of coarticulation, 202; of consonants, 209

Assonance: commonly used in pre-MHG literary language, 94

Attila, 59

a-umlaut: explained, 106, 171*n*

Bacon, Roger, 99

Baltic languages, 5

Bandkeramiker, 40

Baroque style: origin and definition of term, 148 and *n;* examples of, 148-49; parallelism and antithesis in, 153

Battle-axe people, 41

Bavarian, 191; subgroups of, 191; phonetic characteristics of, 192

Belustigungen des Verstandes und Witzes, 155

Benrath line, 54
Berthold von Regensburg, 99
Bible: pre-Lutheran versions printed in *das Gemeine Deutsch,* 128; Luther's translation of, 129-33 *passim;* Low German versions of, 130, 133; Roman Catholic versions of, 134
Bierwisch, Martin, 198
Bingen, Hildegard von, 100
Birken, Sigmund von, 139
Bismarck, Prince Otto von, 171
Bloomfield, Leonard, 195
Blütezeit: MHG, description of, 84; waning of, 96
Bödiker, Johann, 142
Bodmer, Johann Jakob, 153-54, 156, 168
Böhme, Jakob, 150
Boileau, Nicholas, 151
Books: ratio of German to Latin in ENHG period, 127
Brabant: point-of-entry for French culture into Germany, 92
Brant, Sebastian, 136
Breitlinger, Johann Jakob, 153-54, 156, 168
Bremer Beiträge, 155, 156
Brockes, Barthold Henrich, 142
Brugger, Father J. G. C., 176, 186
Buch von der deutschen Poeterey, 140
Bühnenaussprache: artificiality of, 174. *See also* Pronunciation
Burdach, Konrad, 113
Burgundians: migrations of, 43-45 *passim*

Calvin, John, 134
Campe, Joachim Heinrich, 159
Carolingian dynasty: descended from Salian Franks, 65; normalizing influence on OHG, 75
Catechetical style: origin of, 97*n*
Celtic languages: classification of, 5-6
Centum-Satem languages: grouping of, 18
Century of Silence. *See Ezzos Gesang*
Chancery languages. *See Kanzleisprachen*
Charlemagne. *See* Charles the Great
Charles IV, 112, 115, 120
Charles the Bald, 12, 76
Charles the Great: his interest in German, 75; West Franconian native language of, 76; mentioned, 74, 75, 76, 80 *passim*
Chivalry: as an institution, 92

Chomsky, Noam, 198
Christianity: early influence on OHG, 68
City chronicle *(Stadtchronik):* importance of in late MHG, 97
Claius, Johann, 135
Classical style: examples in German literature, 164-65
Clovis (Chlodwig), 70
Cognate: defined, 14
Colonial territories: settlement of, 107-8
Comparative method: defined, 14; used to establish nature of PGmc., 21
Consonants: how differentiated, 201, 203-6
Consonant shift. *See* High German consonant shift
Court. *See* Imperial court
Courtenay, J. Baudouin de, 194
Court epics, 94. *See also* Heinrich von Veldeke
Court poets, 101

David von Augsburg, 99
Demonstrative pronouns: inflection of, 31
Deutsch: first occurrence of, 77; once synonymous with "fränkisch," 77
Deutsches Spracharchiv, 193
Deutscher Sprachatlas, 192
Deutscher Wortatlas, 193
Dialect: universally used in eighteenth century, 146; use of in drama of Naturalism, 186. *See also* specific dialects, e.g., Bavarian
Dialectical materialism: applied to linguistics, 29
Dictionaries: early German, 135*n*, 145 and *n; Deutsches Wörterbuch* (Grimm's), 168
Dietenberger, Johann, 134
Diffusion: defined, 64; does not explain HG consonant shift, 65
Diphthongization: in Rhenish Franconian, 67; similarity in OF and OHG, 68; in MHG and ENHG, 103, 106; in chancery language of the Luxemburgers, 112
Diphthongs: defined, 207; classed as "falling," 208
Dominicans, 99
Druckersprachen. See Printers' languages
Duden: Grammatik der deutschen (Gegenwarts-) Sprache, 194, 195; *Re-*

chtschreibung der deutschen Sprache und der Fremdwörter, 172 and *n*

Dutch: official language of Holland, 92*n*; borrowings into ENHG, 123. *See also* Low Franconian

Early New High German: dating of, 102; analogy in development of, 103; structural characteristics of, 103-6; orthography of, 106; geographic spread of, 107-8; principal dialects of, 109; esthetic qualities of, 135-36

Eastern European languages: loanwords in German, 86, 122

East Franconian, 190

East Germanic: dialects, 37; tribes, migrations of, 43-45 *passim;* dialect features shared with North Germanic dialects, 46-47; dialect features shared with OHG, 48-49

East Middle German: status as literary medium after 1190, 94; influence reflected in chancery language of the Luxemburgers, 113; basis for chancery languages of Prague and of Saxon Electorate, 117; basis for *Lutherdeutsch,* 117, 129

East Middle German dialects: general phonetic characteristics of, 189-90

Eck, Johann, 134, 136

Eckhart, Meister, 100

Edictus Rothari, 60

Eichendorff, Joseph von, 166

Eike von Repgowe, 88, 97, 98

Einhard (biographer of Charles the Great), 75, 76

Einheitssprache, 187

Elbgermanen, 43-44 *passim*

Empfindsamkeit: defined, 156. *See also* English

Emser, Hieronymus, 134

End-rhyme, 73

English (British): statement by Bodmer and Breitinger in praise of, 154; influence of literature on *Empfindsamkeit,* 156; influence on NHG vocabulary, 177-78. *See also* Old English

Enlightenment: early leaders of, 152; as cultural movement, 152; literary style of, 152-53; effect on *Hochsprache,* 153; Lessing most effective champion of, 159

Epistolary style: characteristic of Rococo, 155

Evangelisch: explanation of, 134*n*

Ezzos Gesang: significance for EMHG period, 83

Family names: role of alliteration in, 23

Faust chapbook: illustration from, 121

Finnish: Gmc. loanwords in, 22

Fischart, Johann, 134

Flemish: knights, models of courtly elegance, 92; loanwords in MHG, 92; official language of Belgium, 92*n*. *See also* Low Franconian

Food gatherers: characteristics of, 40

Fraktur. See Scripts

Franciscans, 99

Francke, Augustus Hermann, 150

Fränkisch. See Duetsch

Frankish dialects: as links between north and south, 66; influenced by Gallo-Romance forces, 67; reduction of vowels of final syllables in, 67

Franks: descended from *Weser-Rhein-Germanen,* 44; Ripuarian and Salic (Salian), 65; introduced French elements into German, 68

Frederick the Wise, 114

Fremdwörterbuch, 120

French: influence on MHG, 89; influence on language of the soldier in ENHG, 125-26; widely adopted in seventeenth century, 137-38; used as language of scholarship, 138; political terms borrowed into German, 175-76; resistance to in modern times, 177. *See also* chronological subdivisions of, e.g., Old French

French loanwords in MHG, 90-91; into German via Netherlands, 92; in NHG, 175-76; purged from postal system, 177

Freyer, Hieronymus, 142

Friederich Barbarossa, 88

Frisch, Johann Leonhard, 142

Frisian: emergency of, 44; a Low German dialect, 54, 188. *See also* Old Frisian

Gallo-Romance: influences of on Frankish dialects, 67

Gallehus drinking horn: linguistic importance of, 22

Gauß, Karl Friedrich, 127*n*

Gellert, Christian Fürchtegott, 155, 165

(Das) Gemeine Deutsch, 117; favored by early printers, 128; pre-Luther Bibles printed in, 128; used by Luther, 129; early grammars of, 135; used by few seventeenth-century writers, 146*n*

Gemination (*Konsonantenverdoppelung*): shared feature of West Germanic dialects, 46

Germanic family tree, 38-39

Germanic homeland: prehistoric location of, 20; as established by archeology, 39-42

Germanic languages: enumeration of, 6; classification of, 37; attempts to explain similarities among, 49-51

Germanic loanwords: in Latin, 21; in Finnish, 22

Germanic-Slavic unity: suggested date of, 42

Germanic sound shift: discussion of, 24-25; chronology of, 27-28; causes of, 28-29

Gleim, Wilhelm Ludwig, 155

Glinz, Hans, 194-95

Glosses: importance for knowledge of OHG, 75

Glottal stops: defined, 201n

Goethe, Johann Wolfgang von: stages of linguistic development, 164; mentioned, 156, 158, 162, 163, 173, 174 *passim*

Goethe-Institut, 196 and *n*

Goldsmith, Oliver, 156

Gothic: as representative of PGmc., 24; Crimean, 44; of Italian Goths, 61; specimen text of, 81

Goths: migrations of, 43-44

Gottfried von Straßburg, 84, 93

Gottsched, Johann Christoph: Lessing's criticism of, 160; mentioned, 143, 152, 173, and notes *passim*

Götz, Johann Nikolaus, 155

Grammar: *inhaltbezogene,* 194

Grammars: seventeenth and eighteenth centuries, importance for determining standard language, 140-45 *passim;* twentieth century, 193-98 *passim*

Greek: dialects of, 7; influence upon German Classicism, 163-65 *passim*

Gregory of Tours, 60, 62

Grimm, Jacob: his *Kreislauf* theory for explaining Germanic and HG consonant shift, 63; mentioned, 25, 26, 33, 52, 63, 167, 168, 171, 173 *passim*

Grimm, Wilhelm, 167

Grimm's Law, 25-26

Grunddeutsch, 197n

Gryphius, Andreas, 139, 148

Gueints, Christian, 141

Gutenberg, Johann, 127

Hagedorn, Friedrich von, 155

Hanseatic League: influence on Low German, 118

Harsdörffer, Georg Phillipp, 139

Hartmann von Aue, 84, 95, 111

Hartung, Wolfdietrich, 199

Hauptmann, Gerhart, 186

Heine, Henrich, 160

Heinrich Julius von Braunschweig, 134

Heinrich von Morungen, 95

Heinrich von Veldeke, 94 and *n*

Helber, Sebastian, 135

(Der) Heliand, 54-55; selections from, 82

Herder-Institut, 199

Herder, Johann Gottfried, 161

Hermunduri: migration of, 43

Herodotus, 27

Herrnhuter: pietistic language of, 151n

Hessians: descended from *Weser-Rhein-Germanen,* 44

High German: dialects of, 53

High German consonant shift: described, 56-57; scope of, 57-58; chronology of, 59-62; causes of, 62-64

Hildebrandslied, 75n

Hittite: discovery of, 7; a centum language, 19. *See also* Laryngeal theory

Hochsprache, 185. *See also* Literary standard

Hofmannswaldau, Christian Hofmann von, 148

Holtzmann's Law, 47n

Homilies: defined, 98

Hugo von Trimberg, 110

Humanists: Italian, influence on Luxemburger chancery, 114; Classical influence on ENHG, 120-21

Hungarian: influence on ENHG, 122

Hunter: language of, 126-27

Hutten, Ulrich von, 136

Ickelsamer, Valentin, 135

Imperative: modern modifications in use of, 170

Imperial court: used Romance languages rather than German (1600-1800), 137

Indefinite pronouns: as definite article, 67

Indic: oldest records of, 9; modern dialects of, 9; Schlegels' interest in, 168-69

Indic languages, 9-10

Indo-European: linguistic evidence for, 17-19; location of homeland uncertain, 16-17; possibly related to Semitic and Finno-Ugrian, 19

Industry: effect on NHG vocabulary, 183-84

Ingwäonen. See Nordsee-Germanen; -theorie. See Wrede
Institut für deutsche Sprache, 196
Institut für Grunddeutsch, 197*n*
Iranian languages, 10
Irminonen. See Elb-Germanen
Isogloss: defined, 53
Istwäonen. See Weser-Rhein-Germanen
Italic languages, 11-12
Italy: possible point of origin for HG consonant shift, 61
i-umlaut: shared feature in West Germanic and North Germanic, 47-48; in OHG, 66; as sign of plural, spread of in ENHG, 104

Johnson, Samuel, 159
Journalism: effects of on *Umgangssprache,* 185-86 and *n*
Julius Caesar, 21, 28

Kanzleisprachen: under Rudolf von Hapsburg and Ludwig the Bavarian, 112; under the Luxemburgers, 112-13; under Frederick III, 114; under Maximilian I, 114; of the Saxon Electorate, 114-15; summary, 115-16; specimen of, 116; style of, 117
(Die) Kasseler Glossen: significance of, 78
Klaj, Johann, 139
Klinger, Friedrich Maximilian, 161
Klopstock, Friedrich Gottlieb, 156-57
Klosterkultur. See Monasteries
Knighthood: language of, 88, 93; definition of, 88*n;* education of knights (as discussed in Hartmann's *Gregorius*), 111
Koiné: basis of modern Greek, 7
Kolroß, Johann, 135
Konrad, Pfaffe, 89
Kuchimeister, Christian, 97
Kunstsprache: use urged by Opitz, 148

Labialization (lip-rounding): feature of coarticulation, 208; vowels pronounced with, 208
Lamprecht, Pfaffe, 89
Landfriede: defined, 98*n*
Lanfranc, 89
Langobards: migrations of, 43-44; possible influence of Italian Gothic upon language, 62
Language societies: of the seventeenth century, 139-40; in modern times, 176

Laryngeal theory, 8-9
Laterals: definition and inventory of, 206
Latin: oldest inscriptions of, 11; major periods of, 11-12; influence on OHG, 72-73; influence on ENHG, 120-21. *See also* Latin loanwords
Latin loanwords: in Germanic, as evidence for fixing chronology of HG consonant shift, 28; in Germanic, 35-36; in OHG, 71-72; in ENHG, 120-21
Law (German): codification of, 98
Leibniz, Gottfried Wilhelm von, 138
Lessing, Gotthold Ephraim, 156, 159-61
Lexico-statistical dating (Glottochronology), 42
Limburg dialect, 94*n*
Literary standard: Luther's contribution to, 145-47; Klopstock's contribution to, 157; effect of Storm and Stress on, 162; realized in nineteenth century, 170
Loan translations: definition of, 69*n;* from Gothic in OHG, 69; from Latin in OHG, 72; from French into German via Netherlands, 92; from French into MHG, 90; from Latin into language of Romanticism, 101; from British English into NHG, 177; from American English into NHG, 180-81; from Russian into NHG, 182
Loanwords: Christian, in OHG, 69-70; Germanization of, by seventeenth-century language societies, 140; by Campe, 145*n. See also* under specific languages
Logau, Friedrich von, 139, 159
Lohenstein, Daniel Caspar von, 148
Low Alemannic: status as literary medium after 1190, 94
Low Franconian, 54, 188; suitable terms for, 92*n*
Low German *(Niedersächsisch, Plattdeutsch):* as "uncontaminated" Anglo-Frisian, 50; dialectal groupings of, 53-54; features of in OHG, 66; language of some early city chronicles, 97; principal dialects of (1350-1600), 109; borrowings into ENHG, 123; Bible translations in, 130, 133; as language of the theater, 133; speakers tend to have "purer" pronunciation of High German, 142*n;* major modern dialectal areas of, 188 and *n*
Low Saxon. *See* Low German
Lübeck: importance of dialect, 118
Ludwig the Bavarian, 112
Ludwig the German, 12, 76

Ludwig the Pious, 80

Ludwig von Anhalt-Köthen, 139

Luther, Martin: as "creator" of NHG, 128-29; example of skill as translator, 130; reaction to critics, 131-32; mentioned, 105, 114, 117, 128-36, 147 *passim*

Lutheran-*e*: Roman Catholic objection to, 147

Lutherdeutsch: principal orthographic and grammatical characteristics of, 129*n*; influence on everyday speech, 132-33; distribution and acceptance of, 133-35; early grammars of, 135; used by major seventeenth-century writers, 146*n*

Magdeburg, Mechtild von, 100

Marcomanni (Bavarians): migrations of, 44

Marxism: in linguistics, 29

Mathers, Rodney Harold, 280

Maximilian I, 114

Medieval society: nature of, 88-89

Megalithic builders: characteristics of, 40

Meißen dialect: closest approximation to standard language (1600-1800), 162, 173

Mementô morî: example of EMHG, 84

Mentel, Johann, 130, 134

Merovingians: descended from Salic (Salian) Franks, 65

Merseburger Charms (Zaubersprüche), 74*n*

Metaphor: use of in writings of Mystics, 100; uncritical use of deplored by Gottsched, 153; use of recommended by Bodmer and Breitinger, 154

Middle Franconian: OHG dialects of, 94; as MHG literary medium, 94; NHG dialects of, 188-89

Middle German: modern dialects of, 188-89

Middle High German: chief structural features of, 85-88; as *Standessprache* of the knight, 88; as literary medium, 93, 95; tendency toward standardization of, 93; specimens of *Dichtersprache,* 96; prose, 97; normalizing tendencies of "classic" era of (ended by 1300), 109; literary works in (edited and published by Bodmer), 154

Middle Low German *(Mittelniederdeutsch),* 118

Middle Netherlandish *(Mittelniederländisch),* 119

Migrations: served to extend Germanic boundaries, 20; of Germanic tribes from historic homeland, 43-44; to colonial territories in ENHG times, 107-8

Milton, John, 154

Miners: language of, 126

Monasteries: linguistic influence on OHG, 71

Monophthongization: in Low Saxon and Frankish dialects, 66; in ENHG, 103; in chancery language of the Luxemburgers, 112

Morphology: of adjectival declension in Germanic, 31-33; of preterite in Germanic, 33-35; some features of in ENHG, 103-6; changes in caused by analogy, 104-5. *See also* specific headings, e.g., Nouns

Moscherosch, Johann Michael, 139

Moser, Hugo, 195, 196

Motsch, Wolfgang, 198

Mutation. *See* Umlaut

Mysticism: specimens of language of, 100-1; mentioned, 150

Nasalization: of voiced sounds, 203, 209

Nasals: inventory of, 206

Naturalism: drama of, enhanced status of *Umgangssprache,* 186 and *n*

Nazideutsch, 184 and *n*

Near Eastern languages: loanwords in NHG, 122-23

Negau Helmet: testimony of for PGmc., 21; as evidence for fixing chronology of Germanic sound shift, 27-28

Neologism: defined, 184*n*

Netherlandish: generic term for Dutch and Flemish, 92*n*

Neumarkt, Johann von, 113, 114, 115

New High German. See especially entries for Chapter Seven in Table of Contents

Niedersächsisch. See Low German

Nominalization: trend toward in NHG, 169

Nordgermanen, 43-44 *passim*

Nördlingen, Heinrich von, 100

Nordsee-Germanen, 43-44 *passim*

North Germanic: dialects of, 37; features shared with West Germanic, 46; features shared with East Germanic, 46-47

Notker Labeo: *Anlautsgesetz* of, 79; contributions to OHG orthography, 79-80 and n

Nouns: abstract, used by Mystics, 100-1;

derivatives, increased number of in Modern German, 169; capitalization of, 173

Occlusion: defined, 20
Offizinen, 128
Old English: features shared with Old Frisian, 49; influence on OHG, 70
Old French: and Straßburg Oaths, 12; German influence upon, 55; linguistic features shared with OHG, 67; indefinite article in, 67; vocabulary borrowed into MHG, 89; epics translated into Middle Franconian, 94
Old Frisian, 49
Old High German: features shared with East Germanic languages, 48-49; dialects of, 58 and *n;* made up of *Stammesprachen,* 65; indefinite article in, 67; literature, list of principal documents in, 73*n;* irregular and dialectal, 76; written evidence of the vernacular, 78; conversational manuals, 78; writing of limited by Ludwig the Pious, 80; specimen texts, 81-82
Old Indic: word composition of important for understanding of IE morphology, 10
Old Norse: language of Gallehus horn, 22. *See also* North Germanic
Old Saxon: oldest historical form of Low German, 54; once an Ingvaeonic dialect, 55; specimen text, 82. *See also* West Germanic
Opitz, Martin, 139, 140, 148
Oral (buccal) cavity: description of, 201
Orthography: Notker's system of, 79-80 and *n;* irregularity of in manuscripts, 86 and n; in ENHG, 106-7; of Luther's Bible translation, 130; modern efforts to reform, 171-73
Otfried von Weißenburg, 76, 77

Participles: use of in translating Latin ablative absolute construction in OHG, 73; as used by Klopstock, 157; as used by Goethe and Schiller, 164*n*
Pennsylvania German, 119-20
Persian: influence on vocabulary of ENHG, 122-23
Pfeffer, Alan J., 197
Philology: Romanticists prominent as founders of, 167-68 and *n*
Phonemic change: defined, 24
Phonetic correspondences: systematic, examples of, 14

Phonetics: articulatory (physiological, anatomical), defined, 201
Pietism, 150-51 and *n;* relation to *Empfindsamkeit,* 156
Place names: testimony in Latin of Germanic, 21; as evidence for dating HG consonant shift, 60
Plattdeutsch. See Low German
Pliny (the Elder), 21
Portmanteau word: defined, 181*n*
Porzig, Walter, 195
Prefixes: Klopstock's use of, 157; Lessing's use of, 159; verbal, in writings of Mystics, 100-1, 150
Prenestine fibula, 11
Preterite: Germanic development of, 33-35; standardization of resisted by MG dialects, 105
Printers' languages *(Druckersprachen):* principal types in sixteenth century, 128
Printing, invention of, 127-28
Prokosch, Eduard, 64
Pronouns: in OF and OHG, 67. *See also* Demonstrative pronouns; Indefinite pronouns
Pronunciation: Modern German, not standardized until twentieth century, 174-75
Prose. *See* Middle High German
Proto-Germanic: defined, 20; information about obtained by comparative method, 21; structural changes in, 29-31
Pufendorf, Samuel, 152
Punctuation. *See* Orthography

Quadi (Germanic tribe), 44

Rabener, Gottlieb Wilhelm, 155
Rask, Rasmus, 25, 26
Ratichius, Wolfgang, 140, 141
Rationalism: philosophical system of Enlightenment, 152
Raumer, Rudolf von, 171
Reconstruction, linguistic, 13-16
Reichstagsabschiede: linguistic importance of, 115
Relationship (linguistic): most decisive evidence of, 14
Rhenish Franconian: diphthongization in, 67; as language of Carolingian court, 76
Rhotacism: defined, 49
Rhyme: normalization of in MHG literary language, 94-95

Richardson, Samuel, 156
Riegel, Hermann, 176, 186
Ripurarian: as term for dialect of Limburg, 94*n;* a Low Franconian dialect until twelfth century, 94*n;* a Middle German dialect in NHG, 188; characteristics of, 188-89
Rist, Johann, 139
Rittersprache, 88
Rivius, Johann, 135
Rococo: literary style of, 155
Rollenhagen, Gabriel, 134
Rollenhagen, Georg, 134
Romance languages; emergence of, 12; influence upon language of seamen in ENHG, 125. *See also* specific languages
Romanticism: linguistic characteristics of, 166-67
Romantik: origin of term, 166*n*
Rousseau, Jean Jacques, 161
r-sounds: pronunciations of, 175
Rudolf von Hapsburg, 112
Runes: earliest Germanic, 6; evidence of PGmc., 21, 42
Russian: influence of on NHG, 181-83

Sachs, Hans, 134
St. Augustine: language of, 12
St. Boniface (Winfrid of Wessex): "Apostle to the Germans," 71
St. Francis of Assisi, 99
(Der) St. Georgener Prediger, 99
St. Jerome, 5
Sanskrit, 9; as reflecting PIE accentual conditions, 26; the Schlegels' interest in, 168
Sapir, Edward, 195
Saussure, Ferdinand de, 194
Saxons *(Niedersachsen):* emergence of, 44
Scandinavian languages: enumeration of, 6; borrowings from into ENHG, 123. *See also* North Germanic
Schiedsspruch: defined, 111
Schiller, Johann Christoph Friedrich: features of literary style, 164; retained Swabian accent, 174; mentioned, 156, 162, 163, 173 *passim*
Schlegel, August Wilhelm, 168
Schlegel, Friedrich, 168
Schlegel, Johann Elias, 155
Schmeller, Johann Andreas, 54
Schnurkeramiker, 40
Schönau, Elisabeth von, 100
Schopenhauer, Arthur, 185
Schottel, Justus Georg, 141

Schriftsprache. See Literary standard
Schwabe, Johann Joachim, 155
Scriptoria, 71; as points of origin for OHG literary records, 73
Scripts, 107*n,* 173
Seaman: language of, 125
Second Silesian *Dichterschule,* 148
Sekundärumlaut: in MHG, 85*n;* in Upper German texts, 171*n*
Semantic change: in vocabulary of Mysticism, 101
Semivowels: defined, 207
Sentimentalism. *See Empfindsamkeit*
Sermons (German): collections of, 98-99; by missionaries, delivered in colloquial language, 99; examples of, 99-100
Seuse (Suso), Heinrich, 100, 101
Siebs, Theodor, 174
Sigismund (Luxemburg), 112
Silesia: settlement of, 107-8
Silesian: some phonetic features of, 189-90. *See also* Second Silesian *Dichterschule*
Slavic languages: classification of, 12; verbal aspects reflect conditions in PIE, 13; influence upon ENHG, 122. *See also* Russian
Soldier: language of the, 125-26
Sound shift. *See* Germanic sound shift
Specialized dialects *(Sondersprachen):* rise of in ENHG, 123. *See also* specific entries, e.g., Trade and Commerce
Spener, Jakob, 150
Spigel, Dr. (chancellor under Albrecht, Archbishop of Mainz), 115
Spirants: inventory of, 204-5
Sprache der Gegenwart, grammar of contemporary German jointly published by *Das Institut für deutsche Sprache* and *Das Goethe-Institut* (both BRD), 196-97
Sprachgesellschaften. See Language societies
Stammbaum. See Germanic family tree
Standardization of MHG literary language, 93-95
Stephan, Heinrich von, 177
Sterne, Lawrence, 156
Stops: inventory of, 203-4
Storm and Stress: relation to *Empfindsamkeit,* 156; as a reaction to the Enlightenment, 161; language described, 161-62
Straßburg Oaths: earliest document in French, 12; German version in Rhenish Franconian, 76

Stress accent: became fixed on root syllable in PGmc., 22; importance in history of Germanic languages, 22-23

Structural linguistics, 194-95, 197

Studia Grammatica, publications of the *Zentralinstitut für Sprachwissenschaft* (**DDR**), 198 and *n*

Substantive verb. *See* Verbs

Sühne: defined, 111

Swiss German: reception of *Lutherdeutsch* by speakers of, 134; adoption of certain Upper German features in written form of, 134; Kolroß' grammar of, 135. *See also* Alemannic

Syntax: of OHG, influenced by Latin, 72-73; of ENHG, influenced by Italian Humanism, 113-17 *passim;* of ENHG, criticism of, 117; of ENHG influenced by Classical Humanism, 121; German, influenced by Classical Greek, 163-64

Synthetic structure: defined, 30

Tacitus, 21, 43

Tauler, Johannes, 100

Tense: compound past, in OF and OHG, 67

Tenseness: feature of coarticulation, 202; vowels pronounced with, 208-9

Tepl, Johann von, 114

Territorium: defined, 110*n*

Tersteegen, Gerhard, 150

(Der) Teutsche Merkur, 158

Teutonic Knights: Order of, 108*n*

Thomasius, Christian, 138, 152

Thuringian: some phonetic features of, 189-90

Tieck, Ludwig, 166, 168 and *n*

Tischreden (Luther's): selection from, 129

Tocharian: discovery of, 13; a centum language, 19

Toponymy. *See* Place names

Tournament: contributions of to MHG vocabulary, 91

Trade and commerce: borrowings from Italian, 123-24; from French, 124; from Dutch, 124-25

Transformational grammar, 197-200 *passim*

Tribes (Germanic): settlement of Low German area, 43; location of in sixth century, 55

Trier: point-of-entry for French culture into Germany, 92

Trills: description and inventory of, 206 and *n*

Trubetzkoy, Count Nikolas, 195

Ulfilas, 6, 70

Umgangssprache, 185-87

Umlaut: defined, 59; in OHG and MHG, 85-86; examples of, 85. *See also a*-umlaut; *i*-umlaut; *Sekundärumlaut*

Unio mystica: of Mysticism, 100; of Pietism, 150

Upper German: as reflected in Luther's Bible, 129 and *n*. *See also (Das) Gemeine Deutsch*

Upper Saxony: settlement of, 107-8; dialect considered best by early grammarians, 144; dialect classified as East Middle German, 189; phonetic features of contemporary dialect, 189-90

Urkunden: increase of number written in German, 110-11; defined, 110*n*; geographical distribution of, 111; first occurrences of in city chanceries *(Stadturkunden),* 111-12; in the royal and imperial chanceries, 112-13

Urnfield (cemetery) culture: date of, 41

Urnordisch. See Old Norse

Uz, Johann Peter, 155

Vandals: migration of, 43-45 *passim*

Velum (soft palate): location of, 202

Ventris, Michael, 7

Verbs: Germanic, principle of classification of, 33-34; substantive used as auxiliary in OF and OHG, 67; class changes in ENHG, 106. *See also* Ablaut; Preterite; Tense

Verner, Karl, 26, 27

Verner's Law: as explanation of "exceptions" to Germanic sound shift, 26

Viking period: date of, 42

Vocabulary: Indo-European, loss of in Germanic, 35; native Germanic elements of, 35-37; effects of World War I and II upon, 184-85; post-World-War II innovations, 185. *See also* specific language and *Sprachgesellschaften*

Vocal cords: function of, 201*n*

Vocal tract: description of, 201 and *n*

Voiced sounds: defined, 203

Völkerwanderungen. See Migrations

Voltaire, François, 160

Vowels: weakening of unstressed, 85; criteria for describing, 202; inventory of, 207

Weise, Christian, 151
Weisgerber, Leo, 193-94, 195
Weitenauer, Ignaz, 147
Wenceslas (Luxemburg), 112
Wenker, Georg, 192
Wenn-clauses: in NHG, 170
Weser-Rhein-Germanen, 43-44 *passim*
Westgermanen, 143
West Germanic: dialects of, 37; features in common, 46; features shared with North Germanic, 47-48; implications of linguistic unity of, 151
Wickram, Jörg, 134
Wieland, Christoph Martin: example of literary style, 158
Winckelmann, Johann Joachim, 163
Wolf, Hieronymus, 135
Wolff, Christian, 152
Wolfhagen, Tilemann Ehlen von, 97
Wolfram von Eschenbach, 84, 136

Word-forming potential: developed by Mysticism, 101; German characterized by richness of, 169
Wrede, Ferdinand, 50
Wurmlingen spearhead: inscription on, 60

Yiddish, 119
Young, Edward, 156

Zentralinstitut für Sprachwissenschaft, 197-200 *passim*
Zesen, Phillipp von, 139
Ziegler, Niclas, 114
Zinzendorf, Nicolaus Ludwig von, 151n
Zwingli, Ulrich, 134
Zwirner, Eberhardt, 193